Commoners is both a social history of the s̲u̲............
commons in eighteenth and early nineteenth-century English villages, and a
powerful reassessment of the entire course of English rural history during
that period.

For much of the eighteenth and early nineteenth centuries in England all
occupiers of common-field land and many cottagers shared common
grazing over common fields and wastes. In forest and fen manors, and others
with substantial uncultivated commons or well-defended customs, even the
landless found pasture and collected fuel, food and materials. Here common
right ensured the survival until parliamentary enclosure of a peasantry
whose social relations were in part shaped by access to land, common
agriculture and shared use-rights. *Commoners* describes some of these
villages. It looks at entitlement to commons, the co-operative regulation of
common fields and pastures, and the harvests taken from uncultivated
common waste. It suggests why and where common right survived until
enclosure, and it reviews the contemporary debate on the social implications
of common right and the public policy issues at the heart of parliamentary
enclosure. Finally, it describes a vigorous opposition to enclosure and a
significant decline of small landholders when common lands were enclosed.

In short, *Commoners* makes shared land-use a prism through which to see
both the economies and the social relations of common-field villages. A
work of unusual strength and imagination, *Commoners* challenges the view
that England had no peasantry or that it had disappeared before industrialization: rather it shows how parliamentary enclosure shaped social relations, sharpened antagonisms, and imprinted on popular culture a pervasive
sense of loss.

Past and Present Publications

Commoners: common right, enclosure and social change in England, 1700–1820

Past and Present Publications

General Editor: PAUL SLACK, *Exeter College, Oxford*

Past and Present Publications comprise books similar in character to the articles in the journal *Past and Present*. Whether the volumes in the series are collections of essays – some previously published, others new studies – or monographs, they encompass a wide variety of scholarly and original works primarily concerned with social, economic and cultural changes, and their causes and consequences. They will appeal to both specialists and non-specialists and will endeavour to communicate the results of historical and allied research in readable and lively form.

For a list of titles in Past and Present Publications, see end of book.

Commoners: common right, enclosure and social change in England, 1700–1820

J. M. NEESON

Associate Professor in the Department of History,
York University, Toronto

CAMBRIDGE
UNIVERSITY PRESS

Published by the Press Syndicate of the University of Cambridge
The Pitt Building, Trumpington Street, Cambridge CB2 1RP
40 West 20th Street, New York, NY 10011-4211, USA
10 Stamford Road, Oakleigh, Melbourne 3166, Australia

First published 1993
Reprinted 1995
First paperback edition 1996

Printed in Great Britain at the University Press, Cambridge

A catalogue record for this book is available from the British Library

Library of Congress cataloguing in publication data

Neeson, J. M.
Commoners: common right, enclosure and social change in England, 1700–1820 /
J. M. Neeson.
  p.   cm. – (Past and Present Publications)
Includes bibliographical references and index.
ISBN 0 521 44054 8
1. Commons – England – History – 18th century. 2. Enclosures – England –
History – 18th century. 3. Land tenure – England – History – 18th century.
4. Peasantry – England – History – 18th century. 5. England – Rural conditions –
18th century. I. Title.
HD1289 G7N44 1993
333.2–dc20   92–28461   CIP

ISBN 0 521 44054 8 hardback
ISBN 0 521 56774 2 paperback

CE

To Anna and Douglas

Stand (says the Philosopher) from betwixt me and the Sun, lest thou take away what thou can'st not give me.

Thomas Andrews, *An Enquiry into the Encrease and Miseries of the Poor of England* (1738), p. 38.

Do you know ... what the trees say when the axe comes into the forest? ... When the axe comes into the forest, the trees say: 'Look! The handle is one of us!'

John Berger, *Once in Europa* (1983), p. 69.

Contents

x   *Contents*

Tables

Preface

I began working on common right and enclosure as a graduate student at the Centre for the Study of Social History in the University of Warwick. There I had the good company of Bernice Clifton, Julian Harber, Douglas Hay, Peter Linebaugh, the late David Morgan, Michael Sonenscher and Malcolm Thomas. I did most of my archival work in those years in Northampton, where, thanks to John Lowerson, I found food, shelter and good argument in the house of Valerie and Vivian Church. Their friendship has been a pleasure ever since.

A change of continents since then has deepened those debts and brought others. It is a pleasure to thank Joan Thirsk for her unfailing encouragement and good advice, and to thank John Beattie, Maxine Berg, Reuben Hasson, Michael Havinden, Maureen Lennon, Christine Johanson, Robert Malcolmson, Siân Miles, Nicholas Rogers and Larry Shore for their interest and support. J. M. Martin has been the most exemplary of correspondents, whose interest and generosity have never flagged. Robert Allen, Kathleen Biddick, David Brown, John Chapman, Andrew Charlesworth, Paul Craven, Colin Duncan, R. L. Greenall, Alun Howkins, Bernard Leahy, David Levine, Arnold Rattenbury, Rex Russell, Keith Snell, John Styles and Dorothy Thompson shared ideas, sources and skills with me. I am grateful to all of them.

For listening to me talk about commoners it is a pleasure to thank my colleagues at York University in Toronto, and my students there and in Northamptonshire, at Memorial University, St John's, the University of Warwick and Queen's University at Kingston. Most chapters appeared as papers given to meetings of the Canadian Historical Association, the British Agricultural History Society, the York University Social History and Historical Anthropology

xiii

xiv   *Preface*

Seminar, the International Conference on Nineteenth-Century Agrarian Structures and Performance (McGill and SUNY-Plattsburgh, 1984), the ESRC Working Group on Proto-Industrial Communities' International Conference on Custom and Commerce in Early Industrial Europe (Warwick, 1987), and seminars at Birmingham, Oxford, Queen's (Kingston), Warwick and York.

Edward Thompson suggested the subject and has read drafts ever since. The debt I owe him is immense. Time and again as I prepared chapters for publication I came across references he gave me, xerox copies of documents, books, files of material he had collected and pages of detailed comment on almost everything I have ever written about commons and enclosure. He is the most generous of scholars, the kindest of friends, the toughest of critics. And, though I winced, groaned and argued, I thank him for all these things.

To the Social Science and Humanities Research Council of Canada I am grateful for the timely award of a research grant and a research-time stipend for the years 1987–9. To the archivists and staffs of the Northamptonshire, Bedfordshire, Berkshire, Warwickshire, Cambridgeshire, Oxfordshire, Norfolk, Essex, Staffordshire and Leicestershire Record Offices, and of the Public Record Office, I extend warm thanks for collaboration, often across great distances. They were all helpful, but Clive Burch, Patrick King, F. B. Stitt, Christopher Tongue, Rachel Watson and Kevin Ward were particularly generous with their time. I am grateful, too, to the staffs of the Beinecke and Stirling libraries at Yale, Memorial University Library, Cambridge University Library, the Guildhall, the Bodleian and the British libraries. Elaine Glossop and Leon Gonzales typed much of the manuscript and did so quickly and kindly: I am grateful to them both. For permission to use previously published material in Chapters 8 and 9 I am grateful to JAI Press and Cambridge University Press. For access to papers in their possession I thank Lord Harrowby (Sandon Hall) and Cmdr L. M. M. Saunders Watson (Rockingham Castle).

If no one writes a book alone, no one lives with a book alone either. My husband has lived with this one in one form or another for as long as he has lived with me. He read, he listened, he remained optimistic. Our daughter has lived with it too, and with us. With grace and good humour she bears the burden of being the daughter of not one but two writers. The book is theirs already.

Introduction

No Shire within this Land hath so little waste grounds, for theare is not in manner anie parte thereof but is turned to some profitable use.

> John Norden, *Speculi Britanniae pars Altera; or a Delineation of Northamptonshire; being a brief historicall and choriographicall description of that Country ... by the travayle of J. Norden, in the year 1610* (1720), p. 20.

'The interest which a commoner has in a common is, in the legal phrase, to eat the grass with the mouths of his cattle, or to take such other produce of the soil as he may be entitled to ... '[1] The soil itself, the land, was not the commoner's, but the use of it was. That use, what the law called a *profit à prendre*, was common right. Its history had important consequences for small landholders, rural artisans and landless labourers in eighteenth-century England. Their relative independence of wages and markets, the changing levels of their wages and poor relief, the shifting components of their family incomes, the histories of their trades and manufactures, the balance of power in their villages, their very sense of who they were and how well they lived were all in part dependent on its survival or decline.

Despite this we know relatively little about common right, and less about commoners, and even that is disputed among historians. There are many reasons, but one of them is a failure of the imagination. For good reason: imagining something that has disappeared

---

[1] *Halsbury's Laws of England Being a Complete Statement of the Whole Law of England* (2nd edn), ed. Viscount Hailsham, 1932, IV, p. 607, adapted from 1 Rolle Abr. 406, quoted in 1 Saund. 353a.

1

is difficult; after all loss *is* loss. To begin the journey back to the eighteenth century it may help to start in the present.

After years of thinking about commoners I went to see Laxton in Nottinghamshire last year. I had not gone before because I did not expect much: I knew most of the fields were no longer held in common. In the end I went because I saw a film about it made in the 1940s. For a few minutes on the screen I saw men sowing seed broadcast together, talking across the furrows. The image stayed with me. When I got to Laxton it was the late afternoon. I was tired because it had taken a long time to get there. But when the road dipped down under the railway bridge on the western side of the parish and came up next to the old common, without doubt it invaded an older world. The description of common fields as *open* fields is entirely appropriate. Distances are shorter when fields are in strips. You can call from one to the next. You can plough them and talk across the backs of the horses at the same time. You can see at a glance whose bit of the hedges or mounds needs fixing, what part of the common ditch is choked with weeds. Standing at the centre of the village feels like standing at the hub of the whole system: the fields spread out around you, the decision to sow one with wheat, another with barley is written on the landscape. For all that individual men and women work their own bits of land, their economy is public and to a large degree still shared.

It was even more so in the eighteenth century, when more of a parish was common than in Laxton now, and when pasture, the central common right, was still shared (Laxton has had no herd since the 1940s). The fields were places where people talked while they worked, and they worked together. The countryside was busy not empty. The village pound was a source of constant interest. You could tell the time of day by the regular comings and goings of common flocks and herds along the village roads, and the time of the year by their disposition in the fields and meadows. Fieldsmen, pinders and haywards were often about. Twice a year they made field orders to manage the fields and pastures, and a jury sat to ratify them and to hear complaints. Jurors and fieldsmen met at an inn, in public, with an audience of commoners. They drank together with the rest of the company, or in earshot of them. Then they had the orders cried round the village, before they nailed them to the church door. Once a year the whole parish met together and walked the bounds naming the field marks, remembering the line between what was theirs and what belonged to the parishes around them. Every year after harvest the field officers opened the wheat field to the gleaners and cried the hours of gleaning round the village. Gleaners came in procession, the women and children led by their Queen. After that the herd came into the stubble, followed later by the sheep. And all through harvest and afterwards the pigs and geese picked up fallen grain in the lanes and streets.

So much of the land was in some way shared. You could walk across the parish from one end to the other along common tracks and balks without fear of trespass. Your children could seek out bits of lane grass and river bank for the geese or the pigs; they could get furze or turf, go berrying or nutting in the woods or on the common. John Clare's poetry is about this sharing, this access, this possession without ownership:

> Love hearken the skylarks
> Right up in the sky
> The suns on the hedges
> The bushes are dry
> Thy slippers unsullied
> May wander abroad
> Grass up to the ancles
> Is dry as the road
>
> There's the path if you chuse it
> That wanders between
> The wheat in the ear
> And the blossoming bean
> Where the wheat tyed accross
> By some mischevous clown
> Made you laugh though you tumbled
> And stained your new gown.[2]

The wheat in the ear and the blossoming bean belonged to John Clare because he could see them and touch them and walk through them. He owned this world because it was open to him. It was as familiar as the inside of his house. He knew it as well as he knew his own face.

Clare's Helpston was more pastoral than arable, but still

---

[2] John Clare, 'Love hearken the skylarks', in *Selected Poems and Prose of John Clare* (1967), ed. Eric Robinson and Geoffrey Summerfield, p. 39.

common-field. Commoners in wholly fen or marsh parishes lived as much on the water as the land. More of this kind of economy survives. Jonathan Raban's description of a bit of the Essex marshes captures something of the eighteenth-century marsh and fen before they were drained:

> The marshes were unhealthy but rich. The Dengie people made a lot of money on a small scale, working from a single boat or a plot of drained swamp, selling salt, butter, cheese, corn, fish and timber to London merchants.
>
> With no great houses and no powerful county families, the marshes lay happily outside the usual class arrangements of rural England. They were cultivated by small farmers who were more like European peasants or American settlers than the general run of cap-doffing English tenants. The flat landscape with its mephitic air was no place for trespassing gentlemen; the nearby sea had no bathing beaches; the marshes were difficult to cross, with narrow lanes twisting round the maze of dikes and drains. The people of Dengie were left largely to their own smelly and profitable devices. When the culture of London spread out far beyond the city, and overran counties like Buckinghamshire, Middlesex and Kent, it kept clear of Dengie. Nor did the Scandinavian name of the place add to its charm; its suggestions of dinginess and dung made the marshes sound like a very undesirable address ...
> The Essex dissenters declined to recognise temporal aristocracies, preferring to elect themselves as a spiritual aristocracy in their own right. They were indeed a peculiar people, living at an oblique angle to the rest of England, so far out on the country's watery margin that they had almost run away to sea ...

Daniel Defoe found the ancestors of the Dengie people in their unhealthy marshes in 1722. The men told him that they married at least five, often fourteen or fifteen wives in a lifetime because, while they were bred to the marsh, the women married into the life and died young.[3] There may be some truth in this, certainly the marshes were unhealthy, but the suspicion lingers (and Defoe shared it) that they were practising the ancient art of pulling the foreigner's leg: it would not have been out of character.[4] Even now some of the

[3] Jonathan Raban, *Coasting* (1986), pp. 293–5.
[4] Daniel Defoe, *A Tour through the Whole Island of Great Britain* (1724–6; 1962 edn), I, pp. 12–14; M. J. Dobson, 'When Malaria Was an English Disease', *The Geographical Magazine*, 54 (1982).

independence of commoners survives in the household economies of twentieth-century Dengie:

> The place was a hive of tiny, tax-free private enterprises. Up every lane there was a brick bungalow with a notice nailed to a tree, advertising the spare-time products of the industrious householder. BIRDTABLES ... LACE BEDSPREADS ... POTTERY LOGS SAWN TO ORDER POND LINERS HONEY GOATS' MILK PEDLAR DOLLS ROTTED MUSHROOM COMPOST EGGS LAID WHILE YOU WAIT TOMS GLADS AND CUES REPLACEMENT WINDSCREENS DWARF LOP RABBITS MAGGOTS SWEET CORN TERRIER MEAL HORSE PELLETS KARATE LESSONS HAIRCUT SIR? GOLDEN LABRADOR PUPPIES READY SOON CLAY PIGEONS CREAM TEAS, WELDING & RESPRAYS BABY BUNNIES PULLETS' EGGS BY THE TRAY PORK SAUSAGES AND SHOE REPAIRS CONCRETE TUBS FOR SALE.[5]

The initiative, the versatility, the isolation and the independence of the Dengie people today recall the insubordinate, stubborn, resourceful commoners of the fens in the eighteenth century. They shared the same mephitic air: the air (and the airs) that repelled investigators and improvers. They shared the same amphibian economy. They lived off grazing in summer, fishing and fowling in winter. They got flags, rushes and reeds to make mats and baskets, thatch and down; they caught eels and fish; they snared rabbits and birds; and like the Dengie people of today they sold them.

Most commoning economies were extinguished by enclosure at some point between the fifteenth and the nineteenth centuries. The pace of the change was uneven. Much of England was still open in 1700; but most of it was enclosed by 1840. Commoners did not always object to enclosure, but often they did. Of the smaller commoners many lost land as well as grazing. They lost a way of life too. In Helpston, wheat and beans still grew after enclosure but they did not grow in open fields. They were fenced in with rails and quickthorn. Enclosure – rightly named – meant the closing of the countryside:

> These paths are stopt – the rude philistines thrall
> Is laid upon them and destroyed them all
> Each little tyrant with his little sign
> Shows where man claims earth glows no more divine

---

[5] Raban, *Coasting*, p. 295.

But paths to freedom and to childhood dear
A board sticks up to notice 'no road here'
And on the tree with ivy overhung
The hated sign by vulgar taste is hung
As tho the very birds should learn to know
When they go there they must no further go
This with the poor scared freedom bade goodbye
And much they feel it in the smothered sigh
And birds and trees and flowers without a name
All sighed when lawless laws enclosure came[6]

Despite Clare's deliberate acts of remembrance, historians have differed in their judgements of the meaning or value of common right. John and Barbara Hammond thought that commoners 'lived their own lives and cultivated the soil on a basis of independence' and with a chance at least for the 'humblest and poorest labourer to rise in the village'. Laxton's first historians, C. S. and C. S. Orwin, agreed with them. But Professor J. D. Chambers did not. In his eyes common right was only a 'thin and squalid curtain' hanging between the poor and even greater poverty. His powerful image has endured. And his opinion later took on some theoretical ballast from the work of Garrett Hardin, who argued that the end of common right was due to the inevitable over-use of common lands, itself an economically logical result of sharing property rights in common.[7]

The argument that common right was already in decline in the modernizing eighteenth century is persuasive. It is so not least for the reason I began with: imagining how commoners lived off the

---

[6] John Clare, 'The Mores', in John Barrell and John Bull, eds., *The Penguin Book of English Pastoral Verse* (1982), p. 415.

[7] J. L. and Barbara Hammond, *The Village Labourer* (1911, repr. 1966) pp. 27, 26; C. S. and C. S. Orwin, *The Open Fields* (Oxford, 1938; 3rd edn 1967), pp. 171–4; J. D. Chambers, 'Enclosure and Labour Supply in the Industrial Revolution', reprinted in E. L. Jones, ed., *Agriculture and Economic Growth in England 1650–1815* (1967), p. 117; Garrett Hardin, 'The Tragedy of the Commons', *Science*, 162 (1968), pp. 1243–8. Cf. Bonnie M. McCay and James M. Acheson, eds., *The Question of the Commons: The Culture and Ecology of Communal Resources* (Tucson, Ariz., 1987). The value of common right, and of common of pasture in particular, was again questioned in 1966 by Professor Chambers with Professor Mingay: J. D. Chambers and G. E. Mingay, *The Agricultural Revolution, 1750–1880* (1966), p. 49; see also Gordon Philpot, 'Enclosure and Population Growth in Eighteenth-Century England', *Explorations in Economic History*, 12 (1975), pp. 29–46.

shared use of land is difficult in an age such as ours when land is owned exclusively, and when enterprise is understood to be essentially individual not co-operative. Even in the eighteenth century it was difficult. Enclosers and critics of commons did not always believe their eyes. They noted the value of common lands but concluded that commoners were poor: 'We don't find them', Pennington wrote of fenland commoners, 'in any better condition than the poor in other places, but, if we may judge from appearances, in a great deal worse.'[8] Common right, Chambers and Mingay wrote almost exactly two hundred years later, was 'usually a very limited benefit'.[9]

The historians' excuse is distance, coupled with too great a respect for the achievements of modern agriculture and English landlords. The eighteenth-century enclosers' excuse was the national interest. In its name they deplored the insubordination of commoners, the unimprovability of their pastures, and the brake on production represented by shared property. In the end they won the argument: they identified parliamentary enclosure with the national interest. But whatever its merits, it is well to remember that this kind of enclosure was controversial. It was not public policy until the middle of the eighteenth century, when private Acts began to flow. And for the next fifty years pamphleteers lobbied Parliament with arguments against it. It follows that an important, and successful, function of critics of commons, and later on of the reporters to the Board of Agriculture too, was to change public opinion on the issue of enclosure, to turn it from hostility to approval. These writers were making a case, not conducting an enquiry. In a century-long remoulding like this, exaggeration and licence played their parts. Necessarily, writers could take no account of the support that common pasture had given English agriculture before enclosure. It had to be written out. More than this, the enclosers' view shaped the official record long after the enclosure period itself. Their central argument, that enclosure was vital to the national interest, is not one historians have ignored. In the last resort for some of them it still justifies the extinction of commoners.

But the historian's job is not to argue the national interest. It is to investigate the allegations made in its name so long ago. To this end

---

[8] W. Pennington, *Reflections on the Various Advantages Resulting from the Draining, Inclosing and Allotting of Large Commons and Common Fields* (1769), p. 33.

[9] Chambers and Mingay, *Agricultural Revolution*, p. 98.

several have shown that impressive developments were made in common-field farming in the long run-up to parliamentary enclosure in the late eighteenth century. In the lowland Midlands in particular, convertible husbandry, the adoption of fodder crops sown on the fallows, and the redivision of the common fields produced a flexibility in agricultural practice which led to all-round increases in fertility and production long before parliamentary enclosure.[10]

But common right, a central part of that agricultural system, remains relatively unexamined. Neither its economic nor its social implications for commoners have been discussed in depth. The 'thin and squalid curtain' still hangs in the cottages of common-field villages. The result is that social historians, following the lead of Professors Hobsbawm and Rudé in *Captain Swing*, have accepted the old case for the vestigial nature of common right. And from it they deduce the disappearance of the peasantry well before enclosure.[11] If eighteenth-century England had a peasantry, they say, it was a poor ghost of its former self, barely surviving on wage labour, helped little by common right.

I argue in this book that they are wrong. The case for the inadequacy of common right relied on evidence taken from only part of the contemporary record and that mostly from the pens of those reporters to the Board of Agriculture who supported enclosure and were necessarily hostile to common right. It discounted the large volume of anti-enclosure opinion. It was unaware of the frequency of anti-enclosure protest. It gave little weight to the apostasy of Arthur Young and others who began seriously to

[10] Amongst others: H. L. Gray, *English Field Systems*, Harvard Historical Studies, XXII (1915); W. G. Hoskins, 'The Leicestershire Farmer in the Sixteenth Century', in *Transactions of the Leicestershire Archaeological Society*, 22 (1941–5), 'The Leicestershire Farmer in the Seventeenth Century', *Agricultural History* 25 (1951), and *The Midland Peasant. The Economic and Social History of a Leicestershire Village* (1957, 1965); Joan Thirsk, *English Peasant Farming: The Agrarian History of Lincolnshire from Tudor to Recent Times* (1957), and Thirsk, ed., *Agrarian History of England and Wales*, IV (Cambridge, 1967), ch. 1; M. A. Havinden, 'Agricultural Progress on Open-Field Oxfordshire', *Agricultural History Review*, 9 (1961), pp. 73–4; D. B. Grigg, *The Agricultural Revolution in South Lincolnshire* (Cambridge, 1966); J. M. Martin, 'The Parliamentary Enclosure Movement and Rural Society in Warwickshire', *Agricultural History Review*, 15 (1967); R. C. Allen, 'Enclosure, Farming Methods, and the Growth of Productivity in the South Midlands', University of British Columbia, Department of Economics, Discussion Paper no. 86–44 (1986).

[11] See below, Chapter 10.

question the treatment of commoners from the 1790s onwards. It defined commoners or peasantry too narrowly, regarding occupiers and owners of small amounts of land too little for a farm as essentially outside the pale of landed society.

For all these reasons we have to look again at the lives of commoners and the meaning of common right. We need to know more precisely who commoners were, where they lived, and whether the value of their rights was maintained or eroded before enclosure. We need to be aware of the variety of commoning economies and the reasons for the relative strength and weakness of common right in different unenclosed parishes.

With this knowledge we can learn something about the economic value to commoners of common right: its income value. But the survival of common right had other implications too: for wider economic change in an industrializing society; for property law; for social relations in common-field villages.[12] My concern is primarily with the last: I want to look at common right as a part of the structure of social relations in common-field villages.

Chapter 1 introduces the two themes of the book: income value and social meaning. It looks back past the historiography of common right to the eighteenth-century writers on enclosure – those for and those against. From their debate three things become clear. First, they believed commoners to be numerous and well-dispersed in space and time through the country and the century; second, they thought common right gave commoners an income and a status or independence they found valuable; third, they agreed that the extinction of common right at enclosure marked the decline of small farms and a transition for commoners from some degree of independence to complete dependence on a wage. All eighteenth-century commentators saw a relationship between the survival and decline of common right and the nature of social relations in England.

These themes are then explored. In part I, 'Survival', chapter 2 describes the identity and ubiquity of commoners entitled to common of pasture, perhaps the most valuable common right in lowland England. Chapter 3 considers potential threats to that entitlement before enclosure. The three chapters that follow discuss the value of common of pasture and access to common waste. Two describe how juries maintained the value of common pastures

---

[12] On common right and law see E. P. Thompson, 'Custom, Law and Common Right', in his *Customs in Common* (1991), pp. 97–184.

(readers concerned first with the main line of argument may wish to return to these later). The fuel, food and materials found in unculti-vated common waste, and their social significance, are the subject of Chapter 6.

Part II, 'Decline', is concerned with the economic and social meanings of the extinction of common right at enclosure. Chapter 7 tells the story of enclosure in two villages. It introduces two themes: the loss of land and rights that followed enclosure, and commoners' resistance. Chapters 8 and 9 show that the experience of these villages was not unusual. Chapter 8 argues that commoners in many Midland villages lost land at enclosure, and suggests that a new set of smallholders took their place, with a new agriculture, higher rents, and a new relationship to their landlords and the market. Widespread and longlived resistance to enclosure is the concern of Chapter 9.

In a concluding chapter I argue that commoners were the eighteenth-century survivors of the English peasantry, not yet labourers. What this means is the object of the book, but how I have approached the issue is important.

Lack of imagination is not the only reason why writing a history of commoners is difficult. When my husband's elderly aunt moved out of her house in 1986 she came across a number of prints taken from engravings. One of them, 'Cottage Wealth', was by George Morland, the most prolific and probably the most popular painter in late eighteenth and early nineteenth-century England. In the twentieth century Morland's work has been criticized for its senti-mentality, its flight from realism, but at the time his critics thought him too accurate, too *un*sentimental in his record of village life, unwilling to idealize, reluctant to argue a case. They remarked on his ability 'to present the poor without affectation or idealisation'. But the engravers of Morland's paintings sentimentalized them. They suggested a more prosperous, contented peasantry, and, in the absence of the original paintings, misled later critics.[13] In this print a woman feeds cabbage leaves to three pigs in a stable; she is watched by a donkey and a dog, and from the doorway a child looks out at us. The animals are neither sleek nor skeletal, some plaster has fallen off the stable wall but the window is glazed; the woman is

---

[13] John Barrell, *The Dark Side of the Landscape* (1980), pp. 90, 120–2. Criticism of the French painter of peasant life, Jean-François Millet, followed the same path; see Griselda Pollock, *Millet* (1977), p. 52.

intent on her business. It is a cottage scene, probably painted in the 1780s.[14] If the title 'Cottage Wealth' is ironic, it could as well be a statement of fact. I do not know why this print was brought from Lancashire in the 1860s to Montreal. Nor do I know whether Morland's popularity came from the fact that he recorded the lives of the peasantry or because his engravers fed a sentimentality about rural life pervasive in newly urban England.

Realism or nostalgia? The problem of interpreting Morland's work is one presented to twentieth-century historians by Oliver Goldsmith, John Clare, Thomas Bewick, the later work of Arthur Young, and all the other critics of enclosure and engrossment. But their testimony is vital because on crucial questions they give us the view from below. Morland painted cottagers' livestock, Clare described the breaking apart of customary relationships. No other sources get as close to peasants who left no wills, for whom no inventories were drawn up, who had few family papers, no account ledgers or bills. No one, not even the pastoral trio of Richard Gough, Gilbert White and David Davies, took a census of stock-keeping in eighteenth-century villages.

Instead the evidence of peasant economy comes indirectly. It is implied in the field orders of customary courts, which show the survival and protection of common right, and in the Land Tax returns, which show the survival of small peasant landholding in common-field villages. It is clearer in the resistance of commoners to enclosure on the grounds that they would lose their cows, their lands and their wastes, though the complete map of their resistance will never be drawn. It is implied again in the inventory of useful products found on uncultivated common and waste, and again in the stubborn memory of roast beef and milk and the swift disappearance of both from labourers' diets after enclosure.[15] It is described most directly in the work of pamphleteers, writers to the Board of Agriculture, and guilt-ridden improvers.

I have used all these sources in writing this account of eighteenth-century commoners. Taken together they make a case for the survival into the age of parliamentary enclosure of a numerous and

---

[14] Sir Walter Gilbey, Bt, and E. D. Cumming, *George Morland his Life and Works* (1907), p. 271.

[15] Alun Howkins and Ian C. Dyck, '"The Time's Alteration": Popular Ballads, Rural Radicalism and William Cobbett', *History Workshop Journal*, Issue 23 (1987), pp. 29–34; Board of Agriculture, *General Report on Enclosures* [ed. Arthur Young] (1808), pp. 150–2.

identifiable English peasantry. But no pile of Land Tax returns or field orders is worth as much as the realism of George Morland or the anger of John Clare. The conclusion of this book is that they saw clearly. Others saw too: whether they were defenders of commoners, or supporters of enclosure, writers about common right and enclosure thought they were witnessing the end of peasantry. But Clare and Morland saw the change from where commoners stood: they looked with them, not at them. That there were so few who came so close to the peasantry is the strongest testimony of all to its isolation in the later eighteenth century. By then prescriptions were many (and Morland was criticized for making none), descriptions few.

It is the argument of this book that common right prospered in the eighteenth century where forest, fen, hill and vale villages had generous common pastures, or where they housed many small occupiers of land and cottages.[16] Here, commoners ensured the value of common right with an effective local system of by-laws, and common right offered some independence of wages and markets. More than this: it was a crucial part of the structure of social relations. Commoners were the last of the English peasantry. When, despite their best efforts, enclosure acts extinguished common right from most of lowland England in the late eighteenth and early nineteenth centuries, its loss played a large part in turning the last of the English peasantry into a rural working class.

What the survival of an eighteenth-century peasantry means in more purely economic terms is not the focus of my argument but some implications are clear.

First, the agricultural production accompanying industrialization in lowland England until the 1820s, and for an even longer period in the villages serving the industrial Midlands and north, was generated by *peasant* producers as well as tenant farmers in classic capitalist mode. In other words, agricultural production came not from a social structure on the land of tenant farmers and agricultural labourers but from a synergy of family farm, agricultural business and agricultural labour. A parallel in manufacturing production is the survival of domestic industry into the nineteenth

---

[16] For the disappearance of the *yeomen* in the eighteenth century before enclosure, see Allen, *Enclosure and the Yeoman* (Oxford, 1992), esp. chapter 5. While I agree with Allen that there were often few yeomen in open-field villages at enclosure, the small, commons-using peasantry survived in greater numbers; accordingly the loss of commons at enclosure crucially affected their social relations: cf. Allen, *Enclosure and the Yeoman*, pp. 85–6.

century. It is possible (and Carter shows this in Aberdeenshire) that peasant production actually expanded in some places as population grew and industrialization advanced, just as domestic industry did. Certainly small master or kauf-system rural industry accompanied and supported peasant landholding in some Midland villages where it also encouraged opposition to enclosure.[17] But whether this peasant production was a brake on agricultural productivity or an accelerator is not my concern here. Instead I describe the rules, the priorities and the conduct of common-field farming as behaviour freighted with important implications for social relations.[18]

Second, peasant production may have subsidized manufacturing production and the poor rate – something nineteenth-century English manufacturers came to envy in the economies of their European competitors – and this may have encouraged early industrial growth. In Northamptonshire, for example, the decline of the woollen industry accompanied the enclosure of the common fields.

Finally, commoners' relative independence of wages and the cash economy helps to illuminate the nature of the eighteenth-century agricultural labour market. Their tendency not to work for wages on every occasion goes some way to explain the late eighteenth-century complaint of labour shortage. Their independence also helps to explain the equally common complaint about the poor quality of labour. It throws light on the belief held for half the century that population was falling; and on the fear that military reserves were insufficient. In other words the eighteenth-century labour market worked like one staffed by peasants, not one supplied by wage-labourers.

A consequence is that the rise in labour productivity in agriculture, which seems to have been accomplished over the century without proportionally enlarging the labour force, may have been accomplished in part by turning peasant labourers into agricultural

---

[17] Ian Carter, *Farm Life in Northeast Scotland 1840–1914: The Poor Man's Country* (Edinburgh, 1979). J. M. Neeson, 'Opposition to Enclosure in Northamptonshire c.1760–1800', in Andrew Charlesworth, ed., *An Atlas of Rural Protest in Britain, 1548–1900* (1983), pp. 60–2. For the extension of cultivation in England see Mark Overton, 'Agricultural Revolution? Development of the Agrarian Economy in Early Modern England', in *Explorations in Historical Geography*, eds. A. R. H. Baker and D. J. Gregory (Cambridge, 1984), p. 126.

[18] For open-field productivity see Allen, 'Enclosure, Farming Methods, and the Growth of Productivity', and his *Enclosure and the Yeoman*.

labourers at enclosure.[19] This is not to argue, as some historians have, that a benevolent enclosure movement generated employment for the underemployed. It is to suggest instead that commoners became utterly dependent on miserable wages. And that to earn them they worked harder.[20]

But the history of labour productivity, like the history of land productivity, is not the story told here. My concern is to describe and explain the survival and decline of commoners in eighteenth-century common-field England.

[19] For an explanation of labour productivity earlier in the century see Ann Kussmaul, *A General View of the Rural Economy of England, 1538–1840* (Cambridge, 1990), p. 175.

[20] Gregory Clark, 'Productivity Growth without Technical Change in European Agriculture before 1850', *Journal of Economic History*, 47 (1987); N. F. R. Crafts, 'Income Elasticities of Demand and the Release of Labour by Agriculture during the British Industrial Revolution', *Journal of European Economic History*, 9 (1980); cf. R. C. Allen, 'The Growth of Labour Productivity in Early Modern English Agriculture', University of British Columbia, Department of Economics, Discussion Paper no. 86-40.

1. *The question of value*

... the true interest of a nation, the authority of government, and the liberties and property of the subject, are all best established and promoted, by keeping things in a state in which the bulk of the people may support themselves and their families.

> *An Enquiry into the Reasons for and against Inclosing the Open Fields Humbly Submitted to All Who have Property in them, and Especially the Members of the British legislature* (Coventry, 1767), pp. 5–6

... the province of ninety-nine out of an hundred was to receive, not to give orders.

> John Clark, *General View of the Agriculture of the County of Hereford with observations on the Means of its Improvement* (1794), p. 75.

From the fifteenth century to the nineteenth, evaluations of common right were inseparable from the larger question of enclosure and the engrossment of small farms. For enclosure meant the extinction of common right and the extinction of common right meant the decline of small farms: 'Strip the small farms of the benefit of the commons', wrote one observer, 'and they are all at one stroke levelled to the ground.'[1] Disagreement about the value of common right has always been a debate within this debate. In our own century it is as part of the same argument that the quarrel continues between historians. If I begin with them it is not because they have the most to say about common right but because increasingly they

---

[1] [Stephen Addington], *Inquiry into the Advantages and Disadvantages Resulting from Bills of Enclosure* (1780), p. 14.

have chosen to say the least and in so choosing they have misunder-
stood the full meaning, the real value, of common right.

It was not always so.[2] To the Hammonds, commons were the
hallmark, 'the distinguishing mark', of the old village because they
gave labourers and small occupiers an independence of the wage
that they would lose when the commons were enclosed. Lord Ernle
also thought commons were the lowest rung on the property-owning
ladder. Even E. C. K. Gonner described a social transformation at
enclosure amounting to the end of peasantry that was due in part to
inadequate compensation for the loss of commons. And C. S. and
C. S. Orwin, historians of Laxton, agreed.[3]

But the place of the commons in the creation of a peasantry was
not discussed by a later generation of historians, who disagreed with
the Hammonds and whose interpretation became the new orthodoxy of enclosure history. For them the question of value was not to
be measured in the broad terms of the social relationships engen-
dered by independence of the wage. It was measured as no more
than an *income* dependent on the quality of pasture on open fields
and commons, and the regulation of open-field agriculture.[4] *The
Agricultural Revolution 1750–1880* is the best expression of this
view. Here J. D. Chambers and G. E. Mingay doubted the value of
common pastures. They described 'the impossibility of improving
the livestock, and the risks of wildfire spread of disease among
beasts herded together on the commons and fields' of open villages.[5]
They did so despite a concurrent re-evaluation of open-field agriculture that emphasized its relative dynamism.[6] To accommodate
some of that evidence they argued that where there *was* progress in

[2] See above, pp. 6–7.
[3] Hammond and Hammond, *Village Labourer*, pp. 27, 26; R. E. Prothero, Lord
Ernle, *English Farming Past and Present* (1912; 6th edn, 1961), pp. 306–7; Gonner
was less certain than the Hammonds of the timeless value of common right, and
doubtful of the connection between enclosure and high rates of poor relief. He
thought the end of peasantry was less a consequence of deliberate expropriation
than of the gradual rationalization of agricultural practice of which the extinction
of common right at enclosure was part, E. C. K. Gonner, *Common Land and
Inclosure* (1912; 2nd edn 1966), pp. 362–6; Orwin and Orwin, *Open Fields*,
p. 178.
[4] J. D. Chambers, 'Enclosure and Labour Supply in the Industrial Revolution',
Economic History Review, 2nd series, 5 (1953), p. 336.
[5] Chambers and Mingay, *Agricultural Revolution*, p. 49. The question of disease is
discussed below in Chapter 4.
[6] Chambers and Mingay, *Agricultural Revolution*, pp. 49–52, citing W. G. Hoskins,
'The Leicestershire Farmer', and Havinden, 'Agricultural Progress', pp. 74–82.

open-field farming it was accompanied by the individualization of practice. The result was that the progressive open-field parish looked remarkably like an enclosed one: rights and commons were engrossed into a few hands.[7] But where there was *no* progress in open-field farming, common of pasture was of almost no use: commons were unregulated, cattle were unstinted and overstocked, disease was rife. In short, either rights were virtually useless because practice was so poor, or they were of equally little value because progressive practice was so good that it had virtually swept away the old communal system and common right with it.

As a result the argument exonerated the very controversial means by which common right was extinguished between 1750 and 1850: parliamentary enclosure. If commoners who lost common right at enclosure had long before ceased to benefit from it, or if the stock they fed on commons was inferior and diseased, then enclosure, in taking commons away, impoverished no one. The subsequent popularity of this view spanned the political spectrum of social historians. It appeared that the English peasantry, small and ill-nourished at the start of the eighteenth century, had died by 1750 – before enclosure. Common right has received little attention ever since.[8]

It was, of course, very much a part of the eighteenth-century scheme of things. Though equally enmeshed in the enclosure debate, the value of common right was discussed then in the larger terms later taken up by the Hammonds. And enclosure was as controversial in the eighteenth century as it had ever been. From early on, and particularly from the 1760s to the 1790s, writers declared its legiti-

---

[7] Chambers and Mingay, *Agricultural Revolution*, pp. 49–52.

[8] The exception is K. D. M. Snell's *Annals of the Labouring Poor: Social Change and Agrarian England 1660–1900* (Cambridge, 1985), which *assumes* the value of commons given both widespread complaint about the loss of cows and fuel after enclosure, and the belief that the end of commons would increase the supply of labour. M. E. Turner's work on small owners at enclosure neglects common right and is inconclusive about change: Turner, 'Parliamentary Enclosure and Land-ownership Change in Buckinghamshire', *Economic History Review*, 2nd series, 27 (1975), pp. 565–81; J. A. Yelling gives common right more weight than Chambers and Mingay but draws no conclusion about its importance, in part because 'we have only the judgement of contemporaries to depend upon': Yelling, *Common Field and Enclosure in England, 1450–1850* (1977), pp. 230–2. Historians who noted the dislocation of enclosure and the sense of loss following the end of common right, M. K. Ashby, *Joseph Ashby of Tysoe, 1859–1919* (Cambridge, 1961; 1974 edn); E. P. Thompson, *The Making of the English Working Class* (1963), A. J. Peacock, *Bread or Blood* (1965), did not carry the argument (see below Chapter 10).

macy or illegitimacy in pamphlets, articles and reports. Read together, they become a connected series of exchanges on the nature of enclosure and the meanings of common right, made between members of the political nation. They are the physical survivals of a lengthy public policy debate. Their authors often knew each other, cited, applauded or ridiculed each other. Their work is substantially one text.

Despite this integrity, historians have not examined the subject as a whole. Selective quotation supports one interpretation of the effects of enclosure or another; too often there is no reference to contemporary voices at all. But looking at the debate as an historical event in itself disinters the polemic and illuminates the meaning of common right for eighteenth-century observers. It shows us the world as they saw it. And it also reveals some of the world as it was. It becomes clear that beneath the argument between these writers lay a fundamental agreement. Opponents agreed on the nature of English rural society before enclosure, and they agreed on enclosure's effect: it turned commoners into labourers. Their disagreement was about the worth of each class; neither side doubted that the transformation occurred, and had profound consequences. I shall argue later on that this was an informed debate: individualized agriculture, a new set of smallholders, and a bitter sense of betrayal amongst commoners replaced an economy dependent on common right, petty landholding and communal regulation. In this chapter I want to look at the debate's shared perception of the very different societies common-field and enclosed villages supported.

THE SOCIAL MEANING OF COMMON RIGHT

Common right was defended at the centre of government in sermons, pamphlets, judgements and speeches for three hundred years. Eighteenth-century defenders wrote in the tradition of Thomas More, Hugh Latimer, Thomas Lever, Robert Crowley, John Hales, Sir Francis Bacon, the Levellers at Putney, Gerrard Winstanley and John Moore. These men had condemned depopulation and the loss of commons at enclosure, and Tudor and some Stuart governments agreed with them.[9] They did not condemn

---

[9] Official, intellectual, and some ecclesiastical opposition to enclosure did not prevent it, as Hugh Latimer lamented: Christopher Hampton, ed., *A Radical*

enclosures that benefited poor peasants by reorganizing their land to their advantage. Nor did agricultural writers who supported enclosure – Fitzherbert, Tusser, Norden – approve of enclosure for the conversion of arable land to pasture or the loss of commons without full and proper compensation in land.[10] This was 'bad' enclosure in anybody's terms, and for much of this period it was illegal.

What distinguishes the period from the mid seventeenth century to the 1790s is the development then, not before, of a public argument in favour of enclosure even when it *did* cause local distress. This followed the final withdrawal of official resistance to enclosure in the early seventeenth century: the last Inquisitions of Depopulation were held in the 1620s.[11]

The public debate opened in the 1650s with a series of pamphlets written by two Midland clergymen, Joseph Lee and John Moore, one of whom (Lee) was also an encloser.[12] It is an important debate but short-lived: little public argument about enclosure appears to have followed the Restoration.[13] Timothy Nourse and Daniel Hilman broke the silence in the first decade of the eighteenth century; the 1730s saw the publication of pamphlets by John Cowper, Thomas Andrews, and others, the estate management and husbandry treatises of Edward and John Laurence, and the first few

Reader: The Struggle for Change in England 1381–1914 (1984), p. 109. For official attitudes to early modern enclosure see E. Power and R. H. Tawney, *Tudor Economic Documents, I, Agriculture and Industry* (1924, new edn, 1951), section 1. See also Joan Thirsk, *Tudor Enclosures* (Historical Association, 1958, reprinted 1967, new edn, 1989); Peter Ramsey, *Tudor Economic Problems* (1963), ch. 1; Joan Thirsk, ed., *The Agrarian History of England and Wales, IV, 1500–1640*, pp. 213–39; and John E. Martin, *Feudalism to Capitalism. Peasant and Landlord in English Agrarian Development* (1983; 1986).

[10] R. H. Tawney, *The Agrarian Problem in the Sixteenth Century* (1912, reprinted 1967), pp. 149–50. Levellers at Putney could imagine useful enclosure too: A. S. P. Woodhouse, ed., *Puritanism and Liberty. Being the Army Debates (1647–9) from the Clarke Manuscripts with Supplementary Documents* (1938), p. 339.

[11] J. E. Martin, 'Enclosure and the Inquisitions of 1607: An Examination of Kerridge's Article, "The Returns of the Inquisitions of Depopulation"', *Agricultural History Review* 30 (1982); Mary E. Finch, *The Wealth of Five Northamptonshire Families 1540–1640*, Publications of the Northamptonshire Record Society, XIX (Oxford, 1956), pp. 162–3.

[12] See Joyce Oldham Appleby, *Economic Thought and Ideology in Seventeenth-Century England* (1978), pp. 59–63, and below, p. 43.

[13] Enclosers may have gone unchallenged, thanks to a productive agriculture and a newly stable population, thus Appleby, *Economic Thought and Ideology*, p. 57: 'The fear of famine ceased to haunt the English'. Plenty may have stifled the public expression of opposition to enclosure but not necessarily the local.

private enclosure Acts.[14] Then, in the 1760s, dearth and a strong spate of Acts drove defenders of commons to write against enclosure again. This time more advocates of enclosure felt impelled to answer them than ever before: bad enclosure, first sanctioned in the mid seventeenth century, found its most passionate supporters in the mid eighteenth. To understand how they and their opponents saw commoners, and to understand what they expected enclosure would do to them, I want to pick up the debate in 1700, beginning with the case of the defenders of commons.

Always contentious, Timothy Nourse began *Campania Foelix* with a denunciation of commoners. They were 'very rough and savage in their Dispositions', of 'leveling Principles', 'refractory to Government', 'insolent and tumultuous'. More dangerous than mastiffs and stallions, they needed the same harsh treatment, civility was futile: it was easier 'to teach a Hog to play upon the Bagpipes, than to soften such brutes by Courtesie'. In the flora of English landed society these men were 'trashy Weeds or Nettles, growing usually upon Dunghills, which if touch'd gently will sting, but being squeez'd hard will never hurt us'.[15] As the men, so too the land they lived on: commons gave only a 'lean and hungry soil' to lean and hungry stock ('And as the men, *so are the Cattle*') unfit for the dairy or the yoke.

But Nourse also thought that common-field agriculture supported a larger population than enclosed farms, that it provided soldiers and sailors ('excellent good Food for Powder'), and a supply of labour more valuable than any increase in the supply of cattle. In effect, the very qualities of insubordination and independence that made commoners a nuisance also made them brave and prolific (like mastiffs and stallions). And because these qualities sprang from the commons themselves, their survival was in the national interest.[16]

[14] See below, *passim*.
[15] Timothy Nourse, *Campania Foelix, or a Discourse of the Benefits and Improvements of Husbandry* (1700, 2nd edn, 1706), pp. 15–16. Timothy Nourse, miscellaneous writer, born Newent. BA Oxford 1655–8; holy orders; admirer of Dr Robert South; associated with Roman Catholics, converted in 1672, lost fellowship; returned to Newent and a country life; 'suffered much on the outbreak of the popish plot', died 1699, *Dictionary of National Biography* (1885).
[16] On the national interest see Appleby, *Economic Thought and Ideology*, esp. p. 277. Nourse echoed Shakespeare's King Henry V:
And you, good yeomen,
Whose limbs were made in England, show us here

And commons supported a viable, even admirable way of life too. Commoners were poor but they were not paupers, their cottages and commons were miniature farms. Few had no pasture ('a pretty Plot of Ground like a Meadow') or some field land ('a little Rib of Tillage for Bread-Corn'), or fruit trees ('a slender Orchard').[17] Nourse's description of this economy is as approving as his description of commoners' insubordination was emphatic. He could even recognize in the 'familiar enjoyments' of commoners living in their 'Rural Mansions' a bond with much richer men: they were both property owners. In fact, commoners' rights were older than any manorial lord's.

In 1732 John Cowper argued in terms of the national interest too. Open-field villages were the source of all grain, all manufactures, and abundant cheap labour. Enclosure would devastate all three.[18] The profit of a few landlords was nothing compared to the 'Good of the Whole', for how could wealth be produced but by labour?[19] Cowper knew 'of no Set of Men that toil and labour so hard as the smaller Farmers and Freeholders, none who are more industrious to encrease the Product of the Earth; none who are more serviceable to the Commonwealth; and consequently none who better deserve Encouragement'.[20] And Thomas Andrews followed Cowper in identifying the victims of enclosure as less the needy poor who dominated the seventeenth-century debate (and its twentieth-century re-statement) than the working, productive poor: 'I mean, not only the *Poor*, strictly so called, but also our poorer Sort of *Freeholders, Farmers*, and Manufacturers'. When they lost their commons at enclosure they lost their independence too: 'Stand (says the Philosopher) from betwixt me and the Sun, lest thou take away what thou can'st not give me. For, in those places where the Poor

> The mettle of your pasture; let us swear
> That you were worth your breeding: which I doubt not;
> For there is none of you so mean and base,
> That hath not noble lustre in your eyes.
>
> (Henry V, Act III, Scene 1, lines 25–30)

[17] Nourse, *Campania Foelix*, pp. 15–16, 100, 102, 100, 103–4.

[18] John Cowper, *An Essay Proving that Inclosuring of Commons and Common Field Land is Contrary to the Interest of the Nation* (1732), pp. 1, 5–7, 12, 22–3, 24. Cowper is described as a Surrey farmer in the *Dictionary of National Biography* entry for Edward Laurence.

[19] Cowper, *Essay*, p. 10; here he is answering J. Laurence, *A New System of Agriculture and Gardening* (1726), pp. 45–6, which made a case for the individual's right to profit from enclosure.

[20] Cowper, *Essay*, pp. 3–4, 18.

are deprived of their Common Pasturage, the most comfortable Gift of a Free Country is taken away.'[21]

A generation later, in the 1760s and 1770s, enclosure Bills, often leading to conversion to pasture, began to fill the committee rooms of the House of Commons. In addition poor harvests provoked serious food riots in 1766 and again in the early 1770s.[22] Arguments against enclosure were familiar. But criticism of enclosers as profiteers began to sharpen, and so did the fear that enclosure threatened internal peace.

The familiar arguments were three. A decline in small farmers would weaken England's military strength. Tillage was more beneficial to the public than pasture. And, again, it was not only more productive, it was also 'necessary to the very being of the community'. 'The true interest of a nation' was served by a society in which most people could live without wages. But here is the sharper criticism: enclosure impoverished twenty small farmers to enrich one. It reduced the size of holdings that were once nine or ten acres to only six or seven. Rents rose and prices followed. Commoners became labourers, mere 'tools'. Landlords grew lazy, some 'little better than tyrants or bashaws ... who when they had less wealth were more sensible of their dependence and connections, and could feel both for the poor and the public upon every emergency'. Their claim to the exclusive enjoyment of their land was nothing more than an excuse for 'shutting out' the poor from their rights on the common fields, from gleaning, from getting turf and furze.[23] And the fear: in destroying village relations enclosure also endangered relations in the nation as a whole. It brought about an open dissatisfaction that risked mob rule and encouraged sedition, even Jacobitism.[24]

[21] Thomas Andrews, *An Enquiry into the Encrease and Miseries of the Poor of England; which are shewn to be I, Taxes ... II, Luxury ... III, Absence of Great Men from their Counties ... IV, Inclosures of Commons* (1738), p. 38.

[22] On the chronology of Acts see Michael E. Turner, *English Parliamentary Enclosure. Its Historical Geography and Economic History* (Folkestone and Hamden, 1980), ch. 3, esp. p. 68, Table 10: 39 Acts were passed in the 1730s, 393 in the 1760s, 640 in the 1770s; on conversion to pasture, see pp. 75–6. On food riot see Andrew Charlesworth, ed., *An Atlas of Rural Protest in Britain, 1548–1900* (1984), pp. 88–94.

[23] Anon., *An Enquiry into the Reasons for and against Inclosing the Open Fields Humbly Submitted ...* (Coventry 1767), pp. 5–6, 8, 11.

[24] Anon., *Enquiry into the Reasons*, pp. 10, 12, 14. The author replied to Homer on the question of an individual's rights, arguing that if everyone had the right to exclusive enjoyment then no one had a right to 'dictate to any one of their

Writing, as this author did, in the wake of the 1766 food riots and with the example of John Wilkes before him, 'vox populi' might well be considered 'vox dei'.[25] But the belief that enclosers stole independence from the poor outlived this crisis. As enclosures accelerated through the 1770s, and into the 1780s when inflated poor rates and more profitable alternative investments temporarily slowed them down, the economy of commoners and their distinctive independence were more thoroughly described.

Consider, for example, this account of the economy of farmers' wives, written by an anonymous 'Country Farmer' in 1786. Before enclosure, he wrote, small farms were numerous, rents were low, and the land was tilled, not left for pasture. Because profit did not come easily, farmers turned their hands to everything. Their wives did the same. Their dairies stocked the markets with eggs and poultry. The money they made was spent on shop goods for their families; anything left over they 'used to sink into their own pockets as a kind of pin-money, to buy themselves and children such necessary little articles as required, without applying to their husbands for every trifling penny they might want to lay out'.

But, after enclosure and the foreclosure of mortgages, these families moved to other parishes (if they could afford a settlement) or they left, indentured, for America. The old lingered on in the village. All were 'fenced out of their livelyhood', prey to the ambitious and aspiring.[26] Enclosure depopulated and depopulation led to the social and economic transformation of the village.

Defenders of commons argued that common fields supported the economies of small farmers (and their wives) then, and those of the

neighbours'. Moreover 'though he has only an acre in a field in which they have five hundred ... His one acre may be as important to him and his family, as their five hundred to them', p. 15; and Henry Homer, *An Essay on the Nature and Method of Ascertaining the Specifick Shares of Proprietors, upon the Inclosure of Common Fields. With observations upon the inconveniences of open fields, and upon the objections to their inclosure particularly as far as they relate to the publick and the poor* (1766, 2nd edn, Oxford, n.d.), pp. 5, 6.
[25] Anon., *Enquiry into the Reasons* p. 37. *Vox Populi, Vox Dei: Being True Maxims of Government*, was the title of a frequently printed Whig pamphlet expounding a contract theory of government first published in 1709 and possibly written by Daniel Defoe: see H. T. Dickinson, *Liberty and Property: Political Ideology in Eighteenth-Century Britain* (1977), p. 73.
[26] Anon., *Cursory Remarks on Inclosures, Shewing the Pernicious and Destructive Consequences of Inclosing Common Fields &c. By a Country Farmer* (1786), pp. 19–20, 5–7, 22.

'cottager, mechanic, and inferior shopkeepers' too. They generated independence, thrift, and industry: 'this common-right is an incitement to industry, and also an encouragement to the young men and women to intermarry, and is the means of supporting their children with credit and comfort, and of course renders them very valuable members of society'. The thrifty children of thrifty cottagers became farm servants, saved to get married and stock a cottage of their own, and while the men worked as labourers on neighbouring farms the women tended the livestock at home. In all this they were unexceptional: 'I could mention many cottagers in my neighbourhood ... who keep two or three milch cows, two or three calves a rearing, forty or fifty sheep, two or three hogs ... chickens, ducks, geese and turkies, to the amount in number of fifty to one hundred in a year.' And at the worst of times the honesty and energy of cottagers kept them from theft and the poor rate.[27]

Probably the most published eighteenth-century defender of commons was Dr Richard Price, the Unitarian defender of the American revolution. His *Observations on Reversionary Payments*, first published in 1771, ran to at least six editions.[28] Simply put, Price said that enclosure concentrated wealth. It ruined small farming families and drove them into the towns; it raised prices; it intensified labour and encouraged luxury. Above all, it destroyed equality: 'modern policy is, indeed, more favourable to the higher classes of people', he wrote, 'and the consequences may in time

[27] Farmers used the common only 'from the time the grass begins to shoot to the mowing time'. Cottagers took this for granted; they were fortunate that 'great farmers', and the stewards of large landlords had not conspired to let their cottages decay, in order to engross their rights: Anon., *A Political Enquiry into the Consequences of Enclosing Waste Lands, and the Causes of the Present High Price of Butchers Meat. Being the Sentiments of a Society of Farmers in ------shire* (1785), pp. 43–4, 111, 46, 48. For a discussion of the engrossment of cottage rights see Chapter 3.

[28] In 1786 his adversary, John Howlett (whose arguments are considered next), complained that Price had 'printed and reprinted' his views, so confirming and establishing them without 'seeming to have at all attended to the accounts, of equal authenticity, repeatedly given on the other side of the question'. The reason for the popularity of Price's work may have been his tables for calculating annuities as much as his observations about enclosure, but to Howlett and some radicals (Thomas Spence, Thomas Evans) the latter were more important. Howlett replied to Price's *Essay on the Population of England from the Revolution to the Present Time* (1780), in *An Enquiry into the Influence which Enclosures Have Had upon the Population of this Kingdom* (1781); he refers to *Observations on Reversionary Payments* in the second edition (1786), p. 2.

prove that the whole kingdom will consist of only gentry and beggars, or grandees and slaves'.[29]

These opponents of enclosure writing in the first half of the eighteenth century, and in the first wave of parliamentary enclosures from 1750 to the outbreak of war in 1793, framed their arguments with three observations. First, enclosure was for the conversion of arable to pasture; second, it impoverished small farmers and landless commoners who lost land, use rights and work; third, it diminished the supply of military as well as agricultural and manufacturing labour. Most of them thought that enclosure depopulated, and that depopulation would destroy the basis of both national and local wealth. In contrast, the value of common right lay in its support of a fertile, hardy population employed in the production of corn, in the encouragement it gave to manufacture, and in the military reserve it sheltered. These arguments flowed from fear of depopulation in its narrowest sense – the unpeopling of enclosed villages. But when writers described depopulation they meant *more* than a decline in numbers: they were talking about the disappearance of an entire economy. It was one rooted in hard work, governed by thrift, independent of the poor rate and the wage. Commoners were to be cherished.

Like defenders of commons, writers in support of enclosure in the eighteenth century also argued in terms of the national interest – though they adopted the argument late in the day, and commoners might have argued with their definition of the nation.[30]

The Reverend John Howlett, after Arthur Young, was the most active public supporter of enclosure in the 1780s. He was also a friend of Young, with whom he set up a correspondence, and in whose *Annals of Agriculture* he published for most of his career.[31] Howlett's patron in the 1780s was Alexander Wedderburn, Lord Loughborough, later Baron Rosslyn, an improver with a Scottish enlightenment background and an English legal platform. As a young man Wedderburn had been a pupil and friend of Adam

[29] Price, *Observations* (6th edn, 1805), quoted in Karl Marx, *Capital* (Everyman edn, 1962), II, pp. 158–9; again, engrossing 'is, indeed, erecting *private* benefit on *public* calamity; and for the sake of a temporary advantage, giving up the nation to depopulation and misery', Price, *Observations* (2nd edn, 1772), p. 361, cited in Wilhelm Hasbach, *A History of the English Agricultural Labourer* (1908; 1966 edn), pp. 158–9.

[30] See below, pp. 42–6.

[31] G. E. Mingay, ed., *Arthur Young and his Times* (1975), p. 12.

Smith, and had developed an interest in Scottish agriculture.[32] In England he became Solicitor General in Lord North's administration (1771–4), then Chief Justice of Common Pleas (1780–93), and Pitt's Lord Chancellor (1793–1801). In 1788 as Chief Justice he declared against shared land use and in favour of the exclusive enjoyment of property when he ruled that the right to glean could not be defended at common law.[33]

Loughborough may have been drawn to Howlett's ability as a demographer and statistician, and to his unequivocally improving ideas. In 1781 these led Howlett to repudiate Dr Price's allegation that enclosure depopulated in a pamphlet he dedicated to Loughborough.[34] He wrote in a decade of harvest failure, high prices, riot, the loss of America, and when enclosures slowed from the torrent of the 1770s to a trickle. The significance of Howlett and Loughborough was that together they brought a new, harder line of argument to the enclosure debate. In effect Howlett agreed with the defenders of commons that enclosure reduced farmers to labourers.

[32] John Howlett, *Enclosure and Population* (1973), with an introduction by A. H. John, p. [i]; Wedderburn also wrote an appendix to Howlett's *An Examination of Dr Price's Essay on the Population of England and Wales* (Maidstone, 1781). In Edinburgh he was a founder member of the Select Society and the first editor (1755–6) of the *Edinburgh Review*: John, Lord Campbell's *Lives of the Lord Chancellors and Keepers of the Great Seal of England, from the Earliest Times till the Reign of King George IV* (5th edn, 1868), VII, pp. 339, 358–69; R. H. Campbell and A. S. Skinner, *Adam Smith* (1982), p. 37. On the Select Society as a forum for the discussion and implementation of economic change, including agricultural improvement, by a modernizing elite, see I. Hont and M. Ignatieff, eds., *Wealth and Virtue: The Shaping of Political Economy in the Scottish Enlightenment* (Cambridge, 1985), *passim*, esp. p. 68.

[33] *Steel v Houghton et Uxor* (1788), 1 H. Bl. 51, ER 126, pp. 32–9; for discussion of the case see Peter King, 'The Origins of the Gleaning Judgement of 1788: A Case Study of Legal Change, Customary Right and Social Conflict in Late Eighteenth-Century England', *Law and History Review*, 10 (1992), and Thompson, *Customs*, pp. 139–42. (Smith's understanding of the seasonal marketing of grain is reflected in Loughborough's arguments in 1788.) In London in the mid seventies Wedderburn gave weekly dinners attended by Adam Smith: Campbell and Skinner, *Adam Smith*, pp. 154, 163, 166; in 1776 he published his *Essay upon the Question What Proportion of the Produce of Arable Land Ought to Be Paid as Rent to the Landlord* (Edinburgh, 1776). As Lord Chancellor, so anxious was he to exercise office that after Pitt's administration fell he continued to attend cabinet meetings until 'politely dismissed' (*DNB*). He became Earl of Rosslyn in 1801.

[34] Richard Price was also one of Lord Shelburne's many protégées, and a correspondent of William Pitt. Both Shelburne and Pitt were political opponents of Loughborough at this time, John Ehrman, *The Younger Pitt: The Years of Acclaim* (1969), pp. 86, 261–7. In 1792 Loughborough went over to Pitt, the first Whig to do so: Steven Watson, *The Reign of George III 1760–1815* (Oxford, 1960), p. 580; he became Lord Chancellor in January 1793.

But it was worth the price ('disagreeable and painful as it may be to the tender and feeling heart') because it would encourage population *growth*. In particular, enclosure would provoke a rapid and general increase of labouring and then of indigent poor. Labourers married early ('they readily obey the suggestions of natural constitution'). Marrying earlier they had more children. And the poorer they were, the earlier they married. Fortunately they felt their growing poverty less keenly than those with more money: 'They have already trod the rugged path, and felt its thorns and briars.'

In other words, dependence and unemployment, supposedly the worst consequences of engrossing, were advantageous. They would cause population to grow.[35] And the creation of a proletariat through enclosure was a guarantee of economic growth on a broad front.[36] Enclosure meant larger agricultural and manufacturing populations, greater agricultural production, stable grain prices. The traditional argument was reversed: now proletarianization, instead of damning enclosure and the disappearance of common right, justified it.

Howlett alone connected enclosure and poverty, but the prediction of wage dependence became general. Not every critic of commons followed him in *recommending* the transformation: several writers including Nathaniel Kent and Thomas Stone regretted the loss of small farmers in particular. (The wage dependence of former landless commoners did not concern them.) And Arthur Young from as early as 1784 argued against the uncompensated loss of common right.[37] But, if they did not recommend it, it is important

---

[35] Howlett, *Examination of Dr Price's Essay*, pp. 26–9. Charles Vancouver also argued that labourers would marry earlier ('the gratification of an early and generous passion') as a consequence of enclosure: Charles Vancouver, *General View of the Agriculture of the County of Cambridge* (1794), p. 197. Historians of eighteenth-century demography also explain growth in terms of an earlier age at marriage: see E. A. Wrigley and R. S. Schofield, *The Population History of England 1541–1871: A Reconstruction* (Cambridge, 1981).

[36] In ancient Rome the proletariat was the lowest class in the community, distinct because it contributed only its children to the state. In this sense the word fits Howlett's vision exactly. In the text that follows I use the term to signify the class of wage-dependent labourers that defenders and supporters thought would result from enclosure. Of course, every supporter, not just Howlett, denied that enclosure would depopulate: it would leave the commoners' reproductive function intact and create a class of labourers at the same time.

[37] Nathaniel Kent, *Hints to Gentlemen of Landed Property* (2nd edn, 1776), pp. 218–35; Thomas Stone, *Suggestions for Rendering the Inclosure of Common Fields and Waste Lands a Source of Population and Riches* (1787), pp. 76, 81; A. Young, 'Introduction', *Annals of Agriculture*, 1 (1784), p. 63.

to note that none of these observers of proletarianization thought it
sufficient grounds for opposing enclosure: 'Let no one imagine',
said Young,

> that one word offered in this paper is meant generally against
> enclosing: all contended for is ... that instead of giving property
> to the poor, or preserving it, or enabling them to acquire it, the
> very contrary effect has taken place; and as this evil was by no
> means *necessarily* connected with the measure of enclosing, it was
> a mischief that might easily have been avoided.[38]

And many pamphleteers and most reporters to the Board of
Agriculture *did* recommend the creation of complete wage dependence. They said that the discipline was valuable. They argued that
the sanction of real or threatened unemployment would benefit
farmers presently dependent on the whims of partly self-sufficient
commoners. For them, like Howlett, the justification for ending
common right was the creation of an agricultural proletariat.

Here is John Clark from Herefordshire: 'The farmers in this
county are often at a loss for labourers: the inclosure of the wastes
would increase the number of hands for labour, by removing the
means of subsisting in idleness.'[39] And Vancouver on Devon commoners whose independence meant that it was 'not without much
difficulty that, under such circumstances, the ordinary labour of the
country is performed'.[40] So too in north-west Hampshire, where

---

[38] The exception to the rule is William Pitt, the Midland reporter to the Board of
Agriculture, who recommended that enclosure occur only where it would promote
tillage, but his comments came too late for most of the counties he visited: Pitt,
General View of the Agriculture of the County of Northampton (1809), pp. 60–3.
A. Young, 'An Inquiry into the Propriety of Applying Wastes to the Better
Maintenance and Support of the Poor ...', *Annals of Agriculture* 36 (1801),
pp. 497–547 at p. 515. Sir George Onesiphorus Paul was another supporter of
enclosure, who also advocated allotments of land (of at least one-third acre garden
ground) for the poor: see Esther Moir, *Local Government in Gloucestershire
1775–1800: A Study of the Justices of the Peace* (Publications of the Bristol and
Gloucestershire Archaeological Society, VIII, 1969), p. 62.

[39] John Clark, d. 1807, gaelic scholar, land and tithe agent. Reporter to the Board of
Agriculture for Brecknock, Radnor and Hereford; his *The Nature and Value of
Leasehold Property* was published posthumously in 1808 (*DNB*); Clark, *General
View of the Agriculture of the County of Hereford* (1794), p. 29.

[40] Charles Vancouver, *General View of the Agriculture of the County of Hampshire*
(1813), p. 505. (Charles Vancouver, fl. 1785–1813, American, of Philadelphia.
Invited English settlers to America to farm. Owned 53,000 acres in Kentucky, the
woodlands and forests of which he was busy improving in 1807. Wrote reports for
the Board for the counties of Cambridge (1794), Essex (1795), Devon (1808) and
Hampshire (1813), *DNB*.)

labouring families readily earned a guinea a week in the summer season by travelling a few miles to the Berkshire peat meadows. Work in the forests, wastes and woodlands 'allure many to task-work in such places, cutting wood and raising fuel'. There was summer work in the saltings and fisheries on the coast, and there was constant employment in the transport of timber from the woods to the canals and rivers. Portsmouth and other shipyards drew the best labourers, 'leaving behind but feebleness and debility, to carry forward the common labours of the county'. High wages for task-work led to short days, which then set the standard for agricultural labour. In Devon the working day ended early at 5 p.m., in Hampshire it was over even earlier at 3.30 or 4 o'clock.[41]

Enclosure would change this timetable for good. It would end commoners' relative wage-independence, and make agricultural labour necessary.[42]

Once commoners were dependent, care should be taken to prevent labourers becoming in any way independent of the wage again. Even planting new hedgerows required careful thought. Medlars (*mespilus germanica*), for example, should never be used because 'it is bad policy to increase temptations to theft; the idle among the poor are already too prone to depredation, *and would still be less inclined to work*, if every hedge furnished the means of support'. Equally, cottage gardens should in no circumstance be large enough to take the labourer away from wage work.[43] When evicted from the common by enclosure, said Vancouver, labourers must live in cottages belonging to farms, and at a distance from the corrupt solidarity of the village. Or they might live in large houses of industry, for which the Parkhurst house of industry in Parkhurst

---

[41] Vancouver, *General View ... Hampshire*, pp. 381–5, 496, 505; for more complaints of labour shortage see Peter Foot, *General View of the Agriculture of the County of Middlesex* (1794), p. 31; Clark, *General View ... Hereford*, pp. 27–9; Thomas Rudge, *General View of the Agriculture of the County of Gloucester* (1807), pp. 49–50, 97. (Thomas Rudge, antiquary; born Gloucester; BD Oxford, 1784; Rector of St Michaels etc. Gloucester, and vicar of Haresfield on presentation of the Earl of Hardwick; Archdeacon of Gloucester (1814); Chancellor of the diocese of Hereford (1817); *History of the County of Gloucester* (1803); *History and Antiquities of Gloucester* (?1815), *DNB*.)

[42] Vancouver, *General View ... Hampshire*, p. 496; see also J. Billingsley, *General View of the Agriculture of the County of Somerset* (1797), p. 52; J. Middleton, *General View of the Agriculture of the County of Middlesex* (1807), p. 102; J. Bishton, *General View of the Agriculture of Shropshire* (1794), cited in Hammond and Hammond, *Village Labourer*, p. 31.

[43] Rudge, *General View ... Gloucester*, pp. 97, 50 (my italics).

Forest on the Isle of Wight, built to take seven hundred, was a model. Vancouver saw no harm in potato plots, but he feared teaching commoners to read and write. 'Independence' had become a threat: 'however beautiful it may be in theory to raise the lower orders to a situation of comparative independence', said Rudge, the line 'between the proprietor and labourer' must be drawn firmly. Without it 'neither agriculture nor commerce can flourish'.[44] Labourers must be labourers, not more. Subordination required dependence on a wage: the lesson of the commons had been learnt.

There was widespread agreement, then, between critics of commons and defenders, that enclosure would produce a more biddable, available labouring class. But how did the proponents of enclosure address the other argument of traditionalists: that access to land and common right supported a way of life superior to wage labour?

Critics argued that the living afforded by the common-right economy was inferior because it was primitive. Next to notions of modern agriculture the idea of sharing land in common was barbaric.[45] Toftstead owners in the Boston fen, said Pennington, would be hurt by enclosure, but their economy, like that of poor fenmen, was primitive. It made as much sense to preserve it as it did to leave North America to the Indians: 'Let the poor native *Indians* (though something more savage than many in the fens) enjoy all their ancient privileges, and cultivate their own country their own way. For 'tis equal pity, notwithstanding some trifling dissimilarity of circumstances, that they should be disturbed.' The idea was ludicrous, far better to engross the small farms after enclosure. The greater production of oats alone would be worth more than all the ancient harvest of mats, rushes, reeds, fish, fowl, fodder and fuel.[46]

The President of the Board of Agriculture, Sir John Sinclair, also put the origins of commons in the dark ages, that stage of society when 'Men were Strangers to any higher Occupation than those of Hunters and Shepherds'. The waste was an enemy to be engaged and

---

[44] Vancouver, *General View ... Hampshire*, pp. 505–9. Rudge, *General View ... Gloucester*, p. 50.

[45] John Clark said it was 'the barbarous usage of remote ages', *General View ... Hereford*, p. 69; see also A. Young, *General View of the Agriculture of Lincolnshire* (1813), p. 488.

[46] Pennington, *Reflections*, pp. 34–5, replying to *An Enquiry into the Reasons for and against Inclosing the Open Fields*, p. 40. For a description of the international scope of improving ideology see Thompson, *Customs*, pp. 164–75.

beaten. 'We have begun', he wrote in 1803, inspired by the drama of the war,

> another campaign against the foreign enemies of the country … Why should we not attempt a campaign also against our great domestic foe, I mean the hitherto unconquered sterility of so large a proportion of the surface of the kingdom? … let us not be satisfied with the liberation of Egypt, or the subjugation of Malta, but let us subdue Finchley Common; let us conquer Hounslow Heath; let us compel Epping Forest to submit to the yoke of improvement.[47]

Without 'improvement' labourers could to some extent work or not as they chose, and potentially rich land lay unused. Critics did not always distinguish between small farmers, landless commoners and squatters on wastes. When they did, they described small farmers much as they did poorer commoners. They were unproductive and conservative, either by definition or because the commons killed enterprise. Some worked too hard for the poorest of livings. Others wasted their time at the market, full of their own import-

[47] Sir John Sinclair, *Memoirs of Sir John Sinclair*, II, p. 111, quoted in E. Halevy, *England in 1815* (2nd edn, 1949), p. 230. John Barrell has noted how often enclosure writers associated the cultivated landscape with the civilized, known world, and the uncultivated with the hostile and inhuman: John Barrell, *The Idea of Landscape and the Sense of Place 1730–1840: An Approach to the Poetry of John Clare* (Cambridge, 1972), esp. pp. 75, 94. Many war-time writers, though not all, focussed on waste commons, partly because much common-field pasture already had undergone enclosure. From early on Young had seen little difference between them: stinted fielden commons were as barbaric as any fen or heathen waste. To keep them was no 'less absurd than it would have been, had the Tartar policy of the shepherd-state been adhered to, and the uninterrupted range of flocks and herds preferred to the appropriation of the soil, as the property of individuals': Young 'Introduction' *Annals of Agriculture*, 1 (1784), p. 70. The advantages of nomadic pastoralism are discussed in Bruce Chatwin, *The Songlines* (1987), pp. 16–19, etc.

If Sinclair and Young thought the ancient origin of commons lay in the primitive agriculture of primitive people, the descendants of commoners, nineteenth-century agricultural labourers, disagreed. They deployed the stadial theory differently: commons were ancient but they were far from uncivilized because their *raison d'être* was to protect the commoner. Such barbarity was better than enclosure:

> When Romans reigned in this land, the commons they did give,
> Unto the poor for charity, to help them for to live,
> But now they've taken the poor man's ground, that certainly is true,
> Such cruelty did ne'er abound, when this old hat was new.

For a full text of 'My Old Hat' see Howkins and Dyck, '"The Time's Alteration"', p. 22.

ance.[48] Commoners in general stood in the way of national economic growth. Instead of the nation's pride they were a measure of its backwardness.

This evaluation of the common-right economy allowed many writers to adopt Timothy Nourse's instinctive distrust of commoners, but without his respect for their economy. For most it went further than distrust. Critics of commons loathed commoners with a xenophobic intensity. They were a 'sordid race', as foreign and uncultivated as the land that fed them.[49] Like commons they were wild and unproductive. They were lazy and dangerous. If wastes must be subdued, so must they. Fenland commoners were the worst. 'So wild a country nurses up a race of people as wild as the fen', Young wrote of Wildmore fen in Lincolnshire, in 1813. In Louth he had seen a gang of fenmen, a 'mischievous race', charged with 'laming, killing, cutting off tails, and wounding a variety of cattle, hogs and sheep'. Many were commoners. He knew 'nothing better calculated to fill a country with barbarians ready for any mischief than extensive commons, and divine service only once a month'. Fen commoners drank, they worked only four days a week, they could not be depended upon for the harvest.[50] Pennington said they, not enclosers, were *de facto* engrossers producing nothing of legitimizing value. They might be 'justly called the *Great profanum vulgus* of the fens'. Some were worse: 'these lurk like spiders, and, when they see a chance, sally out, and drive or drown or steal just as suits them, and are the Buccanneers of the country'.[51]

But critics feared and despised forest commoners too, and indeed anyone living on heath or waste. An anonymous writer in 1781

[48] Some improvers made an exception of small farmers, once their lands were enclosed (above at note 37), but some of the most influential improvers argued that they were as much a brake on productivity as landless commoners: Howlett, *Examination of Dr Price's Essay*, pp. 24–6; Clark, *General View ... Hereford*, p. 75; A. Young, *General View of the Agriculture of Oxfordshire* (1813), pp. 94–5.

[49] Identifying commoners as a race was alive and well in the 1850s and later: the few survivors of enclosure were 'relics of that sordid race' who favoured the common-field system, *Agricultural History, Gazetteer and Directory of the County of Huntingdon* (1854), p. 76.

[50] Young, *General View ... Lincolnshire*, p. 488. On drinking amongst commoners other than fenlanders see John Monk, *General View of the Agriculture of the County of Leicester* (1794), pp. 56–7; W. Marshall, *Rural Economy of Gloucestershire* (2nd edn, 1796), pp. 15–16.

[51] Pennington, *Reflections*, p. 37. Crabbe thought the same of Suffolk marsh commoners: 'Here joyless roam a wild amphibious race / With sullen wo display'd in every face': 'The Village' Book I (1783), line 85, in *George Crabbe. Tales, 1812 and Other Selected Poems*, ed. Howard Mills (Cambridge, 1967), p. 3.

called them 'more perverse, and more wretched' than labourers in enclosed villages. Their commons were the 'most fruitful seminaries of *vice*', providing 'habitations of *squalor, famine*, and disease'. He had seen 'sloth the parent of vice and poverty begotten and born of this said right of Common. I saw its progress into the productive fields of lying, swearing, thieving. – I saw the seeds of honesty almost eradicated.'[52] Hampshire foresters were an 'idle, useless and disorderly set of people', whose first act of plunder was to steal the materials for the very roofs they lived under. Their 'habitations', their appearance and their morals were much inferior to those of labourers in tied cottages or houses of industry. The very attraction of wastes was the chance they afforded for 'pilfering and stealing'.[53] In the Black Mountains of Herefordshire, 'IDLENESS, that *fell* ROOT on which VICE always finds it easy to graft her most favourite plants', turned idle commoners into criminals, unlike the labourers in the Golden Valley below.[54]

The industry and independence of commoners was a 'lazy industry' and a 'beggarly independence'.[55] They were thieves by definition:

---

52 Anon., *Observations on a Pamphlet entitled an Enquiry into the Advantages and Disadvantages, Resulting from Bills of Enclosure* ... (Shrewsbury, 1781) p. 5. See also Thomas Scrutton, *Commons and Common Fields* (1887), pp. 138–40, for references to the connection of poverty, common lands and crime in the *General Views* of the counties of Hertford, Gloucester, Shropshire, Essex and Buckingham; also Arbuthnot, *Inquiry into the Connection between the Present Price of Provisions and the Size of Farms*, p. 81; [Report on commons in Brecknock], *Annals of Agriculture*, 32 (1799), p. 632; Gonner, *Common Land* p. 360, n. 1, cites numerous examples of this view; also Vancouver, *General View ... Hampshire*, p. 495; Young, *General View ... Oxfordshire*, p. 239; Laurence, *New System*, p. 46. An earlier pamphleteer complained to Parliament that fen projectors had misrepresented the value of the fens, which was enormous: the seminaries they sheltered had little to do with vice, they were 'seminaries and nurseries' of fish and fowl 'which will be destroyed on draining thereof': *The Anti-Projector of the History of the Fen* [1646], p. 8, quoted in H. C. Darby, *The Draining of the Fens* (1940), p. 52.
53 Laurence, *New System*, p. 46.
54 Clark, *General View ... Hereford*, p. 28. Defenders saw the crime wave moving in the other direction. They argued that the *loss* of commons and conversion to pasture at enclosure generated criminality. See, for example, 'The Old Fashon'd Farmer', writing to Sir John Fielding in the *London Evening Post* on 12–14 January 1775, and asking 'who, in their senses, would force the subjects of their Prince to become thieves, and then encourage the executioners to dispatch them because they would not live honestly?'; similarly 25–27 February 1772; I am grateful to Nicholas Rogers for these references.
55 W. Mavor, *General View ... Berkshire*, pp. 328–9, cited in Tate, 'Handlist of English Enclosure Acts and Awards Relating to Lands in Berkshire', *Berkshire Archaeological Journal*, 47 (1943), pp. 67–8.

they commoned without legal right. At enclosure Parliament had no obligation to compensate them. Instead they must abase themselves, become deferential and 'assume (if anything) the meek and humble tone of those who implore charity for the love of God. As a charity it should be asked – as a charity it should be given.'[56]

Dependence through reliance on a wage was to identify the new structure of agrarian society and ensure the authority of farmers over labourers. It was as essential to the critics' world view as an independent peasantry was to their opponents'. John Clark considered the justice of this in 1794:

> But one man to have so large a tract of land, and so many people obliged to obey his orders? To this it is to be replied, that in farming, as in most other occupations, men of the greatest talents generally get to the head of their professions, while others are left by the way; and whoever will examine the extent of the intellects of the general run of mankind, employed in any branch of business, will find, that Nature, in allotting to each his respective portion of her gifts, had it in view that the province of ninety-nine out of an hundred was to receive, not to give orders.[57]

So both sides of the published debate said that enclosure would ensure labourers' complete dependence on a wage, and encourage the proletarianization of small farmers. Enclosure would end 'independence'. On this question the only argument was whether to welcome or disapprove of the change. Only common right stood between the survival of the common-field peasantry and its proletarianization. This assumption was so thoroughly worked into the social vision of both defenders and critics as to be beyond dispute.

COMMON RIGHT AS INCOME

The other side of independence was income. The structure of the debate about this, the economic value of common right, is very similar to the debate about independence. Critics and defenders agreed that common right provided a living – just as it provided independence. Once again they valued it differently. What defenders

---

[56] Anon., *Observations on a Pamphlet entitled an Enquiry into the Advantages and Disadvantages* pp. 8, 10. This observer claimed that only landowners, not the landless, and few commoners, had common right: p. 9. For another view see below, Chapter 2.

[57] Clark, *General View ... Hereford*, p. 75.

called a sufficiency, critics called meagre and lawless. What defenders saw as hard work and thrift, critics saw as squalor and desperation. One observer's cow with her milky treasure was another's half-starved, ill-bred runt. They were looking at the same things but who saw clearly? From evidence like this what can historians conclude about the economic value of common right?

It seems clear that the motives of the critics of commons make their evaluations of common right suspect. They wanted to raise productivity and to improve the supply and quality of labour. In the harvest-crisis decades of the 1790s and 1800s they led a movement for the easier and cheaper enclosure of wastes. As they saw it, common right stood in the way of modernization. Accordingly, they could not approve of it, and they could not see, in the larger terms of national interest, how common-right economies could be allowed to survive. Most of them were Anglican vicars, professional agricultural writers, or land agents and surveyors. Either they stood to gain from enclosure personally, or their Church, their employers or their readers did. So there are good reasons why critics of commons might undervalue common right.

Nevertheless, unlike some historians, critics of common right did not doubt its widespread survival. In Gloucestershire, Rudge found that occupiers of an acre, or even less, grazed sheep on the fallows, winter and summer, to their great advantage; in Herefordshire, Clark noted that a cottage and a small close brought hill-grazing; in the Hampshire forests, Vancouver thought encroachments of two or three acres meant relative independence; in Devon, labourers living on the borders of wastes and commons were similarly 'independent of the farmers and many of the country gentlemen'.[58] And in Middlesex, Thomas Baird described commoners on Hounslow Heath and Enfield Chase who seemed to live on air, without either labour or any obvious advantage from the common.[59]

Nor did these observers think commons worthless. Rudge talked about their 'considerable advantage'; John Clark had to justify the extinction of common right in Herefordshire on the grounds that the county suffered a shortage of labour: the fit poor must work for

[58] Rudge, *General View ... Gloucester*, p. 104. Clark, *General View ... Hereford*, p. 26. Vancouver, *General View ... Hampshire*, pp. 81, 505.
[59] T. Baird, *General View of the Agriculture of the County of Middlesex* (1793), pp. 22–6, 36; Peter Foot, in looking at the same county, described a thousand acres of unstinted meadow on the Middlesex side of the lea, on which inhabitants turned whatever stock they pleased: Foot, *General View ... Middlesex*, p. 69.

wages even though 'To deprive the *poor* of that benefit, which, in their present state, they derive from the *waste land*, must, no doubt, at first view sound *harsh*'. Similarly, in Middlesex, common rights were 'a matter of some little conveniency as well as emolument'; they had to be sacrificed only for the greater good of the community at large. Common right on Salisbury Plain was probably the best means of using this unimprovable land. In Bedfordshire Thomas Batchelor described the common at Campton cum Shefford (one of many Bedfordshire commons) as fertile and reputed never to run bare; it supported many cottagers with rights for a mare and a colt or a milch cow, two bullocks and twelve sheep each.[60]

But when they came to compare the lives of commoners and small farmers with those of labourers in *enclosed* villages estimates of value changed. Now commons offered no more than a poor living, a thin independence. In fact, reporters contradicted themselves on the subject of value. The enclosure of Corse Chase, a 1,350 acre common in Gloucestershire, Rudge said, would be a 'trifling' loss to local cottagers.[61] Thanks to overstocking, said Vancouver, parish wastes in Hampshire were of little benefit; even forest commoners lived miserably.[62] The value of grazing 'greyhound-like sheep' or 'a parcel of ragged, shabby horses' and getting fuel from the five thousand acres of Hounslow Heath were nothing compared to a regular wage, in Baird's opinion. Here is his description of the cattle on Enfield Chase:

> In the spring the chace is covered with ticks which fasten on the cattle, and by sucking their blood, reduce them so low, that they are incapable of raising themselves from the ground, and in this state they are often carried away in carts, being unable to walk, or stir from the place where they are fallen.

Foot agreed: the many thousand acres of waste in Middlesex were almost worthless. In general, Middleton added, Middlesex commons, 'as in most other places', provided only the worst sort of

---

[60] Clark, *General View ... Hereford*, pp. 27–8. Baird, *General View ... Middlesex*, p. 22. [A. Young], 'Waste Lands' [a digest of the Reports to the Board of Agriculture], *Annals of Agriculture*, 33 (1799), p. 15. In this context see also Pitt, *General View ... Northampton*, pp. 60–1; Thomas Batchelor, *General View of the Agriculture of the County of Bedford* (1813), pp. 224–5; and Young, *General View of the Agriculture of Lincolnshire* (1813), p. 19, on happy commoners living on four to twenty acres each in the Isle of Axholme, enjoying 'vast commons'.

[61] Rudge, *General View ... Gloucester*, p. 251.

[62] Vancouver, *General View ... Hampshire*, p. 496.

firing, and only enough pasture to keep the cattle from starving. The building materials, the ground for a house, the firing and free run for pigs and poultry they offered were only 'trifling advantages'.[63] From Somerset, Billingsley reported that cottagers' cattle were generally stunted. They starved first on the common, then again in the winter for lack of fodder. Commons were no advantage at all, in fact cottagers had more to gain from enclosure than farmers.[64] From Bedfordshire Thomas Stone described the 'diminutive carcases... of sheep that barely get a subsistence' on commons.[65] Young said if he were King he would enclose every waste in the kingdom, thereby exchanging 'the miseries of poverty for chearfulness'.[66] The produce of wastes, said a writer in 1781, was no more than 'gorst, heath, fern, broom, briers, bushes, thistles, moss and various other weeds, with a mixture of some grass'.[67] In the same year Howlett claimed that a thousand-acre heath in his neighbourhood did not 'support a single poor family'.[68] He scorned the idea of the 'Paradisaical Common'; a commoner's child would get a better dowry from a few years in service than all the lambs and wool a cottage could provide.[69] Pennington thought commoners no better off than the poor elsewhere, possibly worse.[70] And both Howlett and Young said that commons brought no relief to the poor rate: in Chailey, Sussex, and Sutton Coldfield, Warwickshire, large unstinted commons drove the poor rate up, not down. Commons were the worst kind of charity.[71]

---

63 Baird, *General View ... Middlesex*, pp. 23, 26; Foot, *General View ... Middlesex*, p. 30; Middleton, *General View ... Middlesex*, pp. 117, 103; the estimate of Hounslow Heath's size is Middleton's, p. 114.
64 Billingsley, *General View ... Somerset*, pp. 51–2.
65 Stone, *Suggestions for Rendering*, p. 53.
66 Young, 'Introduction', p. 61.
67 Anon., *Observations on a Pamphlet Entitled An Enquiry into the Advantages and Disadvantages Resulting from Bills of Inclosure ...* (Shrewsbury, 1781), p. 13.
68 Howlett, *Examination of Dr Price's Essay*, p. 29.
69 J. Howlett, *Enclosures a Cause of Improved Agriculture* (1787), pp. 76–7. This is a reply to the anonymous author of *A Political Enquiry* (1785), though Howlett ignored the author's description of cottagers' children doing the very thing he argued only labourers' children would do: going into service to save wages: see above, p. 24
70 Pennington, *Reflections*, p. 33.
71 A. Young, 'Dairy Farms', *Annals of Agriculture* 5 (1786), pp. 222–4; and 'Mischiefs of Commons', *ibid.*, 8 (1787), p. 347; Howlett, *Enclosures a Cause*, p. 80.

Nathaniel Kent, an admirer of cottagers, argued that commons were of no use to them. Fewer than one in six kept a cow. Cottagers were better off in the care of a good farmer.[72] And Baird claimed that even the fuel from commons, the least doubtful of benefits, would be bought more cheaply when commoners were put to work after enclosure.[73]

Others thought that small farmers lived no better than their labourers: enclosure and proletarianization would be a deliverance, if age was no impediment:

Indeed I doubt it is too true, that he must of necessity give over farming, and betake himself to labour for the support of his family; but on the other hand, we must consider that the condition of a small farmer is very often worse than even that of a day labourer; he works harder, and lives poorer; has all the cares, and little of the proportional profits of the larger farmer; and experience very often shews, that he earns as a labourer a much more comfortable subsistence than before, if not too old to betake himself to his new station.[74]

This comparison between the old system and the new coloured every criticism of common right.

Their opponents said that critics could not see the common-right economy clearly because they were either ignorant or wilfully blind. I shall return to ignorance later. An anonymous defender of commons analysed the psychology of wilful blindness in 1780: *in order to enclose*, an encloser must first deceive himself about the value of commons, he must 'bring himself to believe an absurdity, before he can induce himself to do a cruelty'. So he convinces himself that, because his tenant sometimes fell upon hard times, he always did, that because he 'sometimes loses an horse, or a cow, or his expected train of goslings, and is then distressed to pay his rent, or to

---

[72] Kent, *Hints to Gentlemen*, pp. 112–13, 115, 243, 252.

[73] Baird, *General View ... Middlesex*, p. 22; G. O. Paul, *Observations on the General Enclosure Bill* (1796), p. 40: free fuel from wastes was more expensive in terms of hours of labour lost than bought coal.

[74] Anon., *The Advantages and Disadvantages of Inclosing Waste Lands and Open Fields. Impartially Stated and Considered. By a Country Gentleman* (1772), pp. 31–3; Clark, *General View ... Hereford*, p. 75; Vancouver, *General View ... Hampshire*, p. 81; Howlett, *Insufficiency of the Causes*, pp. 42–3. Compare the twentieth-century view of Eric Kerridge: 'The unsuccessful farmer who became a wage labourer had lost nothing but his chains', *The Farmers of Old England* (1973), p. 150.

procure a sum of money to supply the loss, – that none of them ever yielded his profit or comfort'.[75]

But the motives of defenders of commons themselves may make their evaluation of the common-right economy equally suspect. Their defence was grounded in the fear of depopulation in two senses: an absolute decline in population, including labour supply and military reserves, and a fundamental change in rural society – unemployment, the decline of small farmers, the loss of peasant independence. In defending the old society they might exaggerate its value, construing as independence what was only temporary relief from chronic underemployment. Their picture of rustic harmony and a trusty peasantry may have been no more than (in Gilbert Blane's words) a 'poetical device', an unspecific, idyllic pastoralism.[76]

The motives of both opponents and supporters of enclosure make their conflicting opinions about the income value of common right difficult to weigh. But there are clues to a proper assessment of value in what critics of commons saw, and what they did not see. These are to do with the laziness of commoners, the time they wasted, and their poverty.

First, the complaint that commoners were lazy. We have seen that improvers often noted this. They used laziness as a term of moral disapproval. But what they meant was that commoners were not always available for farmers to employ. We might ask why were they *un*available? In some regions and at some times high wages in non-agricultural occupations made agricultural wages unattractive. But commoners were 'lazy' in the fens too where there were fewer industrial alternatives to farm work, and also in Middlesex where they seemed to live without either benefit from the common *or* labour. In fact (with the occasional exception of small farmers), *every* commoner was lazy, whether wages were high or not. This suggests that they refused to work because they could live without wages, or without regular wages. Their laziness becomes an indica-

[75] Anon., *An Enquiry into the Advantages and Disadvantages Resulting from Bills of Inclosure in which Objections are Stated and Remedies Proposed ...* (1780), pp. 66–7.

[76] [Dr. Gilbert Blane], *Inquiry into the Causes and Remedies of the Late and Present Scarcity and High Price of Provisions in a Letter to the Right Honourable Earl Spencer, KG, First Lord of the Admiralty* (1800), p. 42.

tor of their independence of the wage. And the degree of frustration
critics felt when they saw this laziness may be a guide to how well
commoners could do without it.

Then there is the *time* we have heard critics say commoners
wasted. Most often they wasted it gathering fuel. Wage labour, it
was said, would enable commoners to buy coal. The value of the
common was no more than wood for the fire. Evidently critics did
not know that a waste might provide much more than fuel. Saun-
tering after a grazing cow, snaring rabbits and birds, fishing,
looking for wood, watercress, nuts or spring flowers, gathering
teazles, rushes, mushrooms or berries, and cutting peat and turves
were all part of a commoning economy and a commoning way of life
invisible to outsiders. This is partly explained by the repulsion
critics felt at the very idea of commons. Obviously such an attitude
made any proper investigation of the value of common right
difficult.

But to some extent this ignorance was deliberate. William
Marshall, one of the most prolific writers on English agriculture,
refused to interview anyone. He preferred to rely on his own observations. He also tried to avoid being a transient tourist reliant on
secondhand accounts, a sin of which he accused some Reporters to
the Board.[77] Arthur Young and at least some Reporters did spend
time talking to farmers, but they almost never talked to smaller
commoners. Merely looking at a common or a common-field village
wasn't enough, as defenders said. When critics took things at face
value, they mistook the uncultivated common for infertile heath,
and many did not see common-*field* pasture at all.[78] Critics of
commons in the eighteenth century shared a myopia common
among modernizers. 'We ever must believe a lie', said William
Blake, 'when we see with, not through, the eye.'

---

[77] Barrell, *Idea of Landscape*, pp. 91–3.
[78] The Reverend James Willis, 'On Cows for Cottagers', *Annals of Agriculture*, 40
(1803), pp. 557, 562; on blindness to common-field pastures see Anon., *Reflections
on the Cruelty of Inclosing Common-Field Lands, Particularly as it Affects the
Church and Poor; in a letter to the Lord Bishop of Lincoln by a clergyman of that
diocese* (1796), p. 16. Agricultural 'experts' who defamed wastes were a joke to one
defender of commons. They wrote 'farming romances', whose impractical theori-
zing was about as good a guide to farming as Fielding's *Tom Jones* was to
adolescence: Anon., *A Political Enquiry into the Consequences of Enclosing Waste
Lands*, pp. 3–11. This author also argued that misconceptions about the common-
right economy were rooted in an ignorance of the nature of real commoners,
pp. 109–11.

Nor could they understand the relationship between the commoners' means and their *wants*. Commoners had little but they also wanted less. The result may have been that they lived well enough for themselves, but invisibly and poorly in the eyes of outsiders.[79] The satisfaction of commoners was incomprehensible to supporters of enclosure. Listen to their accounts of the misery of small farmers: they lived worse than labourers; they were no better than their own sows, incurious, deaf to the world.[80] But this state of mind is as credibly ascribed to contentment as it is to misery. In West Haddon small farmers, bitterly opposed to enclosure, argued that they had 'enough'.[81] Oliver Goldsmith thought in the same terms: 'his best riches' were 'ignorance of wealth'. So did every defender of commons who described the self-sufficiency of cottagers. Brigstock commoners argued that their enclosing landlords had enough too and should be satisfied. The poet John Clare said the same thing.

Perhaps having 'enough' was unimaginable to men who wrote about crop yields, rents, improvements, productivity, economic growth, always *more*, as it has been incomprehensible to twentieth-century historians living in constantly expanding market economies, albeit on a finite planet. Something critics might have understood better was the pride of ownership that small farmers also displayed which was the other side of self-importance. Something they missed entirely was the constantly negotiated interdependence of commoners, their need of each other.

When critics of commons weighed the value of common right they did so in their own terms, the terms of the market. They talked about wage labour and the efficient use of resources. But commoners lived off the shared use of land. To some extent they lived outside the market. They lived in part on the invisible earnings of

---

[79] Marshall Sahlins, *Stone Age Economics* (Chicago, 1972; London, 1974), p. 13; Hugh Brody notes that visitors to pre-Famine Ireland also mistook poverty for desperation: Brody, *Inishkillane: Change and Decline in the West of Ireland* (1973), p. 55. Defoe made the point early in the eighteenth century on visiting cave-dwelling commoners in the Derbyshire Peak: inside the cave were two sides of bacon, and pots made of earthenware, brass and pewter; outside was a cow, a pig and a patch of barley ready to harvest: Defoe, *Tour*, II, p. 62.

[80] Some of the tone is captured in this: 'A wicked, cross-grained, petty farmer, is like the sow in his yard, almost an insulated individual, who has no communication with, and therefore, no reverence for the opinion of the world. – To no person is good character of so little importance': *Commercial and Agricultural Magazine* (July 1800), quoted in Thompson, *Making*, p. 219.

[81] See below Chapter 7, pp. 198–9.

grazing and gathering. Much of this was inconceivable to critics, either because they did not look or because they did not want to see. In their eyes commoners were lazy, insubordinate and poor. But when historians come to assess these assessments we have to understand that none of these conditions, except poverty, is a measure of the inadequacy of a living. Even poverty, in the case of commoners, may have been in the eye of the beholder: commoners did not think themselves poor.[82]

Polemical debates settle few arguments without empirical enquiry. Despite this, the evidence found in polemic is both useful and usable. From the enclosure debate we learn that common right was widespread and probably useful enough to offer significant independence of the wage. Furthermore, the breadth of agreement, both between writers and over time, that common right was the only obstacle to complete wage dependence for small occupiers as well as landless commoners is striking. The general expression of this view, coupled with other evidence, suggests to me that these observers were right. This is not to argue that agreement between people who otherwise disagree is an acid test of the truth of a proposition: clearly, this evidence requires corroboration, some of which later chapters will provide. But it is to argue that in the case of common right the testimony found in the words of contemporary observers about social process is strongly presumptive.[83]

The value of knowing that the debaters talked about the world-as-it-was is that it reintroduces to the history of enclosure the role of politics. Defenders and critics were not dealing in imagined or archaic notions of rural England. They were well informed, they talked about real alternatives. So when the critics won the argument for enclosure they helped to change the lives of commoners, and commoners knew it.

PEASANTS OR LABOURERS? SOCIAL CHANGE AND THE NATIONAL INTEREST

The centrality of the debate's very large arguments about independence, loyalty, labour supply, productivity, and the effect of

[82] For a longer discussion see below, Chapter 6.
[83] It is possible that all these writers shared, and expressed in their language, an image of a world that no longer existed. It is possible too that they did not, and this is the argument here. On this point see George Steiner, *After Babel* (Oxford, 1975), p. 21, quoted in Richard Pine, *Brian Friel and Ireland's Drama* (1990), p. 3.

enclosure on the poor rate, marks a shift in emphasis from the seventeenth to the eighteenth centuries. Unlike the earlier debate between John Moore and Joseph Lee, argument about the legitimacy of ending common right in the eighteenth century was more than a conflict between the moral economy and the self-interested individualism of agrarian capitalism.[84] Increasingly it was also a debate over how best to serve the national interest. Or, more exactly, and crucially, a debate about *what sort of society* best served that interest.

This is not to say that ideas of paternal obligation and individual freedom were outmoded. Manifestly they were not, any more than paternal behaviour was obsolete. The argument that the rich had an obligation to the poor was still made (and usually with more grace than any other) but as a way of framing the argument about enclosure it took second place to an argument about country.

In Nathaniel Kent's and Thomas Andrews' eyes the national interest was best served by the industry, independence and patriotism of a flourishing peasantry. In the Reverend John Howlett's it was served best by a multitudinous, fecund, ever-growing proletariat, no matter how poor. But behind both views was a fundamental concern with Britain's economic and political hegemony. This concern was matched by an agreement that Britain's power lay in her navy, her merchant marine and her manufactures as well as her agriculture. The question was how could agriculture serve them best?[85]

[84] For the debate between Lee and Moore see Appleby, *Economic Thought and Ideology*, ch. 3, esp. pp. 55–63. Lee supported an individual's right to enclose, pointing out the public benefits that accrued; he disparaged commons as 'the seed-plot of contention, the nursery of beggery'. Moore argued that the motive for enclosure was greed, which led enclosers to forget their duty to the poor: they 'buy the poore for silver . . . make chaffer and merchandize of them for gain and profit: they use them as they doe their beasts, keep them or put them off for advantage: they buy them, and sell them, as may best serve their turns to get by them'. The observation of a greater eighteenth-century emphasis on national interest than individualism made here does not contradict Appleby's: her description of the triumph of mercantilist over liberal economic ideology in the 1690s is consonant with the shift: see Appleby, *Economic Thought and Ideology*, ch. 9, esp. p. 277.

[85] On the national interest see, among others: Cowper, *Essay*, pp. 10, 22–3; Anon., *An Enquiry into the Reasons for and against*, p. 11; Homer, *Essay*, pp. 35, 38, 41; Anon., *A Political Enquiry*, pp. 36–7 ('agriculture is the parent of industry and wealth. A well conducted system of *farming* is the only root from whence can spring a lasting wealth, power, and happiness to this nation'), pp. 54, 55–7, 98, 104, 122; Henry Kett, *An Essay on Wastes in General, and on Mosswold in Particular* (Norwich, 1792), p. 6; Andrews, ed., *Torrington Diaries*, p. 395.

For this reason it is wrong, I think, to understand the writers on
the eighteenth-century debate to be arguing only or even primarily
about the creation of a labour supply or exclusive property rights –
even though these were almost certainly the *undeclared* priorities of
critics of commons. Labour supply was a concern of all those
writing about enclosure in the eighteenth century, as it always had
been. The effect of enclosure on labour helped to stigmatize or to
legitimize enclosure and the end of common right. Very properly
historians have not let it go unnoticed.[86]

But rather than labour supply or property rights, critics described
alternative societies and asked which best served the national interest. Commoners were not only potential labourers; they were
either property-owners and patriots, or criminals and paupers,
too. Critics expressed a concern with morality and poverty as well as
labour supply. They argued that enclosure would provide solutions
to all three problems. Defenders expressed a concern with common
rights and loyalty as well as work. They argued that rural society *as
it stood* guaranteed both. Ultimately critics' arguments justified the
creation of an abundant supply of cheap labour completely dependent on the wage. But neither critics nor defenders of commons
framed their arguments as solutions for the problem of labour
supply.

In the same way writers did not argue the individual's right to the
exclusive enjoyment of his property: indeed critics, to whose lips this
argument had come most readily in the 1650s and 1730s, increasingly argued the subordination of individual property rights to the
'national' interest and accused *commoners* of selfish individualism.
Ultimately, of course, the legitimation of enclosure did establish
exclusive property rights – much to the benefit of enclosers. But, as
in the case of ensuring a cheap labour supply, if this was their aim
critics chose not to argue it directly.

Why should this concern us here? The debate's emphasis on social
change in the national interest is important because it shows that
critics of commons were willing to recommend a large piece of
deliberate social restructuring, and to be seen doing it. Improving
ideology, the Hammonds wrote, was as deadly to the old system as
greed itself.[87] It was deadly not only because it took away commons

---

[86] Snell, *Annals*, pp. 174–5; N. F. R. Crafts, 'Enclosure and Labour Supply
Revisited', *Explorations in Economic History*, 15 (1978); and see above, pp. 28–30.
[87] Hammond and Hammond, *Village Labourer*, pp. 30–4.

but because it took away an economy and a society too. Critics of commons wanted to improve society as well as agriculture: they wanted to change the structure of rural England.

Whether they were instrumental in producing the change they envisioned is beside the point (though they wrote as if they were, and Parliament passed almost a hundred enclosure Acts *a year* between 1800 and 1814). The causes of wage dependence were many, and the capture of public opinion only one of them. The point is that critics of commons, improvers and enclosers, made an argument that *justified* the change. They made an attack on independence thinkable. To do this, to ensure a consensus that would in turn make labour available and dependent, and common fields and wastes ready for enclosure, they had to malign and denigrate the basis of that independence, the common-right economy.

In making their attack on that economy explicit, they confirmed commoners in their belief that agricultural improvement held no advantage for them, and they legitimized the most rapacious of enclosers in their turning of common rights into mean and demeaning charity. In the end the critics' arguments not only legitimized, but also *publicly expressed* the terms of class robbery. They served the 'national' interest at the cost of the loss of common right, and they offered little compensation to those who paid the bill.

When independence went, and wages and poor relief took its place, social relations inevitably changed. All the old arguments of the defenders of commons come into play.[88] Property does beget content with one's lot, and content begets loyalty to landlords and farmers as well as to Nations. Take away property and you take away, in Thomas Andrews' words, 'the most precious gift of a free country': the independence of commoners. With it went connection,

[88] On property and patriotism see, William Paley, *Works*, 5 vols. (1823 edn), II, p. 59; C. Bruyn Andrews, ed., *The Torrington Diaries. A Selection from the Tours of the Hon. John Byng (later Fifth Viscount Torrington) between the Years 1781 and 1794* (1954), pp. 141–2, 207–8. The lesson was learnt later on, after most enclosure had occurred. Observers contrasted incendiary, landless Norfolk and Suffolk labourers with law-abiding Lincolnshire smallholders; the need to establish internal peace became an argument for providing agricultural labourers with allotments: Young, *General View ... Lincolnshire*, p. 469; and his 'Inquiry into the Propriety of Applying Wastes', pp. 509, 510–11; G. Lawson, 'Hints Favourable to the Poor', *Annals of Agriculture*, 40 (1803), p. 53; Pratt, 'Cottage-Pictures' [1801], in *Sympathy and Other Poems Including Landscapes in Verse, Cottage-Pictures, Revised, Corrected and Enlarged* (1807), pp. 253–5; J. Williams, *The Historical and Topographical View ... of Leominster* (Leominster, 1808), p. 121.

sympathy and obligation. The value of the commons was their social cement. The arrogance of critics was to think they could do without it.

THE END OF THE ARGUMENT

By the late 1790s commoners no longer found anyone to speak for them at the centre of government. This happened when critics of commons won the national interest debate there. It was underlined when Pitt's government ignored a body of opinion in favour of proper compensation for commons. It was confirmed again by the failure of defenders to advocate any real power for commoners themselves.

The critics laid the groundwork for their victory in the 1760s when they began to adopt the national interest argument of the defenders of commons. At the same time they began to transfer the defenders' descriptions of commoners as honest, hardworking and available to the future agricultural proletariat. Newly equipped, critics increasingly defined defenders' concern for the rights of commoners as hostile to the national interest, which was first and foremost to ensure an adequate supply of food. Increasingly, they justified enclosure as an extension of tillage not pasture. Increasingly, it was evident that this sort of enclosure, whatever else it might do, did not immediately depopulate. By the mid 1780s critics had kidnapped the national interest argument. They went on to use it to win support for the very institutional change that defenders had hoped it would prevent.

The result was that from 1793, and particularly from 1795 to 1801, as the war and poor harvests reduced the supply of food, the national advantage of enclosing waste in particular seemed unanswerable. Critics of commons lobbied for an easier and cheaper way to enclose large wastes.[89] Defenders of commons, instead of oppos-

---

[89] See, among others: Sir John Sinclair, *An Address to the Members of the Board of Agriculture, on the Cultivation and Improvement of the Waste Lands of this Kingdom* (1795); Staffs. RO Q/SB Transl. 1800, printed address of the Grand Jury of the County of York, March 15, 1800, to the High Sheriff of the County of Stafford, printed and circulated by the Board of Agriculture, recommending legislation to facilitate the enclosure of wasteland for the production of grain; Blane, *Inquiry*, p. 52; J. Lawrence, *The Modern Land Steward* (1801), p. 30; W. Marshall, *Draught of a General Act, for the Appropriation of Parochial Wastes* (1801), and *On the Landed Property of England* (1804), section II, 'On Appropriating Commonable Lands',

ing enclosure and extolling commoners for their service to the national interest, talked about regulating enclosure, or helping those it had already displaced.[90] They did so because, in the very decade when the defence of commons became unviable, the worst predictions of earlier defenders came to pass. If there was dearth in the 1790s that enclosure might alleviate, there was also a new kind of poverty in the countryside understood by men like the Reverend David Davies and Thomas Bewick in terms of the loss of land and commons.[91]

The public policy defence of commons now seemed futile. But the victory of the critics, coupled with the crisis in the countryside, brought about some agreement on the need for a proper compensation for commoners between enclosers like Young, Sir John Sinclair and Nathaniel Kent, and critics of enclosure like the Reverend David Davies and Viscount Torrington.[92] The breadth of this agreement on compensation, in which opponents of enclosure and its advocates were united, is evidence of the widely agreed upon value of common right. The Hammonds made this point when they argued that every prominent writer on agriculture in the 1790s and early 1800s supported compensation: 'Parliament was assailed on all sides with criticisms and recommendations', they wrote. Their conclusion that 'its refusal to alter its ways was deliberate' may be illustrated by the later careers of two critics whose apostasy reveals

[90] In 1801 John Lawrence wrote that the defenders' ideas 'so generally promulgated some years ago, seem now to have nearly all melted away before the sun of reason and experience'; they were doomed because they had preferred the 'savage state of man' to the 'civilized'; Lawrence, *Modern Land Steward*, pp. 24–5.

[91] The Reverend David Davies, *The Case of the Labourers in Husbandry Stated and Considered* (1795), pp. 56, 81; Thomas Bewick, *A Memoir*, ed., Iain Bain (1862; 1975 edn), pp. 24, 60.

[92] Sir John Sinclair, 'Observations on the Means of Enabling a Cottager to Keep a Cow, by the Produce of a Small Portion of Arable Land', in *Communications to the Board of Agriculture*, IV, no. 18 (1805), pp. 358–67; N. Kent, *The Great Advantage of a Cow to the Family of a Labouring Man* (1797) (broadsheet), and (same title) in *Annals of Agriculture*, 31 (1798), pp. 21–6; Kent practised what he preached: in 1796 his firm of land agents divided up land for cottagers on lands of the Earl of Egremont in Yorkshire: see Pamela Horn, 'An Eighteenth-Century Land Agent: the Career of Nathaniel Kent (1737–1810)', *Agricultural History Review*, 30 (1982), p. 7; Andrews, ed., *Torrington Diaries*, pp. 505–6: looking at the poverty of cottagers without land at Romney Warren near Chicksands Priory 'surround'd by hether they dare not collect, and by a profusion of turnips they dare not pluck', Torrington doubted the charity of his hostess: 'Madam said I, you only apply temporary balm; let them [have land]'.

the officially approved function of critics of commons in the public debate: Arthur Young and John Howlett.[93]

Arthur Young believed enclosure was the best possible route to economic strength and full employment. But when he discovered that full employment and adequate agricultural wages did not follow enclosure, he tried to carry his considerable public with him to demand compensation for the loss of commons. He wanted a legally regulated allotment of land – particularly waste land – to commoners at enclosure. He was immediately marginalized. A committee of the members of his own Board of Agriculture refused to publish his tour of England, in which he described the poverty of enclosed villages. Young described the Board's repudiation in his diary:

> [March 28th 1801] To-morrow will be published in the 'Annals' the first parts of my essay on applying waste lands to the better support of the poor. I prepared it some time ago for the Board, as it was collected in my last summer's journey; I read it to a committee – Lord Carrington [the Board president], Sir C. Willoughby and Mr Millington – who condemned it, and, after waiting a month, Lord C. told me I might do what I pleased with it for myself, but not print it as a work for the Board; so I altered the expressions which referred to the body, and sent it to the 'Annals'.

Even as he published it he doubted its effect:

> I prayed earnestly to God on and since the journey for His blessing on my endeavours to serve the poor, and to influence the minds of people to accept it; but for the wisest reasons certainly he has thought proper not to do this, and for the same reasons probably it will be printed without effect. I think it however my duty to Him to do all I possibly can ... I am well persuaded that this is the only possible means of saving the nation from the ruin fast coming on by the misery of the poor and the alarming ruin of rates. God's will be done![94]

But even in the *Annals of Agriculture* Young wrote less directly than he wrote privately. Compare, for example, his two accounts of Millbrook in Bedfordshire. The enclosure here in 1796 included a 878–acre waste confidently expected to enrich the enclosers.[95] It was

---

[93] Hammond and Hammond, *Village Labourer*, p. 78.

[94] *Autobiography of Arthur Young*, p. 351.

[95] Enclosing the waste was a prime object of the enclosure: see Bedfordshire RO, R 3/1209 (1792).

clearly disastrous for the commoners. In 1800 Young visited the
parish by chance, alone, on his way from Bradfield to Woburn. The
desperate poverty of some of the cottagers, and the neglect of
others, moved him greatly. In his diary he blamed their rich landlord, and advised the return of some of the waste:

> These poor people know not by what tenure they hold their land;
> they say they once belonged to the duke [of Bedford], but that the
> duke has swopped them away to my lord [Lord Ossory]. How
> little do the great know what they swop and what they receive! ...
> How very trifling the repairs to render these poor families warm
> and comfortable! ... What have not great and rich people to
> answer, for not examining into the situation of their poor neigh-
> bours?[96]

But when he wrote publicly about Millbrook in the *Annals*, Young
said only that 'The complaints of the poor chiefly turned on the
points of fuel: [before the enclosure] they got much fern and turf,
now an allotment assigned in lieu of the latter.'[97]

The gulf between the outrage and anger of the first encounter with
Millbrook and the short statement emptied of any emotion at all in
the second is startling. Perhaps Young had learnt something from
the rejection of his *Inquiry*. To escape further ostracism he may have
modified his public views and saved his class analysis of enclosure
for his diary.

The censoring and self-censoring of partial apostates like Young
is important. It suggests a reluctance to alienate the landed interest
for which they had always acted as a lobby. But, whatever the
reason, the reticence, the censorship and self-censorship are all
evidence that prominent critics of commons said privately that their
loss was more disruptive than they said publicly.

John Howlett was also a prominent and well-connected critic of
commons. We have seen that he was unusual in that he could see
that the rural proletariat created by enclosure might be unemployed
and impoverished. In the 1780s he argued that this did not matter
much because, as commoners, they were inured to misery anyway,
and the growth of population in itself was worth the cost. But as
that misery deepened in the 1790s and early 1800s Howlett stopped
talking about enclosure altogether and began to look for ways of
paying agricultural labourers decent wages. He publicly chastised

[96] *Autobiography of Arthur Young*, pp. 332–3.
[97] A. Young, *Annals of Agriculture*, 42 (1804), p. 27.

Pitt for deciding to let the market and the poor rate determine wage
levels, and he publicly doubted the humanity of village elites in the
dispensation of poor relief. He described the Reverend David
Davies' account of newly landless labourers in enclosed villages,
The Case of the Labourers in Husbandry, as 'incomparable'.[98]

Young and Howlett were critics of commons who became critics
of enclosure. For enclosure did not bring about a proletariat of the
industrious, hardy, healthy and moral sort. It took the commons
from the commoners. It drove women out of their employment in
the common-right economy. It drew the men to the pub, where what
small compensation they got for their commons was 'piss'd against
the wall'.[99] Finally, it put them both on poor relief, and stole the
birthright of the common from their children. Knowing this (and
knowing too that it might have been avoided), Young spoke out and
went unheard, as he had expected. Then he left commoners in the
hands of God. Howlett turned to other ways of saving labourers
from poor relief and the tender mercies of the local farmers. Neither
had much success.

Young and Howlett had served their purpose. They had been
successful earlier because they had had things to say that promoters
of enclosure, and Parliament, wanted to hear. They had successfully
taken the arguments of the defenders, and turned them to enclosers'
advantage. They had identified enclosure with the national interest.
But they became ineffective when they had something to say that
enclosers and Parliament did *not* want to hear. Indeed, they were
silenced.

But the obduracy of Parliament in refusing compensation is not

[98] Cited in Hammond and Hammond, *Village Labourer*, p. 77. Howlett published his
accounts of the state of the poor in Young's *Annals of Agriculture* from 1789 until
his death. In these years it seems likely that his connection to Beilby Porteus, the
Evangelical Bishop of London, was closer than his connection to Loughborough,
who sided with Pitt against Whitbread's minimum wage Bill. For the Porteus
connection see Howlett, *Enclosure and Population*, [p. i]. For Loughborough and
Pitt see J. R. Poynter, *Society and Pauperism: English Ideas on Poor Relief,
1795–1834* (1969), p. 59. For the poverty of Essex agricultural labourers (particularly in newly enclosed Audley End) and problems of order in Howlett's
village of Great Dunmow, see T. L. Richardson, 'Agricultural Labourers' Wages
and the Cost of Living in Essex, 1790–1840: A Contribution to the Standard of
Living Debate', in B. A. Holderness and M. E. Turner, eds., *Land, Labour and
Agriculture 1700–1920. Essays for Gordon Mingay* (1991), pp. 69–89.
[99] The phrase, in this instance, is that of opponents of enclosure in the village of
Atherstone: Warwick. RO, HR 35/15.

explained by improving ideology alone. After all, by the 1790s even pamphleteer improvers called for some compensation for the poor. By the late 1790s a new pamphleteer had caught the ear of Parliament. He was the Reverend Thomas Malthus. In 1798 he argued against giving outdoor relief to the poor; in 1803 he argued against giving them land. Saying that Arthur Young contradicted himself in prescribing for England what had ensured poverty in France, Malthus argued that giving land to the poor would lead to more poor relief, not less. The appeal of Malthus may explain the failure of defenders and critics of commons to persuade Pitt of the value of compensated enclosure. A newer ideology than improvement sealed the fate of nineteenth-century commoners.[100]

Defenders in the 1790s had an alternative to asking for compensation for enclosure or higher wages for labourers and work for women. They might have asserted the right of commoners to self-determination. This is not as anachronistic a suggestion as it sounds. Commoners' demands for some say in their own affairs were a large part of the local debate on enclosure.[101] But in the national debate few defenders of commons took this stand, perhaps because the 1790s was a bad decade in which to put so radical an argument publicly. If talk of making enclosers of waste compensate commoners was unacceptable when it came from the Secretary to the Board of Agriculture, the argument that commoners should have the power to prevent or shape enclosure could hardly be successful. Critics of commons were scathing on the subject. Paul put the livelihoods of commoners on a par with the sporting rights of grouse-hunters: in opposing the enclosure of wastes both denied the national interest. As we have seen, Charles Vancouver doubted the wisdom of teaching commoners to read and write, let alone their

---

[100] Thomas Malthus, *An Essay on the Principle of Population, as it Affects the Future Improvement of Society* (1798), and *An Essay on the Principle of Population, or, A View of its Past and Present Effects on Human Happiness* (1803), in Gertrude Himmelfarb, ed., *On Population. Thomas Robert Malthus* (1960), pp. 556–63. Malthus' second edition is known for its optimism compared to the first edition, but this did not extend to commoners. Young replied in 'On the Application of the Principles of Population, to the Question of Assigning Land to Cottages', *Annals of Agriculture*, 41 (1804), pp. 208–31; in 1808 Young took up Malthus again in his Board of Agriculture, *General Report on Enclosures* where he argued (pp. 100–10) that improved agriculture could outstrip population growth. I am preparing a longer discussion of the argument between Pitt, Malthus and Young.
[101] See below, Chapter 9.

having the power to prevent enclosure.[102] Magistrates sending for troops to deal with enclosure rioters expressed themselves more directly: 'if poor people are suffered to make Laws for themselves', wrote James Webster from Bedfordshire in 1796, 'we shall very shortly have no Government in this County'.[103]

But defenders failed to advocate self-determination for another reason too. Nothing in their descriptions of commoners suggests that they thought commoners were equals. If commoners were honest and hardworking, they were also simple, innocent, uncorrupted rustics with strong bodies and English hearts. These are the best qualities of good subordinates but – despite their petty landholding and common right – not the qualities of informed citizens. In ignoring the possibility of self-determination, and in keeping commoners themselves out of the public debate, the defenders of commons ensured the end of the enclosure debate between pamphleteers, in Parliament and at the Board of Agriculture.

Outside these fora of the official body politic, commoners continued to resist enclosure as they always had. Thomas Bewick and John Clare (to name only two) continued to make the public observation that enclosure and the loss of commons turned commoners into labourers. And at the level of radical popular politics the Spencean Philanthropists saw the re-allotment of all the land to all the people as the basis of a new society in which commoners would be neither peasant nor proletarian.[104]

[102] Pennington, *Reflections*, pp. 34–5; Paul, *Observations on the General Enclosure Bill*, extracted in [Young] *General Report on Enclosures*, p. 159; Vancouver, *General View … Hampshire*, pp. 505–9.
[103] PRO: WO 40/17, letter from James Webster JP, 2 August 1796, concerning the enclosure of Maulden, Bedfordshire.
[104] Thompson, *Making*, pp. 176–9, 672–4; Malcolm Chase, 'Thomas Spence: The Trumpet of Jubilee', *Past and Present*, 76 (1977); and *The People's Farm. English Radical Agrarianism 1775–1840* (Oxford, 1988).

I

Survival

2. Who had common right?

Eighteenth-century writers said that commoners were small farmers, artisans, tradesmen, and the labouring poor, many of whom commoned without land. And, although they disagreed about the value of common right compared to a regular wage, they did not disagree about the survival, the useful or barbaric ubiquity of commoners. Far more than these writers, historians have disagreed about the value of common right. How have they described the identity and ubiquity of commoners?

'In the open field village', Gilbert Slater wrote, 'the entirely landless labourer was scarcely to be found.' Accordingly, where land brought common right, commoners were many. The Hammonds went further: few villagers got nothing from the common; it was the 'patrimony of the poor', even those without land might have commons: 'Were there any day labourers without either land or common rights in the old village? It is difficult to suppose that there were many.' Lord Ernle, and J. D. Chambers in his early writing, agreed.[1]

Sir John Clapham also thought that commoners were ubiquitous. But he added two qualifications. First, they commoned by *custom* not right. And custom was illegal. Second, so valuable a custom as to keep a *cow* was rare. In well-populated arable areas the right to graze a cow had never been universal. Arthur Young was wrong, he said, to claim that in nineteen enclosures out of twenty the poor lost commons for their cows: 'Cows were not so common as that.' What

---

[1] Hammond and Hammond, *Village Labourer*, p. 25; Gilbert Slater, *The English Peasantry and the Enclosure of Common Fields* (1907; repr. New York, 1968), p. 119; Ernle, *English Farming*, pp. 304–7; J. D. Chambers, *Nottinghamshire in the Eighteenth Century. A Study of Life and Labour under the Squirearchy* (1932; repr. 1966), pp. 182–5.

was *almost* universal was the usage, the illegal 'sufferance and custom', of turning geese and asses onto the common and into the stubble grazing on the fields.[2]

The later Chambers, with Mingay, argued like Clapham that custom was not law. But they also argued that not every cottage entitled its owner or occupier to common right: 'it must be remembered that even before enclosure *the majority of cottagers had no rights of common*. Such rights did not belong to every villager but were attached to open-field holdings or certain cottages, and only their owners or occupiers were certainly entitled to make use of them.'[3]

And again, unlike Clapham, they argued that agricultural improvement led to the decline of the shared use of commons. Clapham had described their co-existence: eighteenth-century improvers, he said, deplored the *unstinted* common but they 'took no exception' to the widespread usages of poor commoners.[4] Elsewhere Mingay described a general decline of small farmers in the early eighteenth century, a decline which also implies a decline in commoners.[5]

In short, Clapham's many commoners grazed geese and asses (but not cows) on sufferance. Chambers and Mingay's fewer commoners were a minority who commoned as property owners and tenants. Or they were a larger number of labourers whose dwindling commons were not theirs by right but by uncertain and ill-defined custom – a term itself ill-defined to mean mere usage or habit. Since then, J. A. Yelling has taken a more agnostic stand on the question of numbers, arguing that common right is a difficult and unexplored subject. He was not primarily interested in commoners, but like Clapham he argued none the less that the commoner with a cow 'must be

---

[2] J. H. Clapham, *An Economic History of Modern Britain: The Early Railway Age 1820–1850* (Cambridge, 1926; 2nd edn, 1930; repr. 1950), pp. 115–17; also see George Glover Alexander, 'The Manorial System and Copyhold Tenure', *Publications of the Thoresby Society*, 33, *Miscellanea* (Leeds, 1935), p. 294: 'A good deal of foolish talk has been uttered at various times about the iniquity of taking away commons from the poor man and giving them to the rich. The poor man, as such, as a mere inhabitant of a place, free to come and go, had no rights of property in a common, except such as he was allowed by the indulgence of the commoners.'

[3] Chambers and Mingay, *Agricultural Revolution*, p. 97 (my italics).

[4] Clapham, *Economic History*, p. 116.

[5] G. E. Mingay, *English Landed Society in the Eighteenth Century* (1963), p. 99.

reckoned only among the more wealthy of the labouring population'.[6] And M. R. Postgate in a discussion of East Anglian field
systems has described commoners in relation to the foldcourse. The
right to put sheep in with the lord's declined from the sixteenth
century onwards. Increasingly, the foldcourse became the preserve
of the lord and a burden to his tenants. Even where the tenants kept
their usage, the foldcourse was increasingly whittled away at with
severalty.[7]

There are at least three areas of conflict here. First, about
numbers of commoners: were they many or few? And, related to
this, did access depend on the occupancy of property (land or
cottage) or on residence? On this Chambers, Mingay, and later
writers confront the Hammonds and Clapham. Second, about
what they commoned: was it only pigs and poultry or did it include
cows and horses? On this Clapham parted company with the
Hammonds and was endorsed by Chambers and Mingay. Third,
about justification: did commoners common by right or by illegal
usage? Here, the Hammonds made no distinction, talking instead
about *practice*, and Clapham, Chambers and Mingay put custom
outside the law.

If these historians have disagreed about numbers, cows and
legality, part of the reason may be that they were not centrally
concerned with the survival of common right before enclosure.
When we look at the historical record with this in mind, what does it
say? What do customary agricultural regulations, disputes about
common right and contemporary descriptions of practice tell us
about numbers of commoners, the animals they grazed and the
nature of their entitlement? In the first part of this chapter a study of
contrasting forest, fen, hill and vale manors in Northamptonshire
offers some answers. In the second part the commoning histories of
villages throughout the Midlands illustrate the ubiquity of common
right.

[6] Yelling, *Common Field and Enclosure*, p. 229.
[7] On East Anglian lords' 'seigneurial monopoly' of the fold see K. J. Allison, 'The
Sheep-Corn Husbandry of Norfolk in the Sixteenth and Seventeenth Centuries',
Agricultural History Review, 5 (1957); Alan Simpson, 'The East Anglian Fold
Course: Some Queries', *Agricultural History Review*, 6 (1958); M. R. Postgate, 'The
Field Systems of East Anglia', in A. R. H. Baker and R. A. Butlin, eds., *Studies of
Field Systems in the British Isles* (Cambridge, 1973) pp. 281–324.

NORTHAMPTONSHIRE[8]

Eighteenth-century open-field Northamptonshire had a mixed-farming agriculture in which about two-thirds of the land went for crops, the rest for pasture.[9] The county also had a reduced but still significant forest and fenland, relatively buoyant rural industries and a history of enclosure for the conversion of arable land to pasture. Customary village trades, expanding forest industries, lace-making in the east and south-east, and the rushwork and mat-making of the Nene valley were supplemented by the growth between 1740 and 1770 of a worsted industry in the western half of the county, and after about 1780 of shoemaking in the east.[10] Much of the west and south-west of the county where it meets Warwickshire and Oxfordshire was enclosed in the sixteenth and seventeenth centuries, sometimes by agreement, more often by unity of possession when one owner held all the land. These enclosures often led to depopulation and consequently met resistance, most notably in 1607.[11]

By 1720, although one-third of Northamptonshire parishes were enclosed, only 10 per cent of the population lived in them; the rest lived in open villages and towns destined to be enclosed eventually by Act of Parliament.[12] Still open in the mid eighteenth century was

---

[8] The following discussion is based on a study of the royal manor of Raunds to which Ringstead also owed suit, the manors of Moreton Pinkney cum membris (Woodend, Blakesley, Plumpton, Adstone), manors owing suit and service to the court of the manor of Green's Norton (Green's Norton, Duncot, Field Burcot and Carswell), manors of the Duke of Grafton in Whittlewood and Salcey forests (Grafton Regis, Hartwell, Roade, Ashton, Wicken and Bugbrooke, and Shenly and Hanslop in Buckinghamshire), and the Earl Fitzwilliam's fenland manor, Maxey cum membris (Helpstone, Castor and Ailesworth, Etton and Marholm, Northborough, Botelars and Thorolds).

[9] Pitt, *General View . . . Northampton*, p. 76.

[10] *Ibid.*, pp. 240–3; Adrian Randall, 'The Kettering Worsted Industry in the Eighteenth Century', *Northamptonshire Past and Present*, 4 (1971–2); V. A. Hatley and Joseph Rajczonek, *Shoemakers in Northamptonshire, 1762–1911: A Statistical Survey*, Northampton Historical Series, no. 6 (Northampton, 1971).

[11] E. F. Gay, 'The Midland Revolt of 1607', *Trans. Roy. Hist. Soc.*, new series, 18 (1904); W. E. Tate, 'Inclosure Movements in Northamptonshire', *Northamptonshire Past and Present*, 1 (1949), pp. 25, 30; Martin, *Feudalism to Capitalism*, considers events in Northamptonshire central to the Midland revolt due to the extent of enclosure.

[12] John Morton, *Natural History of Northamptonshire* (1712), pp. 15, 17. More than 87 per cent of the county population lived in open villages and towns: John Bridges, *History and Antiquities of Northamptonshire*, ed. P. Whalley (Oxford, 1791). Bridges did not note the population size of a further forty-three parishes

half of the western uplands (where deserted enclosed villages and expanding open cloth villages lay side by side), much of the upland near Northampton, the Nene valley, the royal forests of Rockingham, Salcey and Whittlewood, and the north-eastern heath and fen of the Soke of Peterborough, home of the poet John Clare.

Landed commoners

Land, *common-field* land, whether arable, greensward, or ley, entitled its occupiers to pasture rights in Northamptonshire. By the middle of the eighteenth century manorial courts stinted rights for cows to one for every six to ten acres of arable. They set sheep commons at one per acre, except in the fens, where stints were more generous. Land left as greensward, or laid down as ley, generally entitled the occupier to graze more animals than the same acreage in common arable.[13]

Even the smallest occupiers of land were entitled to pasture. In most parts of the county those with only five acres could graze five sheep every year, more if they lived in fen or forest. Occupiers of less than the minimum acreage for a cow common had the right to graze one cow or a horse for half the year; in some places for the whole year, despite the shortfall. In Raunds in the Nene valley the minimum acreage needed to graze one, two or three cows was lower per beast than the acreage needed to stock more.[14] In some villages the option of renting dead commons was open to occupiers of the smallest of common-field holdings too: a commoner with only two acres might graze five sheep or a cow, paying the price of the additional rights. When extra pasture could be rented in this way, and when browse and other kinds of fodder were available from the waste, keeping a cow was not impossible on a holding of only two acres and a small close, or even less in forest and fen. A larger holding of six to ten acres of common arable land would bring the right to pasture ten sheep and either a cow or a horse. Leaving land fallow in the corn fields, or sowing it with sainfoin or clover entitled a commoner to twice as much grazing. Sowing only one acre with clover in the forest-fringe villages of Stoke Bruerne and Shutlanger

(including the four comprising the town of Northampton), 60 per cent of which were open in 1720 when he compiled his evidence.
[13] Stints are discussed at length in Chapter 4.
[14] Northants. RO, Raunds Parish Records, Overseer's Accounts, 1789.

in 1725 brought common for a cow or a horse; all the other Grafton manors set more sheep commons (and sometimes cattle commons too) for this kind of land. One might suppose that the smallest commoners often left land as greensward because, more than anyone else, they needed fodder.[15] In short, commoners might occupy very little land and yet have grazing for a cow.

But how many landed commoners lived in eighteenth-century England? The best sources can suggest only minimum estimates. In twenty open-field parishes in late eighteenth-century Northamptonshire occupiers ranged from as few as 16 per cent of the village to as many as 68 per cent. The mean figure was 37 per cent.[16] This is a substantial number of potential commoners, but the real figure was probably greater, for two reasons. First, the poor owners of land worth less than 20s per annum were exempt from the Land Tax, and may not appear on the tax returns from which these figures come. If observed, and the exemption was noted in every edition of Burn's *Justice of the Peace*, this provision would have excluded the poor owners of three acres or less, and their tenants.[17] It is possible that such landowners were numerous; certainly in eighteenth-century Northamptonshire the landholding structure was one of large

15 An order made for the manors of Stoke Bruerne and Shutlanger in 1731 set the sheep stint at three sheep for every four acres of arable, and five for every two acres of greensward. A common right for a horse or cow was stinted to six acres of arable land or only three of greensward: Northants. RO, G3347a, 22 April 1731. G3340a, 8 April 1725; see also G3624b, 26 April 1764: an acre of clover sown instead of wheat or barley brought five sheep commons. See below, p. 70.

16 Based on the evidence of a random sample of parishes taken from Slater, *English Peasantry*, Appendix B, list of Northamptonshire enclosure acts, compared to populations noted in the *Census*, 1801, and pre-enclosure Land Tax returns. Proportions of occupiers were: Rounds (42 per cent), Wadenhoe (16 per cent), Whittlebury (23 per cent), Whitfield (36 per cent), Wollaston (43 per cent), Hargrave (68 per cent), Greens Norton (24 per cent), Islip (27 per cent), Chelveston (31 per cent), Hannington (27 per cent), Maxey (48 per cent), Helpstone (64 per cent), Sutton Bassett (25 per cent), Newton Bromshold (30 per cent), Weston by Welland (32 per cent), Abthorpe (44 per cent), Stanwick (39 per cent), Roade (25 per cent), Eye (25 per cent), Lutton (47 per cent). The proportion rises if landlords are included: taxed *landholders* (landlords, owner-occupiers and tenants) ranged from a third to three quarters of the populations of these villages, with a mean proportion of about one half. Commoners' landholding is further discussed in Chapter 10.

17 See the eighteen editions of Burn from 1755 to 1797. See Appendix A, p. 340, for instances of exempt landholders in Burton Latimer and Whitfield in Northamptonshire, Bucklebury, Berkshire, and Bledington, Gloucestershire. Cf. J. V. Beckett, 'The Decline of the Small Landowner in Eighteenth and Nineteenth-Century England: Some Regional Considerations', *Agricultural History Review*, 30 (1982), pp. 102–3.

numbers of owners of ten acres, or less, and relatively few middling
and larger owners with more than forty acres each.[18] Second, the
proportions of landholders derived from Land Tax returns also
exclude the occupiers of sublet land. Again, it seems reasonable to
assume that in common-field villages of scattered landholding, the
subletting of strips for a year at a time was more common than in
enclosed parishes, or, indeed, in highly consolidated open-field
parishes. It was a simple matter to arrange, and rents, at seven to ten
shillings an acre, were low enough to attract very small tenants.[19]
The chances are that in many common-field villages on the eve of
enclosure as many as a half of the villagers were entitled to common
grazing because they occupied land.

Cottage commoners

Besides land, the occupancy of some cottages, inns, millhouses,
farmhouses, and other buildings or sites of former buildings also
brought pasture rights. A cottage in Warmington, advertised for
sale in the *Northampton Mercury* in 1753, carried right of common
for two cows and ten sheep. Without the cottage right, and unless
inhabitants had rights as residents alone, grazing like this required
the occupancy of at least ten or twelve acres of common arable. As it
was, the land sold with this cottage consisted of only two acres of
meadow, half an acre of arable and another half acre of sward, each
of which lay in the common fields. This cottager would have had the
proverbial three acres but with grazing for two cows, not one, and
ten sheep.[20] A 'messuage tenement' sold in Daventry in 1785 came
with a stable 'fit for any trade' and right of common for no fewer
than three horses, three cows and sixty sheep.[21] Inns were also
endowed with common rights for a cow, or a cow and her calf, or a
cow and a horse.[22]

[18] See below p. 250.
[19] Patricia Croot and David Parker make the same observation in 'Agrarian Class
Structure and Economic Development', *Past and Present*, 78 (1978), p. 40.
[20] *Northampton Mercury*, 5 Feb. 1753. A Wilbarston cottage was put up for sale in
1794 with commons for four sheep and one and a half cows, 3 May 1794 (half
rights might be used for half the pasture year, or for one whole year in every two).
Similar advertisements were published for cottages in Walgrave (16 Oct. 1727);
Rothwell (8 Aug. 1767); Irthlingborough (27 July 1767); Brigstock (31 May 1788).
[21] *Northampton Mercury*, 7 March 1785.
[22] Respectively, *Northampton Mercury*, 25 Apr. 1763, 12 Mar. 1791, 3 Mar. 1796,
and 20 June 1763.

The proportion of common-right cottages in the housing stock varied between parishes and from region to region. In Rockingham forest in the 1720s cottages as a proportion of all the forest dwellings ranged from almost all the houses of Stanion and Little Oakley, to a third of those in Brigstock and Geddington, and a quarter of those in Great Weldon.[23] Outside the forest, proportions of common-right cottages in village housing stocks were often smaller: in Chelveston cum Caldecott at enclosure in 1801 the proportion was a seventh, in Wootton and Irthlingborough it was a fifth or a quarter, in Polebrooke a ninth.[24] But the contrast between forest and hill and vale can be exaggerated. Some hill and vale parishes had more cottages than others: a third to a half of the houses in Aldwinkle, Walgrave, Holcot, Kilsby, Titchmarsh, Harpole and Duston had common right.[25]

[23] Northants. RO, Mont. B. X350, Box 10, no. 25, Papers concerning the proposed enclosure of Geddington Chase, 1720; Bridges, *History and Antiquities*. Two generations later, in 1795, little had changed: petitioners for the enclosure of Brigstock, Stanion and Sudborough Green agreed that two thirds of the joint housing stock had common right: there were 181 cottages with common right between them at the Bill's engrossing, *Jls House of Commons*, 1, 21 April 1795; the 1801 *Census* recorded 282 houses. Similarly, in Whitfield, Whittlewood Forest, the proportion of houses with cottage common rights was almost half of the 48 houses counted in 1801: Northants. RO, Whitfield Enclosure Award and map 1796 (flat folders); *Census*, 1801, p. 248.

[24] Six commoners claimed cottage rights for eight cottages in Chelveston: Northants. RO, Chelveston Enclosure Award, 1801, X3475; the number of inhabited and uninhabited houses was 55: *Census*, 1801, p. 247. There were 41 cottage rights in Irthlingborough when enclosure was attempted in 1808: *Jls House of Commons*, 7 Apr. 1808; and 160 houses noted on the 1801 *Census*. Common-right claims were compensated for twenty cottages and farmhouses in Wootton in 1778; there were 101 inhabited and uninhabited houses there in 1801: *Census*, p. 52. There were six cottages in Polebrooke when its Bill was engrossed in 1790, and 55 houses on the 1801 *Census*.

[25] Aldwinkle, 53 cottage rights in 1772, and 87 houses in 1801; Walgrave, 49 cottage rights in 1776 and 99 houses in 1801; Holcot, 64 cottage rights in 1777 and 60 houses in 1801; Kilsby, 40 cottage rights in 1771 and 151 houses in 1801 (but only 72 in 1720); Titchmarsh, 71.5 cottage rights in 1778 and 130 houses in 1801; Harpole, 37.5 cottage rights in 1778 and 177 houses (but only 60 in 1720); Duston, 20 cottage rights in 1776 and 76 houses in 1801 (but only 60 in 1720). Figures for cottage rights are taken from tallies made at the engrossing of each enclosure bill in the *Jls of the House of Commons*; figures for inhabited and uninhabited houses in 1801 are taken from the 1801 *Census*; figures for houses in 1720 come from Bridges, *History and Antiquities*. Cottage rights were counted only when a Bill was opposed at engrossing by someone owning at least one of them. This makes a comparison of proportions of rights in all parishes impossible. For further discussion of the variation in common-right survival *within* hill and vale parishes, see below pp. 67–9, 73–4.

The number of common-right cottages counted by enclosure commissioners or lords of manors at enclosure gives us an estimate of the number of common-right *cottagers*, but it is almost certainly an underestimate. For only narrowly defined legal right was acknowledged at enclosure; more widely enjoyed customary right was sometimes ignored.[26] But the number of cottage commoners exceeded the number of cottages compensated at enclosure for another reason too: cottage rights were divisible. Some evidence of this comes from awards made at enclosure for fractions of cottage rights. Chelveston claims for cottagers' sheep rights ranged from as few as three to as many as fourteen.[27] Wootton cottagers claimed grazing for four sheep and a cow or for exactly twice that number, and claims to rights for farmhouses ranged from four sheep commons to eight, sixteen or twenty.[28] When Raunds was enclosed in 1797, eight cottagers claimed fractions of cottage rights.[29] Earlier, in December 1717, John Clarke of Raunds surrendered into court one third of a cottage, its attached buildings, and one third of the adjacent land. With the property went commons for three sheep and a cow.[30] Similarly, in Brigstock in 1720, cottagers holding their cottages by suit-house tenure held them in a variety of sizes: 53 were full suit-houses, two were half suit-houses, and nine were quarter suit-houses. In all, there were 56 and a quarter full suit-house cottage rights but 64 households of cottage commoners.[31]

How had this division of rights come about? It seems to have happened when cottage rights were shared between the two or more households created when a single cottage was subdivided. Thus in Raunds at enclosure John Hall made two claims, one for the half

[26] See below, pp. 78–9.
[27] Northants. RO, Chelveston Enclosure Award, 1801, X3475.
[28] Northants. RO, Wootton Enclosure Award, Book V, 65, June 1778 and November 1779.
[29] For example: 'a half part of a cottage belonging to my messuage or tenement': Northants. RO, Box 88, no. 1140, Raunds enclosure claims, 1797.
[30] Northants. RO, QCR 47, 2 Dec. 1717.
[31] The tenure was claimed before the Eyre in the reign of Charles I; it required attendance at the three weeks' court in return for wood for houses, gates and fences – house-bote, gate-bote, and hedge-bote (62 loads of thorns) to be taken from Geddington and Farming Woods every year at a low rate: Bridges, *History and Antiquities*, pp. 284–7. Similar tenures were held in Stanion, Geddington and King's Cliffe: Pettit, *Royal Forests of Northamptonshire: A Study in their Economy 1558–1714*, Publications of the Northamptonshire Record Society XXIII (1968), p. 167.

cottage he lived in, the other half he let to someone else.[32] Or it happened when two or more cottages were built on the site of one ancient cottage – some claims made at Raunds were for the sites of cottages now demolished.

The significance of division for the numbers of cottage commoners is twofold. First, when rights were divided and shared among more households – households until that moment having no rights of their own – the number of cottage commoners rose. Second, because cottage rights were divisible, population pressure did not inevitably create a small elite of cottage commoners – the 'ancient' cottagers – and a growing majority of cottagers with no access to commons. Instead, right could spread more thinly when populations grew: tenementized cottages could offer commons to each household within. Divided cottage rights signify the multiplication of commoning *families* – though not the multiplication of rights. They also mean that proportions of cottages in the housing stock of enclosing villages are very much minimum estimates.

The Northamptonshire evidence suggests that officially defined and counted common-right cottages comprised anything from a fifth or a half of the housing stock of some villages in the Nene valley to half or three quarters of others in the royal forests. But the division of cottage rights into fractions suggests that cottage commoners were more numerous than official counts of common-right cottages might suggest. In fact their numbers were also swelled by landless commoners whose rights came as residents, as we shall see.

Landless commoners

Commoners with rights of pasture attached to land they worked or to cottages they occupied were perhaps half of the county population on the eve of enclosure. But there were other commoners who owned or rented no land at all, and whose cottages did not entitle them to compensation for loss of common right in a court of law. They were landless commoners – a term which describes labourers and artisans (and those who were both, depending on the season), small tradesmen, and the part of the village made up by those who were 'poor' in the sense of being unfortunate – the old, the widows with families to support. In some parishes, immigrants and squatters were also landless commoners.

[32] Northants. RO, Box 88, no. 1140, Raunds claims, 1797.

Proof of their enjoyment of right is difficult to find in the usual sources – manorial customs and field orders – the kind of documents that would satisfy an enclosure commissioner or a judge. For this reason they escape the view of historians looking only at manorial or even enclosure papers. The rights of the landless are better documented where they resisted the loss of commons at enclosure. In Northamptonshire, for example, they took part in riots at West Haddon and Warkworth; they also joined in a mob of three hundred when the army brought in the fences for the enclosure of Wilbarston wold; they signed the counter-petitions against enclosure in Wellingborough and Burton Latimer, despite their propertylessness; they tore down notices of enclosure bills from church doors. And they may have been responsible for covert attacks on the hedges and gates of enclosed fields in the years following each enclosure.[33] Of all the complaints against enclosure, the loss of commons by the poorest commoners is heard loudest.

In an untidy paradox, landless commoners were often almost rather than absolutely landless. They were land poor. Some occupied too little land to be eligible for the Land Tax, or they worked an acre or two and escaped payment. Some had gardens, pightles of meadow or small assarts, and yards with stalls or sheds suitable for pigs and poultry, or in some cases a couple of sheep or a horse.[34] Particularly in the unstinted forest commons of Rockingham, Whittlewood and Salcey, or in the northern fens, or in scarpland parishes like Wilbarston, Clipston and West Haddon, which enjoyed large local wastes, these landless commoners swelled the population dependent on land and common rights. The Hampshire reporter to the Board of Agriculture, Charles Vancouver, described commoners in Devon as living on the edges of the waste.[35] The description is metaphorical as well as real. Landless commoners lived at the edges of landed society: they were neither landed nor really landless. At some points in their lives some of them had animals but no land at all. Farmers, for example, paid their servants

---

[33] Labourers were part of the crowds that destroyed the notices of enclosure bills posted in Oakley, Stewkely, Princes Risborough, Towersey and Haddenham in Buckinghamshire: M. E. Turner, 'Some Social and Economic Considerations of Parliamentary Enclosure in Buckinghamshire, 1738–1865' (unpublished Ph.D. thesis, University of Sheffield, 1973), p. 195; and see below, Chapter 9, pp. 283–4.

[34] A pightle is a small piece of land, an assart is an enclosure from the forest or waste.

[35] See Chapter 1, p. 35.

in pasture for sheep and lambs as well as in cash.[36] Landless commoners lived off the land rather than on it.[37]

The Swedish traveller Pehr Kalm's 'sheep-men' were landless commoners: 'A poor man lays by something by labour, or how he can, so that he is just able to buy a few sheep – the more the better.' He found a local farmer who would fold the sheep on the parish fallow field at night in return for a small fee. The sheep-man drove his sheep to pasture during the day on the common-field pastures, and also on to the farmers' own land, 'where he always has freedom to pasture them, because they by the droppings which they leave after them always pay for what they eat'. They ate well in the fields and in bad weather the sheep-man took them home to feed them with 'all kinds of straw and hay' of his own. Any dung he turned to manure, which he sold. They spent most nights in the common sheep fold; but, for fear of harsh mid-winter nights, they were often sold in the autumn and bought again in spring.[38]

If they had no grazing for sheep, then at the least in parishes with uncultivated forest, fen or heath, landless commoners could turn their pigs into the permanent pasture when it was open, and on to the stubble after the harvest, and feed them on acorns and beech-mast from the woods, selling them later in corn markets and at fairs.[39] In 1610 John Norden remarked on the value of North-amptonshire hogs in his *Delineation of Northamptonshire*:

... wch made me most to marvayle weare the great heards of Swyne, a beaste altogether unprofitable, till he come to the slaughter. Then his rustie ribbs in a frostie morninge will please Pearce the ploughman, and will so supple his weatherbeaten

---

[36] Ann S. Kussmaul, *Servants in Husbandry in Early Modern England* (Cambridge, 1981), p. 39.

[37] For a modern attempt at this, albeit without animals, see Anthony Wigens, *The Clandestine Farm* (1980).

[38] Pehr Kalm, *Kalm's Account of his Visit to England on his Way to America in 1748*, trans. Joseph Lucas (1892), pp. 301–3. Atherstone freeholders could let their sheep commons but not horse or cow commons: Warwicks. RO, CR 127/8. The same was true of Sowe in 1722 ('Wee do further Agree that there Shall not a hoof of any Sort of Cattell Sheep only Excepted be Commoned in our fields but such only as Belongs to our Town'): Warwicks. RO, CR 556/299; see also Z 12/1a, 2a.

[39] For harvest pasture see *Northampton Mercury*, 20 Aug. 1796: pigs could be turned into the fields three weeks after gleaning; Northants. RO, YO 578: at Orlingbury in 1711 a new stinting agreement set a fine of one shilling per hog put into the fields before three weeks after harvest; Dorothy Hartley, *Lost Country Life* (1979 edn), p. 330.

lipps, that his whipp and his whistle will hammer out such harmony as will make a Dogge daunce that delights it.[40] In no parish were pigs stinted to the acre, or specifically allowed pasture only if they belonged to landholders, although custom limited their numbers, and regulations governed the ringing of their noses to protect the surface of the land.[41] When Lord Gowran tried to expel the local hogs from Farming Woods Walk in Rockingham in 1747, he was advised that if there was no grant of common for them he could give notice of trespass, which if broken would empower him to impound the hogs *damage feasant*, or sue the owners for trespass.[42] Gowran and his steward believed that there was no such grant because several commoners had paid a small fee for the liberty. But grant or not, the forest commoners had enjoyed the pasture for their hogs, and may have continued to do so, for complaints about their hogs (and their sheep) are heard until enclosure.[43]

The pigs of the forest and waste were the southern counterpart of the geese that had the run of fen pastures in Maxey and Deepingate throughout the century until enclosure in 1809.[44] In Staffordshire, William Pitt described their breeding as the work of 'the poor people' who sold them to farmers to fatten them in their stubbles for the table.[45] He also remarked on their scarcity after enclosure, and supposed that 'they must in future be bred on the farmer's premises'. In much the same way Adam Smith commented on the disappearance of goose-down at enclosure and associated it with the

[40] John Norden, *Speculi Britanniae pars Altera; or a Delineation of Northamptonshire; being a brief historicall and choriographicall description of that county . . . by the travayle of J. Norden, in the year 1610* (1720 edn), p. 20.

[41] See Neeson, 'Common Right and Enclosure in Eighteenth-Century Northamptonshire', (unpublished Ph.D. thesis, University of Warwick, 1978), ch. 2, pp. 113–15. Nor were donkeys mentioned in stints, but they too may have been common. Strangers' cattle and hogs were agisted in Cliffe Bailiwick in 1728: Northants, RO, W(A)4, xvii, 4; Earl Cardigan turned his hogs into Bandy Slade near Corby to fatten them in 1727: 'The hogs in Bandyslade are all very fatt and I think fit to kill when your Lordship pleases': Joan Wake and D. C. Webster, eds., *The Letters of Daniel Eaton to the Third Earl of Cardigan 1725–32*, Letter 153 [30 Nov. 1727] (Publications of the Northamptonshire Record Society, Kettering, 1971), XXIV, p. 129.

[42] Northants. RO, YZ 4959, Letter Mathew Duane to Lord Gowran, 13 June 1747; Lord Westmorland wanted to exclude the hogs too.

[43] Rockingham Castle Muniments, A 3/105/2 and A 3/106.

[44] See Chapter 4, p. 115.

[45] William Pitt, *Topographical History of Staffordshire* (Newcastle-under-Lyme, 1817), Part II, p. 79.

decline of small proprietors in the Lincolnshire fenlands. (The geese themselves were said to have supplied the quills to sign their own death warrants.) In Hinxton, Cambridgeshire, the poor fattened turkeys in the stubbles of the barley, pease and oat fields. Turkeys, feathers, down and piglets were all part of the domestic economy of landless commoners.[46]

That landless commoners could graze cows as often as they could graze pigs or geese or even sheep is less certain. Much depended on where they lived. In villages with plentiful common pasture, cow commons were plentiful too. Labouring families in Cliffe Bailiwick, Rockingham Forest, kept cows, sheep and hogs in the early eighteenth century, and regularly harvested the trees for mast.[47] In Peterborough in the fens in 1701, those who lived in the manor and paid scot and lot were entitled to graze sheep and cows.[48] In 1790, cottages in nearby Peverill's manor still carried unstinted common right. The manor stretched over three parishes – Walton, Werrington and Paston – and two more villages – Dogsthorp and Gunthorp; a 'good 8000 acre common' in the shape of Borough Fen was open to each of them. Bylaws did not define cottages and messuages as being ancient or in any way unlike any other residence in the villages.[49] The Maxey jury in 1738 stinted great cattle at two cows or horses per farmer, and one per cottager. Field orders made no distinction between those cottagers with ancient right to common (if such existed) and those who occupied more recently built cottages.

[46] Adam Smith, *An Inquiry into the Nature and Causes of the Wealth of Nations* (1776; New York, 1937 edn), pp. 227–8; K. J. Bonser, *The Drovers* (1970), p. 73; *Northampton Mercury*, 30 Mar. 1767, on the rising price of feathers (by about 40 per cent) in Lincolnshire as a result of enclosing the commons; and [Rev. James Tyley], 'Inclosure of Open Fields in Northamptonshire. Translation by Miss Dorothy Halton, of a Latin Poem by the Rev. James Tyley, Rector of Great Addington, 1799–1830', ed. Joan Wake, *The Reminder* 3: 94 (Feb. 1928), p. 5, on commoners mourning the loss of their geese in marshlands. See also Cambs. RO, R57.24.1.26 (1792).

[47] Pettit, *Royal Forests of Northamptonshire*, pp. 157–8; and (generally) Paul, *Observations on the General Enclosure Bill*, p. 162.

[48] Juries introduced the residence qualification to deter outsiders from buying cottages for their pasture: Northants. RO, Church Commissioners' Records 278573, 28 October 1701; *Northampton Mercury*, 5 Sept. 1763; Northants. RO, Fitzwilliam Misc., vol. 747, p. 54, 19 Feb. 1767. Any occupier holding property worth 20s rent a year could hire additional dead commons – most cottages would have had a rental value of at least that sum: Pitt, *General View ... Northampton*, pp. 29–31.

[49] 'All the Messuages and Cottages have Right of Common without Stint on the Peterborough and Burrow Fens', *Northampton Mercury*, 22 May 1790.

In the light of the evidence of generous common pasture in the fens, it seems reasonable to suppose that in Maxey too every resident could have common for a cow or a horse. Even some less well-pastured villages provided for the landless. In 1711 a stinting agreement in Orlingbury confirmed the use of the common by the 'poor cottagers as they have usually held and Enjoyed the same they paying the usual price or rate for such Common'.[50] The lord of the manor of Deene – an old-enclosed manor – determined which poor commoners could use a special cottage pasture set aside for the five cows of five poor families. In April 1725 his steward advised him that, 'Widow Sutton I think deserves one more than Richard Wilkins, for though he has 3 children he is better able to work for them than this woman, who besides her own 2 small children maintains her husbands mother, who otherwise must be an immediate charge to the parish.'[51]

In other pasture-poor villages, landless commoners found grazing when their economies meshed with those of richer men. For example, when farmers needed manure to feed their arable they fed landless commoners' sheep on their own land. The small flocks of the Essex sheep-men described by Pehr Kalm played a useful part in the economy of better-off farmers; in much the same way, farmers in Flecknoe, Warwickshire, in 1730, after an outbreak of sheep rot, brought in sheep and shepherds from near and far 'meerly for the Manure' to fold their clay.[52] The interlocking of different common-ing economies also encouraged the breeding of young cattle. In

50 Northants. RO, YO 578, Orlingbury Stinting agreement, 1711. Two Harpole 'Townsmen' might 'sett and lett & dispose of six cows commons in the heath ... to any of the poor inhabitants of Harpole as they ... shall see necessity or occasion for so doing': Nobottle Grove Hundred Roll, 12 Oct. 1743, Northants, RO, YZ 6a.

51 Wake and Webster, *Letters of Daniel Eaton*, Letter no. 10, 20 Apr. 1725, pp. 12–13.

52 Warwicks. RO, Z 12/2a: 'A State of y Case relating to an ynclosure of Flecknoe fields Com: Warwick 1730.' That the sheep of the smallest commoners were welcomed is also demonstrated in Eaton Bray, Bedfordshire, where cottage commoners could fold three sheep for every cow common they possessed, but while the sheep went into the open fields the cows were confined to the common wastes, greens and meads: Beds. RO, P 63/28/1; similarly at both Atherstone and Walsgrave on Sowe in Warwickshire, letting cow and horse commons was forbidden but letting sheep commons was not; at Walsgrave on Sowe the sheep of outsiders could be agisted, but not their cattle: Warwicks. RO, CR 556/299 (Sowe, 1722); HR 35/25 (Atherstone, 1739). Dorothy Hartley remarks that 'sheep seem to have been hurried onto any land that needed fertilising', and they trod the manure in, *Lost Country Life*, p. 67.

Raunds, small occupiers supplied the farmers with lean stock they
had raised on a combination of common pasture and fodder grown
on common-field land laid to grass, land which already had given
them more pasture rights than sown land.[53] In places with this kind
of symbiosis between the economies of small and big commoners, or
places with good common waste, the supply of pasture was sufficient for sheep and enough even for a cow.

Outside the forest, fen and heath, and in villages where no
commons were available for the poor, or where their economies did
not support those of bigger commoners, the likelihood of a landless
family having common right for a cow was not strong – though not
unknown. Right was more often attached to the occupancy of land
than to the status of inhabitant. But in these places a cow common
was less useful anyway. Where would a landless commoner find the
extra fodder to over-winter a cow? Bits of meadow, encroachments
on the forest or chase, good-sized yards and plentiful furze were not
to hand. Here most (though not all) landless commoners were
absolutely landless, not merely land poor. Some parishes granted
rights to occupiers of houses, rather than occupiers of common-
right cottages alone, but the same restriction operated in practice:
without sufficient land of their own commoners could not use their
rights. Instead, the grazing they claimed (and the litter and fodder
they collected) were for pigs and poultry.[54]

In most of these parishes the minimum acreage needed for a
common right was low enough to include most people who could
support a beast for the rest of the year anyway. We have seen that in
Stoke Bruerne and Shutlanger only two acres of ley or one of clover
entitled its occupier to a cow common.[55] In nearby Ashton, Roade
and Hartwell *every* occupier of no matter how little open-field land
could pasture a horse or a cow.[56] In Raunds, common right for a
cow came with the occupancy of land to the value of ten acres of
ploughed land. But three of arable and three of ley were reckoned to
be worth ten of arable land and so carried the right to pasture a cow.
Any shortfall could be made up by paying 6d per acre up to the
necessary ten acres.[57]

[53] *Jls House of Commons*, 19 June 1797.
[54] For a longer discussion see Chapter 6.
[55] Northants. RO, G3624b, 26 Apr. 1764.
[56] Northants. RO, G3626b, 3 May 1764.
[57] Northants. RO, Raunds Overseers' Accounts, 1789.

There were parishes where free, or nearly free, grazing could not be got for love or money, and parishes where common-field economies were not interdependent, but the poor cottager and her cow was not an invention of anti-enclosure propagandists or sentimental, pastoralizing painters. In the fens commoners did not need land to get grazing, and in many parishes with good wastes or good forest pasture cows could be kept without it. In still other villages landless commoners grazed cattle on particular pastures set aside for them. Where rights to pasture were attached inseparably to the occupancy of common-field land or common-right cottages the necessary holdings could be very small indeed, and in some parishes commoners could rent dead commons or agist their sheep with a local farmer. Evidently places where the landless could get pasture for a cow were not a few: they may have been the rule rather than the exception.

These Northamptonshire parishes suggest that anyone occupying commonable land in the common fields of a parish, and in some parishes those occupying none, had common right. And, landed or not, cottagers and those who rented dead commons had common right too. If they could keep a cow at all in these villages they could also put it on the common pastures each year. Clapham was wrong to think that the right to keep a cow was rare, and Young was right to think that it was common. It seems clear that in many villages, though not all, the landholding population was a majority and the commoning population substantial.

Northamptonshire was not a county noted for its extensive wastes: it was a Midland county of mixed agriculture, well connected to the London market. But even here, in the middle of the eighteenth century a substantial commoning class survived on the income from less than ten acres of open-field land, whatever other employment was to hand, and grazing rights. Some cow commoners survived with no land at all.

But they *were* more numerous in some villages than others. What circumstances signalled commoners' survival? Why did they thrive and prosper in some places but not in others?

SURVIVAL: PATTERNS

Land type

Clearly, plentiful useful grazing was to some extent dependent on land type. In forests, fens, heaths, marshes and coastal plains, places where pasture was abundant, commoners were abundant too. In the Northamptonshire fens, housedwellers often had the right to pasture a cow in the eighteenth century; in forest parishes occupiers of no matter how small a landholding often could do the same. Moving out of Northamptonshire into the rest of lowland England, pasture rights in wastes near the New Forest were parish-wide and commoners could supplement them with forest grazing for a fee. In the Warwickshire Arden parish of Astley every inhabitant could keep a horse or ten sheep. Needwood Forest in 1800 supported cows belonging to numerous poor families.[58] Inhabitants of the Lancashire parish of Longton fed sheep, scotch cattle and geese on 750 acres of marsh along the Ribble estuary.[59] At Willingham in the Cambridgeshire fens 109 houses had common right. Every house with half a yardland could common nine great cattle and ten sheep, and, in the West Fen, three cows or two mares or geldings and a cow.[60] Occupiers of 378 common-right cottages in the three townships of the fenland manor of Whittlesey, near Peterborough, had access to more than 7,000 acres of commonable waste in the late seventeenth century.[61]

But it is important to note that widespread entitlement was not

[58] Warwicks. RO, CR 764/1 (1724); *Staffordshire Advertiser*, 11 Oct. 1800: report of a general meeting chaired by Lord Vernon on the subject of enclosing Needwood: 'it would be of material disadvantage in depriving them of keeping cows, by which their families are in great measure supported and kept from the Parishes'.

[59] *Jls House of Commons*, 20 Feb. 1760: 'the same (Pasture grounds) have been immemorially used and enjoyed as Common of Pasture, as well by the Charterers and Land-owners as also by the Cottagers and Inhabitants living within the said Township, for all their Cattle and Geese, without Number, as they were able to keep (but consisting chiefly of sheep and Scotch cattle), without any Molestation from the Lords of the Manor or any of the Landholders within the said Township, to the very great relief and Maintenance of several Families residing within the said Township'. The bill received the royal assent three months later on 15 April.

[60] Cambs. RO, R 59.14.5.9 (1) (1764); R 59.14.5.9 (n) (1790).

[61] Cambs. RO, 126/M91 [temp. 14 Charles II]. Inhabitants' grazing rights were claimed for the 855 houses and 441 toftsteads in Holland Fen in 1765: Guildhall Library, 1765 fol., 'Lincoln Acts etc. Draining, Inclosure, Roads etc.', Claims to common right in Holland Fen, 'The Number of Houses and Toftsteads in each Town in the forgoing List.'

reserved to fens and forests. In hill and vale parishes with substantial wastes, entitlement to common could be equally generous and even landless commoners might keep a cow.[62] At Chipping Norton in Oxfordshire before its enclosure in 1769 every householding parishioner had the right to graze two horses or cows on the 500 acre common; every parishioner had furze.[63] 'Anyone who could get a cow' could put it on Burton Latimer's eight-hundred-acre common on the outskirts of Kettering, in Northamptonshire. Equally landless inhabitants put their cows on the commons at Campton cum Shefford in Bedfordshire. In Abington Piggotts, Cambridgeshire, before enclosure 'every poor man' had a cow common 'by right or permission'.[64] And the same deliberate naming of the poor as beneficiaries occurred at Sutton Coldfield and Sowe in Warwickshire. At Sutton every resident had right of common – some were said to keep twenty sheep each; at Sowe in 1722 the field officers noted, 'wee do allow any poor Inhabitant of our own parish for the Payment of 5s to the Constables Levy shall have Liberty to put one Cow On the Common'.[65] On Somersham Heath in Huntingdonshire in 1773 every poor man without meadow or arable could put 'but one cow apiece' on the droveways and common balks of the commonable fields, or on the common, for a payment of fourpence for each pounding.[66]

---

62 Although large wastes and numerous commoners did not always coincide: in intensively arable eighteenth-century Norfolk villages, large sheep walks were monopolized by single landowners: Postgate, 'Field Systems of East Anglia', pp. 314, 319; but they had not always been so: see Allison, 'Sheep Corn Husbandry of Norfolk'.

63 The 1769 enclosure Act reduced the common from 500 acres to 218. Inhabitants' common right did not end but in 1806 a new order limited commons to one per house, no matter how many tenements it contained, and eligible houses were those in existence in 1769, not later: see A. Ballard, 'The Management of Open Fields', *Report*, Oxfordshire Archaeological Society (1913), p. 133; M. K. Pearson, *Chipping Norton in Bygone Days* (Chipping Norton, 1909), pp. 47–9.

64 Beds. RO, X89/1, Court Book of Campton cum Shefford; Thomas Batchelor wrote that many cottagers kept cows and that bullocks were almost fattened on what seemed to be very little grass, *General View ... Bedford*, pp. 224–5. A. Young, 'Minutes concerning Parliamentary Inclosures in the County of Cambridge', *Annals of Agriculture*, 42 (1804), p. 494.

65 Every four or five years, five or six hundred acres of the waste were enclosed and an acre allotted to each commoner to let or to cultivate; a year later the fences were thrown down and the land became common again, offering better feed. The acre was worth about a guinea if let: Young, 'Mischiefs of Commons', pp. [437–9] misprinted 347–9. Warwicks. RO, CR 556/299 (7), Stinting Agreement, 16 and 30 Apr. 1722.

66 Hunts. RO, HMR 16 (12), Court Books of Somersham Manor, p. 204, 15 Oct. 1773, Duke of Manchester's Court Leet.

And broad access in hill and vale was not always dependent on large wastes either. Even where pasture was relatively scarce, small occupiers enjoyed grazing rights and (for a fee) so did the virtually landless. In Bassingbourne, Cambridgeshire, in 1708, common for a horse came with a payment to the poor rate of 10d a year.[67] More often, the smallest landholders could hire an unused common with a cash payment. When they set a new stint at Wigston Magna, Leicestershire, in 1707, the eveners (fieldsmen) kept the same 'Liberty to provide pastures [commons] for them that have none as Formerly.' No 'poor men that want' should pay more than four shillings for a single pasture. Every yardlander must 'spare and Lett one single pasture every yeare if need be to bee for poor men that shall have occasion for them and have none of their own'. Those with one and a half yardlands must let two of their commons.[68] At Bassingbourne a dead common cost much less: one shilling in 1750, two shillings in 1800.[69]

Other parishes practised a reverse discrimination in the use of commons. Those with the *least* land got the common waste; it was reserved for the near-landless commoners, the poor or the relatively poor, alone. In Soham, Cambridgeshire, no one who owned or occupied land worth £4 per annum (about eight acres) or more could use the reputedly fertile 200-acre common.[70] In Kirtling, in the same county, horse and cow commons were kept for those occupying land worth less than £3 a year.[71] In Laxton, Nottinghamshire, rights on the commons belonged to toftholders – cottagers who might have a close but no common-field land.[72]

Landholding

The more diffuse the landholding in villages like this, the greater the number of commoners. Equally, where occupancy was concentrated in a few hands, commoners might also be few: the town meadow and

[67] Cambs. RO, P 11/8/1, Bassingbourne Town Book, 1 Oct. 1708. See also 14 Apr. 1800 for the stint of two cows per messuage or tenement, on pain of 6s 8d per cow if exceeded.
[68] Hoskins, *Midland Peasant*, p. 239.
[69] Cambs. RO, P 11/8/1, Bassingbourne Town Book, 16 Apr. 1750 and 14 Apr. 1800.
[70] Vancouver, *General View ... Cambridge*, pp. 136–7: each commoner had a right for three cows or two horses.
[71] Cambs. RO, P 101/28/11, 6 June 1798.
[72] J. V. Beckett, *A History of Laxton: England's Last Open-Field Village* (Oxford, 1989), p. 35.

common fields of eighteenth-century Barford were open to the many cattle of only eight commoners – all identified with the title Mr.[73] But, if common right was not confined to fen and forest, nor was it confined to villages of diffuse landholding. Consolidated ownership or occupancy do not automatically signal the exclusion of small commoners or the end of common right. In some villages where *ownership* was well concentrated, *occupancy* was not, and a numerous small tenantry carefully guarded its common right. Elsewhere even parishes farmed by only a few tenants could harbour a large number of commoners for whom common right was an important and well-defended part of village life: in early nineteenth-century Sandy, 90 per cent of the land belonged to two landowners, but 63 freeholders held the rest and worked their lands as gardens, relying on the common for turf, litter, and pasture for their cows, which manured the gardens.[74] In the nucleated, manorial villages of the Warwickshire Feldon families depended on customary right, though quite without land.[75]

Chippenham in Cambridgeshire is another example. Gradually appropriated from the sixteenth century, by 1712 most of the land was owned by a handful of freeholders and a lord; few farms were smaller than one hundred acres. Its historian describes it as quintessentially a parish where the peasantry had disappeared, 'classically appropriated' long before enclosure.[76] But this apparently peasantless village had still in the late eighteenth century forty-five cottages with common right over the fields, and fuel rights in a three-hundred-acre fen – though in the two decades before the enclosure they had lost some access to the heath because the farmers had begun to plough it. In such a consolidated parish, ownership of the cottages was also consolidated: in 1796 the Lord of the Manor,

---

[73] Warwicks. RO, CR 410/Box 1, Memoranda re common rights 1719–76.
[74] Batchelor, *General View ... Bedford* (1813), p. 240. Earlier in 1767 an editorial in the *Northampton Mercury* vindicated the good reputation of a maligned 'Nobleman ... who is supposed to possess the largest Landed Estate in the Kingdom' by saying that 'he has only one single Farm lett at 200£ p.a., all the rest at inferior Rents; and he is particularly careful that none of the poor Cottagers on his Estates shall be oppressed or turned out': *Northampton Mercury*, 30 Mar. 1767.
[75] J. M. Martin, 'Warwickshire and the Parliamentary Enclosure Movement' (unpublished Ph.D. thesis, University of Birmingham, 1965), pp. 134–5.
[76] Margaret Spufford, *Contrasting Communities: English Villagers in the Sixteenth and Seventeenth Centuries* (Cambridge, 1974), pp. 90–1, and her *A Cambridgeshire Community. Chippenham from Settlement to Enclosure*, University of Leicester, Department of English Local History, Occasional Paper no. 20 (Leicester, 1965), pp. 48, 52–4.

John Tharp, owned thirty-two of the forty-five.[77] But the rights had neither fallen into disuse nor were they engrossed by the farmers. Cottage tenants used them until enclosure. More than that, there were other commoners too. Field orders show that before the enclosure the fen had provided every inhabitant with sedge-straw for local use; the open fields offered pasture for cottagers and landholders, and gleaning for the poor.[78]

The fields were enclosed by Act in 1791, and Tharp gave the cottagers about thirteen acres for their right of shack. Within a year the 'principal Inhabitants' of the parish had formed a prosecuting association bound to prosecute any theft of wood, hedges, fences, corn, haulm, turnips or poultry – and to use the poor rate to pay for it.[79] The fen remained open until 1796 when Tharp enclosed it after buying out the owners of the other thirteen cottages. He compensated the former cottage tenants, and the parish poor, with a thirty-six-acre allotment for fuel.

Tharp thought the compensation generous, and it may have been better than most enclosers' compensation to commoners, but the villagers saw it differently.[80] At Lammas, on the evening of 3 August 1830, more than three decades after the enclosure, some entered the enclosed former fen, now a 750-acre farm, and began to dig. When the tenant confronted them, they were alleged to have threatened to chop off his feet with their spades. They went on to claim rights to fuel and litter not only for the occupants of ancient cottages but for *all* the cottage-dwelling poor of the parish.[81] Their claim may well have been good. Tharp denied that anyone other than ancient cottagers had common right, but the field orders corroborate the paupers, the local magistracy refused to prosecute them for trespass, and their case was strong enough to convince an attorney to proceed to King's Bench when Tharp laid an information there for trespass, and to find bail when Tharp prosecuted one of them for theft, in an attempt to frighten the others.[82]

[77] Spufford, *Cambridgeshire Community*, p. 53; Cambs. RO, R55.7.117.16.
[78] Cambs. RO, R55.7.4 (a), 20 June 1757, court leet.
[79] Haulm is defined as thatching straw in the *Oxford English Dictionary*; it may also be the clumps of pease plants left after harvest and used for fodder and litter. Cambs. RO, R55.7.31.1, 18 Oct. 1792.
[80] Spufford, *Cambridgeshire Community*, pp. 53–4.
[81] Cambs. RO, R55.7.117.25, 7 May 1831, King's Bench affidavit of Edward Amos Chaplin, attorney for John Tharp Esquire. Note that all the evidence is from Tharp's side: he may have misrepresented the case of the defendants.
[82] Cambs RO, R55.7.4(a), 20 June 1757; R55.7.117.16, 18–26, 1830–1.

If the paupers were right, this seemingly peasantless village had still in the late eighteenth century a valued commoning economy; one enjoyed not only by the tenants of cottages and the landed, but by those who were neither. But because landholding in Chippenham was so thoroughly consolidated, even though Chippenham is a part fenland parish in which peasants had often survived without land, they and their *use* of the land slip from view. The example of Chippenham suggests that categories of commoning village are difficult to define exactly because even a consolidated parish might retain a significant commoning sector. This example could be multiplied by others in south Cambridgeshire, Bedfordshire and elsewhere.[83]

Clearly too systematic a setting out of the factors (land type, landholding) likely to signal the incidence of common right, though necessary, is also misleading. Forest and fen do not mark the extent of common right. Though they often offered more to commoners than hill and vale parishes they had not become oases of right in a desert of private ownership in the eighteenth century. Nor is the pattern of landownership or occupancy a complete guide to the survival of commoners: villages of petty landholding were strongholds of common right but even consolidated villages had commoners.

Evidence and silence

Boundaries are difficult to draw around commoning for other reasons too. Most evidence of local practice is given by manorial lords and large landowners or their tenants. It comes from enclosure claims and Awards, or from court rolls. Some of the shortcomings of enclosure evidence are already clear: claims made at enclosure for the loss of cottage commons underestimate the numbers of cottagers with right. In addition, enclosure commissioners did not recognize claims based on residence. At the enclosure of Hinxton in 1792,

---

[83] South Cambridgeshire villages consolidated in ownership but well populated by cow-keeping commoners include Abington Piggotts, Long Stow, Guilden Morden, Stretham, Weston Colville, March, Harston, Wimblington: Young, 'Minutes Concerning Parliamentary Inclosures in the County of Cambridge', pp. 318–26, 471–502. In Bedfordshire, Little Staughton had 35 common-right cottages and consolidated landownership; Billington and Stanbridge field-keeping agreements were signed by relatively few, but smaller occupiers were protected: Beds. RO, PM 1684; BO 1326; BO 1337–9.

Serjeant Le Blanc advised the inhabitants not to claim right of common for their sheep in the common fields *as inhabitants*. They must claim as the owners of their houses and lands. Consequently their claims appear to attach rights to property not to residence: the practice of the village was misrepresented in order to conform to enclosers' law not custom.[84]

Moreover, awards made at enclosure reflect only the latest stocking level in the village, not any earlier level, no matter how recent, or any likely future level. Numbers of cottage commoners fluctuated with the economies of commoners: they rose and fell with changes in the economic circumstances of commoners and even with changes in the age structure of villages. But enclosure commissioners relied on proof of present use.[85] They recognized only the current practice, not the past or the likely future practice. Thus in Kettering the late eighteenth-century decline in the weaving trade probably led to the disuse of cottage commons because cottagers could not afford to stock them, but at enclosure in 1804 unstocked cottage rights were not recognized, and so went uncompensated.[86] Rates of stocking commons varied within a lifetime too. It is possible that the more elderly or widowed cottagers did not stock their commons; when enclosure came, unless someone testified to their stocking at some time in the past, their rights went uncompensated too.

Manorial records give an equally incomplete picture. They were often kept by Stewards, who represented the Lords of the Manors, and so may have failed to record all the commoning done in the parish. Rolls, in particular, rarely recorded customs or included field orders.[87] While rights attached to land were relatively safe simply because every landholder, great or small, enjoyed the same stint, rights and customs enjoyed by inhabitants were more vulnerable. Some justification for this might have been found in the common law which, from early in the seventeenth century, no

---

[84] Cambs. RO, R57.24.1.26.
[85] For example: Northants. RO, X3475, evidence given on Timothy Hawks' claim to a cottage common right in Chelveston: one neighbour could not say if he stocked for cottage or land, another thought it was for the cottage.
[86] The commissioners rejected sixty claims of cottage rights made by thirty-six people: R. A. Martin, 'Kettering Inclosure 1804–5', *Northamptonshire Past and Present*, 5 (1977), pp. 416–17.
[87] J. Thirsk, 'Field Systems of the East Midlands', in A. R. H. Baker and R. A. Butlin, *Studies of Field Systems in the British Isles*, (Cambridge, 1973), p. 232, notes this too.

longer recognized residence as grounds for a claim of right.[88] Whether or not this was the case, the steward served the Lord's interest best when he did *not* write them down. If nothing else, they were expensive to compensate, which was why Edward Laurence advised stewards to eliminate common right as a preliminary to enclosure.[89] In the same way stewards did not always inscribe rights attached to cottages in the record of the court. In Atherstone, Warwickshire, in the 1760s, significant cottagers' rights were well attested to by cottagers and enclosers alike, but they were nowhere to be found in the rolls of the manor.[90] At Chatteris in Cambridgeshire, in 1798, rights attached to 163 houses were 'swept away by a clause in the Act requiring them to prove their rights, which they could not'. And the users and uses of Foulmere common in the 1840s were many but the claims commoners made at enclosure were much narrower.[91] The distribution of right known to the fieldsmen and that acknowledged in the records of the manorial court did not have to coincide. Courts were not always impartial. Certainly some of their suitors thought they were not:

> most of the persons composing Your Lordships manorial courts are in various great degrees Your dependents and are consequently influenced to act inconsistently with the feelings, the duties and the interests of themselves and others.[92]

The mismatch of *right*, defined in the manorial court, and *practice*, enjoyed by cottagers and cow keepers, can be explained by the ultimately divergent interests of lord and commoner. It was a conflict marked by the silence of the official record, and consequently one very difficult to identify unless other evidence survives. If the measurement of crime has its dark figure of criminal acts not reported, common right has its dark figure too – of *practice*

---

[88] 6 Coke 59b (77 English Reports 344) [Gateward's case].

[89] Edward Laurence, *Duty of a Steward to his Lord* (1727; 2nd edn 1731), p. 37.

[90] In 1739 the Lord of the Manor, 'in pretending to pursue a case some time since', had taken 'all town books and writings' but refused to show them to the townspeople; he also had custody of the rolls. The commoners asked how they might get them back and were told they should get a Speaker's Warrant: Warwicks. RO, HR35/25, The Case of Atherstone conc. Inclosure of the Com. Fields. – as drawn pr Wm Baxter and Others in Jan. 1738/9.

[91] Young, 'Minutes Concerning Parliamentary Inclosures in the County of Cambridge', pp. 473–81, for evidence of rights at Chatteris before the enclosure; W. Gooch, *General View of the Agriculture of the County of Cambridge* (1811), p. 76; Cambs. RO, 292/015, 292/028.

[92] Staffs. RO, D603/K/16/104, C. Landor to the Marquis of Anglesey, 26 Apr. 1824.

not recorded. This should encourage us to draw the social boundaries of entitlement widely. And it should encourage us not to define
practice as mere usage or 'custom', not a right, too readily.

I said at the beginning of this chapter that when they talk about
common right historians have argued about at least three things.
First, were commoners many or few? (And, as part of this, were
rights attached to residence as well as land?) Second, did small
commoners graze cows and horses, or only lesser stock? Third, was
their use of commons legal or illegal, a right or merely a custom – by
which they meant a tolerated practice, a usage?

The findings made here may be summarized. First, commoners
were many in fen, forest, and heath parishes, and they were many in
hill and vale parishes where wastes were large and the occupancy of
land remained diffuse. But not *only* there: villages with little waste
or where landholding was consolidated might also have commoners.
And in all these places the evidence of survival probably underestimates numbers. Some of this ubiquity came from the attachment of
rights to the status of inhabitant as well as to land, and often the
attachment held until enclosure. Second, smaller commoners grazed
cows and horses as well as lesser stock. Third, landed commoners
and cottagers pastured their stock as of common right, a right
recognized at law. And inhabitants pastured their sheep (and sometimes their cows) by custom – but by custom I mean more than
usage, because, at the local level, custom had the force of law.

The pattern of survival of commoners – their ubiquity in some
places, their scarcity elsewhere – depended on many things including land type, land tenure, prices, markets, wages and rents, but it
also depended on their ability to protect their commons, or on the
inability of landlords to extinguish them without a parliamentary
enclosure. In the next chapter I want to look at this.

3. Threats before enclosure

> Where all things in common doth rest,
>   corne field with the pasture and meade,
> Though common ye doo for the best,
>   yet what doth it stand ye in steade?
> There common as commoners use,
>   for otherwise shalt thou not chuse.
>
> Thomas Tusser, *Five Hundred Points of Good
> Husbandry*[1]

Thomas Tusser was not the only farmer critical of commons, and as time went on criticism like his became more and more acceptable. After mid century it became even easier to justify the exclusion of small commoners in the name of improvement; and pasture shortage or worries about labour supply and compensation at enclosure might move the better-off yeomen, tenants and landlords to curtail or extinguish common right long before enclosure. How successful were they? To answer this I want to look at some of the means at their disposal. I shall argue that – compared to an enclosure Act – they were limited, and that the determination of commoners to resist them was an important factor in their survival. For the efforts of lesser commoners to preserve common right were as tenacious as any attempt by great commoners or lords of manors to extinguish it.

---

[1] Thomas Tusser, *Five Hundred Points of Good Husbandry* (1st edn, 1573; this edn, 1580; repr. Oxford, 1984, with an introduction by Geoffrey Grigson), ch. 52: 'A Comparison betweene Champion Countrie and Severall'.

RESTRICTING ACCESS TO PASTURE

Engrossing common rights

At all times the incentive for landlords to let their land and rights separately, or to let the land and stock the rights themselves, might be strong. Stripping common right from small parcels of land would free the common pasture from the cows and sheep of small commoners. But the law insisted on the integrity of lands and rights. And other commoners resisted any breach.

Perhaps the most important defence was that common appendant itself remained attached to land. Whenever such land was divided or sold, its commons were to be divided exactly and apportioned to each piece of land.[2] As a result, a market in common rights separated from land could not develop. This meant that landlords and large farmers could not engross common rights, and small peasant farming could not starve for lack of pasture. Consequently, the exclusion of small peasants from common grazing without their agreement was difficult without a thoroughgoing enclosure. And, although landlords might have persuaded large owner-occupiers and tenants of the advantage of depriving smaller commoners of pasture rights by engrossment, they could not so easily persuade them of the value of enclosure, which was expensive and would raise rents.

The reason why common appendant remained appendant was that its reputed origin – the need of a lord's tenants for pasture in order to cultivate the land given to them in return for labour service and rent – was so clearly defined in common law. Blackstone noted the origin of the right in necessity, saying 'the law therefore annexed this right of common, as *inseparably incident to the grant of the lands*'.[3] To remove the right from land would make a nonsense of the origin of the grant, and so end the right for everyone. Moreover,

[2] *Halsbury's Laws of England*, 2nd edn, IV, section 1159, p. 621, and section 988, p. 534: 'every little parcel is entitled to a common appendant and the right is apportionable'.

[3] William Blackstone, *Commentaries on the Laws of England*, 12th edn (1794), Book the Second of *The Rights of Things*, ch. 3 of Incorporeal Hereditaments, section III, COMMON, pp. 32–3. My italics. The author of *The Law of Commons and Commoners* (2nd edn, 1720) describes the same origin of the right and agrees that it 'cannot be severed from the soil by grant without being extinguished', p. 21. Mr Brittain of Cold Harbour, near Biggleswade, received similar advice from Edward Rudd in 1806, Beds. RO, X267/8.

in the eighteenth century the law already provided a way of extin-
guishing common right in the shape of parliamentary enclosure.
Judges were unlikely to feel the need to add another remedy.
If they could not separate land and rights, they could separate
cottages and rights. Potentially at least, this threatened the survival
of cottage commoners. In principle it meant that cottage rights
could be bought up by a small number of men. In law, complete
severance from a cottage of a right of common appurtenant to a
cottage was possible if the right itself was for a specific number of
beasts and not for beasts levant and couchant. Once separated it
became *common in gross* and could continue so unless the owner of
the common land on which it was used sold any part of the land in
such a way as to discommon it. What evidence is there that this
practice was common?

Certainly it was not unknown. For instance, when he made his
will in September 1748, Robert Nutt of Burton Latimer, a farmer,
bequeathed the common rights belonging to one house to his children who lived in another. The house he gave to his son Robert he
separated from its common rights, which went instead to 'those to
whom I leave the House wherein I now dwell'. His daughters
inherited this house, and also the rights attached to the other. There
is no indication that Nutt or his family expected the rights to revert
to their original cottage. Again, in 1760, Thomas Streets, a Teeton
weaver, left his house to one son and two cow commons to another.[4]

So moving rights from a cottage to an individual could come
about in this way. But it is difficult to establish how often. It occurs
in wills only infrequently, and when it does the numbers of
commons are small, not large enough to suggest a process of
engrossment.[5] If anything, the evidence suggests that rights were
moved in order to endow children living in cottages that carried no
right, or to enable children leaving home for cottages without right
to take part of the right with them. More certain than the frequency
with which cottage commons were moved about is that when whole
rights or fractions of rights were claimed at enclosure they were

---

[4] Northants. RO, Northants. Wills and Admons., Pr. 26 Mar. 1760; Pr. 11 Nov.
1760.
[5] In a search of eighty-one weavers' wills probated at Northampton between 1750
and 1780, only Streets' will separated house from rights, and even his may have
been understood to transfer the rights from one house to another. Few commoners
left wills; their transactions are better recorded in court rolls, but I have found none
creating common in gross.

always described in relation to real property. In 1797 John Wimpress claimed for 'One third part of a Cottage belonging to a Messuage or Tenement in Middle Raunds'.[6] No claims were made without this kind of identification. It seems that if rights were severed from some cottages they were grafted on to others, not left as common in gross. One might suppose that the attachment of rights to a piece of real property was the best proof of their existence.

A more serious threat to the survival of cottage commoners was the buying-up of *cottages* by farmers and Lords of Manors long before enclosure, followed by the separation of the *use* of rights from the occupancy of the cottage to which they had belonged. Did farmers or their landlords engross cottage rights by engrossing cottages themselves? Certainly cottages were bought and sold, and cottage ownership may well have become concentrated in fewer hands, but it seems that the number of cottage commoners may not have diminished as a result. Attempts to separate the occupancy of a cottage from the use of its rights were resisted in manorial courts and vestries. Bylaws made in the courts of Stoke Bruerne and Shutlanger, Peterborough and Raunds – forest, fen and Nene valley parishes – specified that only the occupiers of cottages could stock for them, not the non-occupying owners.[7] An order made in the Peterborough court in 1701 shows how cottage common rights might be enjoyed only by residents:

> Itm Wee Order that If any person shall come and buy a house in Peterborough and putt Stock into the Common and Doe not inhabitt[,] he and his ffamily[,] and pay Scott and Lott for that [,] he shall for every head of Cattle soe putt into the ffennes pay 10s half to the Lords of the Manor and half to the Poore of this parish for every such Offence.[8]

---

6 Northants. RO, Box 88.1140, Raunds claims, 1797, p. 19. Even when cottage rights were bought as a speculative venture on the eve of an enclosure they were identified by the cottage to which they had belonged: Daniel Abbott in Raunds claimed a right 'belonging to a House by me some Time since sold ... which was formerly the estate of Ezekiel Fowler'.

7 Northants. RO, Raunds: QCR 47, 23 Oct., 11 Dec. 1718; Peterborough: Church Commissioners' Records 272853, 28 Oct. 1701; Stoke Bruerne and Shutlanger: G3347a, 2 Apr. 1731.

8 Northants. RO, Church Commissioners' Records, 278573, 28 Oct. 1701, repeated in 1702. The fine in Stoke Bruerne and Shutlanger was 5s in 1731: all rights were to 'be kept and let only by the persons that occupy the Land in Stoke and Shutlanger fields', G 3347a, 22 Apr. 1731. Similarly in Tiptofts manor in Harston, Cam-

Why were cottage rights to be used only by the occupiers of the cottages and not their landlords? First, there is some evidence that common-right cottagers were a valued part of village society, worthy of protection. They paid a good rent for their cottages and they rarely claimed poor relief. For this reason (and others) the enclosure of Welton in 1754 was a contested one. In part, the cottage landlords who opposed it argued that weaving, gleaning, furze-gathering and agricultural labour together made a viable livelihood for their tenants. This they would lose at enclosure if the expected conversion of arable to pasture went ahead. Instead of paying rent for their cottages they would be thrown onto the poor rate, a rate paid by their landlords. So here is some acknowledgement by cottage-engrossing farmers themselves of the value of cottage commoners. Here is the sturdy commoner described by eighteenth-century pamphleteers: cottage tenants were respectable, they paid their rents, they brought up their children decently, they stayed off the rates. Even if they did not stock their rights they were said to *aspire* to stock them, and aspiration was the ground in which the evils of indolence and sloth could not grow, nor the poverty so burdensome to others.[9] For most of the eighteenth century twenty dairying families lived like this in March, Cambridgeshire. Each cottage had nine acres of mowing ground, enough to keep cows winter and summer. Ten more did the same in Wimblington.[10]

But cottage commoners like these had another advantage too: they would not graze the commons bare. They were unlikely to overstock their rights, they might not even stock them fully.[11] Farmers who could afford to buy up cottages in order to engross their rights were quite different. They were the owners of large

bridgeshire, only the occupiers of houses, cottages and tenements might keep cows, hogs and horses on the commons: Cambs. RO, 132/M23, 2 Apr. 1771.

[9] *The Case of the Petitioners against the Welton Common Bill*, n.d. (*c*.1754) (Northampton Public Library); Northants. RO, Wel. 26; Neeson, 'Common Right and Enclosure', pp. 306–16. The counter-petitioners said seventy labouring families were at risk; in 1754 seventy families paid tithe at St Martin's. The farmers did not stock for the cottage commons, only for their land: Northants, RO, Wel. 26, Welton tithe book. For aspiration to common right see Warwicks. RO, HR 35/15. The enclosure of Mitcham in Surrey was opposed in 1801 in large part because common right supported 'a large number of poor families': S. and B. Webb, *English Local Government*, I, *The Parish and the County* (1906; repr. 1963), p. 59.

[10] Young, 'Minutes Concerning Parliamentary Inclosures in the County of Cambridge', pp. 323–5.

[11] At Atherstone relatively few cottagers stocked their rights: Warwicks. RO, HR 35/25 (1739).

flocks and herds. They might overstock, certainly they would stock
the full stint. In Raunds and Peterborough it may have made sense
to protect the commons by insisting that the use of cottage rights be
restricted to the occupiers of cottages. At Maulden in Bedfordshire
where the occupiers of ancient cottages *could* let their cottage rights,
they could do so only to the occupiers of new cottages, relatively
poor commoners like themselves.[12] The threat to common pasture
came less from the clearly defined rights of cottagers than from the
larger flocks and herds of richer men.

Cottage commons may have survived cottage engrossment for
another reason too. Landlords who separated common rights from
cottages ran the risk of being unable to prove the rights later on,
whereas cottagers who could stock them (whether in part or in full)
might keep the right alive. This came into play most forcefully in the
middle of the eighteenth century because to compensate the loss of
common right the new enclosure commissioners required evidence
of long usage of a cottage common, and of the intention not to
abandon it. Of course, the best evidence was the existence of the
cottage and a tenant stocking for it.[13] The landlords of the March
dairymen were well compensated at enclosure – they were 'greatly
benefited', says Young, 'to the amount of above 100' – though the
dairying families were ruined.[14] But when Sir William Langham
claimed rights for nine cottages in Raunds in 1797 his claim was
rejected on the grounds that he had 'never stock'd any'. Only those
who stocked for their cottages were compensated.[15] Sacrificing
future compensation for common right was something that a large
landowner or a grantee in the royal forests might contemplate (or
adequately guard against) but not something that a yeoman or a
farmer artisan would risk. The separation of cottage common right
from cottage occupancy was in the interest of substantial landowners concerned to encourage labour discipline, to disencum-
ber land that might be enclosed by agreement, or to reduce the
pressure on forest commons.[16] But, outside the forest, pressure on

[12] Beds. RO, R Box 147 (1699).
[13] *Halsbury's Laws of England*, p. 614.
[14] Young, 'Minutes concerning Inclosures in the County of Cambridge', p. 324.
[15] Northants. RO, Raunds enclosure papers: Minute Book, 24 Jan. 1798, Objections
    to Claims; 27 June 1798, State of Claims.
[16] On labour discipline see above, pp. 28–9; Vancouver noted that Isle of Wight
    farmers housed their labourers in cottages on their farms ('who would otherwise
    have other employments to tempt them away') to 'considerable advantage': it gave

village pastures could be dealt with in other ways, particularly by stinting agreements.[17] Evidence of the sort of exchange that did lead to a decline in the number of cottage commoners appears in villages on the very eve of enclosure. At Sonning in Berkshire the Lord of the Manor was advised by his lawyer 'to remove the one or two Cottagers who claim their old encroachments as freeholds' before the Bill went through.[18] Some rights changed hands more peacefully. In Everdon in 1764, as the enclosure Bill became an Act of Parliament, Samuel Bird sold a 'Cottage Common or Common of Pasture for one Cow ... And Also one Sett of Bracks and bushes' both of which were enjoyed in respect of a certain 'messuage Cott or Tent in Great Everton ... not intended to be hereby granted'. He was paid no less than £25. He seems not to have been a cottager selling his cottage right in anticipation of the enclosure Award because in the same year he bought another cottage common, this time for £21. This looks like a small market in cottage common rights, one that probably concentrated them in fewer hands.[19] But sales so late in the life of common right have little significance for a count of the number of commoners. The buying up of cottage rights at enclosure was little threat to the grazing practice of commoners whose rights were about to be extinguished in any case.

Overstocking

If they did not separate cottage occupancy from the use of common right, did the most powerful farmers try to drive smaller commoners

them 'greater controul over the labourers': Vancouver, *General View ... Hampshire*, p. 73. 'Apuleius' blamed the stewards of large landlords for turning out cottagers, *Northampton Mercury*, 22 Aug. 1726.

[17] See Chapter 4 pp. 116–17.

[18] Berks. RO, D/E Do E 35/2, Sonning enclosure proceedings, Letter to Talbot from Wheble, 12 Oct. 1818.

[19] Northants. RO, D8670; another sale of a cottage common right was made in 1762, the year of Towcester's enclosure, D8648. Similar sales were made at Weedon Beck; purchasers expected compensation in land worth 12s a year for cottage commons for a cow and one lot of brakes and bushes. Lewis Brown bought a cow common from John Billing, 'and about seven such purchases were made by various people from Poor Persons who had no land in the Open Fields': Northants. RO, J. W. Anscomb, 'Abstract of Enclosure Awards', Weedon Beck, p. 86. More cottage rights were bought up at the enclosure of Somersham Heath, Huntingdonshire, in order, it was said, to increase the support for the Bill in the House of Commons: *Northampton Mercury*, 22 Oct. 1785. Forthcoming enclosure

off the commons by overstocking? In Cheshunt, in 1799, persistent overstocking had preceded the enclosure and provided its rationale. At Tottington in Norfolk opponents of enclosure accused the Lord of the Manor of deliberately overstocking in order to reduce the value of common right and thence the compensation due at enclosure.[20] But overstocking hurt everyone, big or small. Accordingly, its tactical value was limited to the years in which an enclosure was mooted, and this is when the evidence occurs.

Moreover, manorial courts, vestries and quarter sessions considered overstocking a major offence and they punished offenders with high fines.[21] They did so despite a decision made in 1769 by Lord Mansfield that commoners could not distrain (impound) certain overstocked animals. The remedy, he said, must lie in an action on the case. There were two exceptions to the rule: strangers putting beasts on the common might still be prosecuted locally, and so might commoners with a right for a fixed number of animals. In each case entitlement – or the lack of it – was easily established. But commoners with rights to beasts *per acre* for their commonable land could not be tried by their fellow commoners because their fellows had an interest in the outcome. In particular, establishing guilt required that someone measure the commonable land at issue. Fellow commoners could not do that because 'when the question depends on a collateral fact, or upon a matter of judgement, the party interested can never be a competent judge in his own cause'.[22]

Was this an overstockers' charter? If it was, its value was more as a precipitant of enclosure than as a way to exclude small commoners and so get exclusive use of a finite resource. For even if the decision became widely known and used by overstockers – and this is uncertain – commoners had ways of maintaining the effectiveness of

---

explains the buying up of cottage rights in the 1790s at Elstow too: Samuel Whitbread bought five for about £30 each and received land in compensation: Beds. RO, W 3438; Joyce Godber, *History of Bedfordshire, 1066–1888* (Luton, 1969), pp. 411–12.

20 E. P. Thompson, 'The Crime of Anonymity', in D. Hay, P. Linebaugh, J. G. Rule, E. P. Thompson and C. Winslow, *Albion's Fatal Tree. Crime and Society in Eighteenth-Century England* (1975), p. 314; *Jls House of Commons*, 7 Feb. 1774.

21 See below pp. 145–7.

22 *Hall v Harding* 4 Bur. 2426–33 (98, *English Reports*, 271). The ancient remedies, a writ of admeasurement of common, or taking the lord to assize, prevented distraint. But it is unclear whether these remedies remained open to villagers, or whether they could proceed only by an action on the case, a more expensive and time-consuming remedy.

local sanctions already in place. For example, most villages put their commonable sheep and cattle into one or two common flocks and herds and swore their herdsmen not to take beasts over the stint, and some juries insisted on prior written notice of how many sheep or cattle a commoner intended to put on for the season. Others specified in the by-laws the number of cows or sheep each farmer could common. Even before Mansfield's verdict, overstocking was less likely to happen when it was easy to prevent. And the prevention of overstocking was always better than the cure of impounding after the damage was done. Prevention may have helped control the damage of *Hall v Harding* too. [23]

Minimum acreage requirements, dead commons, agistment and inhabitants' rights

Weapons other than overstocking were more effective when enclosure was not in sight, and more exact in reaching their targets. The principal threats to the land-poor commoner were an increase in the minimum acreage requirement and a prohibition on agistment or the letting of dead commons. For utterly landless commoners the principal threat was the removal of residence as an entitlement to right, and its substitution with property. Let us look at each.

Small occupiers' rights were safe while small occupiers survived. The same appears to have been true of cottagers. In most places commoners did not change the minimum acreages entitling occupiers to common rights when they introduced stints to reduce rates of stocking. Cottage rights seem inviolate. Where minimum acreages were changed it was never to the complete exclusion of the smallest occupiers. At law it could not be because rights appendant to commonable land were inseparable – the smallest fraction of land entitled its occupier to common. Nevertheless, if commoners reduced minimums they could deprive land-poor commoners of even so much as a year's common pasture for one cow. Many parishes took steps to make the reduction less serious. For example, when Raunds commoners raised the minimum acreage for a cow common from seven to ten acres, the fee paid to make up a shortfall

---

[23] For the organization of common grazing see Chapter 4. See Rockingham Castle Muniments, A 6/11, Rockingham by-laws, 5 Oct. 1725, for a listing of the various numbers of cows and sheep to be kept in the common cow pasture and on the fields by four named farmers.

was small, and land laid down to grass entitled its occupier to common at the old rate.[24] As long as commoners could make up the shortfall all was well. At Billington in Bedfordshire in 1772 a stinting agreement reduced the number of common cows for twenty acres of common field to two. This was the usual rate for this time, or a little better. But, in order not to punish smaller commoners, it required those who now could common four cows (occupiers of eighty acres) to let one common to those who had once grazed two cows but now had land enough for only one (occupiers of ten acres).[25]

Other courts were less accommodating. In Little Bowden, Leicestershire, in 1717, a new stinting agreement halved the number of beasts commonable for a yardland. It allowed those whose lands were so small that this new stint virtually extinguished their commons to buy pasture for up to twelve beasts each for ten shillings apiece. But the purchase of extra pasture could be done only with the consent of four named landowners, all of them leaders in the decision to introduce the new stint.[26] Without their permission small occupiers might graze their cattle for only part of the pasture year – the length of time their acres allowed. Even with the farmers' permission the cost of a cow common for the rest of the year was as much as a labourer's weekly wage. And the use of a whole common right year after year would always depend on the consent of the biggest occupiers. The element of discretion introduced here may have worked against small commoners. The different resolution of the problem in Raunds and Little Bowden may be explained by the difference in their landholding structures: Raunds was a parish of many commoners, Little Bowden was not.

One way into the commoning community was to hire a dead common. A dead common could give a landless commoner cheap grazing – it cost anything from 2s to 8s. It was also a way a small occupier could get extra grazing.[27] How it was done varied. In some

[24] Northants. RO, Raunds Parish Records, Overseer's Accounts, 1789.
[25] Beds. RO, BO 1326.
[26] Northants. RO. TLB 84; compare the lower cost of cow commons in Orlingbury and Old, next note.
[27] A cow common cost 3s 4d in Orlingbury in 1775, more in Old: Northants. RO, BS&L OR/6 Orlingbury Town or Commoners Book; O 102, Old Fieldsmen's Book, Accounts, 1738–49, 1754–60, 1766. In 1728 King's Cliffe commoners who could not stock their own rights were said to let their commons in the forest to strangers: W(A)4, xvii, 4. The author of this series of complaints and questions

places it was a private matter, in others the elected fieldsmen set the fee and collected it. Letting (or setting) dead commons to other inhabitants endured in some places but not in others. In North-amptonshire it did so in the fen and forest parishes, but less often in hill and vale parishes.[28] In Raunds the jury introduced a prohibition in 1733 only to withdraw it later in the year, but it reappeared in 1735. In Old the fieldsmen imposed a levy on all the stocking commoners to pay those who did not stock their commons: the commons were not let. Commoners got 5s for an unused horse common in the 1740s, eight in 1766.[29] In Little Gransden, Cam-bridgeshire, fifteen landed commoners agreed not to stock the cottage common in 1740 if the cottagers could not stock it them-selves. Instead they would pay the cottagers 2s for each dead common.[30] But this is not to say that dead commons disappeared from hill and vale parishes. The thirty-five cottagers in the Bed-fordshire village of Little Staughton each had rights for two cows, a heifer and seven sheep from May to Martinmas. They used their sheep commons themselves, but their cow commons they often let for 2s 6d each. We have seen that at Maulden ancient cottagers could let their commons to the occupiers of new cottages; this compensated those unable to stock their rights, and made provision for new cottagers with no right at all.[31]

Agistment too was a way in which landless or almost landless commoners got grazing. Farmers took in cattle or sheep and fed them if their owners had no land, or not enough land, or no winter fodder. Like renting dead commons, agistment was policed. Orders made a distinction between local and out-parish stock. They

about common right in Cliffe Bailiwick wanted a legal opinion on the agistment of strangers' cattle and hogs.

[28] Fen and forest parishes where letting dead commons survived were Helpston, Maxey, Stoke, Shutlanger, Grafton, Ashton, Roade, Hartwell: see Neeson, 'Common Right and Enclosure', pp. 102–3.

[29] Northants. RO , O 102, Old Fieldsmen's Book.

[30] Cambs. RO, P 78/1/1, 7 May 1740; see also Cambs. RO (Hunts. Office), HMR 16 (12), Court Books of Somersham Manor, 16 Oct. 1772: sheep commons were not to be let or sheep agisted. The Wallingford court made a levy in 1778 for dead commons at the rate of 9s per cow and 6d per sheep. Those who used the commons compensated those who did not. There were ninety-seven commoners in all, owning 110 commons; judging from the sum levied, at least two-thirds of the rights appear to have been used by their occupiers, possibly more: Oxon. RO, W/AZ7.

[31] Beds. RO, PM 1684; R Box 147. At Tilbrooke in 1797 each commoner could let only one unused common: Beds. RO, WG 1343.

forbade the agisting of outsiders' cattle even in the forest and fen. In the forest the grantees disliked it because the cattle (and the sheep where they were allowed) drove out the deer. In the fen, graziers might bring in large flocks. But in some parishes even local cattle and sheep could not be agisted; for example, in Kirtling, where commons were reserved for the smaller occupiers, pasture could not be let to anyone else, insider or outsider. In Hemingford Abbots, cottagers might not 'bear or Colour any Cows or steers upon the Commons aforesaid but what are actually his own under paine of forefeitting to the Lord of the Manner for every Cow or steer soe taken five shillings'.[32]

On the face of it, forbidding local agistment, and putting a stop to the letting of dead commons excluded villagers without land or cottage rights from common grazing. They also restricted the number of animals small occupiers might graze to exactly the limits of their land. In effect they reserved the common pastures for farmers, small landed commoners and common-right cottagers. For small occupiers the restriction was no greater than for large – although an unwelcome one. For landless commoners the implications appear to be dire: the orders may signal their decline long before enclosure. But prohibition seems to have occurred in two particular kinds of village. It occurred in hill and vale, where the right to hire additional pasture rights was of little use without land anyway. Or it occurred where inhabitants' grazing rights survived, but letting them to others (local or not) would destroy the value of the right. In Somersham, for example, poor inhabitants could keep a cow on the common-field pastures and on the common waste. But they could not let the right to anyone else, 'it being Contrary to the Old Customs of the said Parish and a great detriment to the Farmers'. The intention of the custom was interpreted to be to give everyone grazing, not to give those who did not *use* it real property to let at will.[33] In both kinds of village – those where hired rights were useless without land and those where everyone had a right already – a prohibition on local agistment or the letting of dead commons probably kept extra commons out of the hands of other *occupiers* rather than the landless. As such it must be seen as a way of reducing

---

[32] Cambs. RO, P 101/28/11 (6 June 1798, Kirtling); Cambs. RO (Hunts. Office), 2537/9, Hemingford Abbots Vestry Book, field orders, 1707.

[33] Cambs. RO (Hunts. Office), HMR 16(12), Court Books of Somersham Manor, 16 Oct. 1772, 15 Oct. 1773, 21 Oct. 1774.

the stocking of *landholders* on common pastures not landless commoners; a way of preserving or improving common land, not of excluding the poorest users of common right.

The last threat to consider is the removal of residence as entitlement to right, and its substitution with property. Gateward's case made this common law. None the less, we have seen that in practice residents' rights often survived, sometimes until enclosure. But did inhabitants elsewhere lose their right to graze cattle in the eighteenth century? There is some evidence that they did. In Eaton Bray, Bedfordshire, in 1798, commoners drew up a stinting agreement and enrolled it in Chancery. In it they deemed ancient any cottage or house occupied for fifty years. Its occupiers were entitled to grazing for two great beasts a year. Cottages occupied for a shorter time carried no common right. In effect the occupiers of anything built after 1748 were not commoners. Inhabitants lost their rights as inhabitants in 1798, if not earlier.[34] At Campton cum Shefford in 1743 some commoners tried to restrict the pool of cottage commons to ancient cottagers, who might then agist a cow for an occupier of a new cottage. They appear to have failed.[35]

Where attempts like this were successful they deprived inhabitants of their common rights before enclosure, though they may not have lost all access to the commons – at Campton the intention was to make new cottagers hire rights from ancient cottagers, as they did in Maulden.[36] We know this must have happened in many places over time because not every inhabitant had common right. But how often did it happen in the eighteenth century? It is impossible to answer with certainty, though these are the only cases found in a wide search. There were reasons why common rights for lesser occupiers and even the landless should remain intact – some of

---

[34] Beds. RO, P63/28/1, 8 May 1797 (enrolled in Chancery 14 Mar. 1798); the cottagers had rights for cows on the common wastes, greens and meads, and for sheep on the fields; whether the date was fixed in 1748 or 1798 is unclear. At Northwold's enclosure in 1798 cottages were deemed ancient if they were older than twenty years; when the decision was made is unclear: it could have been made by the enclosure commissioners at the request of the enclosers or by a jury twenty years before the enclosure: Norfolk RO, MC 62/13, 506 × 8.

[35] Ancient cottages carried rights for three cows or one horse, and six sheep in the fallow: Beds. RO, DDX 89/1, 12 Oct. 1743, 25 Oct. 1743. Similarly, at Stow Bedon's enclosure in 1813 objections made to claims for common right attached to cottages because the cottages were built within the last thirty years were disallowed: Norfolk RO, BR 90/33.

[36] See above, p. 91.

which we have seen at work earlier. The prosperity of small commoners was an advantage to the village trading and manufacturing community, and village traders were themselves commoners. It was also an advantage to those who paid poor rate if access to common right reduced levels of poor relief. Despite the insults of pro-enclosure pamphleteers, who called them idle and unwilling to work, in their own villages commoners were regarded as thrifty, independent, loath to rely on charity.[37] Finally, if kinship in England was – as David Cressy argues – more effective than historians have thought, it is likely that at least some larger commoners felt an obligation to protect the common rights of smaller.[38]

Clearly, to protect their entitlement small commoners had to make themselves heard, and this was easier in some places than in others. Any number of things strengthened their hands. Where their labour was in demand, where their sheep were folded and their calves and geese were fattened by bigger farmers, where farmers thought that commons were good social cement, or kept labourers off the poor rates, where small commoners were willing to threaten big commoners – in all these places the rights of the smallest commoners might survive.

SHRINKING PASTURES

But what if the common was stolen from the goose already? What if the dwindling extent of common pasture made entitlement to common worthless? To consider this possibility we need to look at changes in the extent of common pasture.

In the eighteenth century, common fields lay in most lowland English counties and in some highland ones too. But they dominated the open, villaged landscape of a central belt of counties that covered much of the Midlands, spreading east and north into East Anglia, Lincolnshire and the East Riding of Yorkshire, and south and west into Berkshire, Wiltshire and Dorset. Here, commoners

---

[37] Viscount Cholmondeley's experience that enclosure raised poor rates led him to decide against further enclosures in 1713: J. Thirsk, ed., *Agrarian History of England and Wales*, V, part I, p. 150; Flora Thompson, *Lark Rise to Candleford* (1939; 1973 edn), pp. 80–1; Bewick, *Memoir*, pp. 23–9.

[38] David Cressy, 'Kinship and Kin Interaction in Early Modern England', *Past and Present*, 113 (1986), p. 68; and see below, Chapter 10.

had grazing rights over the common fields themselves and also on uncultivated common wastes.[39]

Common fields became pasture when thrown open to common herds and flocks after harvest and gleaning. Grazing time varied from field to field. It was shortest in the future winter corn field which lay open only until October, though sheep might be let in again to bite down corn that came through too early to be safe from frost.[40] But the new spring corn field (the Lammas field) lay open at different times for cattle, followed by sheep, from Lammas (1 August) for six months until it was ploughed for the spring sowing. And the old spring corn field was open all year if it was to be left fallow; or from autumn to early spring, and then again between hay harvest and winter ploughing, wherever fallow was sown with fodder crops. But common-field grazing was not confined to the fallow field and the after-harvest stubbles. It also lay within sown fields. Here cattle might graze on the 'joynts' or carriageways taken by workers and carts to cross the fields, on the headlands where ploughmen turned their teams in the autumn (unless they ploughed them later on), on strips of meadow lying on the banks of streams bounding the fields, and on the common way circling the field.[41] Still more pasture lay in village meadows where grazing was guarded jealously because the grass was richest. Even the verges of lanes and roads offered grazing.[42]

[39] [Arthur Young], Board of Agriculture, *General Report on Enclosures* (1808); Gonner, *Common Land*; Slater, *English Peasantry*; W. E. Tate, *A Doomsday of Enclosure Acts and Awards*, ed. Michael Turner (Reading, 1978); Turner, *English Parliamentary Enclosure*, ch. 2 and appendices 1–5. H. L. Gray, *English Open Fields* (1955), p. 47, calls common of pasture the 'determining idea' of the open-field system, cited in W. O. Ault, *Open-Field Farming in Medieval England. A Study of Village By-Laws* (1972), p. 16.

[40] Hartley, *Lost Country Life*, p. 55.

[41] Often the balks that divided strips and furlongs were grazed: see Eric Kerridge, *The Agricultural Revolution* (1967), pp. 99–100, and H. A. Beecham, 'A Review of Balks as Strip Boundaries in the Open Fields', *Agricultural History Review*, 4 (1956), pp. 22–24, and see below, p. 137. But not every parish allowed balk and tether grazing, and others watched it carefully: Sowe jury went as far as to warn commoners against leaving 'manes or fringes or Borders of Grass' when they ploughed because grazing them early would reduce the amount of stubble left after harvest: Warwicks. RO, CR 556/299 (5) (16, 30 Apr. 1722). Where juries permitted balk grazing they also regulated it: Orwell commoners might pasture their cattle on their lands' ends privately only between Old May Day and Old Lammas and then they became available to all commoners: Northants. RO, Fitz. Misc., vol. 747, 8 Apr. 1796, p. 162; Cambs. RO, L.63.59.10.

[42] Roade jury stinted street and lane commons at one horse per person in 1732; Alderton jury ordered the highways clear of cattle until after harvest in the same

So commoners found pasture for their herds and flocks on the
uncultivated parts of the tilled fields for some of the year, in the
fallow field all or half the year, early in the sowing seasons of the
corn fields, on the meadows at the critical time between the end of
the hay harvest and the end of the corn harvest or between Lammas
and spring,[43] and on the stubble when the harvest and gleaning were
over, for anything from two or three to six months. In short, the
common fields provided grazing, and were themselves manured, for
much of the year, particularly in the autumn. There was least to be
had of either grass or manure in the winter, especially in the wetter
north and west. Then, with the young stock sold, cattle were penned
in the homesteads, old enclosures or crofts behind village streets.[44]
All this land belonged to individual landholders. In both predom-
inantly arable parishes, and in those with a more mixed agriculture,
it provided some of the best grazing. But the rest of the pasture lay
on the uncultivated common waste, legally the property of the Lord
of the Manor. This was more extensive in highland than lowland
England, but it was not exclusive to the highland. In 1750, one acre
in six in unenclosed Northamptonshire – a county at the centre of
the most intensively cultivated part of the country – was common
waste.[45] Naturally, most waste lay in the northern fenland around

year; commoners in Guilsborough, Coton and Nortoft enjoyed extensive land
commons; a strip of waste two miles long and lying on either side of the
Sleaford–Tattersall road provided twenty-seven acres of common in Lincoln;
wayside grass well manured by pack horses was valuable; drovers regretted the
loss of road pasture when roads were widened at enclosure; enclosure awards
regularly allotted the herbage on public roads to the owners and occupiers of the
adjacent allotments: see Northants. RO, G34321i, G3557a; *Jls House of
Commons*, 25 Jan. 1764; L. D. Stamp and W. G. Hoskins, *The Common Lands of
England and Wales* (1963), p. 115; Hartley, *Lost Country Life*, p. 67; K. J. Bonser,
Drovers, p. 73.

[43] Margaret Baker, *Folklore and Customs of Rural England* (1974), p. 126, citing
H. Harman, *Buckinghamshire Dialect* (1929; repr. 1971), pp. 93–4.

[44] For winter grazing out of the fields in the wetter parts of the east Midlands see
Thirsk, *Agrarian History of England and Wales*, VI, part I, p. 98. For the greater
availability of pasture for sheep from late March to late December see Beds. RO,
WG 1944, rate and stint for commoning in Milhoe, 1693 and 1703. This calendar
of the pasture year is based on the evidence of the Midland manors, whose
regulation is described in this chapter and the next. C. S. and C. S. Orwin describe
a similar seasonal pattern in *The Open Fields*, pp. 47–8, 57–9.

[45] About 11,000 of the 200,000 acres enclosed by Act of Parliament in Northamptonshire between 1760 and 1800 were waste. Another 42,000 acres of waste still
remained open in 1800. The figures are approximate and based on Slater's
calculations in *English Peasantry*, Appendix B, pp. 290–4; on estimates of waste in
twenty-five parishes enclosed between 1760 and 1800 given in the Board of

Peterborough and on the adjacent heaths, and also in the three royal forests, Rockingham, Salcey and Whittlewood. But the scarpland in the west was also well served with rough pasture, and the southern downland was too. Even the Nene valley in the east, an area with the least waste in the county, had substantial meadows. In fact most parishes had some waste, something John Morton saw when he came to describe the county in 1712.[46] So waste common had a place in a range of agricultures; it was part of the forest and fen economies as one would expect, but even in intensively cultivated counties it was part of common-field arable farming too. If it was significant in as cultivated a county as Northamptonshire it was no less important in the rest of common-field England.[47]

Common fields and uncultivated wastes covered a large part of eighteenth-century England then. Every county had some common lands, and within them lay exactly defined common pastures. But were they still organized for common use? Or had agricultural improvement steadily eaten away at the common use of land long

Agriculture's *General Report*, p. 194; and on M. Williams, 'The Enclosure and Reclamation of Waste Land in England and Wales in the Eighteenth and Nineteenth Centuries', *Transactions and Papers of the Institute of British Geographers*, 51 (1970), pp. 57–9. These sources suggest a waste acreage of 9 per cent. But the Board's figures underestimated the acreage of waste enclosed between 1760 and 1800 by about 2,000 acres when it omitted the enclosures of wastes in West Haddon and Denton and underestimated the size of Wollaston's waste. In addition it listed no waste smaller than 100 acres. But we know from the evidence of by-laws and the complaints of reporters to the Board of Agriculture, as well as enclosure Awards, that many small commons survived until enclosure. We may estimate a seventy-five-acre waste for two thirds (100) of the 150 enclosure Acts passed between 1750 and 1800, an average of only 50 acres per parish or 7,500 in all. This is a conservative estimate given the larger number of parishes enclosed in this period. If this is roughly accurate, wastes in Northamptonshire in 1750 covered 62,500 (11,000 + 2,000 + 42,000 + 7,500) acres out of a total of perhaps 400,000 acres of unenclosed land, or 15.6 per cent.

Dr John Chapman's 10 per cent sample of enclosure awards in England and Wales suggests that 10.6 per cent of Northamptonshire enclosure was of waste land, but his sample is designed to show national and regional trends not individual county acreages, and the chances of a 10 per cent sample taking account of the largest wastes in the county are small. In addition, his figure for Northamptonshire is over 2 per cent below the mean common and waste figures for similar counties (personal communication).

[46] Morton, *Natural History of Northamptonshire*, pp. 9–10.
[47] Most enclosure of arable land took place in the Midland counties of Huntingdonshire, Northamptonshire, Buckinghamshire, Leicestershire, Rutland and Warwickshire, but even here the maximum arable acreage enclosed was 79.25 per cent for Huntingdon. At least 20 per cent of the land enclosed in these counties was common pasture and meadow: J. Chapman, 'The Extent and Nature of Parliamentary Enclosure', *Agricultural History Review*, 35 (1987), p. 30.

before it became enclosed? Certainly farmers worked at improving their pastures and feeding their lands, shared or not. Where soils allowed, they sowed fodder crops on the fallow. They turned arable land to greensward. They made temporary and permanent closes in the common fields. But what did their activity mean in terms of common grazing? Was it diminished? Was it improved?

Fodder crops, greensward and half-year land

The work of Michael Havinden on Oxfordshire and of Mark Overton on East Anglia has demonstrated the gradual adoption of fodder crops in early modern villages. Havinden shows the process at work in open fields, Overton the individual initiatives of men working what appears to be *de facto* enclosed land. Of course, the two were not exclusive. In Northamptonshire, farmers both introduced clover and sainfoin on their own accounts (with the consent of the parish) and signed agreements to introduce them through the parish.[48] In terms of the availability of common pasture the effect of the spread of fodder crops on the fallow was to reduce grazing space because the field was sown not grazed for part of the year. Lost common grazing time ran from April until May or June, sometimes later. But this was less serious than it sounds.[49] First, while their lands were fenced off, field orders forbade commoners to pasture the animals to which their newly sown land would ordinarily entitle them, so other commoners enjoyed the usual ratio of common pasture to cattle.[50] Second, the quality of pasture may have

---

[48] Havinden, 'Agricultural Progress in Open-Field Oxfordshire'; and 'The Rural Economy of Oxfordshire, 1580–1730' (unpublished B.Litt.thesis, University of Oxford, 1961). Mark Overton, 'The Diffusion of Agricultural Innovations in Early Modern England: Turnips and Clover in Norfolk and Suffolk, 1580–1740', *Transactions of the Institute of British Geographers*, new series, 10 (1985); Neeson, 'Common Right and Enclosure', pp. 107–12. Agreement was necessary because custom might be invoked against sowing the fallow: see Berks, RO, D/EHy L5, for an opinion given in 1733 that it was unlawful to enclose or hitch land which was customarily grass in the fallow year.

[49] For the argument that fodder crops made strips, commons and rotations obsolete see Doreen Warriner, *The Economics of Peasant Farming* (Oxford, 1939: 1964 edn), p. 10. In Havinden's opinion hitching all the fallow field was rare: Havinden, 'Rural Economy of Oxfordshire', pp. 268–9.

[50] In 1727 the jury at Temple Balsall, Warwickshire, set a fine of £1 19s 11d for failing to abate commons when land was not thrown open: Warwicks. RO, CR 1317/1; see also Berks. RO, D/EHy L5. Sometimes, when land was thrown open after hay harvest, juries rewarded occupiers with rights for more cattle than usual, to be put on the common pasture at that point. But if the closes were not thrown

improved, particularly when the fodder leys were sown by parish-wide agreement, because they provided better grazing than the bare fallow when the fieldsmen threw the sown closes open again after hay harvest. At the same time more fodder had been grown for the winter. Sowing the fallow with fodder crops did not lower the value of common right; instead it may have raised it.

Commoners also put field land down to greensward – that is, they took arable land out of cultivation and left it to grow natural grass for a number of years. Their intention was to improve grazing. Once again, the parish as a whole, or most of it, made the decision to lay land down to grass.[51] And again, like the sowing of fallow leys, the spread of greensward did not reduce grazing on the fallow. Instead it increased the quantity of grazing in every field, for everyone. And, also like fallow leys, greensward gave a better bite than post-crop pasture – something recognized in many villages where orders allowed more common rights for greensward than for crop land. Together, temporary fallow leys and greensward increased the value of common grazing and the total amount of feed in the parish, and in doing so still remained a part of communal agriculture.[52]

Commoners also agreed that common-field land might be put down to enclosed pasture permanently on condition that it be common for half the year from the end of the hay harvest.[53] Creating 'half-year' land required a more formal agreement than sowing the fallow because more stood to be lost. Common rights

open until *after* the occupier had pastured his own cattle on them there was no entitlement to extra commons: see below, pp. 121–2. By-laws made in 1798 and 1814 by commoners in the hamlet of Stanbridge, Leighton Buzzard, carefully limited the sowing or cropping of the fallow: Beds. RO, BO 1337, 1338.

51 The 'Inhabitants ffreeholders and Landholders' of Ravensthorpe drew up a new set of orders on parchment on 1 January 1724, in which they declared that all jointways in the fields were greensward and must be twelve poles wide. In another agreement in 1761 they stipulated the size of balks to the arable acre, and put a 20s per acre fine on anyone who had converted greensward to tillage in the last twenty years, again on parchment: Northants. RO, D8323a, D8323b.

52 Maxey commoners could sow wheat and beans in enclosures in the common fields in 1799; they paid a fee for the privilege and abated their common grazing. The jury made the order for the first time on the eve of enclosure and set high fines for breaking the fences, both of which suggest that the practice was part of the move to enclose and an unpopular one even in the fens, where abundant common pasture lay outside the fields: Northants. RO, Fitz. Misc. vol. 747, p. 177, 14 Apr. 1799.

53 Or longer: an agreement made at Ampthill in 1781 allowed two closes to become several from Candlemas to Michaelmas – an eight-month period, see Beds. RO, WE 802.

had to be vigilantly maintained. In particular, commoners vigorously resisted attempts to turn the temporarily enclosed grass to
winter-sown arable because it both shortened the length of time the
closes were common and reduced the quality of the grazing. For this
reason, when Mr Hodsden of Sydenham sowed his forty-acre leys
with wheat in 1752 his neighbours turned their cows into it in order
to provoke a law suit in which their rights would be vindicated:
'This they did on purpose to make him the plaintiff, to sue them for
damages: and if he does not, they will most certainly do the same in
all the common land and not suffer any of the tenants to plough in
what they call their half year.' Commoners threatened Lord Dartmouth's tenants at Lewisham with the same action.[54]

Vigilance was also necessary because, with time, sowing the leys
could bring into question the half-year right itself.[55] For 240 years,
cottagers in Harold, Bedfordshire, had enjoyed a right of way to
another common through a half-year pasture close in the tenure of
John Knight, tenant to the Earl of Hardwick. The grazing may not
have amounted to much but the right was clearly theirs, and access
through the close was threatened if the land should be under crop
for three of the six months it was common. So when Knight
ploughed and sowed it for the second season in 1770 the cottagers
'(who before, had entered into a Combination to oppose the
Farmers)' turned their cows into the ripening wheat, and followed
them with whips and sticks to beat off the ears of any still standing,
'which, had they spared, and arrested Mr Knight for Damage, in
case he had done any, they would have been thought better of by all
sorts of people'. Maybe so, but destroying a crop worth £90 was
cheaper and more effective than taking its owner to court.[56]

Sowing cornfields with grass also threatened common right. The

[54] *HMC Dartmouth III* (Ser. 20, 1896, 15th Report, Appendix I), p. 167, Rev.
William Lowth to Mr Baron Legge, 'in Lincoln's Inn Fields', 25 Dec. 1752.
Hodsden claimed that he and Dartmouth's tenants had sown the half-year lands
for the previous sixty years.

[55] In Hampshire, Vancouver saw lands 'laid into severalty which heretofore were
subject to a half-yearly inter-commonage': Vancouver, *General View ... Hampshire*, p. 121.

[56] Beds. RO, L 24/231, 234. The cottagers were accused of insisting on their pasture
in order to get compensation for it at enclosure, which they were said to be
deliberately promoting. But enclosure was thirty years away (1797), and these
cottagers would have been most unusual if enclosure was their objective: below,
Chapter 9. Hardwick was busy trying to divide Flitton moor two years later, an
attempt vigorously and successfully resisted (it was eventually enclosed in 1796,
despite another riot), Beds. RO, CRT 100/27/3–4.

sheepmaster and some of the farmers of Hinxton, Cambridgeshire, did this in the 1790s, then, after the hay harvest, fed the land with their sheep until the corn harvest, at which point they let in the common herd. By then the land was exhausted. Again, as they had in Lewisham and Sydenham, other commoners protested. They took their case to Mr Serjeant Le Blanc, who advised them that, if the Hinxton by-laws said that land was commonable from the time of harvest until sowing, that is, if the by-laws implied the fields were arable, they had a strong case. But if they simply said that land was commonable from Lammas to December they did not; instead, farmers might do as they pleased for the rest of the year.[57]

Piecemeal enclosure

The spread of closes – permanently enclosed pastures – within open fields also took land out of the common stock, and, unlike half-year lands, it did so forever. Common-field land became enclosed piecemeal. Historians have thought this destructive of communal agriculture because creating exclusive property rights over the land removed it from the purview of the commoners, and because it deprived the common fields of enough pasture to feed the arable.[58] Without a census of piecemeal enclosure the degree to which common fields became *de facto* enclosed pasture will remain uncertain, though it is clear enough that it varied greatly from place to place. Here it is possible only to indicate some of the limits within which it occurred.[59]

First, for practical reasons the extent of piecemeal enclosure was probably greater in parishes with only a few middling or large owners and their tenants than in those with many small owners and occupiers. Given the opportunity to enclose piecemeal, small commoners faced the same predicament as they did at parliamentary

---

[57] Cambs. RO, R 57.24.1.26.

[58] Chambers and Mingay, *Agricultural Revolution*, pp. 49–52. For a complaint that piecemeal enclosure of common waste and common field led to a shortage of dung for the common fields at Claydon, Buckinghamshire, in 1648, see John Broad, 'The Verneys as Enclosing Landlords', in John Chartres and David Hey, eds., *English Rural Society. Essays in Honour of Joan Thirsk* (Cambridge, 1990), pp. 32–3.

[59] For a discussion of the scope of piecemeal enclosure in some Midland villages, and the difficulty of establishing an explanation for it, see Yelling, *Common Field and Enclosure*, ch. 5; for its varied pace in the eighteenth-century Midlands, see Turner, *English Parliamentary Enclosure*, pp. 138–45.

enclosure later on: they worked too little land to readily give up their pasture rights over the rest of the common fields and waste. They might enclose small amounts but not large, or they might share a close.[60] Second, some landlords, and particularly Lords of Manors, discouraged the spread of permanent closes except when it suited them.[61] Third, when it did take place, the procedure required an agreement negotiated with the rest of the parish both to dis-common and to set up rights of way to the closes. If the parish was divided about the issue, or if villagers came to regret losing common right over the new closes, it was easy to make trouble for the enclos-ing owner, or his tenants.[62]

Permanent closes had another disadvantage too when compared to temporary closes. They were inflexible: their value was limited to the pasture they gave.[63] In contrast, turning arable to pasture temporarily allowed some flexibility in response to changing markets. It always had. Variable proportions of arable and pasture characterized English agriculture long before enclosure enabled farmers to convert to pasture or sow as they chose. The late seven-teenth- and early eighteenth-century extension of pasture changed a ratio of arable to pasture generated in part at least by the inflated grain prices of the previous century or more. It was as much a response to the concurrent falling price of grain and the rising cost of labour as a result of the march of progress towards a more perfect

[60] On shared closes see A. R. H. Baker and R. A. Butlin, eds., *Studies of Field Systems in the British Isles* (Cambridge, 1973), p. 287.

[61] Edward Laurence advised Lords of Manors against allowing freeholders to enclose parts of the common fields because it would lead to conversion of arable to pasture: Laurence, *Duty of a Land Steward*, Article XIV, leading John Cowper to observe that only the rich were permitted to enclose to this end: *An Essay*, pp. 20–1. Lords might attempt piecemeal enclosures in their own interest (and Laurence advised stewards to eliminate common rights before enclosure because they were expensive to compensate) but stand in the way of freeholders; War-wicks. RO, CR 1291/601, for legal advice to tear down the fences of an illegally enclosed common in 1801. Agricultural writers in general disliked piecemeal enclosure: see Yelling, *Common Field and Enclosure*, p. 81.

[62] Beds. RO, CRT 100/27/3–4 (transcript), for the fear of tenant farmers that they would be held responsible for the enclosure of part of a common; and see W. James and J. Malcolm, *General View of the Agriculture of Buckingham* (1794), p. 29, for the reassertion of common rights fourteen years after an agreement to enclose. For instances of agreements to enclose small amounts of land piecemeal in Buckinghamshire see Turner, *English Parliamentary Enclosure*, pp. 141–2; on the difficulty of enclosing piecemeal see T. S. Ashton, *An Economic History of England: The Eighteenth Century* (1955; 1969 edn), p. 38.

[63] Closes in open fields were almost always made for meadow or pasture land; Havinden, 'Rural Economy of Oxfordshire,' p. 228.

agriculture.[64] Similarly, the spread of tillage during the Napoleonic wars was a response to the same kind of stimulus, this time the rising price of grain.

Accordingly, proportions of untilled grassland in open fields in the course of the eighteenth century varied with time, place and prices. Eric Kerridge notes the seventeenth- and early eighteenth-century expansion of common pasture in Northamptonshire. Commoners laid land to grass in the fallow year at a rate per acre of field land, or they laid 'a stretch at the ends of the ridges ... to augment "the headleys"'. The rationale was to expand dairying or keep more beasts.[65] A century later, field pastures in Rothwell, Northamptonshire, covered a quarter of each field. Crops were good, the wheat 'generally heavy and bent under its own weight, or laid by the rain, three to four quarters per acre, and other crops in proportion'.[66] The advantage of periodically but temporarily laying down the fallow, or part of the common field, rather than permanently establishing pasture closes, was that these temporary enclosures allowed this relatively cheap flexibility as well as the retention of common right.

Turning ley to grain was lucrative. The saying went, 'to break a lea makes a man': first he made something from selling his stock, then from the good corn crops he got from the ley. But, unless the sward thickened quickly, making a ley was correspondingly expensive: 'To make a lea breaks a man'. He had to forgo the near-annual crop and then begin to strike a new balance between pasture, stock

---

64 Though F. M. Eden thought there was indeed a perfect balance between pasture and arable, one that would have to be reached through the painful but necessary means of enclosure: see Eden, *The State of the Poor* (1797), I, p. 421, cited in Marx, *Capital*, II, p. 840. For evidence of falling prices and conversion to pasture see G. E. Mingay, 'The East Midlands', in *Agrarian History*, ed. Thirsk, V, part I (Cambridge, 1984), pp. 124–6. On the agricultural depression see G. E. Mingay, 'The Agricultural Depression, 1730–50', *Agricultural History Review*, 8 (1956); on its regional location see J. V. Beckett, 'Regional Variation and the Agricultural Depression, 1730–50', *Agricultural History Review*, 35 (1982); for national and regional price indices of grains, other field crops and livestock, and for wage rates and their purchasing power from 1640 to 1749 see Peter J. Bowden, *Agrarian History*, ed. Thirsk, V, part II, Appendix III, Statistics (Cambridge, 1985), pp. 851–79; for rising real wages from 1640 to 1740 see Wrigley and Schofield, *Population History*, pp. 408, 418.
65 Kerridge, *Agricultural Revolution*, p. 101. And see Marx, *Capital*, II, pp. 829–30, on the cyclical appearance and disappearance of the English peasantry in step with the alternation of English agriculture between cattle breeding and grain growing.
66 Pitt, *General View ... Northampton*, pp. 65–9; he found the crops 'extremely respectable' in 1806.

and grain.[67] It was a thing to be undertaken when prices or declining fertility demanded it. Consequently, on the convertible soils found in much of the Midlands permanent closes may have been unattractive not only to the smaller occupiers who needed their common rights but also to middling farmers. For these reasons permanent closes were probably fewer than temporary ones except in proto-permanent pasture lands farmed by only a few large occupiers. Diffuse occupancy probably discouraged piecemeal enclosure; consolidated occupancy, at a time of high prices for livestock, may have encouraged it.

Finally (and for the extent of common pasture most significant of all), although permanent enclosures within common fields may have reduced the ambit of communal regulation, because common-field land was taken out of the system, they did not devalue common right itself. The amount of common pasture open to each common-able beast was unchanged, or even grew because, in return for permission to enclose, owners gave up common right. They took their animals as well as their land out of the common system.[68] Accordingly, for every acre of open-field land enclosed like this the number of commonable mouths to feed also dropped. Indeed, when larger owners enclosed some of their field pastures and relinquished their common rights they became less likely to overstock the common pasture with their large herds and flocks. Numbers of stock may have fallen disproportionately for another reason too. The bigger farmers most likely to withdraw land from the common system were also those most able to stock all their rights. As a result, they may have been the most consistent users of commons. But when they moved some of their stock into closes they may have become less reliant on common pasture in general and so have commoned more sporadically, leaving more of the common-field pastures to lesser occupiers.

When they did so they left much of the regulation of common fields in the hands of lesser commoners, who could organize pasture, and everything else, in their own best interest. Eric Kerridge has described early modern demesne farming and common-field

---

[67] Carolina Lane, 'The Development of Pastures and Meadows during the Sixteenth Century', *Agricultural History Review*, 28 (1980), pp. 29–30. Hartley, *Lost Country Life*, p. 56.

[68] For example, Berks, RO, D/EHy L5 (1733). The piecemeal enclosure of common *waste* did devalue common right, unless the waste was of little value.

farming as separate endeavours in which demesne flocks and herds did not share field pasture. As a result, although common-field farmers were not necessarily backward, demesne farmers were more likely to innovate, and, through innovation, to modernize.[69] But there may be another conclusion to draw. It is possible that the withdrawal of large tenants from common pasture empowered middling and small commoners. They won more control over the stocking of their fields. And the fields themselves were free of the largest flocks and herds. This may be the process at work in the parish of Ampthill in Bedfordshire. By mid century severalty was well advanced but the common rights of other occupiers were also well established. Ampthill Hills provided turf and grazing for their horses, cattle and hogs, and the Moores provided sheep pasture from which the sheep of four gentlemen landowners were excluded by agreement. Ten non-occupying landowners had agreed in writing not to common, and so not to starve their tenants of pasture. Cottages were not engrossed into a few hands; instead sixty-one people owned the eighty-two cottages, and their rights to fern were well documented.[70] Thus, where significant piecemeal enclosure did occur, the result may have been an invigorated common-field agriculture co-existing with a proto-enclosed one. And where this happened the two agricultures may have fed one another.

Redividing common fields

If fodder and temporary or permanent piecemeal enclosure did not change the ratio of mouths to acres on common pastures, they did – to varying extents – reduce the total acreage in common pastures every year. This also happened when parishes redivided their two or three common fields into four or more. The extent of the fallow shrank with each extra field in the rotation. Unless it was supported by forest commons, a six-field system offered only half the fallow grazing of a three-field system – though it also produced more fodder crops. The incidence of redivision varied from place to place though three-field systems were more common than six overall. To

---

[69] Kerridge, *Agricultural Revolution*, pp. 17–19, 39, 219–20, 256, 326; for an argument that the withdrawal of demesne from the common-field system weakened the latter by reducing grazing and gleaning see Finch, *The Wealth of Five Northamptonshire Families*, pp. 154–5.

[70] Beds. RO, BS 818, pp. 8–9, by-laws, 11 May 1750; and WE 802 (1781).

some extent field patterns were specific to different agricultural regions. In the best redlands of the Midlands, for example, or in the most fertile areas of the valleys like the Avon and the Stour, six- or eight-field systems were commonplace; in Warwickshire, Wootton Wawen and Snitterfield each had eight fields;[71] while in Felden Warwickshire, the three-field system with its large carefully regulated common pastures remained until enclosure, as it did in scarp and plateau Northamptonshire.

But field-systems also varied *within* agricultural regions. Two, three and four common-field systems occurred within single agricultural regions in Lincolnshire, for example, often in neighbouring parishes.[72] Nor was there a uni-directional trend to redivision in the eighteenth century. Instead some juries consolidated fields. In Northamptonshire the Aynho jury reduced their six fields to four in 1756, 'so as to have three crops and then a fallow in each field, which fallow shall be commonable at the same times that the fallows are now commonable'.[73] The conclusion must be that markets, prices and the need for pasture changed more than once in the long run-up to enclosure, and, with them, the number of fields in a parish and thus the extent of commonable pasture did too. But even a six-field rotation in a vale parish like Raunds afforded considerable common pasture, enough to cause a riot at the prospect of losing it at enclosure in 1797.

Encroachments and enclosing waste by agreement

The common-waste equivalent of the piecemeal enclosure of common fields was encroachment. Commoners generally disliked it.

[71] Gray, *English Field Systems*, pp. 129–30. Gray estimated that about one sixth of Oxfordshire was fertile redland but not all of it was farmed in six-field rotations – four courses were usual. Martin, 'Warwickshire and the Parliamentary Enclosure Movement', pp. 30–2. On the regional incidence of different field systems see Baker and Butlin, *Studies of Field Systems*.

[72] For the neighbouring co-existence of two-, three- and four-field systems within the same agricultural region see Rex C. Russell, *The Logic of Open Field Systems. Fifteen Maps of Groups of Common Fields on the Eve of Enclosure* (Standing Conference for Local History, 1974); map no. 11 shows that the three neighbouring parishes of Market Rasen, Middle Rasen and Kirkby cum Osgodby had two, four and three open fields each.

[73] Northants, RO. C(A) 2828, 3 Oct. 1756. On this point see Ian Beckwith's description of the various incarnations of the fields at Corringham, Lincolnshire: 'The Re-modelling of a Common-Field System', *Agricultural History Review*, 15 (1967), pp. 108–12.

When John Cookes, gentleman, of Hatton in Warwickshire enclosed an acre from Shrewley waste in 1674, the freehold, copyhold and customary tenants of Rowington manor made him enter into a bond to open it before 1 September and not fence it off again.[74] Encroachments on the waste were a point of friction between the encroachers, who sometimes had the support of the lord of the manor (who took an annual acknowledgment from them), and commoners, who lost grazing acres as a result.[75] Again, commoners resisted encroachment where they could, and where it was a serious threat. Stony Stratford commoners went to law against encroachers in 1580, 1656 and again in 1733. In 1712 an attempt by the lord of the manor and a London merchant to enclose Hemingford Abbots' common was defeated by an action in Chancery brought by the commoners.[76]

When lords tried to enclose part of the waste by agreement they met similar resistance, and if the task was accomplished at all it was done through a process of negotiation taking months or years. Defoe describes the attempts of an eminent Buckinghamshire emparker whose pales were torn down and burnt several times until he entered negotiations with local cottagers and farmers. Even then they had to pull down the fences again before they came to a settlement. 'How they accommodated it at last, I know not', said Defoe, 'But I see that Mr Gore has a park, and a very good one *but not large*.' Defoe went on to explain the significance of the story: 'I mention this,' he wrote, 'as an instance of the popular claim in England; which we call right of commonage, which the poor take to be as much their property, as a rich man's land is his own.'[77] Given

---

[74] Warwicks, RO, CR 1008/92.

[75] Cottages on Shropshire wastes became the property of the lord after twenty years: Scrutton, *Commons and Common Fields*, I, pp. 138–40, citing the *General View … Shropshire*. At this point lords might begin to raise the rent: *Northampton Mercury*, 26 Aug. 1726.

[76] Turner, 'Some Social and Economic Considerations', p. 29. In 1717 twenty-seven commoners in Kempston, Bedfordshire, bound themselves to share the legal costs of repelling an encroacher on the banks of Hardwick Brook: Beds. RO, X 122/14, cited in Godber, *History of Bedfordshire*, p. 363. Pressure on the north Warwickshire commons in the eighteenth century drove commoners to draw up agreements to enter encroachments and lay them open, and to consider what else they might do to deter them: Warwicks. RO, Studley agreement, 1806, CR 849, 889, cited in J. M. Martin, 'Economic and Social Trends in the Rural West Midlands 1770–1825' (unpublished M.Com. thesis, University of Birmingham, 1960), p. 159. Cambs. RO (Hunts. Office), 2537/9, Memorandum 25 Mar. 1712.

[77] Defoe, *Tour*, II, pp. 15–16, my italics.

this attitude, negotiations could come to nothing: in 1775, when James Leigh Perrot marked out a larger part of the waste for an enclosure than the jury of Wargrave had intended, and was confronted with the fact, he 'desisted and took in no part of the waste at all'.[78] From the commoners point of view, much stood to be lost. Commoners sharing Flitton Moor put their reasons very plainly when regulation and partial enclosure were proposed in 1775. And their insistence on their own control of the resource is an insistence seen earlier in this chapter, when commoners upheld the proper use of half-year land, regulated fallow cropping and argued over the terms of agreement for the partial enclosure of common-field land. At Flitton Moor they said:

> Sir ... we want no stint, we want no separation – we have been used time out of mind to inter common we never differ about one another's stock; and if we do *dig it up* to our own hurt, we *only* hurt ourselves – We do not desire anybody to interfere. The Common is our own ...[79]

In the end two mechanisms destroyed common appendant to land. In parishes in which landholding was diffuse the largest landlords and most substantial freeholders had to resort to the institutional means of a parliamentary enclosure, which automatically extinguished common right and gave enclosure commissioners a free hand to offer as little compensation as they wished, with little redress. In other open parishes, where land consolidation had gone ahead early, the workings of the land market, perhaps the transformation of tenure, and the defeat of small commoners by larger interests, reduced the number of landed commoners before enclos-

---

[78] The enclosure of Corby Woods in Rockingham Forest required extended negotiations with the commoners: see Daniel Eaton, *Letters of Daniel Eaton to the Third Earl of Cardigan 1725–32*, ed. Joan Wake and D. C. Webster, Publications of the Northamptonshire Record Society, XXIV (Kettering, 1971), Letters 54, 55, 134, 139, 145, 147. Berks. RO, D/EN E3. Similar difficulty met the attempt to buy out commoners at Northmore in Oxfordshire in 1672: Berks. RO, D/EL1L1. Halsbury comments on the difficulty of enclosing a common by agreement, because both agreement itself was elusive and identifying all the commoners was difficult: *Halsbury's Laws of England*, IV, Section 1173.

[79] Beds. RO, CRT 100/27/3–4. Commoners at Maulden, said to be the worst behaved in the Flitton disturbance, still enjoyed the unstinted common ten years later. An advertisement for the sale of three acres of arable and a farmhouse there in 1785 mentioned 'unlimited right of common on the extensive Commons': *Northampton Mercury*, 28 Mar. 1785; Maulden commoners resorted to riot again at enclosure in 1796: Godber, *History of Bedfordshire*, p. 418.

ure. The result was either that farming in severalty made common pasture unnecessary, or that it became the preserve of a few large farmers – though significant numbers of cottage, resident and land-poor commoners might remain, as they did in Chippenham and Sandy.[80]

But in comparison to land consolidation and enclosure the attempts of large landowners to undercut common right were unsuccessful. Only in forest villages was it worthwhile for grantees to buy up cottage rights in order to keep commoners out of the forest, and this they tried. But attempts to negotiate the end of pasture rights, or to bludgeon commoners into sales, failed in Northamptonshire forests as often as they did in Windsor Forest and on Waltham Chase.[81] They hit the stone wall of commoner intransigence. Only parliamentary enclosure in the 1790s and 1850s would rid the Northamptonshire and Oxfordshire forests of the encumbrance of shared-use rights, in much the same way as it would extinguish common right and decimate petty landholding in the most populous fielden parishes.

[80] See Chapter 2, pp. 75–7.
[81] E. P. Thompson, *Whigs and Hunters. The Origin of the Black Act* (1975), p. 239.

4. Ordering the commons

Many cottagers and occupiers had common grazing rights. But the very frequency of their entitlement raises the question of their value: did the right to pasture a cow survive because it was worthless, and, being worthless, was worth no one's time to extinguish? Were common pastures as bare and disease ridden as polemicists for a general enclosure Act, and some agrarian historians, have argued? Or were they as fertile as their defenders claimed, and even some enclosers admitted? An answer depends on how well common-field villagers cared for the common pastures. The balance they struck between the good upkeep of the pasture and its maximum use was crucial.

THE LAW OF THE COMMONS

Common pastures were useful only if they were not overstocked, and the animals fed on them prospered only if their grazing was well regulated and the risk of disease kept to a minimum. The upkeep and renewal of the pasture, the fencing and mounding of the fields, and the adoption of fodder crops as communal resources were operations decided upon and enforced by manorial courts and vestries. The by-laws or field orders ratified here regulated the working lives of more people, more often, than any other kind of law in common-field parishes. It involved more officers and more frequent enforcement too. It forbade abuse of the pasture, or use by those without rights, and it survived until all the fields and commons of a manor or a parish were enclosed.[1]

[1] For example, although some of the parish of Grafton Regis was enclosed in 1727 by private Act, the remaining open land was regulated at the court into the 1760s. The criminal law functions of manorial courts may have declined substantially from

The field orders that are our evidence were relatively ephemeral documents. Their archival survival depends on how the steward of the court or the vestry dealt with them. Those generated in manor courts survived better than those produced in public vestries or similar local meetings. Northamptonshire stewards bundled up the field orders with the first drafts of the court proceedings. They rarely enrolled them formally with the fealties, surrenders and admissions that formed the other business of the court. At best they copied them into books. This casual treatment suggests that the orders were not of abiding importance: courts made them at least twice a year, often for that season only, and those that were standing orders became too familiar to need preservation. Once or twice a year fieldsmen read them publicly and then nailed them to the church door. Only occasionally were new arrangements important enough to require permanent preservation in the rolls. When most field orders were of short-term significance, and when their real importance was local, orders not preserved by stewards rarely survive.[2]

Because orders made in manorial courts survive best, orders from the well-manored county of Northamptonshire form the basis of what follows. They come from the manors of the honour of Grafton, the royal manor (and later the vestry) of Raunds, and the fenland manors of Maxey cum membris. They represent the major geographical regions of the county, and they form relatively unbroken runs in this period. Orders made in manors and vestries in other Midland counties supplement them.

The manors of the Duke of Grafton lay in and on the borders of the royal forests of Whittlewood and Salcey in south east Northamptonshire, and further west in the centre of the county, south of Watling Street. The two courts of Grafton and Moreton Pinkney administered manors that shared a mixed agriculture in the eighteenth century, but with different emphasis on the balance of stock and crops. In the forest the thin grey loams lying on limestone encouraged more crop-growing than pasture, in the Moreton

their thirteenth-century levels but their land-transfer and field-regulatory functions did not, though most of the latter were the daily concern not of the steward but of the jury and the commoners – as they had been at other times too: see Barbara Hanawalt, *The Ties that Bound* (Oxford, 1986), pp. 266–7.

[2] When a parish contained more than one manor, agricultural decisions were more likely to be made at a village meeting than at the several manorial courts, with the result that records may have survived even less well, certainly after enclosure: see J. Thirsk, 'The Common Fields', *Past and Present*, 29 (1964), p. 3.

manors a light red loam over sandstone produced better grass and would encourage complete conversion to pasture later on.[3]

The fenland manors in the north of the county also owed suit to a common court – Maxey cum membris – rather than to individual, local ones. Their mixed agriculture, dominated by sheep husbandry, relied upon the use of large commons by several parishes, and the annual communal regulation of drainage. Of all the manors discussed here, those in the forest and fen were the last to be enclosed, few of them before the first decade of the nineteenth century. They also shared the largest permanent pastures and the most generous common rights.[4]

Finally, the royal manor of Raunds lay in the Nene valley in eastern Northamptonshire, on the border with Bedfordshire. The Raunds court dealt also with business from neighbouring Ringstead and Hargrave. In contrast to the mixed agriculture of the forest and mid county manors, and to the sheep of the fen, the Nene valley supported a less mixed, more wholly arable agriculture. After enclosure it would become more pastoral.[5]

Despite the range of common-field mixed farming agricultures in these forest, plateau, fen and clay vale parishes, they regulated their pasture commons in similar ways. This was so despite the partial enclosure of Grafton Regis, despite differences in the structure of landowning and landholding, and despite the differing size of manors and numbers of suitors.[6] Instead, the variety of manors is marked by differences of emphasis on particular kinds of work, of dates at which they brought in new stints, and of rates of stocking.

Perhaps the need they shared to regulate the pastures supporting their economies was more significant than their differing agricultures. The effective regulation of common pasture was as sig-

---

[3] The following forest area manors were considered: Grafton Regis, Hartwell, Roade, Ashton, Wicken, Potterspury, Shutlanger, Stoke Bruerne and Blisworth. The manors to the west were those of Moreton Pinkney cum membris: Moreton itself, Woodend, Blakesley, Plumpton and Adston. All belonged to the honour of Grafton, together with another group centred on the court of Greens Norton, lying between them.

[4] Suitors from Helpston, Castor and Ailesworth, Etton and Marholm, Northborough, and Botelars and Thorolds attended Maxey cum membris court. For a description of the economy of early modern forest villages, see Pettit, *Royal Forests of Northamptonshire*.

[5] See Pitt, *General View ... Northampton, passim*; W. Whellan's *History, Gazetteer, and Directory of Northamptonshire* (1849).

[6] Landholding in Raunds, Maxey, Helpstone and Roade is discussed below in Chapter 8.

nificant for productivity levels as the introduction of fodder crops and the turning of tilled land back to pasture, perhaps more significant. Careful control allowed livestock numbers to grow, and, with them, the production of manure.[7] Whether fertility grew as quickly in common fields as in enclosed is not at issue here.[8] Field orders make it very clear that common-field villagers tried both to maintain the value of common of pasture and also to feed the land.

OVERSTOCKING

The practice of setting stints to limit the number of animals pastured was central to this regulation. Without stints, graziers, butchers and farmers operating with large flocks and herds could run the commons bare every year. It is a common but incorrect assumption that stints were ineffective or that large areas of common waste were unstinted altogether and so overrun,[9] but almost all the Northamptonshire manors made stinting orders early in the century, some of which were elaborations of still earlier practice. Juries made reassessments from time to time throughout the century, and in most cases abated – limited – stints even further. Exceptions to this rule were the unstinted permanent commons of Blisworth Plain, Stoke Plain and the Outgang in Maxey, though we shall see that this did not mean they were overrun.[10]

---

[7] For a longer, more detailed discussion of the wide range of regulation see Neeson, 'Common Right and Enclosure', ch. 2. On the significance of fodder in common fields see Havinden, 'Agricultural Progress'. Manure was not cost-free of course; it may be said more accurately that livestock recycled nitrogen (personal communication from Mark Overton).

[8] See D. N. McCloskey, 'The Persistence of English Common Fields', in W. N. Parker and E. L. Jones, eds., *European Peasants and their Markets* (Princeton, 1975), p. 87, and references cited therein.

[9] For example, from the eighteenth century to the present: Nourse, *Campania Foelix*, pp. 98–100; Hilman, *Tusser Redivivus, passim.*; Anon., *The True Interest of the Land Owners of Great Britain or the Husbandmen's Essay* ... [n.d., early eighteenth century], pp. 14–28; [Young], Board of Agriculture, *General Report on Enclosures*, pp. 3–8; Gonner, *Common Land*, pp. 39, 337–8; Ernle, *English Farming*, pp. 158–9, 188; A. H. Johnson, *The Disappearance of the Small Landowner* (1909; new edn with an intro. by Joan Thirsk, 1963), p. 96; C. W. Chalklin, *Seventeenth-Century Kent* (1965), p. 226; and J. V. Beckett, *The Aristocracy in England* (Oxford, 1986) p. 172, who describes common pastures as 'overstocked and poorly maintained'.

[10] Advertisements of unstinted commons appeared in the *Northampton Mercury* for Raunds, 3 Feb. 1724, for horse commons only (they were stinted five years later: see below); Silverstone in Whittlewood Forest, 19 Mar. 1764; Paulerspury, also in Whittlewood in September 1797; and Denton, 20 Mar. 1769 (for horses only). Advertisements for unstinted *cottage* common rights appeared as part of property

Introducing a stint did not change the grounds on which rights could be claimed, it merely lowered the number of animals a commoner might graze. Four Grafton manors set newly restrictive stints in 1726, 1731 and 1739. Seven, including three of these, did so again in the 1760s.[11] By the mid 1760s the general level was one sheep per acre of arable, perhaps twice as many for leys, and one cow for ten acres of arable in Blisworth, Stoke and Shutlanger. In Potterspury it was one for twenty acres.

Raunds' stints followed the same pattern of a progressive abatement over the century as those in the Grafton manors. Horse commons in the mid 1720s were unstinted.[12] The stint ordered a few years later in 1729 may have been the first of its kind. For ten acres of arable a commoner could pasture one horse, on pain of 6s 8d per default.[13] An order of 1735 relaxed the stint somewhat and favoured smaller occupiers. It allowed a horse common for the first seven acres, not ten, although only a full twenty acres brought two horse commons. The stint of cows, set at the same time, was three for the first twenty acres of arable or ley, and two for each score thereafter. Sheep stints were set at one per acre.[14] Orders made in 1740 and 1741 upheld the stints.[15] A gap in the field orders between 1741 and 1789 means that there is no way of knowing if they abated the stints during that period. Raunds commoners agreed to their last new stint in 1789.

In Maxey and the other fenland manors, stints appear more stable. It is possible that Maxey itself set new stints for sheep in 1738 and for horses and cows in 1767, but no orders of the previous stints exist with which to compare them. Certainly the common arable was stinted, and commoners also enjoyed some unstinted permanent fen common. Sheep stints varied with the value of an occupier's land, at the rate in 1738 of two for every pound paid in rent annually, or

for sale in forest and fen parishes only, thus Geddington 30 October 1790 (on Geddington Chase in Rockingham Forest); Peterborough, Dogsthorpe, Newark and Peakirk, 16 Mar. 1724 and 22 May 1790 (all rights were to the pasture of Borough Fen). The newspaper also advertised unstinted commons in other Midland counties over the century.

[11] Northants. RO, G3297a, 13 Apr., 1726; G3347a, 22 Apr. 1731; G3626c, 3 May 1764; G3624b, 26 Apr. 1764; G3618b, 25 Apr. 1765; G3626b, 3 May 1764; G3618b, n.d., 1765; also see Neeson, 'Common Right and Enclosure', pp. 89–95.

[12] *Northampton Mercury*, 3 Feb. 1724.   [13] Northants. RO, QCR 52, 1729, n.d.

[14] Northants. RO, QCR 56, 3 Oct. 1735.

[15] Northants. RO, QCR 59, 13 Dec. 1740; QCR 60, 23 Apr. 1741.

every pound value of an estate.[16] Orders stinted geese too. In 1737
those with rights in the North Fen could keep only three old brood
geese and a gander there. The jury repeated the order in 1767 with
the additional regulation that geese must wear a horn round their
necks branded with the first two letters of their owner's name and
the town brand. Whatever geese were bred from them could stay
with them – presumably while they were young. Maxey's war with
Deepingate over its stocking of geese in the fen may have already
begun in the sixties (it continued into the 1790s), hence the close
identification of parish geese.[17] First mention of the stint for great
cattle comes in 1767 when farmers could common two cows or
horses and cottagers only one.[18] Strict stinting of a formerly unstinted common in Maxey called the 'Outgang' began in 1778. Hitherto
the common had been unstinted or stinted at too generous a rate.
The result was that it was soon eaten up.[19] Now farmers could stock
four cows or horses and cottagers two. Horse commons in nearby
Helpston, unlike those in Maxey, varied according to the amount
of land held, not with the status of the occupier. Six acres of arable
or meadow brought a right for one horse in 1720 and 1722. The jury
also set sheep commons by the acre, at twenty or twenty-five for
every ten acres in the East or the North field. Leys were worth more
sheep commons than tilled land. And a cottager could put four
sheep to pasture.[20]

Stints like these imply careful regulation, and the absence of stints
implies the absence of regulation. Not surprisingly, unstinted
commons were a favourite target of the supporters of enclosure,
who described them overstocked with the beasts of poor commoners
or powerful farmers. But the absence of a stint did not mean that
common rights were unlimited or that they were free to all comers.
It meant that the level of stocking was determined by the number of

[16] Northants. RO, Fitz. Misc., vol. 746, pp. 88–9, 14 Nov. 1738, similarly Northborough and Deepingate; Northborough sheep were still stinted at this rate in
1767: Fitz. Misc. vol. 747, p. 52, 19 Feb. 1767.
[17] Northants. RO, Fitz. Misc., vol. 747, p. 49, 17 June 1736; and p. 54, 19 Feb. 1767.
Fines in 1736 stood at 5s for each goose overstocked and 6d for each gosling.
[18] Northants. RO, Fitz. Misc., vol. 747, p. 52, 19 Feb. 1767.
[19] Northants. RO, Fitz. Misc., vol. 747, p. 104, 22 Oct. 1778. It was to be laid (closed
to cattle) at New Year every year and fenced by the neighbouring farms. An order
of 1776 had set the right for an unlimited number of 'dry and milched cows',
although they could not be rotated (new cattle replacing the first put on etc.): Fitz.
Misc., vol. 747, p. 97, 28 Oct. 1776.
[20] Northants. RO, Fitz. Misc., vol. 746, p. 9, 5 Dec. 1720; and p. 24 (1722).

common rights immemorially attached to land or cottage or residency: the original, unabated level of stocking. Further qualifications could include the ability to winter animals commoned in summer (levancy and couchancy), or status as a householder or cottager. Commons in the Peterborough fen were 'unstinted' early in the century, but only residents of the manor paying scot and lot could enjoy them.[21]

Even when commons were truly *sans nombre*, without number, they were territorially limited to inhabitants of a particular parish or group of parishes: the forest manors, for example, claimed unstinted rights over forest commons but jealously defended the right against neighbouring manors, whose commoners would have liked the same access. Moreover, access to forest commons was intermittent not constant; it was interrupted by coppicing and confined to particular months of the year. At all times it was regulated by stock-taking or 'drifts': trespass and overstocking were offences in manors where rights were unstinted, just as they were in stinted manors.[22]

'Common without stint', then, did not inevitably signify commons grazed bare, or thin, malnourished animals, any more than enclosed farms inevitably signified higher grain yields. Good husbandry was not born of Act of Parliament. Commoners ran some unstinted commons bare, some commoners could not agree: at North Crawley in Buckinghamshire in the 1740s much of the parish was enclosed by agreement, but the occupiers rented small bits of the remaining common-field land to qualify for unstinted commons 'and thereby Ruin and Starve' other commoners' cattle. Nothing short of brute force, legal action, or the threat of it, would stop them, and that was unforthcoming.[23] But elsewhere it *was* forthcoming. Bucklebury commoners, suffering the same problem in 1733, looked for a legal opinion. The advice they received was that because their common was governed by the rule of levancy and couchancy they had grounds for an action. In other parishes commoners took down fences and drove their cattle through young

---

[21] Northants. RO, Church Commissioners' Records, 278573, 28 Oct. 1701; also the following year.

[22] Ashton, Roade and Hartwell enjoyed unstinted rights until the 1760s, but orders dealt with trespass etc. long before: see below pp. 145–6.

[23] A. C. Chibnall, *Beyond Sherington* (1979), p. 54; Turner, *English Parliamentary Enclosure*, p. 146.

grain in order to force the issue.[24] In still others we might reasonably guess that angry commoners used the subtle and not-so-subtle pressure of village opinion. Until enclosure they could engage in a war of attrition with a good chance of wearing down their opponents. If going to law in the eighteenth century required a long purse, breaking by-laws required a thick skin, and more.

Unstinted commons were thus not infertile *per se*, but were in fact the support of animals that manured the common fields.[25] None the less, the introduction of stints for the first time did show a new level of concern to preserve or improve the value of the common. Unstinted commons were vulnerable to approvement by the lord of manor, his taking bits of the common for his own use, leaving only what he deemed reasonable for his tenants. Introducing a stint protected the common by ensuring that it remained large enough to accommodate the number of beasts the tenants were entitled to. It also protected lesser commoners from the commercial activities of graziers and butchers. This may explain why commoners voluntarily stinted their commons, and called for regulation when lords were slow to act.[26]

The field orders of some two dozen parishes in four sets of manors in four commoning regions suggest that juries set stints quite regularly, abated them progressively, and enforced them with temporarily heavier fines. Juries reduced most stints gradually, often with the intention of preventing overstocking by occupiers of large holdings. Stocking rates differed between manors, even between adjacent manors, but most clearly between the fens and elsewhere.[27]

Every manor protected its pasture from out-parishioners' or outsiders' cattle by its laws against trespass. Equally dangerous was the taking in of animals from other manors by a commoner for a fee

[24] Berks. RO, D/EHy L5: the overstocker was a farmer, Lovelock, who rented little land in Bucklebury and much in Marlstone yet threw all his cattle on to the unstinted Bucklebury common. See pp. 100–1 above for examples of commoners deliberately provoking law suits to protect their commons.

[25] See pp. 119–20 below.

[26] On approvement and unstinted commons see Tawney, *Agrarian Problem*, pp. 250–1; Gonner, *Common Land*, pp. 101–4. On prudent levancy and couchancy in an unstinted common see: Anon., *Political Enquiry into the Consequences of Enclosing Waste Lands*, pp. 41–2; and see Thirsk, *English Peasant Farming*, p. 116, for the resurrection of levancy and couchancy following overstocking by big farmers.

[27] For four acres of ploughed land juries allowed ten sheep commons in Helpstone in the 1720s, three in Stoke Bruerne and Shutlanger in 1731, four in Raunds in 1735: see Neeson, 'Common Right and Enclosure', pp. 100, 96, 91.

(agistment); or the annual lease of unused commons (dead commons) to strangers. Agistment and the letting of commons were problems every court dealt with by setting high fines and narrow limits within which the temporary transfer of commons was acceptable. Raunds and some of the Grafton manors forbade the letting of dead commons to anyone but occupiers in the parish. They also compensated commoners for their dead commons by levying a fee per head of common stock on the other commoners. This compensated commoners not using the commons, and relieved pressure on the pasture.[28] In Stoke and Shutlanger the field tellers required notice in writing of an intention to let a common to a fellow parishioner at least three days before animals were put on the common, on penalty of 5s per horse, cow or sheep. Fen commoners in Helpston in 1720 could let the commons, but only to a maximum of ten sheep and one horse.[29]

In Maxey, field orders forbade agistment, not the letting of dead commons. In 1736 the fen reeves fined one agister 30s for taking in a number of out-parishioners' stock, and in 1767 they set the fine at 11s for each offence.[30] Agisting foreign cattle led to the danger of overstocking with diseased or very hungry sheep and cattle. It was particularly a fen problem because the fen pastures were broad and attractive, and their very size made detection difficult. For this reason field reeves offered rewards to informers and required proof of ownership when they suspected agistment.[31]

FEEDING THE PASTURE

At certain seasons commonable animals fed from the common alone. Sheep in particular were away from their owners' pens and

[28] Northants. RO, QCR 55, 26 Oct. 1733 (this order was crossed out but two years later it reappeared in more detail); QCR 56, 3 Oct. and 13 Nov. 1735; QCR 60, 23 Apr. 1741; Raunds Parish Records, Overseer's Accounts, 1789; G3626b, Grafton Regis, Roade, Ashton and Hartwell orders, 3 May 1764. Payments for unused cow commons were generous in Old, Northamptonshire, and unstocked horse commons were probably compensated at the same rate. Disbursements for both totalled several pounds most years: Northants. RO, O 102, Old Fieldsmen's Accounts, 1738–49, 1754–60, 1766.

[29] Northants. RO, G3347a, Stoke Bruerne and Shutlanger orders, 22 Apr. 1731.

[30] Northants. RO, Fitz. Misc., vol. 746, pp. 80–1, 4 Nov. 1736; vol. 747, p. 51, 19 Feb. 1767.

[31] For example, in Peterborough manor those suspected of agistment had to swear on oath that the animals commoned were their own or forfeit 6s 8d per cow or horse and 2s 6d per sheep 'for the Good of the Comon'. Informers received 5s 8d

closes for long and continuous periods, spending both day and night on the commons. What they took from it was matched by the value their manure returned to the pasture, especially when they were folded within hurdles and moved over the fields from week to week.[32] Long folds also firmed the surface of the land, trod in the manure, and killed the weeds.[33]

Well aware of their value, juries carefully regulated sheep folds. In Ashton, commoners could not take their sheep out of the fold at night and put them on other lands for the five months from late April to Michaelmas, nor might the sheep lie elsewhere unless 'it be a very Raine night'.[34] Maxey commoners kept their sheep in the North Fen and folded them there all week except on Mondays and Thursdays when they could fold them on their own land in the common fields. More frequent folding outside the fen carried a fine of 10s in 1802.[35] Juries here used folding almost exclusively for the benefit of the broad, uncultivated commons, and only partly for the benefit of the smaller common-field pastures.

Further south, on the fringe of Salcey forest, Stoke Bruerne and Shutlanger occupiers had the right to graze an unstinted number of sheep on the extensive Stoke plain as well as a stinted right of common on the fields and meadows. However, both flocks of sheep were folded on the fields at night, separately, increasing the total fold quite substantially. The flock moved around the commonable lands as flocks did on other manors, but with the advantage of larger numbers than the stinted common-field pastures could feed alone.[36] If this occurred in other manors with large unstinted

for each horse, less for sheep: Northants. RO, X5107, Peterborough Court Leet and Court Baron, 26 Oct. 1736; and see below, pp. 134–5, 136.

[32] Sir John Sinclair, *The Code of Agriculture* (5th edn, 1832), pp. 431–2. See also Northants. RO, Fitz. Misc., vol. 747, p. 192, 13 May 1802, orders concerning the sheep kept in Maxey sheep pen.

[33] Orwin and Orwin, *Open Fields*, p. 144.

[34] Northants. RO, G3317a, 25 Apr. 1731, on pain of 3s 4d. Folding often began on St George's day, 23 April; in 1754 a second order extended the common fold to the feast of St Luke on 18 October in the late autumn: G3435, 18 Oct. 1754. Folds in Norton and Potterspury lasted almost eight months, running from May Day to St Luke's, 'excepting wet nights or washed sheepe in there wool', on pain of 5s: G3380c, 28 Apr. 1724.

[35] Northants. RO, Fitz. Misc., vol. 746, p. 3, 1720; vol. 747, p. 192, 13 May 1802.

[36] Northants. RO, G3347a, 22 Apr. 1731; similar orders were made for Blisworth: G3448b, 19 June 1739. Not even this practice was unique to East Anglia: cf. B. M. S. Campbell, 'The Regional Uniqueness of English Field Systems? Some Evidence from East Norfolk', *Agricultural History Review*, 29 (1987), pp. 17–18. Feeding sheep on the Roade commons during the day and keeping them in another

commons as well as stinted common-field rights it is another reason
why unstinted common does not signify poor practice: the existence
of unstinted flocks actually *improved* the quality of pasture in the
common fields. Stinting alone was a means of protecting the
pasture, but the unstinted commons could provide the means of still
more fertility. At Potterspury the practice of folding sheep survived
enclosure, to the surprise of the Reporter to the Board of Agriculture.[37]

Earlier in this chapter, in looking at stints, we saw that commoners adopted fodder crops. Sowing fodder enabled them to keep
more livestock, more livestock meant more grain.[38] But sowing
fodder could also improve the value of common right. For both
reasons juries set particular stints for ley or greensward in all these
manors, usually a more generous stint for this kind of land than for
arable land.[39] Often they organized a general laying down of
ploughed land that had been greensward, setting and assessing fines
against offenders.[40] Courts preserved the size of balks and jointways
in the same spirit.[41] Sometimes they turned arable to pasture *pro
rata*: in 1725 the Stoke jury ordered that 'every fift acor of arable
Land in Stoake field be left unplowd til midsmer day oan the penalty
of 10s for every defalt'.[42] This also extended the length of time such

parish at night (a problem arising from agistment, or the letting of dead commons,
or from occupiers farming in more than one parish) incurred a 5s fine in 1723:
G3275, 2 Oct. 1723.

[37] The advantages of common folds are discussed in 'On Folding Sheep: Extract of a
Letter from Mr Ellman to Sir John Sinclair', *Annals of Agriculture*, 38 (1801), pp.
5–10. Pitt, *General View ... Northampton*, p. 177.

[38] If not the reason for the adoption of fodder crops, their effect on fertility must
have been clear by the first decades of the eighteenth century. On adoption of
fodder crops see Overton, 'Agricultural Revolution?'.

[39] See above, p. 114. In Stoke Bruerne two acres of ley conferred the right to
pasture five sheep whereas two of meadow allowed only two commons for sheep,
and two of 'plough land' only one: Northants. RO, G3624b, 26 Apr. 1764. See also
Blisworth G3348b, 19 June 1739; Potterspury, G3546d, 26 Apr. 1766; Ashton,
Roade, Hartwell G35426b, n.d. [1760s].

[40] In 1731 the Stoke jury ordered that all greensward in the common fields ploughed
in the past twenty years be sown with grass seed on pain of 10s: Northants. RO,
G3347a, 22 Apr. 1731. The Moreton Pinkney court confirmed a similar order in
1733: G3442, 27 Oct. 1733. In January 1724 a Ravensthorpe court put a fine of 20s
per acre on anyone not laying down old greensward ploughed in the last twenty
years; the orders were to last for twenty-one years. The manor is on the scarp
north west of Moreton Pinkney: Northants. RO, BG 177.

[41] See Ravensthorpe *ibid.*, 'for every reputed half acre land ... as much land, as shall
make a Baulk belonging to it full four foot wide in every part thereof ... '.

[42] Northants. RO, G3340a, 18 Apr. 1725.

pasture was available. In 1740 the jury repeated the order: it told everyone putting a score of sheep into the common pasture to leave one and a half acres of their fallow land unploughed until 15 May.[43] Raunds jurymen also took the direction of sowing leys into their own hands in 1740 when they ordered that the church headland – usually a cart way as well as common pasture – should be laid down for greensward with trefoil and rye grass, and that carts should in future take a new route.[44] Later in the century occupiers decided to lay down 'as ley or grass' two out of every twenty field acres; this was done expressly for 'the improvement of the sd Commons'.[45]

Encouragement for the sowing of leys was implicit in every order which set a high stint for ley lands. But the Stoke and Shutlanger jurymen elaborated the practice in 1725 by setting a generous stint (a cow or horse common to every occupier) for each acre of clover sown in the wheat field and left uncultivated for several years.[46] In 1764 they set the stint at five sheep per acre of clover. The land would lie unploughed for three years:

> In Case any person in Either of ye parishes Chuse to Sow one Acre More or Less with Clover in their Wheat or Barley Crop to lie in pasture in ye Bean Field Year and Not to be plowed up in ye Fallow Year till their is a break in Either of ye Corn Fields to keep 5 sheep.[47]

Helpston jurymen directed that occupiers sow every tenth land in the fallow field with clover at the rate of 14 lbs of seed to the acre in 1797; those holding less than a land were to sow in proportion.[48] In this way commoners further protected the stock of common pasture.

Sowing fallows was a familiar practice on the Grafton and Raunds manors, and it was productive of better pasture as well as fodder crops. But while the temporarily enclosed fallow land was taken out of common use its occupier's rights were abated.[49] Whenever commoners took land out of the fallow for vetches or

[43] Northants. RO, G3493a, 17 Apr. 1740; those who pastured more sheep, or fewer, were instructed to leave their lands unploughed in proportion to their commons.
[44] Northants. RO, QCR 59, 11 Dec. 1740. Also QCR 60, fallow orders, April 1741.
[45] Northants. RO, Raunds Parish Records, Overseers' Accounts, 1789.
[46] Northants. RO, G3340a, 8 Apr. 1725.
[47] Northants. RO, G3624b, 26 Apr. 1764.
[48] Northants. RO, Fitz. Misc., vol. 747, p. 171, 10 Apr. 1797.
[49] M. A. Havinden remarks on this lowering of stints on sainfoin leys sown in the township of Spelsbury near Woodstock: 'Agricultural Progress', p. 76.

turnips the fieldsmen enforced a lower stint until the land returned to the common stock. When it was common again the occupier enjoyed a higher stint, unless grazing it privately.[50] Similarly, the jury of the fen manor of Longthorpe ordered a separate stint for leys and an abatement when they were taken out of the common pasture: all common-field land sown with cinque foil within the previous seven years could be stocked at the rate of two sheep per acre, providing 'the same be not eaten or Stocked with Sheep from the time that the Same is Mowed until 10 Days after Harvest is in or else to Stocke but one Sheep for an Acre as Ley ground'.[51] Other courts made similar orders.[52] Helpstone jury allowed occupiers of fallow land to enclose it temporarily for clover on condition of sowing one half acre for the benefit of the community for every acre they sowed for themselves.[53] Jurymen in general seem to have recognized the spiralling value of land sown with clover. Where farmers were willing to share it they were rewarded with extra commons, where they were not their withdrawal of fallow from the common stock was matched by a reduction in their rights.

DRAINAGE, DISEASE AND BREEDING

Flexible stints, the supervision of letting common rights or the agisting of cattle and sheep, the organization of sheep folds, and the incorporation of fodder crops all protected or improved the common pastures. Other operations were more routine, but, like them, they were concerned with the communal upkeep of the pastures. Among many such practices were those surrounding drainage, disease and breeding.

Annual orders to scour ditches and drains leading to ponds and rivers show that these common-field parishes drained their field pastures.[54] Clearing existing drains could be done by occupiers of

---

[50] Potterspury, Grafton Regis, and Ashton, Roade and Hartwell all ordered such abatements: Northants. RO, G3626c, 3 May 1764.

[51] Northants. RO, Church Commissioners' Records, 278573, Longthorpe field orders, 22 Oct. 1701; cinque foil was stinted as meadow.

[52] Northants. RO, G3618b, n.d., 1765 (Ashton, Roade and Hartwell); G3546d, 26 Apr. 1766 (Potterspury); Raunds Parish Records, Overseers' Accounts, 1789 – one sheep was abated for every acre of turnips sown; Fitz. Misc., vol. 747, p. 171, Helpstone orders, 10 Apr. 1797 – four sheep per acre taken in were to be abated.

[53] Northants. RO, Fitz. Misc., vol. 747, p. 186, 18 June 1799.

[54] One instance from many such orders is from the fenland parish of Longthorpe, where the common drain from Burton's Gap to the river and another from 'Mr

the land through which they ran at no cost, but digging new trenches and establishing new water-courses needed more elaborate tools and hired labour. Aynho commoners raised £9 9s 10d with a levy of 6d per cow common and 6d per thirty-two sheep commons to cover the cost of draining part of the Cherwell in 1737.[55] Fieldsmen in Old in 1756 spent almost a quarter of the year's labour bill for keeping up the field drains and wells.[56] Some parishes bought their own draining ploughs, covering the three guineas cost with a levy.[57] In all, there was greater control over a neighbour's ditches and drains before than after enclosure.[58] Arguments could be settled with the field officers in what may have been a speedier, more equitable way.

Proper drainage helped ensure healthy stock. But common flocks and herds were at risk from more than wet land. The dangers of disease and indiscriminate breeding are large subjects, and enquiry into them is complicated greatly by the passage of two centuries. The incidence, epidemiology, and even the names of many eighteenth-century animal diseases are uncertain. It is none the less clear that breeding and disease – sheep rot and cattle plague in particular – were common concerns for juries and fieldsmen in eighteenth-century villages.

Nevertheless, Reporters to the Board of Agriculture, and other supporters of enclosure in the eighteenth century and earlier, criticized the condition of common flocks and herds, and their criticisms have been echoed by twentieth-century historians. Besides alleging

Baxter's Orchard' to the pond were ordered to be scoured and repaired in October 1705. The fieldsmen could levy a fine of 1s per yard of unrepaired drain from the occupiers of land adjacent to the drains who did not do their duty. The order described the fine as a 'usual' one; it was to go to the Lord of the Manor: Northants. RO, Church Commissioners' Records, 278573, 16 Oct. 1705. Clear drains in fenland were crucial, but not only there: see Stoke Bruerne orders, G3341e, 16 Oct. 1725; Moreton Pinkney orders, G3422, 27 Oct. 1733. Most orders included exact directions about scouring. See also O 102, Old fieldsmen's accounts: here drainage was a constant preoccupation in the middle of the century.

[55] Northants. RO, C (A), 2828, 'A Levy for Scouring ye Charwell in Oxhey 1737'; another levy for a drainage plough was made at Hemingford Abbots in 1704: see Cambs. RO (Hunts. Office), 2537/9.

[56] Northants. RO, O 102, Old fieldsmen's accounts, 1756.

[57] J. Mordaunt, *The Complete Steward* (1761), quoted by W. E. Tate, 'Enclosure Movements in Northamptonshire', pp. 28–9; the Hemingford Abbots jury ordered a levy in 1707 of 2s 6d per score of arable acres to provide a horse for the town plough and draining ploughs: Cambs. RO (Hunts. Office), Hemingford Abbots Vestry book, 2537/9.

[58] See Scrutton, *Commons and Common Fields*, p. 117.

malnourishment, both have argued that common pasture led to promiscuous breeding and the spread of disease. They single out sheep rot in particular, but they leave a more general impression that the unregulated mixing of animals in large common pastures caused contagion and made control difficult – if it was attempted at all. In contrast, in enclosures, said Arthur Young, 'There is a much better chance of escaping the distempers to which cattle of all kinds are liable from being mixed with those infected, particularly the scab in sheep.'[59]

Their criticism depends on two relatively unexamined assumptions: first, that little intelligent attempt was made to control animal diseases in common pastures; second, that most if not all diseases were transmitted by animals in close proximity, and that therefore post-enclosure separation of herds must have contained infection. Neither of these assumptions appears to be well founded.[60]

First, juries used by-laws and fines to prevent the spread of disease. They did everything they could to prevent contagion – which they believed, as much as did enclosers, was the origin of all infection. In the case of horses, by-laws supplemented statute. Horses were particularly likely to bring infection into a parish simply because they moved beyond the parish borders more often than other animals. Fines for grazing mangy horses were high, and in Peterborough if an animal escaped detection by the fen reeves anyone could drive it off the common and claim the reeves' half of the fine.[61] In Withern with Woodthorpe the owners of sheep 'not

---

[59] On sheep rot as an open-field disease see seventeenth- and eighteenth-century assertions cited in Gonner, *Common Land*, pp. 339–40; Ernle, *English Farming*, p. 150; Chambers and Mingay, *Agricultural Revolution*, p. 49. The historians' case that common pastures encouraged and spread disease is made by (among others) Robert Trow-Smith, *A History of British Livestock Husbandry 1700–1900* (1959), p. 186, and Chambers and Mingay, *Agricultural Revolution*, p. 49. Neither cite any evidence. Gordon Philpot argues that animal disease on open waste, when transmitted to people, accounted for high mortality and low fertility between 1650 and 1750: 'Enclosure and Population Growth'; Young, *General View ... Oxfordshire*, p. 100. On forest pasture, J. Donaldson, *General View of the Agriculture of the County of Northampton* (Edinburgh, 1794), pp. 39–40; on cottagers' cows on commons, Godber, *History of Bedfordshire*, p. 363.

[60] I am preparing an extended version of the argument of the following pages.

[61] Northants. RO, G3283b, 13 Apr. 1726, Hartwell orders; see also Moreton Pinkney presentments, G3428a, 2 Oct. 1731; X5107, Peterborough Court Baron and Court Leet. Helpstone set the same fine for commoning a 'Glander'd Mangy or Farcion' horse in 1722, Fitz. Misc., vol. 746, 1722. Putting 'scabbed' horses, or horses with mange, into common or common fields was prohibited by an Act of 32 Hen. VIII, c.13, 'which offence shall be inquirable in the leet, as other common

perfectly clear' of the scab were fined, and the sheep quarantined.[62] In Roade the jury ordered hogs away from the horse pool when they were over ten weeks old, to keep the water clean. Washing them in the pool brought a fine of 2s 6d.[63] Juries saw dead animals as sources of contamination too: a Peterborough by-law ordered commoners to carry away the carcasses of animals dying on the fen within two days of their death, and to pay a charge of a shilling per carcass.[64]

Fines and presentments were one means of limiting contagion in common herds and flocks; another, paradoxically, was the very practice of keeping animals in common herds. Paid herdsmen and women almost constantly supervised common cattle and sheep.[65] They collected the cattle each morning from their closes and pens and drove them to the pasture together. Shepherds supervised flocks all day, and during the night too, sometimes folding the sheep within hurdles, where they were easier to watch. It was still possible to graze a diseased animal on the partially supervised pastures where horses or cows could be tethered, but for very short periods; and when there they were in contact with only small numbers of other animals, not the whole herd. Even then, with so much at stake, the vigilance of other owners of common-pasture beasts must have equalled or exceeded that of any officer. Infection was everybody's business, and detection was made easier by the very public assembly, movement and supervision of common flocks and herds.

In other measures, most parishes forbade the agistment of out-

annoyances be': see R. Burn, *The Justice of the Peace and Parish Officer* (14th edn, 1780), p. 501.

[62] Lincs. RO, Withern with Woodthorpe by-laws, 30 Mar. 1792. The by-law preceded an Act passed in 1798 to encourage the detection of scabby and mangy sheep on commons, 38 George III, c.65. The Act, brought by Sir William Lemon, provided that, on the evidence of an informer, a Justice of the Peace could order infected sheep pastured communally to be impounded and their owners punished. The rationale for the Act was that the incidence of 'contagious disease' was growing: see *House of Commons Sessional Papers of the Eighteenth Century*, ed. Sheila Lambert (Wilmington, 1975) Bills, 1797–8, vol. 116, p. 249. The Bill was presented to the House of Commons in April 1798, *Jls House of Commons*, 23 Apr. 1798, p. 482.

[63] Northants. RO, Church Commissioners' Records, 278573, Peterborough Court, 27 Oct. 1708; also 20 Apr. 1704; 10 Sept. 1704; 16 Apr. 1706. An order made for Longthorpe manor at the court baron in 1708 gave 5s of a fine set for grazing a 'stoned or mangey horse' to the fen reeves and 6d to the Lord of the Manor.

[64] Northants. RO, X5107, Peterborough Court Baron and Court Leet, 20 Oct. 1742.

[65] See below, pp. 134–8. Atherstone and Maulden employed herdswomen: Warwicks. RO, CR 128/7, Oct. 1719; Beds. RO, R box 147, 1630.

parishioners' cattle.[66] Nothing could prevent occupiers taking them into their closes for profit – but this was a post-enclosure as well as a common-field problem. There remained the problem of cattle moving through a village, or cattle staying in a village overnight on their way to market. Clearly the danger was greatest in parishes on trade routes, especially those with rich uncultivated commons outside the village, good festering grounds for an epidemic like cattle plague. But even along the drove routes it was possible to employ people to be on the lookout for strangers' cattle, and to insist on the separation of out-parish and local livestock. A frequent order forbade the substitution of one animal for another once it had been put on the pasture: newly purchased beasts could not replace older ones. All the manors resisted this use of commons as 'running commons' – pastures opened to limited numbers, but allowing replacement. The reason juries usually gave for this order was that new beasts ate more than their share.[67] But newly bought animals might also bring infection, and their exclusion from the commons helped control disease. Late in the sixteenth century in the Lincolnshire fens, commoners lay the blame for the introduction of disease on foreign cattle brought into the parishes in droves and pastured there by the manorial lords. Two disputes at Frampton in 1575 and Burton Coggles in 1580 were resolved by the lord either agreeing to end the practice for a few years or by the landholders agreeing to make him a separate grazing ground in return for the extinction of his common rights everywhere else.[68] Finally, animals bought in the spring stood little chance of immediate access to the common pasture anyway because most of it became available only after harvest, by which time the symptoms of many diseases would have appeared. In all these ways commoning parishes minimized the risk of infection brought in from outside. Common-field juries policed the risk of contagion with as much attention to detail as any farmer watching his herds and flocks after enclosure.

The field orders show juries taking the risk of contagion in common pastures very seriously. Within the limits of current knowledge they did what they should.

The second largely unexamined assumption of enclosers and historians is that post-enclosure separation of herds and flocks limited outbreaks of disease by reducing or preventing transmission.

---

[66] See pp. 91–2, 117–18.   [67] Northants. RO, G3626b, 3 May 1764.
[68] See Thirsk, *English Peasant Farming*, p. 38.

Perhaps the most important point to make is that the limited understanding of how many diseases spread made prevention difficult both before and after enclosure. In 1769, after more than twenty years of cattle plague in Europe, Salomon de Monchy noted the inability of most farmers to understand that infection could spread in any number of ways, on clothes for example:

> They have not, as I know, by experience, the least idea of the extreme subtilty of this pestilential *virus*, because it is not perceptible by their senses. They cannot comprehend, and therefore will not believe, that these infectious particles can adhere to their cloaths ... Thus either through ignorance, or downright enthusiasm, they make no scruple to visit their neighbours, where the infection appears, or even rages, and to go into the cow-houses ...[69]

Late eighteenth-century farmers did not know that cattle plague spread in any way other than simple contagion. Like Arthur Young, they believed or hoped that isolating or destroying infected animals was enough. But disease in animals is produced by a wide range of organisms, and spread by many different means, of which contagion – direct contact with an infected host – is only one.

The epidemiology of some of the major eighteenth-century animal diseases shows the extent of the problem of containing them. Brucellosis ('contagious abortion', although the term may also have been applied to leptospirosis) is spread by infected dung, but also by infected bulls in sexual contact, on food, by human contact, and in water. Clearly most of these sources of infection were not affected by separation into herds after enclosure; and the long incubation period of the disease (30–60 days, and up to six months in some cases) made it very difficult to prevent the introduction of diseased animals into uncontaminated herds either before *or* after

[69] S. de Monchy, *Remarks upon the Mortality among the Horned Cattle* (Rotterdam, 1769; trans. London, 1770), pp. 26–7; for the limited understanding of the infectious nature of disease from the mid eighteenth century until the 1840s see N. Goddard, 'Agricultural Literature and Societies', in Mingay, ed., *Agrarian History of England and Wales 1750–1850*, VI (Cambridge, 1989), p. 361. Despite this, farmers fumigated their clothes when their own beasts died from rinderpest in the 1711–14 outbreak: see Bonser, *Drovers*, p. 95. Sophisticated government interference policed the contagious spread of the disease in the early and mid eighteenth century: see J. Broad, 'Cattle Plague in Eighteenth-Century England', *Agricultural History Review*, 31 (1983).

enclosure.[70] Leptospirosis, with symptoms similar to brucellosis, is spread not only through contact with urine in damp earth, but very often through contaminated watercourses, and can also be spread by other animals, notably rodents, which serve as intermediary hosts.[71] Again, the fences of enclosed farms could not eliminate transmission.

Rinderpest, the devastating cattle plague of the mid eighteenth century, and a continuing scourge until the 1870s, may find hosts in wild animals, which then serve as reservoirs of the disease.[72] This disease – deadlier than foot and mouth – is spread by a virus which may be carried in offal, skins, meat, manure, grooming tools, food, blankets, water and so on. Sources of infections are wherever diseased cattle have been, thus markets, pens, and the very roads of the drove routes themselves were as dangerous as any common pasture – or any enclosed one.[73]

Scrapie in sheep presents one of the problems of brucellosis: a very long incubation period (nineteen months to three years) which makes it difficult to exclude from any flocks, private or common, without excluding all new animals. Certainly scrapie can be spread through shared contaminated pasture, but it is transmitted also by lambs infected before birth.[74] A similar threat is presented by the spores of blackleg, another common eighteenth-century disease, which can lie dormant in pastures for up to eleven years.[75] The difficulties of control even in an enclosed agricultural area are great. Where the vector of the disease is a tick, as in the case of redwater (bacillary hemoglobinuria), enclosure may have helped reduce the incidence if it led to the clearing of scrub and heath: habitats of the kind necessary to the tick, which does not survive in clean pastures.[76] But, again, this is not a disease affected by fencing of herds;

[70] B. Halpin, *Patterns of Animal Disease* (1975), pp. 1, 13, 57; Trow-Smith, *British Livestock Husbandry*, pp. 187–8; G. W. Stamm, *Veterinary Guide for Farmers*, ed. R. C. Klussendorf (New York, 1975), p. 170.
[71] Halpin, *Patterns*, pp. 7, 95.
[72] Halpin, *Patterns*, pp. 1, 5, 135; Trow-Smith, *British Livestock Husbandry*, pp. 34, 186–7, 317–18.
[73] W. C. Miller and G. P. West, *Black's Veterinary Dictionary* (10th edn, 1972), pp. 180–3. The spread of the disease by water suggests how little respect cattle plague had for fences.
[74] Halpin, *Patterns*, pp. 7, 117; Stamm, *Veterinary Guide*, p. 323.
[75] Stamm, *Veterinary Guide*, p. 139; Trow-Smith, *British Livestock Husbandry*, p. 187.
[76] Trow-Smith, *British Livestock Husbandry*, p. 188; Halpin, *Patterns*, p. 110.

and the assumption that common pastures were necessarily unkempt is not correct.[77]

Bloat, another major ailment of eighteenth-century livestock could not have been affected by enclosure because it was not communicable. It was caused by over-rich grazing. Another, sheep rot, associated with the liver-fluke and wet ground, like redwater depended on the state of the pasture and also on the weather.[78] The association was known (though not the mechanism); commoners took their sheep off wet commons and juries watched drains and ditches, using orders and fines to keep them scoured and the water flowing.[79] They did this as well as any enclosers who followed them, for we know that post-enclosure improvements in drainage came fifty years after most enclosures were complete.[80] In at least one respect common grazing was safer than enclosed because many parishes had both high and low pastures and could move their flocks between them as they saw fit; after enclosure fewer individual farmers had this advantage.[81]

Sheep rot may serve to re-emphasize this general point: that the vectors, reservoirs, hosts, incubation periods, and other character-istics of both vector-borne and environmentally caused diseases differ greatly, and call into serious doubt the simple assertion that the direct contact of animals in common pastures made livestock there more diseased than livestock in enclosed pastures. Contagion was not the only source of infection. Even the movement of cattle along local roads at different times of the day exposed one herd to the infections of another, and it did so as much *after* enclosure as before.

Moreover, enclosure had no effect on the most serious source of epidemic infection – the marketplace. Unless all the parish sheep

[77] Fuel harvests cleared them annually: see Chapter 6.

[78] Halpin, *Patterns*, p. 109; the weather also affected the spread of cattle plague – drought encouraged it: see P. J. Bowden, 'Agricultural Prices, Wages, Farm Profits and Rents', in J. Thirsk, ed., *Agrarian History of England and Wales*, V, part II (Cambridge, 1985), p. 51.

[79] In the wet 1730s, Flecknoe shepherds 'would upon any Shower more than ordinary take their Sheep away again for fear of Rotting them and so the Land lay unfolded in manure': Warwicks. RO, Z 12/1a, 2a; and HR 35/7. Sinclair, *Code of Agriculture*, pp. 183, 194.

[80] Edward Harrison, 'An Inquiry into the Nature of the Soil, and the Circumstances which Induce and Prevent the Rot', *Annals of Agriculture*, 40 (1803), p. 546; Mingay, *Agrarian History*, VI, pp. 599, 641, 941.

[81] E.g. West Haddon and Long Buckby: Morton, *Natural History*, pp. 9–10.

and cattle were kept for subsistence alone, and were conceived, born, raised, bred and slaughtered without travelling outside the parish fields, markets were a constant source of disease, and they were at least equally potent after enclosure. Markets continued to act as a source of infection, and continued to be the main source of epidemics.[82]

The irrelevance of enclosure is also suggested by the fact that its chronology and that of the great diminution of animal disease differ. Endemic diseases, and great pandemics like foot and mouth, rinderpest, and pleuro-pneumonia, decimated British livestock through the nineteenth century, long after the enclosure of virtually all common fields and most wastes. Between one and two million sheep were lost to sheep rot in the wet winter of 1830–1.[83] Imported animals were the source of several epidemics, and imports rose most rapidly after 1846. Rinderpest, brought by Russian cattle to Hull in 1865, had caused the death or slaughter of almost half a million cattle by 1867.[84] The agencies which ultimately brought control were new veterinary techniques and rigorous enforcement of stringent rules for the destruction of beasts affected by the most serious, highly infectious diseases.[85] The fences and hedges which the enclosers claimed would curb disease did little to halt the spread of the most destructive pandemics of the nineteenth century. In the twentieth century the most recent outbreaks of foot and mouth disease in England in 1967 were widely spread by the wind.[86]

But one indirect way in which common pastures may have weakened animals, and so exposed them to disease, or diminished their value in other ways, remains to be discussed: the cumulative effect of allegedly unscientific (or wholly uncontrolled) breeding.

Like the spread of disease, the 'impossibility' of improving animals on common pastures by selective breeding was contempo-

[82] The 1839–41 outbreak of foot and mouth disease began in the dairies serving London; thanks in part to government inaction, it spread to the rest of England in the space of a few months: Goddard, 'Agricultural Literature and Societies', pp. 359–60.

[83] T. S. Cobbold, *Entozoa* (1864), p. 171.   [84] Bonser, *Drovers*, p. 98.

[85] Trow-Smith, *British Livestock Husbandry*, p. 186; on destruction: John Broad, 'Cattle Plague in Eighteenth-Century England', *Agricultural History Review*, 31 (1983).

[86] Halpin, *Patterns*, pp. 61–8; N. St G. Hyslop, 'Observations on Pathogenic Organisms in the Airborne State', *Tropical Animal Health and Production*, 4:1 (1972), pp. 28–40, which also notes that rinderpest may be spread in aerosols over short distances.

rary belief and has become the received wisdom of some agrarian history. But, in Northamptonshire, the Raunds court, the Grafton juries and the fenland manors all closely controlled breeding. Bulls did not run free. Nor was selective breeding impossible, for rams and bulls were allowed on to the common only at stated times, so a farmer could take his animals off, or breed them previously. Statute law excluded undersized horses capable of breeding from common pasture, by-laws reinforced it and kept off ridgel sheep and lambs too.[87]

In Raunds two or three bulls were provided for the commoners' cattle every year by the owners of particular lands. The three responsible in 1716 were so on pain of ten shillings. In 1740 only two were responsible and the fine had doubled. In the same year the fieldsmen presented one farmer for failing to provide a bull and boar that year, and again two years later, and they presented another for charging a fee for the bull he was supposed to provide free.[88] Later in the century, in 1789, as part of a new agreement, the jury ordered that proper bulls must be provided and 'kept with the herds', not in farmers' yards.[89] Moreton Pinkney commoners made a levy of 2d per common to pay for common bulls in 1737.[90] The forest manors of the Duke of Grafton alone seem to have made no orders concerning common bulls or breeding cattle, perhaps because sheep husbandry was more important. Further east, Moreton Pinkney's jury regulated both the provision of bulls and the entry and exit on to pasture of rams and ridgel sheep.[91] Fenland manors also con-

[87] Putting stoned horses 'above the age of two years, not being 15 hands high' on commons was an offence in most counties under the Act of 32 Hen. VIII c.13; in other counties (notably the south west and the north) the limit was 14 hands: see Burn, *Justice of the Peace* (14th edn, 1780), II, p. 500. A ridgel sheep was an ungelded male sheep with only one descended testicle, and as such was capable of inseminating ewes: see Trow-Smith, *British Livestock Husbandry*, p. 241. Any ungelded male animal could be a ridgel.

[88] Northants. RO, QCR 46, Oct. 1716; QCR 59, 13 Dec. 1740; QCR 60, 23 Apr. 1741 (an order setting out who was to supply the bulls for that year); QCR 41, 15 May and 1 June 1742, the culprit was Robert Ekins. In many manors provision of a bull and boar was an obligation placed on manorial lords or rectors from which they were freed at enclosure by a clause in the Act.

[89] Northants. RO, Raunds Overseers' Accounts, 1789, p. 3. Parish bulls were a feature of medieval agriculture: see Trow-Smith, *British Livestock Husbandry*, p. 125.

[90] The levy was due within a month of the court's sitting, on pain of 1s for each default: Northants. RO, G3423, 23 May 1737.

[91] Northants. RO, G3419a, 14 May 1731. 'Item we order yt all Rams and Rigels be kept out of the Common fields from the 1st Day of September now next ensuing untill a full fortnight after St. Michael & we order yt no Rigel go in till St. Andrew on penalty of 5s each defaultant': Northants. RO, G3420a, 18 Apr. 1732.

trolled breeding: in Helpston any rams kept by the commoners in the season should be worth at least 20s, and at no time should a ridgel sheep be worth less.[92] In 1704 the Longthorpe jury kept ridgel sheep off the common altogether.[93] Fen parishes also regulated cattle breeding. The jury at Castor and Ailesworth, for example, ordered the 'tithmen' to keep two bulls for each parish in the common pasture in 1725. They allowed other bulls into the common only after the harvest.[94] As in Raunds, commoners in Maxey bred their cows on bulls kept by local farmers as an encumbrance on their lands.[95]

Commoners had the choice – in Raunds, the fenland manors, and in the non-forest Grafton manors – of using the bulls provided by levy, or by certain farmers, or of breeding their cows away from the common with bulls they hired or owned themselves. Poorer commoners might choose the former as the only way open to them, but more substantial commoners who owned a number of cows could do as they pleased. On the common pastures breeding was closely controlled. Juries allowed bulls and rams on to commons only at specific times, and they timed their entry in order to give notice of their arrival. They carefully regulated or forbade entry on to the commons of inferior animals capable of inseminating sheep, cows or horses. In principle, the risk of unplanned breeding was no greater than on enclosed land. Parish bulls – whether provided by farmers, rectors and manorial lords or hired by subscription – may have been inferior, aged and ailing, but there are no complaints to this effect anywhere in the dealings of the courts. Whether they were, or were not, farmers wishing to breed better stock could do so, and still enjoy their common of pasture. Breeding organized with this care cannot be called 'promiscuous'.

Field orders suggest that juries made every effort to keep common pastures in good heart. They set stints, they encouraged fodder crops on fallows, they resisted the uncompensated or damaging loss of common pasture. This seems to have been true also with respect to the known dangers of disease. It would be strange to find it otherwise. The critics' image of scabby and pitiful beasts, uncared

[92] Northants. RO, Fitz. Misc., vol. 746, 1722.
[93] Northants. RO, Church Commissioners' Records, 278573, 22 Oct. 1701; 21 Apr. 1704; April 1708.
[94] Northants. RO, Fitz. Misc., vol. 746, 14 Nov. 1725.
[95] Northants. RO, Fitz. Misc., vol. 746, p. 60, 1731.

for and promiscuously herded together, does not accord with the deep concern for property so clear in the regulation of all common rights in these parishes. In fact it is hard to imagine how common-field agriculture could continue production without a system of rules like the field orders. The upkeep of common pasture in particular was the central concern of these orders. Common pastures defined the common-field system. For many commoners they were crucial resources. As such they were protected.

5. *Enforcing the orders*

There were dangers to common pasture and the common stock that orders alone could not avert. Mere rules could be ignored, and it may have been in the interest of some commoners that they should be. Encroachment, half-year land, piecemeal enclosure and approvement could spark local conflict. Higher fines put on new stinting agreements for the first few years suggest that not everyone wanted to abate their commons. In these instances orders needed the strength of effective enforcement. If they were broken, the appropriate fines had to be imposed and collected. Enforcement was crucial.

To some extent the very constancy of regulation – the regular meetings of courts, the introduction and progressive lowering of stints, the adoption of ways to improve pasture – suggests a live system, not a dead one. This impression is strengthened when we look at the structure of enforcement. Field orders were made effective in two ways. First: by organizing common grazing to make orders difficult to break. With this in mind juries ordered drifts, brands, common herds, cowkeepers, shepherds, and tether-grazing. Second: by ensuring detection, if, despite the organization of grazing, by-laws were broken. So juries appointed field officers, tried offenders and imposed fines.

ORGANIZATION

Of all the threats to the value of pasture, overstocking and trespass were probably the worst. They were most difficult to detect in fen and forest pastures. In the manor of Peterborough, for example, the agistment of out-parish stock was the major cause of trespass.[1] In

---

[1] The manor included part of the town but also stretched north to embrace large fen pastures. Records of drifts survive for the 1730s, 1740s and 1750s.

smaller pastures foreign stock would stand out from the common flock or herd. For this reason Peterborough, and other parishes with large commons, staged periodic 'drifts'. During a drift the field officers drove all grazing animals out of the widespread common pastures, herded them together, and counted them to detect interlopers and fine their owners. At the same time they raised a levy on every head of stock to pay for the upkeep of the fields and commons. The reeves drove the pastures for great cattle and sheep, and for pigs too. Drifts were major undertakings for which extra men were employed, and horses hired; and they were relatively expensive.[2] In some years juries made only one drift for each kind of animal, in others more for one than another, and in some years they drove each off the commons several times.[3]

In the Grafton manors enforcing the stint began even before the pastures opened. In 1740 the jury ordered Stoke Bruerne and Shutlanger commoners to give the field tellers written notice of which cattle they intended to put in Stoke Meadow, and then brand them.[4] Two years later it forbade the driving of cattle into the meadow by any route other than the common highway, on pain of 5s for each offence.[5] Branding the cattle was a precaution taken in the Whittlebury shack field after harvest.[6] In 1764, when commoners stinted the pastures of Ashton, Roade and Hartwell, the jury made a new order in the same vein as those made earlier in Stoke and Shutlanger: commoners must tell the field tellers of each of the three towns whether they intended to stock a horse or a cow for each

---

[2] They cost Peterborough commoners a quarter of the whole fieldkeeping bill of £8 6s 2d in 1737: Northants. RO X5107, 'The Fenn Reves Dr to Thos Watkinshon', Nov. 1737 to Oct. 1738. In 1736 the cost of drifts exceeded the revenue from drifts and other levies. But the successful capture of agisted animals could produce useful revenue: Peterborough fines for agisted horses stood at 16s 4d each, for cow at 6s 8d, and for pigs at 3s 4d; informers got 5s for a horse, less for cows and pigs: Northants. RO, X5106, 26 Oct. 1736.

[3] Northants. RO, X5106. At Atherstone in Warwickshire the field officers drove the commons every three weeks in the 1705–6 season; in 1719 the court set a 10s fine for failure to do this; drifts occurred every month in Astley in the 1720s; Warwicks. RO CR 128/4; CR 764/1.

[4] Northants. RO G3493a, 17 Apr. 1740.

[5] Anyone found laying planks or bridges across the ditches and into the meadow in order to drive cattle in covertly became liable to a fine of 10s: Northants. RO, G3494a, 14 Oct. 1742.

[6] If commoners let these valuable post-crop common-pasture rights, whoever hired the common must do the branding or clipping, although the penalty for neglect still lay with the commoner: Northants. RO, G3621h, 30 Apr. 1764.

common; and, once made, the decision could not be changed in the course of the following year.[7]

Town brands, which the tellers used to distinguish local from out-parish animals, were also a feature of forest manors or of manors sharing or disputing a common. They made it possible to identify animals at a glance and difficult to introduce beasts belonging to outsiders, for a few days' feed. Fen parishes used brands as well as drifts. In an attempt to curtail agistment in 1767, Maxey jury warned commoners against using their personal brands on foreign cattle.[8] Earlier regulations ordered the branding of geese going into the North Fen.[9] Inter-parish disputes over fen geese illustrate the difficulty faced by manors with very large permanent commons. In 1767 and 1780, Maxey commoners complained of the illegal depasture of geese from Deepingate, James Deeping, and Market Deeping. These parishes circumvented branding orders by employing men to 'attend and watch' their geese, and give the alarm at the approach of Maxey fieldsmen.[10] Fen pastures were big enough to allow neighbours to remove their stock before they could be impounded. Branding was most effective in detecting overstocking and agistment committed within the manor by its own inhabitants. Large fen pastures were better served by the vigilance of field officers, and by frequent drifts.

An additional safeguard surrounded the common cattle of parishes with smaller pastures like Moreton Pinkney, Stoke Bruerne and Shutlanger, and Raunds: a town cowherd supervised all the common cattle, gathered together in one herd. In Moreton commoners could not put their cows out 'after the Heard brings them home at night till the Heard is ready to looke after them in the morning'.[11] Because the cowherd stayed with the herd all day, watching it and monitoring the entry and exit of the cattle to the pasture, it was difficult to put on illegal cattle, or to graze some cattle in the morning and replace them in the afternoon with another set of cattle of the same number – thus feeding very hungry cattle both morning and afternoon. Cowherds were also some

---

[7] Northants. RO, G3626b, 3 May 1764.
[8] Northants. RO, Fitz. Misc., vol. 747, p. 51, 19 Feb. 1767.
[9] Northants. RO, Fitz. Misc., vol. 746, p. 78, 17 June 1736.
[10] The court threatened prosecution on further information: Northants. RO, Fitz. Misc., vol. 747, 12 Oct. 1780.
[11] Northants. RO, G3362a, 5 Apr. 1725.

protection against cattle straying into the neighbouring corn fields; they could alert the pinder to overstocking or trespass. We have seen that they could exclude diseased animals; they could also enforce the knobbing of cows' horns – which otherwise damaged the bark of trees, other animals, and even the surface of the pasture. The Stoke Bruerne and Shutlanger cowherds were specially charged to look out for unknobbed cows going with the herd.[12] There were two herds in Raunds in 1789, and private herds ('by-herds') were tolerated only when formed for the purpose of moving cows to private pastures, but to them alone.[13]

Within the common fields lay balks, headlands, uncultivated corners and slades used as pasture at certain seasons, for although the crops were growing in these fields the strips of grass could be grazed with care.[14] But tether-grazing could lead to trespass if animals broke free or were let into the young grain intentionally. To avoid this the Grafton courts set times of the year at which commoners might use balks and headlands, and they limited the length of tethers with which cattle were flit. At Ashton in 1754 the jury kept cattle off the narrow balks altogether and field officers could impound beasts found tethered on balks less than four feet wide until their owners paid a fine of 4d. Commoners might graze great cattle in Roade in the grass of the meadow and the sward of the South field only between 1 November and 21 December, and only if they were attended by a keeper to keep them off the tilled lands.[15] Although copious orders setting out the width of balks and joint-ways survive for Raunds manor, a 1789 order forbidding the tethering of horses on balks during the harvest is the only regulation of tether-grazing that survives.[16] The Maxey court introduced supervisory regulations late in the century in 1799, when it ordered that horses and cattle on the green or in the streets must be attended, except during harvest, but no orders regulating balk grazing seem to have been made.[17] It is possible that the court forbade it, as the Laxton court had, but more likely the availability of fen pasture

---

[12] The horns of cows were sawn off and then tipped or 'knobbed' with wood: see Neeson, 'Common Right and Enclosure', pp. 135–7; Northants. RO, G3347a, 22 Apr. 1731.
[13] Northants. RO, Raunds Overseers' Accounts, 1789, p. 3.
[14] See above p. 95.
[15] Northants. RO, G3293a, 24 Oct. 1726.
[16] Northants. RO, Raunds Overseers' Accounts, p. 2, 4 May 1789, on pain of 3s 4d.
[17] Northants. RO, Fitz. Misc., vol. 747, p. 177, 24 Apr. 1799.

made balk grazing less important.[18] Certainly Maxey commoners
used other small pastures near land likely to be damaged if animals
were to stray into it.[19] In Helpston the custom of tethering on balks
survived into the 1790s at least. Tethering elsewhere in the corn
fields, like the meadows, was regulated, and a 1722 order forbade
the turning of animals loose into the highways.[20] Grazing on balks
and other dispersed pastures could not be as efficiently supervised as
grazing in the cow pasture or on the post-harvest fields – hence the
danger of rotating stock on scattered pastures deplored in the 1765
Orders of Ashton, Roade, and Hartwell.[21] But these pastures were
small and easily watched from a distance. This, together with the
obligation to employ a boy to watch the animals, and orders to keep
them firmly tethered, made supervision easier.

Agisting out-parishioners' cattle, using the common as a short-
term pasture for animals on their way to market, and overstocking
in general were three points of conflict managed (as we have seen) by
organizing grazing with regular drifts, brands and common herds to
make the offences difficult to commit. But the courts also tried to
prevent or prosecute these abuses of the common by appointing
supervisory officers and imposing fines.

DETECTION

Fieldsmen – field tellers, eveners, field reeves, haywards – were
responsible for the day-to-day business of the common fields.
Because their work required less close regulation than did the
offences of trespass and overstocking, little of it is recorded in the
court's proceedings. Instead, the fullest descriptions survive in their
accounts, in the details of expenses and disbursements, in the record
of men hired and work completed. Unfortunately the useful lives of
account books were short and few survive. Raunds, Maxey and the
Grafton manors all employed field officers but no records of their

---

[18] Orwin and Orwin, *Open Fields*, p. 136.
[19] In 1806 they could tend three head of stock at a time at Lolham Bridge and More
     Dykes, providing they did 'no damage to the property of other Persons':
     Northants. RO, Fitz. Misc. vol. 747, p. 213, 1 May 1806.
[20] In 1797 the court ordered that horses should not be tethered after sunset in the
     corn fields, and if tethered in the meadow they were to be staked on their owner's
     land and fastened with a rope no longer than the width of that land: Northants.
     RO, Fitz. Misc., vol. 747, pp. 170–1, 10 Apr. 1797; Fitz. Misc., vol. 746, p. 25,
     November 1722.
[21] Northants. RO, G3618b, 25 Apr. 1765.

activity remain. However, the Northamptonshire parish of Old is well represented in the monthly accounts made by its two field officers between 1738 and its enclosure in 1767.[22] Agriculture in Old was a mixed one of sheep and arable, worked over cold black clay in the north of the parish and red clay and gravel in the south.[23] Three men held the office of field officer there between 1738 and 1754, working together in pairs. Two served for more than ten years, another for six, and then again in 1754 after a ten-year gap. At each changeover one man remained in the office to provide continuity.[24] Fieldsmen were overseers or supervisors: they managed the fields but employed other men to do the work they thought necessary. In any one year the Old officers employed between five and nineteen named men, and occasionally women and children too. In addition there were unnamed shepherds, ploughmen and gangs of men who mowed thistles or cut trenches. Their work ranged from simple tasks like scaring crows off growing grain to more skilled ones like draining slades and setting new watercourses.[25]

In a year the fieldsmen focussed on three priorities: fencing, drainage, and keeping the pasture clean. The first required setting quick-thorn, weeding it, stopping up gaps through which cattle or sheep might escape and mending gates and setting hurdles. Drainage involved the seasonal building and freeing of dams, the digging of trenches and the opening up of waterways and clearing of ditches. Cleaning the pasture entailed cutting back hedges, mowing thistles, catching moles and supervising the carrying of thorns and furze from the waste in the autumn.

Added to this was the constant need to watch over sheep as they grazed the pease field, to keep them out of the other fields; to watch the cow herd; to scare crows off the young corn; to clear out wash pits used for the sheep; to knob the cows' horns; and to arrange the crying of the orders, or the crying of the gleaning after harvest. The officers usually spent about £5 a year on the cost of labour alone; in

---

[22] Northants. RO, O 102, Wold Fieldsmen's Accounts, 1738–67.

[23] Whellan's *Directory*, Orlingbury Hundred, Old; of all the manors discussed here Old's agriculture was closest to Moreton Pinkney's.

[24] Treshman Chapman and Edward Corby were field officers between 1738 and 1744; Edward Corby and William Watts between 1744 and 1754; Treshman Chapman again and George Cannell, 1754.

[25] The 1738 accounts mentioned six men by name; the 1740 accounts mentioned six, three others were not named; in 1745 nineteen men and women were employed; eleven in 1754; five in 1755 and 1756; fifteen men and women and four children in 1766, a year before enclosure.

some years they spent more.[26] Materials such as wood, quick thorn, rye-grass seed, powder and shot for crow scaring, and compensation to the owners of dead commons were additional expenses. Each year the fieldsmen let the various leys belonging to the parish, and made a levy on every head of common stock to cover the cost of the year's maintenance of the fields and the compensation for dead commons.[27] They paid two men for not exercising their right to put cows into the common pasture before the common herd. Levies brought in anything from £5 to £8 a year and were set at 2d and 4d per cow in the 1740s, rising to 1s in 1762. Letting leys such as the church headland, Podigal Slade bottom, Walgrave Field freeboard, and the 'Hedge next Walgrave Mear' – often by the rood – added another £4 to £7.

But the Old jury appointed the fieldsmen to police the fields too, and occasionally the officers entered receipts for fines taken at the pound door or thereabouts: overstocking offences brought in £1 16s 1d in 1755, 8s 9d in 1758 and a high £3 3s 6d in 1767, the year of the enclosure. Carting over the grain fields at the wrong time, or along the wrong routes, was also an offence: in 1741 Chapman and Corby fined two men 1s and 5s each for this. In an otherwise meticulously detailed account book (with occasional lapses in the 1740s) the small number of fines imposed is remarkable – quite possibly the seriousness of field offences meant that few men took the risk of breaking the orders, or that fieldsmen in Old exercised discretion by warning offenders at first and imposing a fine only when they paid no heed.

To oversee the pasture was the special responsibility of pinders – pound herds – who worked under the supervision of the fieldsmen. In manors like Old and Grafton Regis the fieldsmen were pinders too, no special officer was appointed, and the rewards of the job went to them. Commoners paid the Grafton pinder, John Joans, 2d a 'pinlock', meaning that he could take 2d of the fine he charged the owner of any overstocked or trespassing animal when he claimed it from the pound.[28] The Ashton hayward earned 6d for every sheep

---

[26] Labour costs ranged from a low of £3 7s 11d in 1738 to a high of £7 5s 0d in 1754; there is no sign of declining expenditure before enclosure.

[27] In 1741 dead horse and cow commons were compensated with £7 13s 9d; this fell to £4 6s 3d in 1742, rose to £12 5s 6d in 1762, and stood at £6 8s 0d in 1767.

[28] Northants. RO, G3290a, 7 Apr. 1731. At Grafton the combination of duties may have been a result of the half-open, half-enclosed state of the parish.

he found folded outside the common fold in 1731.[29] The new stinting agreement made for Ashton, Roade and Hartwell at the Grafton court in 1764 provided that the two field tellers in each parish should receive 1s each every day they were out.[30] The pinder got a double pinlock in Roade for each unringed pig he impounded in 1726.[31]

These examples of payment by results – by the number of animals detected, or the number of days spent checking the common-pasture beasts – found no counterpart in the orders made for the Moreton manors. But they were familiar in Raunds, where the mole catcher – Thomas Crick – got 2d from the occupiers of closes for each mole he killed on their lands, in addition to his yearly salary of 25s for keeping the common fields and pastures free of moles.[32] Similarly, new orders made in November 1735 set the reward for the detection of great cattle and sheep illegally pastured: the fieldsmen would get 'one Shilling a piece for their trouble for every pound Shott they shall make to be paid by the owners of the Sd Cattel so impounded'.[33]

Enforcing field orders in the broad fen pastures required the employment of more officers than in the pastures of the southern loams and clays. Three fen reeves and a pinder, all supervised by the constable, were at work most of the year in Maxey and each of its member manors throughout the century. The court employed extra field keepers as the need arose.[34] The separation of duties apparent in the other manors was repeated in Maxey, where the pinder was almost wholly responsible for the detection of trespassing cattle and sheep, while the fen reeves (in common with the Moreton field keepers) supervised the upkeep of the pastures' fabric, the employment of labour, drifts, and the laying open and haining of the fields.

29 Northants. RO, G3317a, 25 Apr. 1731.
30 Northants. RO, G3626b, 3 May 1764. The tellers were Robert Coock, John Marriott, Edward Longstaff, Peter James, Thomas Denton and Abraham Barritt.
31 Northants. RO, G3292a, 24 Oct. 1726; Grafton Regis, G3290a, 7 Apr. 1725. Unringed pigs damaged the pasture; to avoid this they were ringed through the nose at two months or ten weeks.
32 Northants. RO, QCR 52, 1729. The court set the annual salary and fee for each mole caught in 1729 for the following six years; the money was to be raised with a levy on all the occupiers of common lands.
33 Northants. RO, QCR 56, 13 Nov. 1735.
34 Northants. RO, Fitz. Misc., vol. 746, p. 43, 3 Oct. 1727. In 1722 six overseers supervised the enforcement of the Helpston orders, Fitz. Misc., vol. 746, p. 26, 1722.

But the separation was never complete. Each officer concentrated his attention on one area of the administration of the fields, but was not powerless in the other areas. Both pinders and fen reeves charged fines for Deeping cattle trespasses in the North Fen in 1741, and each took 2d a head. Both were required to fine the same out-parish cattle pastured in the fields of Maxey cum membris no more than 1d per head in the same year. The inhabitants of Market Deeping and James Deeping and Maxey cum membris usually agreed to charge a small fine for any of their respective cattle which strayed into each others' pastures. The courts warned both field reeves and pinders to charge no more than this for fear that the other manors would do the same.[35] By 1767 the fine for cattle found in the North Fen was 3d. Again, both pinder and reeves were responsible for detecting them, and each was liable for a 1s fine every time he took more.[36] Pinders worked alone in detecting other kinds of animal trespass. Like other courts, fen courts paid their pinders by the number of animals they detected. They also identified six major kinds of trespass, each of which could be committed by either cows, horses or sheep.[37]

Breaking stints, stocking without right, agisting out-parish cattle, or pasturing cattle fully armed were all offences for which penalties included a sum for the pinder as a reward 'for his Trouble'. These are instances of paying the field officers by results, and this was perhaps the most usual form of payment in Maxey, Raunds and in the honour of Grafton. It might explain the zeal John Clare saw in Helpston:

> And pinder too is peeping round
> To find a tennant for his pound
> Heedless of rest or parsons prayers
> He seldom to the church repairs
> But thinks religion hath its due
> In paying yearly for his pew.[38]

But parishes adopted other forms of payment too. Occasionally they gave special land-use rights to the officers for the duration of their office: a cottage and one acre of meadow land went with the job of

[35] Northants. RO, Fitz. Misc., vol. 746, p. 108, 2 Nov. 1741.
[36] Northants. RO, Fitz. Misc., vol. 747, p. 51, 19 Feb. 1767.
[37] Northants. RO, Fitz. Misc., vol. 747, 19 Feb. 1767.
[38] John Clare, 'A Sunday with Shepherds and Herdboys', *Selected Poems and Prose of John Clare*, pp. 94–8.

hayward in Grafton and Hartwell. They were worth 24s a year and belonged to the Lord of the Manor.[39] In 1721 the Ringstead haywards enjoyed a similar right to the produce of a meadow.[40]

But in Moreton Pinkney the jury imposed sanctions to inspire efficiency. In 1733 it emphasized the duty of the officers to obey the court, or pay 1s every six weeks for neglect.[41] The Moreton court employed three fieldsmen, each of whom it could punish for dereliction of duty. The jury raised the fine significantly ten years later when it lowered the level of stints.[42] Fieldsmen now forfeited 10s if they failed to search the fields for animals breaking the new stint. Raunds jury enforced new or controversial orders in much the same way. When they widened the common-field balks in April 1741 they also ordered that any 'field searchers' failing to warn anyone whose balks were too narrow, on the request of another commoner, should pay a fine of 6s 8d.[43] Juries held fieldsmen responsible for failing to enforce other orders too. Raunds jury fined Moses Perseswell, hayward of Ringstead manor £1 2s 5d in 1733 for taking waifs and strays to Major Creed of Oundle, 'which usuly belonge to ye maner of Raundes'.[44] This may signal a dispute between Raunds and the major, who was one of the manorial lords of Ringstead, over the ownership of strays, and the wider issue of Ringstead's obligation to do suit and service to the Raunds court.[45] Nevertheless, juries considered field officers responsible for not enforcing the orders because their part in doing so was crucial.

Officers were paid, and they worked full time for some seasons at least, but they may have been corruptible too. Whether they discharged their duties honestly, or compounded with offenders by agreeing not to impound their animals in return for a larger sum than what would have been their share of the fine, is hard to say. Manorial courts recognized that their officers might take bribes: an

[39] R. Lennard, *Rural Northamptonshire under the Commonwealth* (Oxford, 1916; repr. New York, 1974), p. 46.
[40] Northants. RO, QCR 48, 16 Oct. 1721: fieldsmen presented Richard Dyson of Williot Mill for 'withholding The hewards dole in Ringstead from them'.
[41] Northants. RO, G3422, 27 Oct. 1733.
[42] Northants. RO, G3462a, 11 Apr. 1743.
[43] Northants. RO, QCR 60, 23 Apr. 1741.
[44] Northants. RO, QCR 55, 26 Oct. 1733.
[45] Northants. RO, QCR 59, 1740: Ringstead suitors who failed to attend incurred a fine of 3s 4d, Raunds suitors only 4d. Earlier, in 1725, when the officers failed to bring their Bills, two Ringstead men were presented for not appearing at the adjourned court: QCR 50, and see below, pp. 147, 150–1.

order made in the Grafton manor of Blisworth in 1764 provided for
'a Double Penalty on each Breach of Order which shall be provd
against them showing any favour or Affection to any Landholder in
any Case whatsoever'.[46] There were four field tellers in Blisworth. It
could not have been easy to disguise consistent breaking of the stints
and orders, for, unless all the tellers conspired together, sooner or
later another teller, or a commoner not in receipt of a bribe, would
notice the presence of surcharged cattle or unringed pigs or strays.
Indeed, the risk involved was not a small one precisely because
common pasture was a valuable resource; any complicity in its
devaluation affected all the other commoners in the village. In these
circumstances, neglect of duty – whether through corruption or
carelessness – could have important economic consequences for the
commoners. As a result, their self-interest may have ensured the
enforcement of orders.

Providing incentives to enforce the orders and punishing officers
who neglected their duties are two indications of how seriously
juries took the need to enforce the field orders. But more significant
was the fact that these men were employed and paid on a regular
basis. The number and variety of the fieldsmen's responsibilities
could be fulfilled only by the presence of one or another of them in
the common fields most days. Their work involved the constant
supervision of the fields. For this reason, pinders, haywards, field
tellers and fen reeves had to be compensated in some fashion, if not
for their full-time work all year round, then at least for full-time
work for part of the year. In an age when enforcing the criminal law
was a part-time, unpaid occupation, and prosecution was a private
matter, the superior organization of the enforcement of common-
field orders is a measure of their communal importance.[47]

FINES

When the careful organization of common grazing, the employment
of fieldsmen, and commoners' self-interest all failed, fines and
presentments in court remained. They were the ultimate defence of
the whole system of common-field regulation.

[46] Northants. RO, G3625c; once again the new penalty was part of the newly set
stinting agreement. Juries were cautioned against corruption too: G3623b, 24 Apr.
1765, Stoke Bruerne jury list.
[47] Compare Douglas Hay and Francis Snyder, eds., *Policing and Prosecution in
Britain, 1750–1850* (Oxford, 1989), ch. 1.

Like a fine for illegal parking, the penalty for breaking a field order could be paid at one of two points: almost immediately, or after a trial. The procedure began with the charging of a single fine wherever the offence was detected, or at the pound door in return for the release of the offending animals. It ended at the twice-yearly meeting of the manorial court, or at quarter sessions, where a refusal to settle out of court usually raised the fine ultimately imposed. A Blisworth order made in 1764 illustrates this ascending scale:

> We further Consent and Jointly agree for the Penalty's made upon any or either of the aforesd Order's to be paid upon the Spott Catcht or a Pound Door to the foreman of our Jury And We agree for the same to be spent at his Pleasure by the Consent of the Majority of the Landholders. And in Caste That any Landholder shall make any Neglect or Refussall of the forfeitures as aforesaid Shall Come Under the Penalty of Paying Double Paines upon Breach of each Order made as aforesd, unto the Steward of his Graces Court.[48]

Juries used fines such as these to prevent or punish agistment, trespass and overstocking. They also raised them in order to enforce new stints. They wanted to make protest prohibitively expensive. When Raunds introduced the first stint of horse commons in 1729 the penalty for breaking it was 6s 8d.[49] Juries set a new high level of fines at Ashton, Roade, and Hartwell in 1732. Although the commonable land of these three parishes remained without stint until 1764, the custom of the manors restricted the number of animals that could be pastured by right. By 1732 commoners had broken these limits so the jury agreed that, after each commoner's right to pasture had been examined, further breaches would be fined at the rate of 10s per animal per day. They announced the penalty before it could come into effect, using it both as a warning before the rights were verified and a punishment after they were settled, and they appointed four men from Roade, four from Hartwell and five from Ashton to verify rights before Candlemas, on pain of a guinea

[48] Northants. RO, G3625c, 9 May 1764.
[49] Northants. RO, QCR 52, October 1729; subsequent fines were lower: QCR 56, 3 Oct. 1735. In 1724 the Greens Norton court set the fine for breaking a new sheep stint in Duncot and Burcot at 10s per default; similar restinting in Whittlebury put a fine of 3s 4d on stocking any animal over the stint, sheep as well as cattle: G3379a, G3379b, 2 May 1724.

each.[50] When the jury introduced the first stint of the right to pasture in 1764 it set the deterrent fine even higher at no less than £5 for every rejection of the stint, and five shillings for each overstocked animal after impounding.[51]

Most years in all but the fen manors it would have cost 6s to retrieve a dozen sheep from the pound; in the fens is cost 20s. Two or three cows caught overstocked would cost from 3s to 15s, depending upon which manor set the fines and whether a new stint was introduced. Overstocking was only one of the offences so punished, trespass usually carried a higher penalty, and agistment was punished even more severely.[52] High fines, coupled with an efficient body of fieldsmen and a parish of watchful commoners, made breaking the orders expensive. Impounding itself was a penalty because while the animals remained in the pound cows could not be sold or milked by their owners, and horses could not be ridden or used to draw carts and waggons. For this reason one offence sometimes followed another as occupiers tried to rescue their animals without paying the fine. As a result, pound breach brought heavy penalties because it threatened the whole system of fines. When a Raunds farmer committed trespass by driving eighteen cows into the grass and grain of Nordale one night in 1729, the fieldsmen captured the animals and took them off to the pound. As they were on their way, his son rescued most of them, but in doing so he raised the penalty for the incident by two thirds.[53] Less

---

50 Northants. RO, G3432i, 1 Nov. 1732.
51 Northants. RO, G3626b, 3 May 1764. The £5 went to the lord of the manor, the 5s belonged to the manor; 1s was paid to the field tellers each day they went out to check each commoner's stock: G3379b, 2 May 1764. Grafton manor juries introduced new stints and new fines in Whittlebury and Greens Norton, Duncot and Burcot in 1724; in Ashton, Roade and Hartwell in 1732; in Moreton Pinkney in 1743; and in Blisworth, Stoke Bruerne and Shutlanger, and again in Ashton, Roade and Hartwell in 1764: G3379b; G3379a; G3432i; G3462a; G3626c; G3624b; G3625c. Most courts set fines for each offence and for each animal overstocked, but Moreton Pinkney and Ashton, Roade and Hartwell courts collected them for each day over which the offence was committed. Like short-term high fines, this happened when new stints were set.
52 See pp. 92, 118, 149–50 for fines for agistment. In a parish with otherwise low fines, putting a cow on to the pasture without a common right was punished with a 5s fine in Blisworth in 1739: Northants. RO, G3448b, 19 June 1739.
53 Northants. RO, QCR 52, Raunds orders, 1729; the trespass fine was £1 7s 6d, the rescue fine 17s 6d. Violently taking away trespassing horses from a pinder, a landowner or an occupier in Castor and Ailesworth in the fens doubled the fine in 1725: Fitz. Misc., vol. 746, p. 36, 4 Nov. 1725.

serious infringements of similar trespassing orders brought lower fines.[54]

The Raunds court punished other offences too. It is possible that several incidents happening in the 1730s, 1740s and early 1750s were part of the long dispute fought sporadically with Ringstead occupiers over their obligation to do suit and service at Raunds. We have seen that the court fined the Ringstead hayward in 1733 when he took the waifs and strays to Major Creed of Oundle, lord of Ringstead manor, instead of to the Raunds pound.[55] In 1740 it fined two gentlemen of Ringstead and eighteen tenants (including some gentlemen) for their absence from court. Such absences were usually excused (essoined) for a small fee by prior arrangement, but none of those charged had bothered to apply for the favour in 1740.[56] In 1753 Oliver Cox junior made a pound breach of Ringstead stock from the Raunds pound, closely following a common trespass committed by the Ringstead shepherd in Raunds fields.[57] Cox was one of the men fined in 1740 for his absence from court. A third challenge to the custom of the manor came from within the parish in 1740 when – as we saw earlier – Robert Ekins failed to provide the customary bull and boar, an obligation attached to the land he occupied. The court amerced him 13s 4d. At the same time it fined another yeoman a shilling for charging his neighbour for the use of the common bull that it was his duty to provide free.[58]

Challenges to the court's authority like these could be handled there or at the higher courts of quarter sessions and assize. In Ravensthorpe, field officers were empowered in 1724, by agreement of the commoners, to distrain property or initiate law suits to

---

[54] The court amerced five men 1s each in 1718 for riding down a furlong and carting down a headland. Offences like these were probably dealt with on the spot, but these offenders were outsiders and may have hoped to escape punishment altogether by refusing to pay when first caught: Northants. RO, QCR 47, 23 Oct., 11 Dec. 1718.

[55] Northants. RO, QCR 55, 26 Oct. 1733.

[56] Northants. RO, QCR 41, 15 May and 1 June 1740: the jury fined Cox and Allison 5s each; the rest paid 1s each. The gentlemen were Sir James Langham, the Reverend John Sharp, William Barton and Paul Ives. None were presented at the next court: QCR 60, Apr. 1741.

[57] Northants. RO, QS Grand File, Thomas à Becket, 1752; 1753. Raunds jury prosecuted two Ringstead farmers in 1770 for their refusal to scour a common water course: QS Grand File, Thomas à Becket, 1770.

[58] Northants. RO, QCR 59, 13 Dec. 1740.

recover fines still unpaid after twenty-one days.[59] The more usual course, however, was for courts to prosecute serious offences like pound breach at local quarter sessions by the ordinary means of indictment. The Raunds court protected itself quite tenaciously throughout this period, both in resisting the counter-claims of Ringstead commoners, and in dealing with internal assaults on stints and orders – the offences most characteristic of the business recorded by the court.[60]

Records of Moreton court presentments survive more completely, although they too are best documented in the first half of the century before its enclosure.[61] Here presentments often served to warn offenders.[62] In October 1733 the jury fined Hercules Franklyn 10s for not laying down his lands' ends and jointways to grass, but also told him that the fine would be remitted if he complied in time. At the same court Thomas Smith paid 5s for breaking up the old greensward for cultivation.[63] Presentments for failure to scour ditches or lay down land to grass appeared here as often as presentments for trespass in Raunds. Penalties for the latter were high but they were often amerced to 5s or 6s.[64] Occasionally a name appeared

[59] Northants. RO, BG 176, Ravensthorpe Orders, 1 Jan. 1724. It would require examination of *nisi prius* records of assize and the other civil records of the courts of Westminster to establish whether such suits took place, and how often. I have found no evidence in other sources that this was in fact the case.

[60] It is possible that the court recorded these prosecutions because they were matters of long-term importance; other more routine presentments may have been dealt with, and forgotten, requiring no written record. For similar actions see Northants. RO, QCR 46, Oct. 1716, and QCR 60, 23 Apr. 1741. Records of orders and presentments end in 1741, although the court continued to deal with land transfers and fealties. This may indicate when the public vestry took over the agricultural regulation of the two parishes, but records of the vestry do not survive before 1789. Certainly field regulation continued: prosecutions were brought before Northampton quarter sessions in 1751, 1752, 1753, 1768, 1770 and 1788. In 1789 the vestry filed a new set of stints for the next six years in the Town Book, alterations could be made only at a 'Public Vestry', Northants. RO, Raunds Overseers' Accounts, 1747–1806.

[61] Moreton Pinkney was enclosed by an Act of 1761; Blakesley was enclosed in 1760; Woodend was enclosed later in 1779. Adston and Plumpton were not enclosed by Act of Parliament.

[62] In spring 1728 the court ordered John Beauchamp, esquire, of Adston to fill up a pit lying near the highway in Adston before the Michaelmas court; at the same time it told Henry Tucker to scour his ditch on pain of 5s: Northants. RO, G3360a, 4 May 1728.

[63] Northants. RO, G3422, 27 Oct. 1733.

[64] For example, G3380b, April 1724: the fine for the trespass of one cow in the wheat field of Potterspury was 20s but the jury amerced it to 5s. Other examples of trespass: G3341e, 16 Oct. 1725, and G3428a, 2 Oct. 1731. The fine for pound

more than once in the presentments, but no one man or set of men seems to have made a habit of breaking the orders.[65] To be absent from court without notice was an offence in the Grafton manors, as it was in Raunds. Juries amerced suitors from 2s 6d to 5s, though the Roade jury fined an absent juryman 10s in 1763. Less substantial suitors paid lower fines of a few pence each.[66] As the years went by, fines rose but absenteeism seems not to have threatened the authority of the court in any of the manors.[67]

Trespass, overstocking and pound breach were the most common offences presented to the Maxey court, as they were in Raunds.[68] Overstocking with geese incurred high fines in 1738 and again in the 1770s and 1780s, but throughout the period the jury imposed the heaviest fines for agisting cattle.[69] This was Richard Addington's offence in 1736 for which the court fined him £1 10s 0d. Then it fined him an additional 3s 4d for not branding his horses. Two years later the fieldsmen presented him for keeping a by-herd and fined him 2s 6d. Overstocking was Miller John Frisby's offence in 1733, and again in 1736. At the 1736 court the jury also presented him for not paying his levy for the 'New Cutt of a River through the Church lands'. These offences cost him £1 6s 8d at the two courts. Equally severe was the fine imposed on

---

breach was 3s 4d, though a rescue of five sheep from the pound cost one offender only 6d in 1724: Northants. RO, G3379b, 2 May 1724; other pound breaches: G3422, 27 Oct. 1733; G3326a, 29 Apr. 1730.

[65] Both Henry Tucker and Jonathan Furniss committed more than one infringement of the field orders in the 1720s and 1730s: Northants. RO, G3356a, 27 Oct. 1729; G3428a, 2 Oct. 1731; G3360a, 4 May 1728; G3356, 27 Oct. 1729.

[66] Northants. RO, G3493a, 17 Apr. 1740; G3362a, 5 Apr. 1725; G3606a, 21 Apr. 1763; and G3357a, 24 Apr. 1730.

[67] Other presentments were for putting 'scabbed horses on the common' (three men were fined 1s each, a fourth was fined 2s); G3428a, 2 Oct. 1731; for breaching the Assize of Bread (the baker, Josiah Wilson, was amerced 6s): G3277a, 30 Sept. 1723; for flitting mares contrary to the orders of the last court (fine 2s 6d) and for not mounding lands or ploughing leys (5s and 6d respectively): G3341e, 16 Oct. 1725; and for not hedging a hadeway within the allotted time (1s): G3428a, 2 Oct. 1731.

[68] The court amerced Thomas Dunston 1s for trespass in 1720; it fined John and Samuel Laxton and Thomas Bradley between 3s 4d and 10s each for the same offence later on in 1736; Northants. RO, Fitz. Misc., vol. 746, p. 2, 1720; and 4 Nov. 1736.

[69] Northants. RO, Fitz. Misc., vol. 746, Michaelmas 1738 (10s fine); vol. 747, 22 Oct. 1778 (fines ranging from 9s to £4 19s 0d); vol. 747, 12 Oct. 1780 (presentment of Deeping parishes, no fines mentioned).

John Baker of James Deeping in 1736 for pasturing cattle without a right: he paid £1 19s 11d.[70]

Men such as John Frisby of Maxey, Henry Tucker and Jonathan Furniss of Moreton, George Chamberlain of Etton and Woodcroft, and Oliver Cox of Ringstead, who broke orders on more than one occasion, were a nuisance in open fields – although their fellows were not unknown in enclosed parishes too, where they maintained their fences poorly, let their cattle wander, or left their ditches unscoured. Frisby himself was guilty of breaking three orders. But he was a nuisance rather than a persistent threat. We hear no more of his delinquency. A powerful incentive to obey the orders lay in the fieldsmen's right to impound trespassing animals until they received full satisfaction for the offence. In such circumstances pound breach was the only resort left to the determined offender – and pound breach was an offence. Another way of dealing with one man's personal ambition to profit more from the common lands than anyone else was to make a public order specially for him: a jury at Etton and Woodcroft in the fens personally instructed George Chamberlain not to keep more than six sheep and no by-herds in 1735.[71] Verbal warnings may have been given at court more frequently. But if juries failed to prevent such men choosing which orders they would observe and which they would ignore, they could take the case to quarter sessions. Evidence from the manors of Raunds and Ringstead, and from Moreton Pinkney, shows that this was what they did.

Events in Raunds and Ringstead in the early 1750s led to the prosecution of a series of pound breaches at quarter sessions rather than in the manorial court. At the Epiphany sessions in 1751 the jury charged Robert Ekins of Raunds with trespass. He had let his sheep go into the wheat field, rescued them when the fieldsmen impounded them, and then refused to pay the fine. Four fieldsmen, two haywards and the constable signed the Bill. A year later the parish charged Ekins and four others with pound breach again. Thus far five men had been brought from the parish to quarter sessions because they had refused to pay their fines. At the same time the Raunds fieldsmen charged a Ringstead shepherd with trespass. The following year they charged another, James Weekley, and Oliver Cox (who had failed to do suit and service to the Raunds

---

70 Northants. RO, Fitz. Misc., vol. 746, 4 Nov. 1736.
71 Northants. RO, Fitz. Misc., vol. 746, 2 Apr. 1735.

court in 1740) with pound breach.[72] The fieldsmen prosecuted James Weekley again in 1768, with four other men, for trespass in the lands of his own parish of Ringstead. Weekley himself had to answer an additional charge of trespass in the ley and meadow lands.[73] Two years later in 1770 Raunds jurymen returned to quarter sessions once more to prosecute two Ringstead farmers for neglecting and refusing to scour the watercourse running from Lubering Spring in Ringstead to Oak ditch in Raunds, 'to the very great detriment and damage of the Meadow ground belonging to the inhabitants of Raunds'.[74]

There is not enough here to tell us what caused the determination to break the orders on one side and the determination to prosecute the offenders on the other. But there is enough to show that fieldsmen used the sanction of quarter sessions. Pound breach, in particular, found its way there. In the period 1750 to 1803 twenty-two cases from twenty-one parishes were brought to Northampton's quarter sessions. Occasionally the prosecution included allegations of assault or of the destruction of the pound itself.[75] The resort to quarter sessions does not mean that local juries were impotent. Rather, quarter sessions was the last resort, and as often used by enclosed as open parishes: in over a third of the twenty-two cases of

---

[72] Northants. RO, QS Grand Files, Epiphany 1751; Thomas à Becket and Michaelmas, 1752; Thomas à Becket, 1753.
[73] Northants. RO, QS Grand File, Michaelmas 1768.
[74] Northants. RO, QS Grand File, Thomas à Becket 1770. Yet another Ringstead pound breach was prosecuted at the Michaelmas session in 1788, QS Grand File.
[75] Northants. RO, QS Grand Files. Earlier prosecutions were made of offences in the following parishes: between 1694 and 1702, Middleton, 1697 (Thomas à Becket); Newnham, 1698 (Thomas à Becket); Oundle, 1698 (Thomas à Becket). Between 1750–5 and 1765–1803, Raunds, 1752 (Michaelmas); Rothwell, 1753 (Michaelmas); Milton Malzer, 1753 (Thomas à Becket); Ringstead, 1753 (Thomas à Becket); Thorpe Achurch, 1768 (Epiphany); Rushden, 1775 (Thomas à Becket); Moreton Pinkney, 1776 (Thomas à Becket); Great Weldon, 1776 (Thomas à Becket); Titchmarsh, 1776 (Thomas à Becket); Cosgrave, 1780 (Epiphany); Blisworth 1780 (Epiphany); Little Weldon, 1779 (Michaelmas); Thorpe Malsor, 1781 (Michaelmas); Finedon, 1778 (Thomas à Becket); Fotheringhay, 1785 (Michaelmas); Yardley Hastings, 1786 (Epiphany); Ringstead, 1788 (Michaelmas); Creaton, 1790 (Michaelmas); Cottesbrooke, 1797 (Michaelmas); Braunston, 1791 (Thomas à Becket); Badby, 1795 (Thomas à Becket); Maidford, 1771 (Michaelmas); Brigstock, 1803 (Thomas à Becket). Most prosecutions were made in the second half of the year when the harvest fields were ripening, and later, as the post-harvest pastures became available. Assaults and pound destructions were alleged in the following cases: Ringstead, 1753; Oundle, 1698; Newnham, 1698; Badby, 1795; Thorpe Achurch, 1768.

pound breach prosecution occurred after enclosure.[76] This offence, and others, survived enclosure, and village pounds survived too – witness to the need for some common regulation even in highly individualized farming.

In Raunds, the Grafton manors, and at the court of Maxey cum membris presentments most often dealt with common trespass and pound breach, and to a lesser extent with the failure to scour ditches, build mounds, or to lay down adequate balks. In addition, all the courts punished absent suitors. Generally, the fines were amerced to reflect the size of the damage done. In other words the penalty imposed depended on the number of cattle rescued or overstocked, or the extent of the trespass, of the failure despite warnings to scour ditches or build fences. If the ability of offenders to pay their fines entered into the calculation it did so almost naturally because the most serious offences were committed by the most substantial landholders, simply because they owned most animals. Amercements at court varied from 1s for early eighteenth-century offences, or for single offences committed by poorer commoners, to the £4 or £5 amerced Deeping men for putting geese on Maxey common. In between were a number of fines of one or two pounds charged to substantial farmers, most often for common trespass or for neglecting to clean waterways or repair fencing.

In each manor, field officers brought squires and farmers, or landowners and rectors to court, or accused them of failing to do suit and service, or of disregarding customs to provide bulls and boars, and, once there, they fined them quite substantial sums. The courts prosecuted some of the biggest gentlemen and farmers, including the Lord of the Manor of Moreton Pinkney, the Raunds' yeomen, Miller John Frisby of Maxey, John Beauchamp, esquire, of Adston, and the agents of Major Creed of Oundle. Indeed this may have been where their vigilance was needed most because the trespass of substantial farmers' cattle was more dangerous than the occasional trespass of a cottager's cow, and the failure of farmers to fence or drain their lands was more serious than that of someone whose lands amounted to only a few acres.[77] Nor do the courts seem

[76] Northants. RO, QS Grand Files: Creaton, 1790; Moreton Pinkney, 1776; Badby, 1795; Braunston, 1791; Yardley Hastings, 1786; Fotheringhay, 1785; Thorpe Malsor, 1781; Cosgrave, 1780; Brigstock, 1803.

[77] For stints put on Peterborough butchers see Northants. RO, Church Commissioners' Records, 278573, Peterborough Court Baron, 28 Oct. 1701 (48 sheep); 20

to have come to a crisis in which the same men were repeatedly presented, and repeatedly failed to appear at court, or to accept the fine charged them. Nor does it seem that the system itself broke down; presentments continued to be made throughout the century until enclosure, and sometimes after. Henry Homer looked on the loss of courts and regulation in enclosed villages with some regret: 'Where courts are regularly held, and Bye-Laws are enforced under certain Penalties and Restrictions, offences will be less frequently committed.' This supporter of enclosure admitted that where land was best suited to arable the common-field system worked well enough.[78]

NEGOTIATION

It is likely that this usually well-regulated, time-tested system suffered periodic crises: when the pasture supply was too small for its stock of animals, when an increase in the number of animals raised did not exactly match the expected increase in other sources of fodder.[79] But there is no evidence of a collapse prior to enclosure in any of the manors studied here. It seems reasonable to conclude that the regulation of common of pasture was necessary, and that this was a fact well understood by all commoners. For the one or two men who wanted to run the common bare for the sake of a greater profit at the next market, there were many more who understood the basic agricultural law of feeding the land in order to feed oneself.

They knew too that they could discuss and perhaps resolve common problems. Negotiation was as vital to common-field agriculture as pasture itself: commoners could do little without it. To sow the fallow, to lay down balks, to reduce stints, to prosecute overstockers, they had to discuss, negotiate and make agreements. To scare off men like John Lovelock, a substantial farmer in Marlstone who rented a few acres in Bucklebury in order to graze all his cattle on its commons, Bucklebury commoners had to raise

Apr., 10 Sept. 1704 (48 sheep); 16 Apr. 1706 (40 sheep); Oct. 1707 (40 sheep); 27 Oct. 1708 (48 sheep).

[78] Homer, *Essay*, p. 8. William Marshall also noted the survival of manor courts in the west Midlands after the extinction of copyhold tenure where 'their utility is experienced': *Rural Oeconomy of the Midland Counties* (2nd edn, 1796), p. 15.

[79] On pasture shortage in the eighteenth century as an incentive to enclose see Turner, *English Parliamentary Enclosure*, ch. 6.

money to get a legal opinion. To sow grass seed on the fallow they had to make a new agreement because the custom ran only to corn, even though they abated their commons. They would have to talk to each other.[80] This is not to argue that relations in common-field villages were always cordial, consensual and co-operative. 'Grudges and Piques betwixt some particular Men upon the Account of Trespasses and Incroachments made on each other' were in the very nature of a common-field village.[81] Tusser was right to suggest that the communal organization of agriculture was riven with dispute, noisy with argument. But he was wrong to think that argument was *never* resolved; and to think that argument prevented regulation – the two could co-exist. In fact argument is an indication of the life of a community. People argue about what matters to them, about what affects and connects them. David Sabean has argued that it is exactly this argument that defines community:

> What is common in community is not shared values or common understanding so much as the fact that members of a community are engaged in the same argument, the same *raisonnement*, the same *Rede*, the same discourse, in which alternative strategies, misunderstandings, conflicting goals and values are threshed out.[82]

Argument, then, far from preventing the effective regulation of agriculture, is an index of the degree of connection and interdependence in a common-field village – an index of its shared life – and a way to resolve disputes. If common-field villagers did not argue, then they did not need or depend on one another. It is unlikely that setting a new stint was a tranquil process – why else set unusually high fines for breaking it in its first year? It is unlikely that observing the many rules of common-field parishes was done with a consistently glad heart. Some of the success of common regulation depended on officers who were paid by results, and who were looked upon with the fondness we reserve for traffic wardens. Some of it depended on the sharp eyes and ears of neighbours. In common-

---

[80] Berks. RO, D/EHy L5, 'The Case of the Bucklebury Ffarmers and Mr Polenger's Opinion thereon', 28 Dec. 1733. They learnt that Lovelock was guilty of 'Chaseing and rechasing', which was illegal; he could pasture only as many cattle as he could overwinter on the land he held in Bucklebury.

[81] Anon. *The True Interest of the Land Owners of Great Britain*, p. 18.

[82] David Sabean, *Power in the Blood. Popular Culture and Village Discourse in Early Modern Germany* (Cambridge, 1984), p. 29.

field villages ordering the fields and enforcing the orders were constantly negotiated activities. And they affected the livelihood of most of the members of a parish. All of this means that court meetings were likely to be times when commoners contested particular orders, challenged the justice of some decisions, and resisted some fines. 'Grudges and Piques' were to be expected. But they do not mean that the system did not work. Doubtless it worked better in some places than in others. There were common-field parishes where the ability and ambition of a small number of men to dominate a majority of small occupiers wrecked any attempt at strict regulation. In some parishes there was simply not enough regulation – villages where stints were too generous, for example. This was the complaint at Cheshunt in Hertfordshire, in 1799, the year of its enclosure – a complaint put in an anonymous letter and sent to the Lord of the Manor:

> We cannot but say that there is plenty of room for Alterations for We cannot see why that Ruskins and a few more of them should run our Common over while there is no room for another to put anything on it [if] thou hadst made an Alteration in the rights of Commoning thou instead of being contempabel whould thy Name been as Oderriferous Ointment pour'd forth to us *the voice of us and the maguor part of the parrish is for a regulation of commons rights.*[83]

But this variety of efficiency in common-field regulation may have ranged no wider than did the various efficiencies of enclosed farming. And a lack of regulation before enclosure in some places cannot imply a lack everywhere. No failure to regulate occurred in the manors studied here – if the variety, complexity and progressive alteration of orders, and the regularity and social breadth of presentments mean anything at all. Here, juries drew up their orders with some care, and regularly enforced them for a century before enclosure. They may not have been exceptional in this because not all large farmers or butchers and graziers would have wanted to prejudice the parish's livelihood for their own profit. The experience of an ancient tradition of shared land-use stood against it. Even where this experience went for nothing, there must have been men who realized that their own interest, as well as that of poorer commoners, suffered from the abuse of common right.

[83] PRO, HO, 42.46, Anonymous letter sent to Oliver Cromwell, Esq., Cheshunt Park, Herts., 27 Feb. 1799. My italics.

Common-field pasture was too important, and the fear of trespass in the corn fields too great, to encourage persistent and unchallenged overstocking.

Except, that is, in the year of an enclosure. In an earlier chapter we saw that when enclosure looked certain some commoners began to challenge, break or ignore field orders. In Tottington, Norfolk, counter-petitioners against enclosure told the House of Commons that the Lord of the Manor had deliberately overstocked the common in order to reduce the compensation he would have to give them when the Act was passed.[84] In Cheshunt 'that Ruskins' and a few others monopolized the common in the very year that the Lord of the Manor was more concerned with the enclosure bill than the field orders. When enclosure was in the offing, regulation may have taken a back seat. Enclosure transformed relationships in common-field villages – changed the terms of the argument – as soon as it looked certain. But it is important to note that *enclosure* was the reasons for this change in behaviour, not the common-field system.

And it was in the context of enclosure that improving opinion in general began to deplore commons' management: 'that Ruskins' – the overstocker, the trespasser, the agister, the unscrupulous champion who 'robbeth by night / and prowleth and filcheth by day' – stalks the pages of enclosers' account of the common fields from Tusser on.[85] For this reason, as critics of common fields, they missed the point. They failed to look at the system in its own terms. If we do this, we see at once how imperative was the *need* for common pasture to work efficiently, and therefore how vital was effective regulation. We remember the centuries of agricultural production generated by the common fields. Simply put: common pastures had to serve the common stock adequately, and grain had to be grown. In the end, common fields gave way to enclosed farms. But this does not mean that 'good' agriculture triumphed over 'bad', like some conquering hero in a gothic romance. It means that one mode of agricultural production gave way to another. ('Backward' agriculture itself is an astonishingly narrow concept. It assumes that productivity alone defines the many relationships, social as well as economic, that agriculture represents.) In the end, enclosers

---

[84] *Jls House of Commons*, 7 Feb. 1774; and see above Chapter 3, p. 88.
[85] We have seen that when improvers talked only about commons, not commons in the context of enclosure, they were remarkably *un*critical: see above, Chapter 1, pp. 35–6.

enclosed for a number of reasons, chief among them the prospect of higher rents, a belief in the efficiency of larger, consolidated holdings, and an emotional and intellectual commitment to a more individualized production, to private enterprise. The conquering hero is more accurately described as an investing landlord or an enterprising freeholder. But neither the higher rents nor the (arguably) more efficient units of enclosed villages, nor the change in the *zeitgeist* of the agricultural establishment should be taken to mean that before enclosure agriculture was *necessarily* badly run or backward. Communal regulation did not mean inadequate regulation. The system may have been less productive, if we define productivity in terms of agricultural production, though we should note that the jury on this is still out. And while it considers evidence that the greatest growth in crop yields in the eighteenth and early nineteenth centuries may have predated enclosure by several decades, the most conservative recent writing shows a caution altogether new.[86] But equally productive or not, the common-field system was an effective, flexible and proven way to organize village agriculture. The common pastures were well governed, the value of a common right was well maintained.

[86] The old assumption of higher grain yields is now a matter for argument: see R. C. Allen and C. O'Grada, 'On the Road Again with Arthur Young', *Journal of Economic History*, 48 (1988), pp. 93–116, and references to the debate cited therein. In taking stock of the effect of enclosure, contributors to *The Agrarian History of England and Wales*, VI, argue that it brought benefits that took 'a generation or two' to appear. They were 'compactness', 'flexibility', tithe commutation, new roads, the new organization of old closes, and the end of common grazing, (p. 969); and, again, 'compactness', and 'flexibility' but also 'efficiency' and waste reclamation (p. 598); but not higher grain yields. Any improvement in yields as a result of enclosure between 1795 and 1812 was 'modest' (p. 138). For a defence of common-field farming see Thirsk, *Agrarian History of England and Wales*, IV, p. 179.

6. *The uses of waste*

I always admire the kindling freshness that the bark of the different sorts of tree and underwood asume in the forest – the 'foul royce' twigs kindling into a vivid color at their tops as red as woodpigeons claws   the ash with its grey bark and black swelling buds   the Birch with its 'paper rind' and the darker mottled sorts of hazle black alder with the greener hues of sallows willows and the bramble that still wears its leaves with the privet of a purple hue while the straggling wood briar shines in a brighter and more beautiful green   odd forward branches in the new laid hedges of white thorn begin to freshen into green before the arum dare peep out of its hood or the primrose and violet shoot up a new leaf thro the warm moss and ivy that shelter their spring dwellings   the furze too on the common wear a fairer green and here and there an odd branch is coverd with golden flowers and the ling or heath nestling among the long grass below (coverd with the witherd flowers of last year) is sprouting up into fresh hopes of spring   the fairey rings on the pasture are getting deeper dyes and the water weeds with long silver green blades of grass are mantling the stagnant ponds in their summer liverys.[1]

The fuel, food and materials taken from common waste helped to make commoners of those without land, common-right cottages, or pasture rights. Waste gave them a variety of useful products, and the raw materials to make more. It also gave them the means of exchange with other commoners and so made them part of the

[1] John Clare, *Selected Poems and Prose of John Clare*, p. 162; the 'foul royce' (foul-rush) is either dogwood (*Cornus sanguinea*) or the spindle tree (*Euonymous europaens*) (*ibid.*, p. 206).

network of exchange from which mutuality grew. More than this, common waste supported the economies of landed and cottage commoners too. It was often the terrain of women and children. And for everyone the common meant more than income. This is a large subject dealt with only in an introductory fashion here.[2] The work of Dorothy Hartley and Richard Mabey indicates how many were the uses of the natural products of common lands, and how ingenious, sophisticated and effective those uses were. This richness is daunting enough but, even more than common of pasture, writing the history of food, fuel and materials from commons suffers from a shortage of the kind of records that establish its economic history. Though there is no lack of evidence of use there is a dearth of evidence that would plot the history of the income value of each commodity. The reasons are obvious. Many things – nuts, berries, some kinds of wood and browse – commoners had for the taking. Others were part of an eighteenth-century black economy hidden from the sight of even forest officers and estate stewards and so never entering their account books. For this reason I am not trying to establish the history of income value here for anything except fuel. Instead I want to establish the fact of the taking from commons, and to describe the range of materials taken. Of course, the value of wasteland commons, like the value of common pasture, was more than this. Even a small waste had its social meaning as well as its income value, and this too is the subject of this chapter.

I

What would burn well from an eighteenth-century common? There was dry fallen wood in forests and woodlands; turf on downs; furze (or gorse) and bracken (fern) on most heath, hill and vale wastes; peat in peat meads and heathland. Even the leaves from the trees were dried and used by the poor or sold 'to keep a slow fire alive in the hearth'; and growing trees were harvested like any other crop.[3]

---

[2] I shall give a longer account elsewhere of the uses of waste in common-field and common-waste villages.

[3] On leaves and live beech roots: Kalm, *Kalm's Account of his Visit to England*, pp. 304, 279. On turf or peat: Godber, *History of Bedfordshire*, p. 418; R. N. Salaman, *The History and Social Influence of the Potato* (1949), p. 491; D. Hartley, *Food in England* (1954), pp. 43, 48; peat in common meadows along the river Kennet in Berkshire, Tate, 'Handlist of English Enclosure Acts and Awards

Furze was particularly abundant. It gave a fierce, hot flame; it warmed cottages, fuelled bakehouses, lime-kilns and brewers' pots. But almost anything could be put in the fire, including tree roots (taken alive or dead) and any woodcutting chips, shavings, trimmings or sawdust.[4]

Forest commoners were well placed for getting fuel, although not all forests were well wooded, and heath parishes, for example, offered excellent resources too. All the Northamptonshire forests were reservoirs of fuel for forest commoners. Some manor customs attached fuel rights to ancient cottages, for example occupiers of fifty-four cottages in Brigstock in Rockingham Forest each had the right to sixteen loads of brakes a year. And eighteenth-century accounts of rights made by forest administrators note that commoners had the right to take only certain kinds of wood: snapwood – wood easily snapped off a tree or pulled down with a pole and a hook – or the lops and tops of trees, or dry and fallen wood, but not the timber itself. With the exception of specific grants of estovers (repair wood) to some copyholders, the crown did not expect commoners to harvest trees. Sometimes they lost them anyway: after the great ice storm of February 1766 commoners collected hundreds of loads of fallen timber in Wychwood.[5] But the sanctity of timber was also a matter of dispute on particular occasions or at certain times of the year, when the protection of the most profitable wood in the forest and the customary behaviour of commoners were at odds. Maytime celebrations of the accession of George II in Whittlewood Forest led to the felling by commoners from twenty or more villages of hundreds of timber trees or 'coronation poles'. First they danced around them, then they sawed them up for fuel, some of which (it was alleged) they would sell. They claimed it was an old practice, a custom, and eradicating it proved difficult because gentry and commoners stood firm against forest officers.[6]

Relating to Lands in Berkshire', p. 69; the loss of peat at enclosure mentioned in several Berkshire enclosure Awards including Elcot in Kintbury (1780), Marcham (1818), Midgham (1814), Speen (1780), Woolhampton (1815), Ham Marsh, Thatcham (1826); burnt for ashes to dress land at Newbury, Bell, *To Meet Mr Ellis*, p. 62.

[4] Kalm, *Kalm's Account of his Visit to England*, pp. 147–8, 230; Richard Mabey, *Plants with a Purpose. A Guide to the Everyday Uses of Wild Plants* (1977), p. 79.
[5] Mary Sturge Gretton, *Three Centuries in North Oxfordshire* (Oxford, 1902), p. 202.
[6] James Herbert Cooke, FSA, 'Timber-stealing Riots in Whittlebury and Salcey Forests, in 1727–8', *Northamptonshire Notes and Queries*, 1, pp. 123–201; also

Grantees were concerned about more than the loss of wood: entering the forest for fuel was a cover for poaching, and poaching became a strong argument for the closing of woods to commoners early in the century. In the 1720s the Duke of Montagu complained bitterly that 'woodstealers' used 'the pretence of some small privileges, as of gathering dead Wood' as 'Cloaks for ye Greatest Villainies, in destroying the Wood and the Game'. Only the enclosure of Geddington Chase, the erection of a workhouse in Brigstock, and the transformation of wood stealers into wood buyers would put a stop to it. But Lord Gowran, grantee of another walk, to whom Montagu described this plan, feared that on enclosure the commoners would simply direct their activities to his woods, and the plan stalled.[7] Most common right in Rockingham was extinguished by enclosure in the 1790s.

Certainly, commoners and grantees defined what might and what might not be taken from the forest differently. As a result it was the cause of lengthy disputes in which forest commoners gained some of their experience in negotiation, much as fielden commoners did in the regulation of their common fields. Rights to fuel in particular were most specific on paper (usually the grantee's estate management correspondence or copies of court roll). But, although certain cottagers had grants and although certain kinds of wood were in dispute, most inhabitants could get fuel of some sort: specific grants seem not to have precluded a more general enjoyment.

By the end of the century grantees in royal forests in Northamptonshire were trying to restrict access to particular days. The warden of Salcey Forest advertised open days in 1785 as Mondays and Thursdays, 'these being the only Days allowed by ancient Custom of the said Forest'. Notices specified the kind of wood to be taken more narrowly too. The Salcey warden defined fuel to include only the fallen, broken and dry wood on the forest floor, not the green and growing underwood.[8] In Whittlewood the 'poor inhabit-

Harrowby MSS (Sandon Hall), vol. 437, doc. 69, p. 81, on the taking of timber from Hardwick Heath and the difficulty of ending the custom.
[7] Northants. RO, Mont.B, X350, box 10, no. 25, Geddington Chase enclosure papers, 'Some Reasons Offer'd to the Commoners in Ye Chase, 1721', and 'Mr Wargrave's Reasons Why a Cow Common set off ye Chase will be an advantage to Lord Gowran'.
[8] *Northampton Mercury*, 9 July 1785: the warden of Salcey Forest promised prosecution to those taking green wood 'under Pretence of gathering up the Rotten and Dead wood'. See Cambs. RO, P141/6/4, for an attempt to regulate the taking of

ants' of Silverstone, Whitfield and several other parishes enjoyed the right to dry fallen wood, which they could gather on two days every week.[9] But commoners made frequent and illegal expeditions into the forests for wood on other days and nights of the week. Proximity and custom made raids easy and habitual; and commoners probably believed that they had the right to more and better wood than the 'sere and broken' or 'rotten and dead' fallen boughs they were expected to take by wardens and keepers.[10]

Commoners took wood for fuel from private woods too. Indeed they seem to have made little distinction between forests and woods. Discussing this in the nineteenth century, Richard Jefferies described access to private woods as a privilege offered to the local poor, not a right they believed to belong to them regardless of who owned the wood.[11] He may have been wrong; certainly eighteenth-century evidence suggests that long usage made it a right in the minds of commoners who exercised rights over wastes and royal forests too.[12] Private woods were merely an extension of the area over which commoners could move: they crossed them daily, watching nuts and berries ripen, picking up dead wood or browse, and probably taking a few rabbits and hares too. Forest commoners in particular would find the distinction merely formal. Charles Vancouver noted that commoners in the Hampshire woodlands took snapwood 'pretty freely'; in fact they had been 'observed to visit most of the demesnes, and private as well as other woodlands through the county'.[13] They did not recognize (although they may have understood) the nice distinctions of property owners. Instead there is a deliberate and confident assertiveness about wood gathering in areas where wood abounded, or had once done so. The co-existence of turbary in forests and commons, with the hedges,

firing, and to restrict it to 'the actual poor of the parish' after the enclosure of Snailwell in 1805.

[9] PRO, CREST 2/1051, fuel claims made on the enclosure of Whittlewood Forest; J. E. Linnell, *Old Oak* (1932), pp. 189–91. They kept the right until the 1850s when the forest was enclosed.

[10] A survey of prosecutions for wood stealing taken to quarter sessions indicates that they grew rapidly at the end of the century: Northants. RO, Quarter Sessions Grand Files, 1760–1800.

[11] Richard Jefferies. *The Gamekeeper at Home* (1878; 1948 edn), p. 107.

[12] See Neeson, 'Common Right and Enclosure', pp. 62–6, for a case of wood stealing in the non-forest parish of Greens Norton, in which commoners, including the overseers of the poor and the justice of the peace, stood by the wood stealers and against the farmer who informed on them.

[13] Vancouver, *General View ... Hampshire*, p. 389.

spinneys and woods of landowners, made the getting of wood in particular seem to be a general right, or, at least, to borrow a metaphor from another product of commons, fair game. For example, even outside the forest, timber trees became maypoles. At Cottesbrooke near Creaton common field in 1761, commoners cut down an oak in a spinney belonging to Sir John Langham 'with a Design, as is supposed, to erect the same as a May-Pole in some Neighbouring Parish'. Sir John offered a five-guinea reward and upped it to twenty a fortnight later.[14] A year later two more oaks were cut but not carried away from a spinney in Teeton in Ravensthorpe.[15] More of what landowners called the audacity of wood gatherers can be seen in their use of the law to prevent their own prosecution: in 1769 Henry Clark wrote from Chipping Campden in Gloucestershire in some distress.

I have been with the woodfallers and hands great part of the time but the wood stealers, and other Theves, pesters me sadly, the world never was, for badnes as tis now. There is many reasen for it but the worst and cheaf reasion is, the law for taking of horses. No farmer in our Roods can do his busines with so few horses as 4 and if his hedges are pulled gaits and herdles took away trees loped or roots stole if the farmer as putts the laws in execution, the first time he takes a hors above 4 the horse is took out from his dung cart and the rouge as took him wood have 1611 pound, so what ever is dun must be put up so they grow from thing to thing and in time every Honest man must be destitute of everything needfull.[16]

It would take many years, if it happened at all, before this idea of *right*, no matter what its origin, was worn down into a privilege, and before commoners would accept that privileges could be taken away. Until then the Earl Spencer had to resort to threatening anyone (including his own servants) caught nutting in his woods with being 'taken before a Magistrate and sent for a Soldier'.[17] But the threat of the law here in Althorp – unlike the threat in Chipping

[14] *Northampton Mercury*, 18 May 1761, 1 June 1761.

[15] *Northampton Mercury*, 10 May 1762; the night of 1 May was mischief night too: R. W. Malcolmson, *Popular Recreations in English Society 1700–1850* (Cambridge, 1973), p. 82.

[16] Harrowby papers (Sandon Hall), vol. XXXVI, fos. 12, 13, Henry Clark to Hon. Sir, Court House Camden, 11 Mar. 1769. Clark refers to 7 Geo.III, c.42 s.38 (1766), which forbade the use of carts with more than four horses when wheels were only 9 inches.

[17] *Northampton Mercury*, 23 Aug. 1779.

Campden – was bluster. Impressment was not a lawful punishment for trespass. The Earl could not make good his promise. Instead, he and other landowners advertised the closing of their woods and gave notice of their intention to deal with trespassers; at least ten Northamptonshire woods were closed – on paper – in the last decades of the eighteenth century, often in the decade or so after an enclosure.[18]

In east Midland hill and vale parishes little timber or underwood was left to take by the end of the sixteenth century.[19] But private woods remained to be regularly, if illegally, culled; and commoners found other kinds of material to burn. They took the less substantial fuels that grew on the heaths and commons that remained in even hill and vale parishes. Of these, furze was particularly important. Commoners at Bow Brickhill in Buckinghamshire thought enough of it to riot when their common was enclosed, despite winning the relatively large compensation of 230 acres of furze and firing land.[20] Pehr Kalm describes boys on Ivinghoe common scything it down with small scythes when it was still quite short, raking it in heaps with whatever else it grew with, and binding it into bundles with the supple shoots of blackberry bushes:

> We saw several heaps of such bundles, which lay here upon the plain, and which were to be carried home for fuel. This furze with its thorns, had the effect that, when one walked where it grew, it tore great scratches on the shoes, and where it encountered the stockings, they were not respected. It pricked the legs savagely. We afterwards saw boys in many places in this district cut down the same in the above-described way for fuel.[21]

And in Hampshire Charles Vancouver noted that even at the heart

[18] *Northampton Mercury*, 26 Aug. 1776, 1 Sept. 1778, 8 Sept. 1787 (Nobottle Wood in Great Brington); 13 Sept. 1788 (Moseley grounds in Harlestone); 8 July 1765, 23 Aug. 1794, 12 Sept. 1795 (Sywell Wood); 30 Aug. 1788 (Hardwick Wood); 6 Sept. 1773 (Berry Wood in Upton); 23 Aug. 1793 (Fallam Woods in Braunston); 28 Aug. 1790 (Horton Woods); 16 Aug. 1794 (Stowe Wood in Stowe Nine Churches, and Dodford Woods in Farthingstone); 4, 8, 25 Aug., 9 Sept. 1802 (Daventry Wood). The newspaper carried warnings for Bedfordshire woods too, for example: *Northampton Mercury*, 7 July 1798, enclosure and notice of trespass for Deadmonsey Woods, Whipsnade, Bedfordshire; and the woods of Lord St John near Melchbourn throughout August 1794.
[19] Thirsk, 'Field Systems of the East Midlands', p. 249.
[20] *Northampton Mercury*, 4 Apr. 1791.
[21] Kalm, *Kalm's Account of his Visit to England*, pp. 199–200; Kalm reported that bracken was preferred to furze as a fuel for its stronger heat (p. 208). For the use of brambles for binding see also Mabey, *Plants with a Purpose*, pp. 54–5.

of the chalk district commoners gathered furze from the valleys and low grounds that cut across it.[22]

Lops and tops, snapwood, dry and fallen wood, furze and bracken were all taken from forests, wastes and private woods by the inhabitants of common-field and forest villages in the Midlands. Whether it was allotted in bundles per household or regulated by days or was there for the taking, all of it was valuable. In the 1790s the Reverend David Davies of Barkham in Berkshire reckoned that a family could cut enough fuel for a year in a week and that farmers would cart it in exchange for the ashes. It was essentially free, being cut in slack moments, but to replace it after enclosure would cost anything from £1 15s to £4 3s, or £2 8s on average – roughly the wages of four or five weeks' agricultural labour. In short, Davies put the value of common fuel – in this case probably furze – at 10 per cent of a labourer's wages.[23] Earlier in the century, at Atherstone in the Warwickshire Arden, opponents of enclosure valued the fuel and sand the women collected at £3 3s a year, and a child able to work brought in the same again – together they earned almost a third of a labouring family's income.[24] Perhaps the income value of fuel in common-field England ranged from Barkham to Atherstone.

Value also varied with the availability and price of other fuel. In Northamptonshire, until the Grand Junction canal brought coal to Blisworth from the Staffordshire and Warwickshire collieries, the price of coal in the county was high, and that of all kinds of wood correspondingly expensive: the saying went 'He that must eat a buttered faggot let him go to Northampton.'[25] Faggots cost 18s to 20s for six score and stackwood cost 16s to 18s a waggon load. As the cheaper coal began arriving in the 1790s the price of a waggon-load of furze fell by a third to 14s from 21s.[26] The high cost of bought fuel in Northamptonshire made the right to gather furze from commons particularly valuable to poor commoners. Within two years of the enclosure of an 800-acre waste at West Haddon in 1765, parishioners found themselves subscribing to a fund for low-priced fuel for the poor.[27]

---

22 Vancouver, *General View ... Hampshire*, p. 390.
23 Davies, *Case of the Labourers*, pp. 15, 181, 185.
24 Warwicks. RO, HR 35/15; they earned more than a third when gleaning is added.
25 William Andrews, ed., *Bygone Northamptonshire* (1891), p. 215.
26 Pitt, *General View ... Northampton*, pp. 146, 228–9.
27 *Northampton Mercury*, 16 Jan. 1767; for a discussion of the enclosure of West Haddon see Chapter 7 below. Not every Midland county was short of coal:

But commoners took more than fuel from commons, and some of the wood they took had other uses. They cut furze, reeds, and weeds for fodder and litter, and for firing ovens, bakehouses, lime-kilns and woolcombers' pots as well as cottage hearths. Besides fuel, furze had many uses. As fodder it was bruised for horses and bullocks and might get them through the winter until April or May:

> I observed last winter in the frost, that bullocks would eat young twigs of the goss, at least 14" long; and I had several in April and May, in this rough land, that were lusty, without eating a handful, all the winter, of any kind of fodder.

It had the advantage of growing on what was otherwise poor land. Bucklebury commoners petitioning against the enclosure said that they used furze for winter feed for cattle and had no other source of fodder.[28]

From underwood came quick-growing hazel to make hurdles for folding sheep, to mend hedges and make fences. The thin tributary branches made good beanstakes, and a long hazel rod tied around with holly sprigs made a good chimney-sweeping brush.[29] Brushwood, like hazel, was unfit for browse for deer so forest keepers lost nothing when commoners took it. In Needwood Forest many 'help themselves to small quantities of it who live adjacent to the forest and it has never been thought an object worthy of notice'. Commoners took trouse – pollard loppings and small underwood – for repairing fences too. Again, the custom was reasonable, did no injury, and the wood was not sold by the crown anyway.[30]

On heathland there was a fern – bracken – harvest for ash. Poor

charterers in Needwood Forest in Staffordshire had the right to take firewood from the forest but appear not to have bothered because there was plenty of coal, which was cheaper than the cost of cutting, preparing and carrying wood: Staffs. RO, William Salt Library, 11/339/1/50, 'Needwood Forest. Extracts of Records Relating to Estovers in Needwood Forest, Dec. 7, 1790'.

28 Berks. RO, D/EHy E9/1, Bucklebury petition against enclosure 1834; 'A Letter to the Editors, on the Uses of Furze or Goss as Food for Cattle', *Museum Rusticum et Commerciale*, 2: 39 (1764), pp. 118–19; Lawrence, *Modern Land Steward*, pp. 380–3; 'On the Use of Furze, by his Grace the Duke of Richmond', *Annals of Agriculture*, 41 (1804), pp. 193–6; and a late example of furze as fodder before and for a while after enclosure: George Bourne, *Change in the Village* (1912; 1966 edn), p. 144.

29 John Steward Collis, *The Worm Forgives the Plough* (1973), pp. 291–3; Peter H. Ditchfield, *Country Folk: A Pleasant Company* (1974), p. 232; Hartley, *Food in England*, p. 42.

30 Staffs. RO, William Salt Library, 11/339/1/50, 'Needwood Forest. Extracts of Records Relating to Estovers in Needwood Forest, Dec. 7, 1790'.

commoners in Charnwood Forest burnt it to make ash balls to make lye for soap.[31] Its high potassium content made it valuable as potash in glass-making and bleaching too. Though thin and light, bracken was burnt in brick kilns.[32] It also made a better litter than straw in the winter because it held less moisture; and when stalls were cleared out it could be composted and ploughed in, like manure made with straw. Its resistance to moisture also made it a good base for a haystack, when set over stones, helping it dry quickly. Rats and mice had no appetite for it, so the hay was somewhat free of them too. And after it was cut, bracken, like furze, left behind a crop of fine grass, good for grazing. It was good for packaging material too, cheaper than straw; and a good cover for root crops.[33]

Rushes, reeds and useful grasses of all varieties were abundant not only in the fens but in still water in brooks and wet places on common-field commons throughout the temperate zone. Different kinds of grass performed the same functions in different areas; whatever was to hand was used.[34] Reed itself was plentiful and valued most as thatch for roofs and also to cover the stacks, ricks and clamps of all kinds of crops and vegetables.[35] Rushes – bulrushes – were equally plentiful, waterproof, and woven into baskets, mats, hats, chair seats and toys of an enormous range of sizes, functions, shapes and qualities. Like reed, rushes were used for agricultural thatch. Dorothy Hartley tells us that they were also good for bedding, as a netting in the plastering of walls, and a wrap-

---

[31] For bracken see Nigel Webb, *Heathlands* (1986), p. 12; Neeson, 'Common Right and Enclosure', pp. 56–9; and Wigens, *Clandestine Farm*, p. 92. And on ashes sold to farmers see Douglas Hay, 'Poaching and the Game Laws on Cannock Chase', in D. Hay, P. Linebaugh, J. Rule, E. P. Thompson and C. Winslow, *Albion's Fatal Tree: Crime and Society in Eighteenth-Century England* (1975), p. 203. On small commoners' common of fern see T. R. Potter, *The History and Antiquities of Charnwood Forest* (1842), p. 23; Marshall described the forest as bare of wood in the 1790s, though not of furze: *Rural Oeconomy of the Midland Counties*, I, p. 65.

[32] L. Rymer, 'The History and Ethnobotany of Bracken', *Botanical Journal of the Linnaeus Society*, 73 (1976), cited in Webb, *Heathlands*, p. 51.

[33] Hartley, *Lost Country Life*, pp. 67, 153–4, 183; Pehr Kalm makes the same claims for furze as well as bracken, *Kalm's Account of his Visit to England*, pp. 208, 268; Webb, *Heathlands*, p. 50. For a 1755 Needwood Forest commoners' case re furze and pasture see D. Hay, *Crown Side Cases in the Court of King's Bench* (forthcoming, Staffs. Record Society).

[34] Mabey, *Plants with a Purpose*, p. 127.

[35] Dorothy Hartley, *Made in England* (1939; 1987 edn), p. 50; on regional varieties of thatch reed, pp. 54–5; Gilbert White, *The Essential Gilbert White of Selborne*, ed. H. J. Massingham (Boston, 1985), p. 249.

ping for soft milk cheeses.[36] They made cheap, bright rushlights too: Gilbert White reckoned that labouring families got more than five hours of 'comfortable light' for a farthing, and reported that a pound and a half of rushes gave a year's light because they were used chiefly in winter: 'working people burn no candle in the long days, because they rise and go to bed by daylight'. The soft rush he described, *juncus effusus*, was ubiquitous; it grew in most moist pastures, by streams and under hedges.[37]

Commons might provide sand for cleaning, but (like rushes) common *fields* might provide it too: fourteen-year-old Ann Adkins of Brigstock went to gather some from Brigstock field in 1785 and was killed when a large stone covering the pit fell on her.[38] Sand was strewn on cottage floors once a week, raked into patterns and left to absorb dirt, dust and grease. It was a good abrasive for scouring pots and pans too – so too was wood ash from the hearth. Different qualities of sand had different uses: some from the Oxfordshire parish of Kingham was fine enough to clean pewter, and retailers sold it at a penny a pound.[39] But, to commoners willing to get it for themselves, sand was free for the taking. From the Nene valley Morton reported the uses of penny-earth dug from the common fields, ground and mixed with water and moulded into jersey-combers' comb pots, plastered on the sides and roofs of ovens – where it was remarkably fire resistant – smoothed as a coping on stone and earthen walls, and even – with some skill – moulded into chimney stacks.[40]

Even the loose wool caught on thorn bushes lived again in blankets and suits of clothes. The agricultural improver, John Arbuthnot, thought that briars and bushes plucked as much as half the wool from common-field flocks, but Dorothy Hartley describes a gentler, less polemical shedding of fleece, particularly from the old ewes:

[36] Hartley, *Made in England*, pp. 50–1, 70. Bulrushes also made leaky barrels water tight. Pehr Kalm noted the chair-seat industry of the poor in Essex: *Kalm's Account of his Visit to England*, p. 157.
[37] Gilbert White, *The Natural History of Selborne* (1788–9; 1977 edn), pp. 180–3; White did a very careful cost accounting of the fat needed for rush-lights too.
[38] *Northampton Mercury*, 25 Apr. 1785.
[39] Caroline Davidson, *A Woman's Work is Never Done. A History of Housework in the British Isles 1650–1950* (1982), p. 122, cites R. Plot, *The Natural History of Oxfordshire. Being an Essay towards a Natural History of England* (Oxford, 1677), p. 74.
[40] Morton, *Natural History of Northamptonshire*, p. 66.

The scanty winter fodder thins the hairs, so that a weak length comes near the skin, and the weight of the old fleece, the summer heat and the seasonal growth of the animal, make the old fleece slowly drop off.

The ideal time to shear sheep is when the old wool is about to drop, but shepherds leave it unshorn on old ewes, particularly those that lamb early, in order to keep them warm. The result is that by August 'the old ewes trail around the lambing pastures, with disreputable clots of wool dropping off them'. This was the kind of wool commoners gleaned from the common pastures for spinning. It was doubly good because not only was it free but it was tapered at both ends and so made a fine, even thread. The fleece of a small ewe weighed about nine pounds in-the-grease, a third of this picked-over greasy fleece (two pounds of washed wool) would make a plain jersey for a man. Any short, loose wool left over after carding went into batting for quilts or became the stuffing of carriage pads and saddles.[41]

And, while fuel and materials were important supports of a commoning economy, food was too. It included hazel-nuts and chestnuts, often sold for city markets. An acre of coppice in years when the hazel bushes were not cut could yield up to 30 cwt of hazel nuts.[42] They were hawked around the village and sold in towns.[43] William Ellis noted that they could be kept until Candlemas if they were buried in boxes in the earth. As well as nuts there were mushrooms in the autumn for soups and stews, or dried, threaded on string and hung by the chimney piece. For the gentry the truffle-hunter brought truffles at 2s 6d a pound.[44] There were herbs for cooking and healing: wild chervil, fennel, mint, wild thyme, marjoram, borage, wild basil, tansy. And there was all manner of young leaves for salads and vegetables: young hawthorn, wild sorrel, chicory, dandelion leaves, salad burnet, catsear, goatsbeard, greater prickly lettuce, corn sow-thistle, fat-hen and chickweed,

[41] Arbuthnot, *Inquiry into the Connection between the Present Prices of Provisions and the Size of Farms*, p. 8. Dorothy Hartley, *Water in England* (1964), pp. 288, 190; and personal communication from Ms Jane Henderson.

[42] Mabey, *Plants with a Purpose*, p. 78; *Gilbert White's Journals*, ed. Walter Johnson (Cambridge, Mass., 1970), p. 130.

[43] John Clare, 'Nutting', *Selected Poems and Prose*, p. 138; and Linnell, *Old Oak*, p. 21.

[44] Bell, *To Meet Mr Ellis*, p. 29; *Gilbert White's Journals*, pp. 246, 165, 175, 179, 380, 388, 404, 347; Monk, *General View ... Leicester*, pp. 57–8.

yarrow, charlock and goosegrass.[45] William Jones, a Charlbury weaver and farmer, recorded in his diary his walk with his sister up to the cider wells in Wychwood Forest 'to get water crase at ye pools'.[46] There were nettles in the spring. When picked very young and boiled or steamed they were used as a spring tonic: at Ivinghoe 'they here maintain that nettles prepared this or any other way, and eaten, are very wholesome, and purify the blood'.[47]

There were berries too: elderberries, blackberries, barberries, raspberries, wild strawberries, rosehips and haws, cranberries and sloes for jellies, jams and wines.[48] Bilberries were a valuable crop in Staffordshire; Swinnerton Park was 'much resorted to during the season by many of the poor for the purpose of gathering bilberries, which they sell to the nearest towns and villages'.[49] There were crab apples too, and dandelions and primroses for wine and tea.[50] And there were birds, rabbits and hares for stews and for sale, and the fish and fowl of fenland villages caught in autumn and winter when the land was lost under water.[51]

If animals were food from commons, animals were fed from commons too. There was space for geese, cows and sheep, and for

---

[45] Richard Mabey, *Food for Free* (1972), *passim*.: these herbs and salad greens are plants with regionally specific common names that grow in the Midlands and the south and east of England, though some may be found elsewhere too. For medical herbs see Bell, *To Meet Mr Ellis*, p. 39: 'Rue, Henbane seeds, Camomile, Rhubarb, Nettle seeds, Box Daucus or Wild Carrot seed, Bay, wild Thyme, Herb Centory, Elder Flower, Onions, Parsley root, Burdock Root, Fennel Root, Marsh Mallow, Winter-Savory, St John's Wort, Lettuce, Wood Sorrel, Plantain, Five Leaf Grass, Strawberry Leaves, House-Leek, Blackberry-Briary-Leaves, Dandelion, Primrose Leaves, Sage, Mint ... Wormwood, Fumitory, Scurvy Grass'.

[46] Sturge Gretton, *Three Centuries in North Oxfordshire*, p. 201; *Gilbert White's Journals*, pp. 398, 419.

[47] Sturge Gretton, *Three Centuries in North Oxfordshire*, pp. 574–82; Kalm, *Kalm's Account of his Visit to England*, p. 258; Rosamond Richardson notes the sale of nettles in eighteenth-century markets: *Hedgerow Cookery* (1980), p. 149.

[48] *Gilbert White's Journals*, pp. 246, 313, 344, 339, 362, 363, 364, 386; Bell, *To Meet Mr Ellis*, p. 29.

[49] William Pitt, *Topographical History of Staffordshire* (Newcastle-under-Lyme, 1817), p. 385.

[50] Grieve, *Modern Herbal*, pp. 43–4.

[51] For the value of hares and rabbits to the economy of Cannock Chase see Hay, 'Poaching and the Game Laws on Cannock Chase', pp. 203–4, 223; and Bell, *To Meet Mr Ellis*, p. 61; for rooks eaten at Selborne, *Gilbert White's Journals*, p. 96. In the fens, getting eels and hunting was regulated by confining each to particular days: H. E. Hallam, 'The Fen Bylaws of Spalding and Pinchbeck', *Lincolnshire Architectural and Archaeological Society*, 10 (1963), pp. 40–56, cited in Thirsk, 'Field Systems of the East Midlands', pp. 251–3.

hogs there was a beechmast harvest, and acorns. Gilbert White measured the value of mast in January 1787:

> The crop of beech mast was prodigious, and of great service to men's hogs, which were half fat before they were shut up. Between mast and potatoes poor men killed very large hogs at little expense. Tom Berriman's hog weighed 16 scores; yet eat only seven bushels of barley-meal: whereas without the help above mentioned, he would have required 20 bushels.[52]

When commoners had fuel, food and materials from commons they also had access. Open-field parishes were particularly open to commoners and to drovers who used the common-field routes because of the wayside grazing. The 'woodstealers' who crossed Rockingham Forest daily did so by a maze of paths from any of which they might stray to get a rabbit or a hare.[53] In the fens commoners could steep hemp in haff toles in dykes or lakes.[54] Commons, fields and wastes offered space too, for football pitches a mile long, and for weavers' cloth stretched on the hooks of tenter poles to shrink to an even width.[55]

But access also meant walking, looking and being. 'The first thing that a Forester asks of you is that you should say how beautiful the place is, no matter what time of year', says Dennis Potter of the Forest of Dean. And:

> This is the children's Forest too. A place to collect birds' eggs and build secret cabins in the thickest parts of the Wood, to climb trees and search out and occupy abandoned quarries or old, disused pits, smelling with stale, silvery mud caked over the rusted rails. Adults, too, have always had this background and this release, and they appear not to take it for granted: surprise still revolves through the year – the myriad greens, the walks down an old stony road to the rapids, the bracken turning and

---

[52] For geese living for months on commons see *Gilbert White's Journals*, p. 351, and in the Northamptonshire fen, above, Chapter 2, pp. 67–8. For beech and oakmast collected annually see Bell, *To Meet Mr Ellis*, p. 60; *Gilbert White's Journals*, p. 395. On the need to age acorns before feeding them to hogs see Kalm, *Kalm's Account of his Visit to England*, p. 249. White, *The Essential Gilbert White of Selborne*, p. 356.

[53] Northants. RO, Mont. B., X350, Box 10, no. 25, Geddington Chase enclosure papers, 'Some Reasons Offer'd to the Commoners in Ye Chase, 1721', and 'Mr Wargrave's Reasons Why a Cow Common set off ye Chase will be an advantage to Lord Gowran'.

[54] Hallam, 'The Fen Bylaws of Spalding and Pinchbeck', pp. 40–56.

[55] Hartley, *Water in England*, p. 292.

crumbling into a dusty and universal golden brown, and, even in winter, the stark black trunks and icy stubble has its own bitter loveliness.

The solitariness of the forest was a vital and sympathetic backdrop to the close intimacy of the village.[56] Most hill and vale common-field villages had no wastes as large as this, and most commons of a hundred acres or less were not beautiful enough to invite admiration. But the fields themselves provided some of the space and the loveliness of Dean. They did so because they were large and unbroken by hedges and fences, and because they were accessible, cut through with paths, balks, joynts and carriageways – cut through too by even older routes: Saxon estate boundaries, green lanes like those crossing the borders of Oxfordshire and North-amptonshire – the through routes of pre-history – and woodways, the tiny lanes from villages to former woodlands.[57] Commoners owned them through access even if they owned nothing by law. John Clare, who in his loneliness sometimes thought himself the only aesthete in Helpston, describes a general appreciation of the open-ness of common fields:

> How fond the rustics ear at leisure dwells
> On the soft soundings of his village bells
> As on a sunday morning at his ease
> He takes his rambles just as fancys please
> Down narrow baulks that interscet the fields
> Hid in profusion that its produce yields
> Long twining peas in faintly misted greens
> And wingd leaf multitudes of crowding beans
> And flighty oatlands of a lighter hue.[58]

II

By the end of the eighteenth century the amount of uncultivated wasteland in common-field England was relatively small. In the Mid-lands, waste in counties like Northamptonshire and Oxfordshire was not much more than a tenth of the entire area, although it had been

[56] Dennis Potter, *The Changing Forest* (1962), pp. 19, 21; for the children's common waste see Bewick, *Memoir*, p. 11.
[57] Ashby, *Joseph Ashby of Tysoe 1859–1919*, pp. 37–8. W. G. Hoskins, *The Making of the English Landscape* (1955; 1970 edn), pp. 238–42.
[58] John Clare, 'Sunday Walks', in Eric Robinson and David Powell, eds., *John Clare* (Oxford, 1984), pp. 76–7.

larger at the start of the century. How large is uncertain, but in Northamptonshire in 1750, before parliamentary enclosure, roughly one acre in six of the unenclosed land was common waste; by 1850 almost no waste would remain. The proportion of waste in west Midland counties with few common fields was much higher.[59]

Within common-field England, forest, fen, heath and scarp commoners took more from the waste than commoners in the most arable of fielden villages. Though even the fenland courts restricted some commodities to particular cottagers and landowners, fen harvests were evidently very valuable. Commoners named particular days for down gathering, for getting reeds, peat turfs and rushes for ropes. They took sedge too, and willows and osiers, and more.[60] On the Hampshire downs Gilbert White was certain that, when commoners resisted the temptation to hunt:

> Such forests and wastes ... are of considerable service to neighbourhoods that verge upon them, by furnishing them with peat and turf for their firing; with fuel for the burning their lime; and with ashes for their grasses; and by maintaining their geese and their stock of young cattle at little or no expense.[61]

Obviously, the produce of commons ranged from the abundance of the fen, forest and downs to the relative scarcity of the river valley.[62] Many parishes had very little common waste. But even a small waste offered something. In the most densely cultivated parishes a hundred acres of furze meant fuel every winter, some fine grazing in the spring, and space for a game of football or for courting. Moreover, common fields themselves provided more than grazing. At Brigstock commoners took sand from the field, and at Fenny Compton in Warwickshire forty-eight commoners petitioning at

[59] See above, Chapter 3, pp. 96–7. Williams, 'Enclosure and Reclamation of Waste Land', pp. 57–9. In the west Midlands at the end of the eighteenth century, Staffordshire may have had as little as one thousand acres of common field and 140,000 acres of common waste: David Palliser, *The Staffordshire Landscape* (1976), p. 126, citing Pitt, *Topographical History of Staffordshire*.
[60] Hallam, 'Fen Bylaws of Spalding and Pinchbeck'. Rights to fen products were for inhabitants; strangers without land could have grazing for a year; single men could have grazing only. But, in Cottenham in 1662, lotts of turf belonged only to cottagers and owners, though inhabitants could dig for clay and gravel: Cambs. RO, R.50/9/39 (1662); also R.50/9/39/11 (1757).
[61] White, *Natural History of Selborne*, p. 24.
[62] Alan Everitt, 'Farm Labourers', in Joan Thirsk, ed., *Agrarian History of England and Wales*, IV, (1967), pp. 404–5, makes the same distinction between areas of abundant and scarce commons; Thirsk, 'Field Systems of the East Midlands', pp. 232–80.

enclosure for proper recompense for the loss of fuel drew the attention of the commissioners to the fact that it lay in parcels of land intermixed in the *fields*. It should not be allotted to any one proprietor:

> there are in the fields of Fenney Compton aforesd Several Pieces of common lands Such as Obwell Hill, Tite head hill, Rush Slade, Holwell, the Mortar pitts and Several other Pieces of Greensward Some bearing Bushes which the poor had always for fetching and had liberty to fetch time immemorable and all the Rest of the Common land was or ought to have been applied to the use and Benefit of the Poor And not any known right to any one Proprietor And as we are apt to think this thing may not have been Represented before unto You –
>
> We ... Pray that you ... allott the poor somewt in lieu of their rights as well as Rich[63]

If the benefits of commons varied with geography did they also support only some members of a village? Looking back from enclosure, the poor seem to have felt the loss most, and advocates of compensated enclosure in the 1790s were particularly concerned about their plight.[64] But the poor were among the worst placed to withstand the loss of commons. And the evidence of usage *before* enclosure, suggests that many commoners valued the common, not only the poorest. This is important because it means that common usage of commons was not a charity for the weakest in the village, it was a resource for almost everyone.

Take furze, for instance – the fuel most often mentioned in hill, vale and heath parishes. Enclosure awards compensated the poor in particular for its loss.[65] But before enclosure most householders

---

[63] Warwicks. RO, D8053, vi.

[64] [Young], *General Report on Enclosures*, Appendix IV, pp. 158–63, citing Paul's *Observations on the General Enclosure Bill*, pp. 22, 31, 40. Nevertheless, more than half of 130 Warwickshire Awards made no award to the poor, and the worst instances of neglect occurred *after* 1800, despite the best efforts of Young *et al.*: Martin, 'Warwickshire and the Parliamentary Enclosure Movement', p. 137.

[65] At the enclosure of Broughton, for example, enclosers compensated not only the local poor but those of five neighbouring parishes with some sixty acres of land because they had lost the right to cut furze; the parishes were Broughton, Kettering, Rothwell, Pitchley, Weekley and Warkton: Northants. RO, Anscomb's Abstracts of Enclosure Awards, p. 125. For other instances of claims for fuel made at enclosure see Neeson, 'Common Right and Enclosure', pp. 56–7, and Northants. RO, Anscomb's Abstracts of Enclosure Awards, Braunston, Duston, Piddington and Hackleton, East Haddon, Byfield, Watford and Murcott,

gathered it, not only the poorest. Thus at Moreton Pinkney in April
1727 the jury tried to restrict the right to those whose property was
worth less than £5 a year – those with ten acres or less – but it
changed the regulation in October to allow anyone in the parish to
cut furze and bushes provided they 'carry them home upon their
backs not useing any waggons carts or horses'. The same restriction
appeared in fenland as well as hill and vale. In effect it limited the
amount a household might take. Some might not bother, but they
would be the richer households, not the families of husbandmen and
middling commoners.[66] In some parishes those who had no settlement were excluded altogether. At Raunds in 1740:

> noe Certificate person shall ... cut any ffurz from the Comon
> under the penalty of 5 shillings for each default and that no
> person shall fetch any furz from the old meadow with a Cart and
> Horse or Horse under the penalty of Ten Shillings for each
> default.[67]

Gathering furze and other fuel was worth the time of more villagers
than the poorest: a servant to a gentleman living in Great Harrow-
den put too much furze on the kitchen fire in March 1790 and set the
chimney ablaze – furze clearly burnt well in gentlemen's hearths
too.[68] At Berwick Prior in Oxfordshire the right to furze belonged to
the poor inhabitants but also to the occupiers of particular pieces of
property; for example, the Innkeeper of the Chequers Inn in 1773
had the right to grazing for a cow and a plot of ground upon
Berwick Furze. At enclosure some cottage commoners claimed a lot
of bushes or brakes pertaining to their cottages – and cottages with
rights brought higher rents than those without since they were the
better cottages of the village, not tenements for the poorest villagers.[69] And, as we have seen, furze had many uses: it was more

Great Doddington, Weston by Weedon in Weedon Loys, Weedon Beck, etc. Also
see M. K. Ashby, *The Changing English Village* (Kineton, 1974), p. 210.
[66] Northants. RO, G3315a, 10 Apr. 1727; G3361a, 23 Oct. 1727; in 1743 the penalty
for using a cart was 20s a load: G3462a. For the fens see Church Commissioners'
Records 278573, October 1701. For hill and vale see QCR 59, 13 Dec. 1740
(Raunds); and X3851 (1745–54; Boughton and Pitsford). Cumnor inhabitants also
had the right to take furze, again, only on their backs: Orwin and Orwin, *Open
Fields*, p. 57, n.1.
[67] Northants RO, QCR 52, 1729; QCR 59, 13 Dec. 1740.
[68] *Northampton Mercury*, 13 Mar. 1790.
[69] R. E. Moreau, *The Departed Village: Berwick Salome at the Turn of the Century*
(1968), p. 23; Northants. RO, Moulton Inclosure Letters, August–December 1772
(Accn 1969/14/92).

than a domestic fuel. We have seen that bakers burnt it in their ovens and lime-burners used it to fire their kilns. In Bedfordshire it brought a profit of 45s 6d an acre.[70] It was worth having.

There are other examples of the use of commons by the whole village community, or, at least, by a substantial part of it. In Selborne, the 'Little farmers' used rushlights in their kitchens and dairies when nights were long, not the very poor 'who are always the worst oeconomists'.[71] Even the Earl of Cardigan thatched his hay-stacks with rushes. His steward promised to get the work done as soon as he could in September 1726.[72] And, like furze, dung for manure (and perhaps for fuel too) which belonged to the 'parishioners' of Chipping Norton could be carried from the fields and commons only on their heads and backs. The restriction probably excluded those working in the parish but not born there – the certificate poor – but it also prevented local farmers with carts coming into the fields and carrying off more than their share. It seems unlikely that the richest commoners would bother to carry off dung themselves, though they might send a labourer who was a local man to do it for them, but husbandmen would certainly find it worth their while. Similar restrictions applied to the furze on the heath. And only parishioners could take stone and gravel, on pain of a high fine of a pound to the lord of the manor and 2s 6d to whoever detected the abuse of the by-law.[73] These rights were valued by most commoners, not kept for the poor alone.

Commoners took all of the fuels, foods and materials described here for their own use. But many they took to sell. Commons (like common fields) gave employment as well as some subsistence. This included money made from the seasonal crops of flowers, berries and so on that women took round the village or to nearby towns. But it also meant the full-time employment of rush-workers, mat-makers and others who got the raw materials for their work from the commons. For example, in Kettering the flags and rushes in the brook in the common fields were the livelihood of Samuel Martin and his wife, who had the foresight to try to prevent its loss at enclosure. They wrote to the solicitor for the enclosure that they had made enquiries at nearby Brixworth about the enclosure there and

[70] Batchelor, *General View … Bedford*, p. 466.
[71] White, *Natural History of Selborne*, p. 182.
[72] *Letters of Daniel Eaton 1725–1732*, p. 58, Letter 75, 20 Sept. 1726.
[73] Ballard, 'The Management of Open Fields', pp. 137–8.

had found that the lords of the manor had lost their 'rilety' to flags
and rushes when it was not set down in the Award. At Kettering the
same would happen if the Award did not reserve it. Worse, they had
heard 'the gentlemen talk of haveing the Brook cut another way and
if they do it will quite Destroy them'. 'I ham a man', wrote Samuel
Martin, 'quight advanced in years and got notting to get my bread at
and my Wife likewise As she is been brought up in it from her
youth.'[74]

So commons were still useful in the common-field Midlands, and
if they were useful here then they were even more so in the wasteland
parishes further north and west. And they were valued by more than
the poor: most families used the waste; it was a vital part of the
economy of women and children. This begins to establish the
boundaries of income value, a value that clearly varied from village
to village. Common right could double a family income.[75] But what
was the social meaning of using common waste?

III

Living off the produce of commons encouraged frugality, economy,
thrift. Productive commons had always been the insurance, the
reserves, the hidden wealth of commoners – they were the oldest
part of an ancient economy. They gave commoners the fuel, food
and materials that kept them out of the market for labour and out of
the market for consumption too. And the more productive the
common the more independent the commoners.

The habit of living off commons made the habit of regular
employment less necessary. For commoners it was customary to
make a living first out of the materials on hand; after all, the
common came first, wage labour was a relatively recent arrival. This
is not to deny the existence of wage labour; earning wages was
necessary, but until they became the lion's share of income they
were supplementary not central to a commoning economy. Looking
for regular, constant employment was unnecessary where commons
were rich reserves. It is no accident that the loudest complaints
about the unavailability of commoners for work come from the

[74] Northants. RO, Lamb and Holmes, Kettering Enclosure Papers, XIV, 16.
[75] Jane Humphries, 'Enclosures, Common Rights, and Women: The Proletarianization of Families in the Late Eighteenth and Early Nineteenth Centuries', *Journal
of Economic History*, 1 (1990).

Hampshire downs and the East Anglian fens.[76] Time there was customarily spent on other things as well as work for wages. Grazing a cow or a donkey, getting in a store of fuel, finding repair wood and thatch, or gathering winter browse for a cow or pigs and food for the larder were other older kinds of employment. This time was never available to employers, it was never purchasable. Doubtless, for the poorest commoners thrift made a virtue of necessity; but the products of commons, and the habit of using them, made thrift possible.

One consequence was that commoners who were able to live on a little were unlikely to develop expensive wants. As long as they had what they thought of as enough they had no need to spend time getting more. From this freedom came time to spend doing things other than work, as well as the ability to refuse work. This is the evidence for the accusation by critics of commons that commoners were lazy, that they spent too much time at the market or going horseracing. Even Gilbert White regretted the idleness and sporting of Hampshire commoners. Though otherwise steady, they succumbed too easily to the 'allurements to irregularities' that took the shape of rabbits and deer.[77] Clearly sporting, indolence, laziness, taking time off, enjoying life, lack of ambition (all the words are loaded with values of one kind or another) had their origins in other things as well as a life outside the market economy. In particular, celebration and recreation had economic functions as well as social. They established connection and obligation, and I shall return to this in a moment. But the effect of having relatively few needs was liberating of time as well as paid labour. Having relatively few needs that the market could satisfy meant that commoners could work less. Karl Polanyi might say that thrift spared commoners the 'humiliating enslavement to the material, which all human culture is designed to mitigate'.[78] In other words: commoners had a life as well as a living.

George Bourne, who wrote most compellingly about thrift, also argued that the life commoners got was particularly satisfying. On one level, satisfaction came from the varied nature of the work.

---

[76] See above Chapter 1, pp. 32–4.

[77] White, *Natural History of Selborne*, p. 24. For a longer discussion of the observations of laziness and lack of ambition see above Chapter 1, pp. 39–41.

[78] Karl Polanyi, 'Our Obsolete Market Mentality', *Commentary*, 3 (1947), p. 115, cited in Sahlins, *Stone Age Economics*, p. 28.

Commoners had a variety of tasks, many calling for skill and
invention, and they had a sure knowledge of their value. But there is
more to it than versatility and the interest it ensures. Bourne is
tentative in his description of how this life was unlike that of
agricultural labourers because he knew he was describing something
that had almost disappeared. Seeing it clearly was almost impossible. But his description reminds me powerfully of the recurrent
themes of John Clare's poetry. Bourne thought that a commoner's
sense of well-being came from a sense of ownership or possession, a
feeling of belonging, and an overwhelming localness. This was not
the ownership of a few acres (though that is surely important too)
but the possession of a landscape. This is the source of the outrage
Clare felt at the ploughing up of Helpston pastures, and of his
contempt for 'owners little bounds', and the reason for his shock
when enclosers changed everything.[79] Bourne puts it like this:

> From long experience – experience older than his own, and
> traditional amongst his people – he knew the soil of the fields and
> its variations almost foot by foot; he understood the springs and
> streams; hedgerow and ditch explained themselves to him; the
> coppices and woods, the water-meadows and the windy heaths,
> the local chalk and clay and stone, all had a place in his regard –
> reminded him of the crafts of his people, spoke to him of the
> economies of his own cottage life; so that the turfs or the faggots
> or the timber he handled when at home called his fancy while he
> was handling them, to the landscape they came from.

Like Clare, Bourne's commoner 'did not merely "reside"' in his
parish:

> he was part of it and it was part of him. He fitted into it as one of
> its native denizens, like the hedgehogs and the thrushes. All that
> happened to it happened to him.[80]

Commoners were the 'human fauna' of their lands. They lived with
its seasons, they knew its history and its geography, they felt a sense
of belonging in the routines of every day spent on it:

> when, on an auspicious evening of spring, a man and wife went
> out far across the common to get rushes for the wife's hop-tying,

[79] John Clare, 'The Mores', in *Selected Poems and Prose*, p. 170:
Fence now meets fence in owners little bounds
Of field and meadow large as garden grounds
In little parcels little minds to please.
[80] Bourne, *Change in the Village*, p. 80.

of course it was a consideration of thrift that sent them off; but an idea of doing the right piece of country routine at the right time gave value to the little expedition. The moment, the evening, became enriched by suggestion of the seasons into which it fitted, and by memories of years gone by ... And thus the succession of recurring tasks, each one of which seemed to the villager almost characteristic of his own people in their native home, kept constantly alive a feeling that satisfied him and a usage that helped him. The feeling was that he belonged to a set of people rather apart from the rest of the world – a people necessarily different from others in their manners, and perhaps poorer and ruder than many, but yet fully entitled to respect and consideration.

Bourne goes on to say that he misses the best part when talking about the commoner as an individual: he was one of a tribe.[81] All that the commoner did, others did too. Going to get rushes was doing what was appropriate, what the village did, what ought to be done. Each usage of common waste created a sense of self: it told commoners who they were.

Each usage had other meanings too. Every commoning economy provided the materials for small exchanges – gifts of things like blackberries, dandelion wine, jam, or labour in carrying home wood or reeds. Some were given for good reason, others for no particular reason at all. But they were all significant because, in peasant societies, gifts helped families with little other reason for contact to make connection with each other, and through connection to establish a kind of safety net. This was necessary because, apart from common land, commoners got their livings from rural industry and from paid labour. Both activities bound them to employers, or, if they were self-employed artisans, to a customer or a middleman. But neither relationship offered much security if things should go wrong. Access to a common made it possible to establish a relationship through the exchange of goods with other commoners. In short, gifts created bonds of obligation and the common was a better source of gifts than an inadequate wage; it provided more opportunities for giving (and thus receiving) than days spent working for a farmer.[82] Finally, gifts also reassured people of each

[81] Bourne, *Change in the Village*, p. 81.
[82] Pino Arlaachi, *Mafia, Peasants and Great Estates: Society in Traditional Calabria* (Cambridge, 1983), pp. 47–54. George Bourne dates the decline of thrift in his village from the loss of the common creating a need to make regular payments to a

other's solvency because the ability to give required possession in the first place. In this way they established a kind of equality between people. As a result they enabled charity when solvency turned to insolvency simply because the assumption could be made that this person is like us, but has fallen on hard times. Perhaps here lies the origin of the kindness of charity before the end of commoning that M. K. Ashby noted in Tysoe.[83]

This exchange was not always made between equals. Like common-field regulation, customary courts, and disputes over common rights, commons provided opportunities for building relationships of obligation with farmers and gentlemen too. For this reason time spent searching for wild strawberries, mushrooms, whortleberries and cranberries for the vicar, or catching wheatears for the gentry, was time well spent not only in the sense of earning money but also in the sense of establishing a connection.[84] And the exchange could work in both directions. In Hampshire the turf that commoners pared off the heaths gave them free firing. But it gave them more because the farmers carried it home from the heaths for them. In return the farmers got 'so much of the ashes as the labourer may be able to afford, after manuring his garden, potatoe or cabbage patch'. The observer of this, Charles Vancouver, was at pains to note that though the commoners took the turf as a right the farmers made no 'positive claim' on the ashes.[85] In this exchange lay a relationship that included personal knowledge and some recognition of mutual need.

But connection was established by other means as well as the exchanges represented by gifts and shared labour. Gathering, like gleaning, had its seasons. And because it had seasons people tended to work together to bring each harvest in, and often to mix work with pleasure. June saw the start of the peat season which went on into October; and late June and July was the time to get wild

---

benefit society such as the Oddfellows or the Foresters; commoners had never needed regular wages, labourers did: Bourne, *Change in the Village*, p. 92. We might add that experience in communal agriculture may have encouraged the making and the joining of such organizations.

[83] Chatwin, *Songlines*, pp. 112–13. Ashby, *Joseph Ashby of Tysoe*, pp. 278–9.

[84] *Gilbert White's Journals*, pp. 312, 313, 388, 404, 408, 102, 128; Richard Mabey, *Gilbert White. A Biography of the Author of The Natural History of Selborne* (1986; 1987 edn), pp. 28–9.

[85] Vancouver, *General View ... Hampshire*, pp. 389–90.

strawberries, cranberries and to cut bulrushes.[86] August was the month when men and boys cut the furze and forest fuel. In late August and early September girls and boys went nutting; it was also the time to hunt for mushrooms. In October they brought in the acorn harvest and herded pigs to the beech trees for the mast harvest.[87] Men cut the reed in winter and boys played football on the green.[88] In March or April they set fires on the heath to burn off the old furze or ling and encourage new growth to 'afford much tender browse' for cattle.[89] In May children went to the meadows to get primroses and violets, and Clare describes the mixture of sociability and practicality that must have marked all these gatherings:

> – For they want some for tea and some for wine
> And some to make a cucka ball
> To throw accross the garlands silken line
> That reaches oer the street from wall to wall.[90]

All these occasions of contact, familiarity and exchange established some obligation, some connection on the basis of equality – a mutuality between landless commoners and everyone else. Literally and metaphorically they met on common ground.

IV

Mutuality did not disappear with the extinction of common right, but after enclosure landless labouring families with only meagre wages to depend on could not build this kind of insurance relationship with gifts and exchanges. Or they could not build it as easily: sharing cottage pigs and the produce of cottage gardens were ways of maintaining ties but they were survivals of a kind of exchange that was more elaborate and richer in substance before enclosure. Without commons, labouring families had to rely on the solidarities men and boys built up at work on local farms, and on the mutuality created by women and girls helping each other every day in the

[86] Mabey, *Plants with a Purpose*, p. 129; *Gilbert White's Journals*, pp. 262, 263, 293, 312, 313 etc.

[87] Kalm, *Kalm's Account of his Visit to England*, pp. 147–8, 230; *Gilbert White's Journals*, pp. 395, 340, 212, 344, 165, 175, 179.

[88] Mabey, *Plants with a Purpose*, p. 128; John Clare, *Selected Poems and Prose*, p. 18.

[89] White, *Natural History of Selborne*, p. 25, though White also thought fire in the roots of the biggest bushes 'consumes the very ground'.

[90] John Clare, 'Sport in the Meadows,' in *John Clare*, p. 120. See below, pp. 324–5.

village and at home – the caring for children, for women in child-birth, for the sick and the old, the sewing together, and in some villages the spinning and hatmaking, the lacemaking – work done together both outdoors in village streets and indoors, sharing cottage candles. These bonds were there long before enclosure, but after enclosure they were the strongest bonds left. Significantly, they tied together people of the same economic standing. The mutuality of commons and common-field villages had cut across class lines.

Commons and the fruits of commons did not always disappear at once. Enclosers may have let the reclamation of waste land wait for several years during which former commoners may have continued to take what they wanted. Or memories might last much longer. Helmdon villagers still thought a local stone pit commonable in 1896, driving its owner to surround it with thorns, barbed wire and an old gate padlocked with a chain, 'as people looked on it as their right and fetched stones without my knowing'.[91] And the 'moucher', like the poacher to whom he was related, was a familiar figure in the nineteenth century. To gamekeepers he was a man for whom trespass was a livelihood and paid labour a last resort. His work year followed the natural rhythms of woodland. In January he went fowling for linnets, cut briar stocks for grafting and gathered moss for flower pots; in February he got snail shells and turfs for town bird cages; in March he went cattle droving or caught lizards to sell for pets, sold posies of spring flowers and cropped turnip tops too. He had most to do in summer, getting dandelion leaves, sow thistles, parsley and clover to feed rabbits, and taking worms, grubs and flies to town for fishing bait, with all manner of young birds, mice and snakes. The autumn meant berrying, getting mushrooms, finding sloes.[92] These are all things commoners did in the eighteenth and nineteenth centuries. In some places, wooding – gathering bits of dead wood from fields and former commons – went on into the twentieth century. Peter Ditchfield describes village women in the 1970s as dedicated gatherers:

> Our village women are always 'wooding'. One I know, who is over 80 years of age, constantly goes, taking with her an old per-

[91] Edward Parry, 'Helmdon Stone', *Northamptonshire Past and Present*, 7 (1986–7), p. 269.
[92] Jefferies, *Gamekeeper at Home*, pp. 104–7, 110, 119; Wigens, *Clandestine Farm*, pp. 38–9.

ambulator and bringing it back heavily laden with what one would imagine an impossible load.

Former common land still had its uses.[93]

But in common-field England the arrival of parliamentary enclosure reduced the scope for wooding. Forests were enclosed and private woods closed up. There were no more Monday and Thursday admissions to Whittlewood and Salcey. The nuts in some woodlands were cut down by keepers and thrown on the ground. And even where woodland remained the uses of freely gathered wood became fewer and the users less numerous. Above all, villagers in enclosed parishes took their wood or their berries under different circumstances. After enclosure they had to enter fenced land that had been allotted to one or more of the local farmers or landlords, they may have had to ask for permission, and their enjoyment was uncertain. They were gathering as a privilege not a right. As time went on they were more and more unwelcome: getting nuts and wood gave alibis to poachers, berry pickers frightened the pheasants, furze became prized as a cover for game birds. The new fruits of woodland were trespass notices in newspapers, a higher yield of gamekeepers, some spring guns and man traps. These are the circumstances that gave birth to mouchers and the solitary figures of old women with prams. Unless they gathered as of right, like the remarkable Grace Reed who preserved the right to Groveley Wood for the inhabitants of Barford St Martin, they gathered on sufferance.[94] No matter how much *they* believed they owned the right, the fact was that at law they did not. By the end of the nineteenth century even the word gleaning had taken on the sense of theft.[95]

---

[93] Ditchfield, *Country Folk*, p. 203. Of course in the meantime enclosure may have *interrupted* usage, which then resumed after the 1870s as land lost its social and economic value and landowning grew more dispersed.

[94] W. H. Hudson, *The Illustrated Shepherd's Life* (1910; 1987 edn), pp. 138–9; R. W. Bushaway, '"Groveley, Groveley and All Groveley": Custom, Crime and Conflict in the English Woodland', *History Today*, 31 (1981), pp. 37–43.

[95] By *c*.1880, in slang terms a gleaner was 'a thief of unconsidered trifles': Eric Partridge, *A Dictionary of Historical Slang*, abridged by J. Simpson (1972) p. 378; note also the history of 'wool-gathering'.

II

Decline

7. Two villages

For a very long time commoners had lived with the possibility and
the reality of enclosure but in the middle of the eighteenth century
enclosers began to use private Acts of Parliament to enclose whole
parishes. Gone was the slow, negotiated process of piecemeal
enclosure in which closes or woods were taken out of the system and
common rights were abated by general agreement. In its place came
a process that dispensed with the need for much agreement and
enclosed an entire parish in five to ten years, and when it was done
all common right had gone.[1]

We have seen that commoners had always negotiated or resisted
enclosure, as they had always negotiated the rules of their shared
agriculture. Not surprisingly, some resisted parliamentary enclosure
too. Opponents of enclosure had a tradition to call on, a solidarity
that had worked well before. But in the end (and for some parishes
the end was not until the nineteenth century) they were unsuccessful
and enclosure went through. When it did, many small commoners
lost land as well as common right. Resistance, changes in landholding, and their significance, are the subjects of the second half of this
book.

I want to begin by looking at two Midland common-field villages
that were enclosed by Act of Parliament in the eighteenth century:
West Haddon and Burton Latimer. They illustrate an argument
made earlier: that hill and vale parishes, though not areas of abundant common waste like the fenland or forest, might still support a
commoning economy until enclosure.[2] Thus in Burton Latimer any

---

[1] Only enclosure by unity of possession, when one owner who held all the land of the
parish enclosed it, came close to a parliamentary Act in its speed, and even then the
Lord had to wait for leases to fall in, or buy out and evict his tenants.
[2] See above, Chapter 2, pp. 72–7.

inhabitant who could afford a cow could get grazing for it, and in West Haddon half the village population owned or occupied land to which common right was attached. Equally, for both villages manufacture provided an alternative to agricultural labour. And for both an unusually large number of enclosure records remain – records that throw light on the contentious, politicizing process of enclosure and the changes in landholding that it produced. So these villages illustrate arguments that will be made later too.[3] Neither village is typical, but no village is that, and West Haddon and Burton Latimer usefully illustrate in microcosm commoning economies and an experience of enclosure that other Midland villages shared.

WEST HADDON, NORTHAMPTONSHIRE, 1761–7

West Haddon was a village with the business of a market town, sitting comfortably in 3,000 acres in the scarpland of western Northamptonshire. The land is a mixture of deep loam and light sandy soil, a good soil but a heavy one, with a short working season and so best suited to pasture now. A century ago it was almost equally arable and pasture and in the 1760s it was rather more arable than that.[4] West Haddon and all but two of its neighbours were enclosed in the 1760s and 1770s, the heyday of Northamptonshire enclosure; and, as well as in their own, nearby Guilsborough and Watford were involved in West Haddon's battle over enclosure.[5] Centuries before, five villages within a radius of five miles of West Haddon were 'lost' at least partly for reasons of enclosure.[6] Possibly some people made a connection between the old depopulations and the new enclosures,

[3] Chapters 8 and 9 are county-wide studies of resistance to enclosure and landholding change at enclosure.

[4] Whellan's *Directory*, p. 366. Land Utilization Survey of Britain, *Land Classification* (map), drawn from information collected between 1938 and 1942 (1944). The annual wheat acreage dropped by 150 acres after enclosure, [Young], *General Report on Enclosures*, Appendix XI, 'Culture of Wheat', p. 243.

[5] Watford was the scene of a Swing riot in 1830: E. J. Hobsbawm and George Rudé, *Captain Swing* (1969), pp. 224, 227, 350. Posts, rails and fences were burnt at Guilsborough and Watford in 1764 and 1768: *Northampton Mercury*, 20, 27 Feb. 1764, and 15 Feb. 1768. See also Chapter 9, pp. 278–9.

[6] K. J. Allison, M. W. Beresford and J. G. Hurst, *The Deserted Villages of Northamptonshire*, Leicester University Department of English Local History, Occasional Paper no. 18 (Leicester University Press, 1966): they were Downtown in Stanford on Avon, Sulby, Elkington, Althorp, and Silsworth in Watford; the date of the Downtown depopulation is uncertain, Elkington's was between 1350 and 1450; the other three are thought to have occurred later.

men like Joseph James of West Haddon, who said enclosure was 'a very wicked thing and cant answer it to his conscience'. But depopulation was a common enough contemporary fear in any case; and there were many other reasons to resist enclosure.[7]

The population in 1761 must have amounted to 600, including a landholding population of 315. In the same year 59 people claimed right of common attached to cottages or lands in the parish that they owned, representing (when their families are counted) perhaps 260 parishioners. In all, half of the population depended for its livelihood on land in the sense of owning it or working it as tenants.[8]

Set at the crossing of the Northampton–Rugby and Daventry–Market Harborough roads, the village was an easy overnight stop for drovers moving down from Staffordshire into Northampton and a useful place for the woollen manufactory which employed half the men there by 1771.[9] Other men identified in the Militia Lists as labourers may have worked as weavers for part of the year too. Not all weavers and woolcombers depended on wool alone for their livings, for at least one fifth and probably more held a few acres of land as well. Nehemiah Facer, for instance, a woolcomber with five children, was allotted almost an acre at enclosure and rented another four or five besides. Richard Robins was a weaver who had three children and paid tax on an acre of land after the enclosure. His neighbour John Newton, another weaver, paid tax on a house and a small close of less than two acres after enclosure. Jonathan Robins was compensated with about eight acres on enclosure together with another acre for his cottage right. Before enclosure he

---

[7] Northants. RO, ZA 9053, List of the proprietors for and against the enclosure of West Haddon, n.d., probably 1761.

[8] In 1720 Bridges, *History and Antiquities of Northamptonshire*, estimated 134 houses in the parish (multiplied by a household factor of 4.3 this comes to 576); the 1801 *Census* gives a population of 806. The landholding figures are taken from the Land Tax return of 1759 on which 73 landholders appeared. This figure could be larger, for some landowners appearing on the return may have paid their tenants' tax for them, so making the listing of the tenants' names on the return unnecessary. The landownership figures are taken from the list of landowners for and against enclosure drawn up in *c*.1761: Northants. RO, ZA 9053.

[9] Northants. RO, Militia Lists, West Haddon, 1771. Out of 151 men 129 were identified by occupation on the list, the rest being either infirm or already drawn; 49 of the 129 were weavers, 13 more were woolcombers: 48 per cent were working in the woollen trade. Another 10 per cent were labourers; 9 per cent were servants; 8 per cent were farmers, husbandmen or graziers; 15 per cent were tradesmen of one sort or another (tailors, carpenters, victuallers, bakers, 5 butchers, masons, blacksmiths and 3 cordwainers).

had paid tax on a small estate of owned and rented land of over twenty acres; after it he worked only half as much. He too was a weaver in 1771.[10] Nine weavers and woolcombers can be traced back from 1771 to 1766 who held some sort of land, usually no more than a couple of acres, though occasionally as much as twelve or twenty. Seven weavers can be traced back even further to the 1759 Land Tax return, when they paid significantly more tax than they did after the enclosure.[11] No labourers or servants can be traced in this way, although the incompleteness of the Land Tax lists may hide a small number who did hold land.

Opponents of the enclosure of West Haddon made the first protest that we know of in January 1761 with a Petition to the House of Commons claiming they were 'intitled to a considerable Part of the Land in the said Parish, to the amount of Eight Yardland and upwards, intended to be inclosed; and that the inclosing of the said Fields will be very injurious to the Petitioners, and tend to the Ruin of many, especially the poorer Sort of the said Parish ... '.[12] The Bill was the first of three brought into the Commons between 1761 and 1764 and it was dropped less than a month later on 2 February. The second was ordered a year later but got no further. Eventually, a third Bill introduced in January 1764, three years after the first, became law on 19 April the same year. The two-year lull between the second Bill and the successful third Bill may have been a time for consolidating support, or perhaps of buying up more land, or simply one of waiting for opposition to die down (ten of the opponents of enclosure actually died in 1763).[13] But opposition did not abate and another petition was read against the third Bill in the Commons on 5 March 1764. Opposition had grown from the ownership of eight yardlands to the ownership of twelve.

Counsel for the Bill and counsel for the petitioners against it were heard at the second reading, and they in turn examined witnesses from both sides, with the result that the Bill was sent into committee

---

[10] Northants. RO, Land Tax, West Haddon, 1759, 1766; Militia Lists, West Haddon, 1771. Edward Cave (1 acre), William Vaux (1 acre), John Hipwell (1 acre), and William Page alias William Walton (over 20 acres) were the other weavers.

[11] Northants. RO, Land Tax, West Haddon, 1759, 1766. They were William Martin (3 acres), Edward Cave (3 acres), William Hipwell (3 acres), Henry Newton (3 acres), John Newton (3 acres), Nehemiah Facer (11 acres), Jonathan Robins (24 acres).

[12] *Jls House of Commons*, 20 Jan. 1761.

[13] Northants. RO, Abstracts of Enclosure Awards made by J. W. Anscomb, I, p. 33k.

with the direction that 'all the Members who serve for the Counties of Northampton, Leicester, Warwick, Oxford and Buckinghamshire' be admitted to the discussion. According to both the Hammonds and W. E. Tate, such a direction was often used when serious opposition to an enclosure Bill was feared, and no Bill ever failed to get through when this direction was followed.[14] Opposition to the enclosure in Parliament ended with this order, for at the engrossing of the Bill the Journal of the House of Commons reported that no one had appeared before the Committee to oppose the Bill after 5 March.[15] The Bill received Royal Assent with the owners of three-quarters of the land in favour and the owners of one fifth opposed; the owners of some four yardlands and four cottages did not sign the Bill and fourteen of the eighteen cottage commoners were against it.[16]

Fourteen months later the fence posts and rails were burnt as they lay in the fields ready for construction, and those already erected were pulled down and burnt. Invitation to the riot came in an advertisement for a football match printed in the *Northampton Mercury* on 29 July 1765:

> West Haddon, Northamptonshire, July 27th 1765. This is to give notice to all Gentlemen Gamesters and Well-Wishers to the Cause now in Hand, That there will be a FOOT-BALL Play in the Fields of Haddon aforesaid, on Thursday the 1st day of August for a Prize of considerable value; and another good prize to be played for on Friday the 2nd. All Gentlemen Players are desired to appear at any of the Public Houses in Haddon aforesaid each day between the hours of ten and twelve in the Forenoon, where they will be joyfully received, and kindly entertained etc.[17]

The same paper reported on the following Monday:

> We hear from West Haddon, in this County, that on Thursday and Friday last a great Number of People being assembled there, in order to play a Foot-Ball Match, soon after meeting formed themselves into a Tumultuous Mob, and pulled up and burnt the Fences designed for the Inclosure of that Field, and did other

14 *Jls House of Commons*, 5 Mar. 1764; W. E. Tate, 'The *Commons' Journals* as Sources of Information Concerning the Eighteenth-Century Enclosure Movement', *Economic Journal*, 54 (1944), p. 84; Hammond and Hammond, *Village Labourer*, p. 40. Tate, in this instance, corroborates the Hammonds.
15 *Jls House of Commons*, 16 Mar. 1764.
16 Northampton Public Library, Enclosure Act no. 131, West Haddon.
17 *Northampton Mercury*, 29 July 1765.

considerable Damage; many of whom are since taken up for the same by a Party of General Mordaunt's Dragoons sent from this Town.[18]

In planning, execution and result the football match was highly successful, and as a way of opposing enclosure it was as well organized as the counter-petition taken to Parliament the year before. The advertisement gave those hoping for some sort of retaliation two days in which to prepare. But they were not the only people who might be interested in taking part: other 'Well-Wishers to the Cause now in Hand' were expected from outside the parish. By advertising the event as a football match, men from neighbouring parishes could be brought in, told of the affair in the inns during the morning, and invited to join in the afternoon's business. It seems unlikely that drink alone would justify the destruction of property (though drinking together was significant).[19] Rather, those who took up the invitation had to be well-wishers in the exact meaning of the word: supporters, friends, fellow commoners. To make the burning legitimate they needed to share a sense of what was right. Perhaps opponents of enclosure in West Haddon thought that enclosure was reason enough to invite them to a riot.[20]

The advertisement also made the enclosers look foolish. The very publicity of the event served as a taunt. More than that, enclosers themselves were very fond of notices; they put them on church doors and in the press very regularly. On this occasion anti-enclosers in West Haddon got to the *Northampton Mercury* before them.[21]

Commoners planned the riot for a crucial point in the agricultural year, and at an important date in the enclosers' calendar. It was the

[18] *Northampton Mercury*, 5 Aug. 1765.
[19] For some meanings of drinking together see Robert Bales, 'Attitudes towards Drinking in the Irish Culture', in D. Pitmann and C. R. Snyder, eds., *Society, Culture and Drinking Patterns* (1962), p. 175, cited in Roy Rosenweig, *Eight Hours for What we Will* (Cambridge, and New York, 1983): in Ireland mutual aid at harvest time was acknowledged with drink not money because it had 'no utilitarian taint, but indicated good will and friendship, and because it was not in any sense "payment in full", but implied a continued state of mutual obligation'.
[20] *Northampton Mercury*, 29 July 1765 and 2 Sept. 1765: Francis Botterill of East Haddon was one of the men accused of advertising the football match. He came from an open parish five or six miles away on the Northampton road, which was enclosed in 1773, eight years later. Some other men arrested cannot be traced back to West Haddon; they too may have been out-parishioners.
[21] *Northampton Mercury*, 26 Aug. 1765: it was customary to announce the enrolment of an Award in the press. Sir Thomas Ward did this for West Haddon in the closing sentence of his reward notice for the arrest of persons involved in the riot.

end of the last common-field harvest, when the fences were brought into the fields to wait for their construction until the harvest was in. Landed commoners saw each other daily as they worked together bringing in the crop. The gleaners waited, expecting to clear the fields as the corn was taken off. The commoners' cattle were penned up waiting for entry on to the stubble. Posts and rails lay in piles at the corners and ditches of the new allotments. It was a time when all those who had opposed the enclosure must have been most aware of the changes to come. It was an ideal time for a riot.

Gathering up, stacking and burning the fences was expected to take both the Thursday and Friday, and it did. Enclosers put the cost of the fences destroyed at £1,500, which was a serious loss.[22] This was not necessarily all the fencing needed to separate all the allotments made in the Award. Only enclosers most anxious to fence their estates (and best able to pay for it) would have had their posts and rails brought into the fields so that they could put them up at the earliest possible moment. If some landowners were involved in the riot, as others suspected, they would not have brought out their fencing at all.

Fencing itself was expensive to buy, and it cost time to put up. Failing to fence within a year brought heavy penalties, which were written into the Act itself. To enforce any enclosure Act the commissioners had a battery of weapons they could use against opposition. In West Haddon those neglecting to fence their allotments could have their lands seized, let to tenants, and the rents spent by the commissioners on fencing.[23] Landowners could also find their neighbours setting up posts and rails on their land, two feet from the boundary ditches. Acts permitted this to protect the hedge growing between the ditches. And the fence could stay on the neighbouring

---

[22] *Ibid.*
[23] Northampton Public Library, Enclosure Act no. 131, West Haddon, p. 16. Payment of the cost of the Act, the surveyors' fees and the commissioners' costs had to be made by each owner within whatever time period the commissioners decided, upon pain of distraint of goods, chattels, rents and profits (pp. 23–4). Allotments under three acres could be fenced free of charge to the owner, if the commissioners decided there was need. They awarded three such estates (two of about an acre and one of nearly two acres) but none was fenced free. Two were awarded to cottage commoners, who could have had their allotments fenced if they had accepted a joint plot of land; if they wanted individual plots they had to pay the fencing costs themselves (pp. 5, 16). William Pitt estimated the cost of fencing with ditch and hedge as 1s 6d the running yard at the turn of the century: Pitt, *General View ... Northampton*, p. 224.

land for up to seven years.[24] A landowner who held a small amount of land, and used it for pasture, would lose a border of a couple of feet around his holding if his neighbour wanted to protect his hedge or keep out stray cattle. If the first landowner was opposed to the enclosure as well, he might find his anger sharpened by this additional grievance. Fencing, then, was the most accessible, easily damaged property of the enclosers, and it was also a symbol (none better) of the transformation of the parish and its customs which was about to begin.

Disguising the fence burning as a football match had special significance because among the land to be enclosed at West Haddon was a common or wold covering 800 acres, or almost a third of all the open land in the parish. Commoners had very likely played other games of football on it in the past and enclosure would bring the end of this sport as certainly as it brought the end of common grazing, the kids of bushes taken off each year, and all the other uses of the common.[25] Football had been the occasion of riot in Kettering some years before, when Lady Betty Germaine's mills were destroyed in protest at the price of bread. West Haddon commoners must have known of the earlier incident for Kettering lies only twenty miles away. And a third football riot, this time against the drainage and enclosure of fenland, occurred at about the same time as West Haddon's in the village of Werrington on the other side of the county.[26]

On 12 August the editor of the *Mercury* offered a reward for the capture of the advertisers of the football match. In the issue following, the 'proprietors' of West Haddon offered another for 'the commitment' of Francis Botterill of East Haddon, a forty-year-old woolcomber suspected of preparing the advertisement and John Fisher, the younger, of West Haddon, a thirty-year-old weaver,

---

[24] Northampton Public Library, West Haddon, Enclosure Act no. 131, p. 15.
[25] Northants. RO, Enclosure Awards B, 92, West Haddon. The total acreage enclosed was 2498a 3r 18p, exclusive of 47a 1r 31p used for making roads; for commons as pitches, and the loss of them at enclosure, see Malcolmson, *Popular Recreations*, pp. 107–10; the wold may have been used by weavers as a space on which to tent cloth – weavers in nearby Yelvertoft used theirs like this: Northants. RO, D9613, D4799.
[26] E. P. Thompson, 'The Moral Economy of the English Crowd in the Eighteenth Century', *Past and Present*, 50 (1971), p. 116. PRO, KB1/16, Trans. 1766, Mich. 1766. For a discussion of football as a communal sport see David Underdown, *Revel, Riot and Rebellion* (1987), pp. 75–6.

thought to have helped pay for it.[27] Notice of a third reward appeared four weeks after the riot, two days after the enclosure Award was enrolled with the Clerk of the Peace in Northampton. This was offered by Sir Thomas Ward of Guilsborough, a West Haddon landowner and Justice of the Peace.[28] Threatening prosecution under the Black Act, and estimating the cost of the damage at £1,500, Ward offered another £20 on conviction of any 'Persons of Property' concerned in giving encouragement to the rioters by giving 'monies, gratuities or promises of Rewards'.[29] One of these 'Persons of Property' may well have been Richard Beale, who was arrested four days after the riot, before any of the reward notices appeared in the press. He was charged with having promised the rioters half a hogshead of ale and a guinea to indemnify them 'if they would Burn and Destroy the Posts and Rails'.[30] He and the other eight rioters tried may have been arrested by the dragoons at the height of the trouble. He (and possibly the others) was imprisoned from 8 August 1765 to 31 March 1766 waiting for the assize to be held. After seven months in gaol, Beale, William Braunt, Matthew Murden and John Ward were acquitted; five other men received sentences of two to twelve months' imprisonment.[31]

A year later Beale himself brought an action for unlawful imprisonment against John Bateman, the Justice from a neighbouring parish who had committed him.[32] He charged Bateman with maliciously imprisoning him by committing him to gaol 'as for a Felony and Offence not Bailable by Law', although his offence was a misdemeanour. Beale had offered securities for his freedom; Bateman had ignored them. The Justice then saw to it that on 11 August, three days after his arrest, the gaolers loaded Beale with 'heavy Irons and Fetters', in which he remained for over seven months. Bateman did this with a warrant issued on that day for another unspecified misdemeanour. Beale was no landowner,

---

27 *Northampton Mercury*, 19 Aug. 1765. Twenty pounds was offered in this reward.
28 Northants. RO, Land Tax, West Haddon, 1759 and 1766; he owned about 129 acres in West Haddon after the enclosure.
29 *Northampton Mercury*, 26 Aug. 1765.
30 Northants. RO, QS Grand File, Epiphany 1767.
31 *Northampton Mercury*, 31 Mar. 1766. The sentences were: Samuel Loale, twelve months; Roger Wood, four months; Joseph Wood, three months; William Richardson, three months; Edward Clark, two months.
32 Northants. RO, QS Grand File, Epiphany 1767: the source for filling the gap between the August riot and the prosecution of nine men arrested at the assize held on 26 March 1766 and reported in the *Northampton Mercury* that week.

although his ability to prosecute the magistrate and to offer bail on
his own behalf suggest that he was not without means. His land
consisted of two or three acres rented from an unknown West
Haddon landowner.[33] Beale's prosecution of Bateman was unsuccessful. (The Justice, of
course, did not wait seven months in irons for the verdict.)[34]
Bateman was a familiar figure in the West Haddon area, a Justice
who owned land in Guilsborough, Coton, Ravensthorpe and Haselbeach, and in Kibworth Beauchamp, Leicestershire.[35] Bateman may
have known Richard Beale. Certainly he knew Sir Thomas Ward
who advertised the reward in order to catch men like Beale, 'persons
of property' who may have paid for the riot. Ward and Bateman
were neighbours in nearby Guilsborough and both were Justices –
Ward being a particularly meticulous one who kept a diary for the
fifty years he held office.[36] John Bateman was himself a constant
litigant with his neighbours great and small, including Richard
Clarke, who owned a large estate in Guilsborough and Coton and
claimed a church way over Bateman's land. It was in this dispute
that Bateman called upon the support of Sir Thomas Ward when the
case came to Common Pleas.[37] The circumstances of Richard
Beale's arrest and detention and his imprisonment on a charge that
could have been heard at the forthcoming quarter sessions, instead
of next year's assizes, might suggest that Ward's helpfulness to
Bateman was reciprocated. And Bateman may have been concerned
to discourage riotous opposition on his own account, for the enclosure of Guilsborough was going ahead at the same time just four
miles away, and had itself run into trouble. Someone had stolen four
of Bateman's gates and locks early in 1764, the year of Guilsborough's enclosure Act, and someone had burnt Richard Clarke's
posts, rails, brakes, one gate, and seventy perches of hedging from

[33] Northants. RO, Land Tax, West Haddon 1757, 1766. He did not receive any
allotment in the enclosure Award; nor was he listed on the Militia List in 1771,
1774 or 1777.
[34] Northants. RO, QS Grand File, Epiphany 1767. Beale's indictment was found No
True Bill either because he dropped it (for any number of reasons) or because the
Grand Jury threw it out for lack of evidence or legal error.
[35] Northants. RO, Bateman (Guilsborough) papers, *passim*. QS papers, 26 Geo. II
1753, Michaelmas: list of JPs' land.
[36] Warwicks. RO, Ward-Boughton-Leigh, CR 162, 688, 689.
[37] Northants. RO, B(G) 28–9, 50. Case of the King vs. Moses Irons *et al.*, 25/3/23
Geo. II [1750].

the open fields a week later.[38] Either way, Bateman's respect for common right was not high, for on at least one occasion his commoner neighbours had suffered from his attempts to take his own common-field land out of the common stock.[39]

None of those charged in the West Haddon riot can be identified as landholders in West Haddon or even as being eligible for service in the Militia in 1771. Only Francis Botterill and John Fisher (who escaped trial with a reward out for them) can be traced, the former as an East Haddon woolcomber and the latter as a West Haddon weaver.[40] The anonymity of the other nine may be an accident due to the incomplete survival of records, but more likely they were not men of property at all. Their involvement was either temporary and fired by a dislike of enclosure, or they were cottagers, landless and land-poor commoners and friends of commoners. The opponents of enclosure who can be identified tend to be those who owned land and whose names occur as part of the parliamentary opposition to enclosure rather than the football match. Broadly, opposition came from the landowning tradesmen and artisans who may have augmented their land by renting more (the victuallers, butchers and weavers), elderly cottagers of modest means, and cottagers in general. Support for the enclosure came from the farmers, husbandmen and graziers, the landlords, and the biggest landowners.[41] The one farmer known to oppose the enclosure, John Underwood, rented four yardlands cheaply in the common fields.

38 *Northampton Mercury*, 20, 27 Feb. 1764. Nor did opposition cease; Clarke's barn was broken into and yet more posts, rails and other wood were taken in the night in February 1774 – these posts and rails may have been intended for subdividing his newly enclosed fields: *Northampton Mercury*, 28 Feb. 1774.
39 Northants. RO, B(G) 40, 45 [1750]. He had gone to the trouble of getting an opinion on his rights in the matter. Like many landowners he kept a notebook of legal opinions on the land laws: B(G) 250.
40 *Northampton Mercury*, 19 Aug. 1765.
41 Opponents included two victuallers, two butchers, a tailor, a woolcomber, a weaver, a cordwainer and a farmer. Supporters included three gentlemen, two clergymen, two farmers and a husbandman: Northants. RO, Militia Lists, West Haddon, 1771. These were the occupations followed six years after enclosure; before enclosure they may have been a little different. For example, the artisans or journeymen against enclosure owned more land before than after and may have earned more money from its use than from shoemaking, weaving etc. On the relationship between enclosure and the expansion of trading in Warwickshire see J. M. Martin, 'Village Traders and the Emergence of a Proletariat in South Warwickshire, 1750–1851', *Agricultural History Review*, 32 (1984). Identifiable opponents account for only nine out of the twenty-nine landowners who opposed enclosure; identifiable supporters account for eight of a total of twenty-six.

Reasons

Although the broad justification for opposition was the harm enclosure would do 'the poorer sort' in the parish, commoners gave a variety of particular reasons. Some they offered to Thomas Whitfield, the Lord of the Manor and major landowner, when he interviewed them. (Other reasons they kept to themselves.)[42] Fully one-third told him no more than that enclosure would be of no benefit to them so they had no reason to support it. Richard Hipwell owned only a cottage common worth the pasture of a cow and the privilege of getting sixty kids of bushes from the common; he thought 'it will be of no service to him to inclose'. Richard Parnell owned more, twenty-seven acres, but said he too could 'live upon it as it is and is not certain it will improve by inclosing'. Thomas Smith, a butcher with twenty acres of land some of which he rented, said he too could 'live as well on it now as if inclosed'.

Another third said they were too old, or were judged too ill to consent to enclosure. Four men said they could not think of so great a change at this point in their lives: John Branston owned sixty-three acres but considered himself 'too old and childless'; though he believed the 'fields would greatly improve' he still did not 'care for the trouble of inclosing'. Laurence Currin owned less land, nine acres and his cottage common, and he too said 'that he was nearly eighty and was not so ambitious as to have his estate increased though he believed it wou'd improve'. Thomas Towers, a victualler, was 'near seventy and therefore would not consent'. Of these elderly men, only John Kenny, who held the smallest amount of land – four and a half acres – openly doubted that enclosure would be an improvement. Whitfield judged one woman 'not right in her senses' and so unable to explain her opposition; another called herself 'too Old and Childish' but still objected to enclosure. Between them they owned three cottages with rights and almost a third of all the land in the opponents' possession – three yardlands.

This group of six strengthened the anti-enclosure party in a way not often considered. A couple would not have lost much in the event but they said they felt themselves too old to bother. It is hard to exaggerate the size of the change brought about by enclosure, and anticipation must have made it seem even bigger. Even if they grew

---

[42] Northants. RO, ZA 9053, West Haddon list of proprietors, n.d., probably 1761.

the same crops, or pastured the same number of beasts, they still had to work on at least some new land and to find enough capital or profit to pay for the cost of enclosure itself. Buying the wood for fences, carting it, putting the fences up, planting hedges, keeping cattle away from the new quicksets and off the old pastures on roads and wolds were new tasks that needed some of the old communal institutions. In some parishes gangs of men employed by the commissioners put up fencing and the commissioners charged for it with a rate per yard, but this was not the case in West Haddon. Old men and women who could not count on their children or their neighbours may have lacked the energy and ability to reorganize their livelihoods. Change of any size might have been unsettling and unwelcome; a newly individualized farming was designed for enterprising younger landowners who had capital behind them, not for farmers used to common-field agriculture with its joint responsibilities and its familiar routine, or cottagers used to common pasture. Moreover, farmers' livelihoods now depended on their adaptability – on how good their decisions were on where to grow their crops and grass and where to put their cattle, how much to sow, how much to invest in additional pasture. Perhaps it was not a time for old men and women.[43] But some replies expressed a lack of interest due to more than old age: John Branston, for instance, had *enough* for himself and, having no heir, needed no more; Laurence Currin 'was not so ambitious' to own a better estate even though he knew it might improve. The others may well have had sons and daughters to inherit their land but still argued their *own* age as a reason for not backing the enclosure. Those with children opposed to enclosure might use their own age and health as a way of deflecting any blame from them – for their sons were quite possibly tenants of land let by the enclosers and badly placed for protest. The replies suggest both that sufficient land to live on was enough land and that great age or infirmity was a useful, simple, unanswerable excuse covering any number of more pertinent reasons to give the Lord of the Manor. Thomas Towers, a victualler with a cottager son, said simply that he was too old to contemplate enclosure, but he may have had more reasons than one.

There were four men, all cottagers with smallholdings, who believed enclosure to be unjust and said so. Robert Earle, owner of a

---

[43] On this point, and the difficulties of reorganization *all* farmers faced, see [Young], *General Report on Inclosures*, pp. 31–2. Slater, *English Peasantry*, pp. 129–30.

cottage and nine acres, told Whitfield 'that he thinks it a very wicked thing to inclose'; Joseph James agreed it was 'a very wicked thing and cant answer it to his conscience'; David Cox went further to say that 'it was a bad thing to inclose and would not answer but would tend to ruin ye nation'; James Green declared that he 'would not meddle either way'. Each of these men owned nine acres, according to Whitfield, and one owned a cottage as well, but three of them no longer paid tax in 1766 after the enclosure and so probably no longer owned or rented land then. The fourth, Robert Earle, paid only half as much tax as before, perhaps on his cottage alone.

Four more men gave no greater satisfaction to the investigator than that they had pledged their support to their neighbours and would stand by them. The victualler John West – named by the Common's *Journals* as presenting the Petition against enclosure – and his brother William both replied that they would consent to the enclosure if all their 'Neighbours that had been against it' would. John Worcester, a woolcomber, said shortly that he would sign against the Bill this year 'because he signed against it last year'. Nathaniel Parnell had promised John Underwood to join the opposition and intended to keep his promise. Perhaps these answers are no more revealing than the excuses of old age or infirmity given by some others – they have some of the same sense of evasion and suggest that only one reason out of a number was grudgingly given. But in all of them the commoners made the Lord of the Manor recognize the solidarity of the opposition. In all of them the commoners expressed a solidarity older than the present emergency.

More specific were the reasons given by Thomas Ford, Benjamin Robins and William Page: the first two said bluntly that too much was allowed in lieu of tithe, the third said simply that although he thought the land would be improved by enclosure he himself 'has no money to spare to inclose with'. Many more landowners may have agreed with Thomas Ford and Benjamin Robins that the tithe compensation was excessively generous but preferred to say it quietly rather than to Whitfield, who was himself the Impropriator of the tithe as well as the largest landowner. Enclosure costs too would have deterred more men than William Page: in the event they came to about £1 an acre before fencing.[44]

In Ann Tabernar's answer to Whitfield are signs of the patient

---

[44] Northants. RO, Enclosure Award, Book B, 92, West Haddon.

Table 7.1. *West Haddon: landowners for and against enclosure*

Acreage	For	Against
2 – 9	6	18
10 – 17	2	1
18 – 45	8	10
Over 45	10	1
Totals	26	30

Source: Northants. RO, ZA 9053; Land Tax, West Haddon, 1759.

resistance that he would come to know well. She said simply that 'she had some trees growing on her land and if they would defer the inclosure till they were full grown she would Consent but wou'd not till then'. Oak trees take a very long time to mature.

In the case of Benjamin Collis, William Moulton, John Priestly and Thomas Boyes, either they refused to give reasons for their opposition or such as they did give were not recorded.

A commoning parish of many smallholders and cottagers, like West Haddon, stood to lose more from the extinction of common right and the cost of enclosure than one of prosperous landlords and substantial tenants. Moreover, the particular economy of West Haddon – its combination of weaving, woolcombing, drove-route trade and pasture – meant that artisans, innkeepers, and tradesmen, as well as cottagers and small farmers, depended on the common. Measuring the extent of their loss starts with a comparison of the property of those favouring the enclosure, and those opposing it.[45]

[45] There are two sources for the study of landholding in West Haddon before enclosure: the list of owners for and against enclosure made by the enclosers in 1761 or thereabouts (which included their lands), Northants. RO, ZA 9053, and the 1759 Land Tax return. Post-enclosure landholding can be studied using the 1765 Enclosure Award and the 1766 Land Tax return.

There are some difficulties attached to the use of the returns made before 1780 because the assessors did not distinguish between proprietors and occupiers until then. Pre-1780 returns are lists of taxpayers who may have been tenants, or landlords, or owner-occupiers. Comparison of the list of owners (ZA 9053) with the returns can distinguish owners from tenants and owner-occupiers from landlords in most cases. But it is possible, returns in other parishes would suggest, that occasionally a landlord paid his tenant's tax for him. This was unusual because tenants most commonly paid their own tax and deducted it from their rents: W. R. Ward, *The English Land Tax in the Eighteenth Century* (Oxford, 1953), p. 7. The sort of landlord of whom this was true was the substantial owner of several hundred acres who owned a number of farms including some he farmed himself. (John Harper in Burton Latimer, for example, paid his tenants' tax with his own: Northants. RO, H(BL) 649, Account Book, p. 144.) In West Haddon only three

Landholding and opinion about enclosure

The owners of a quarter of the land in West Haddon opposed the enclosure: there were thirty of them and they held four hundred acres between them. Supporting enclosure were twenty-six men and women who owned 1,200 acres. The remaining eight hundred acres in the parish were heathland known as the Rye Hills, good for grazing, gathering bushes and other fuel, and perhaps for tenting woven cloth.[46] With only one exception, landowners against enclosure were the smaller commoners, owners of yardlands (36 acres), quarterns (9 acres), or less. Table 7.1 shows the distribution of land between supporters and opponents in 1760.

Half of all West Haddon's occupiers – perhaps a quarter of the village – also owned some of the land they worked, and most of them opposed enclosure. Opposition was greatest amongst the smaller of them (eighteen out of twenty-two opposed it), but it was not confined to them: six of the fifteen larger owner-occupiers also petitioned against enclosure.[47]

men owned more than a hundred acres in the pre-enclosure period; two were clearly landlords (Sir Thomas Ward and Thomas Whitfield), but the third (Thomas Worcester) may have been a landlord paying his tenants' tax, although he appears to be a yeoman farmer with a farm of three yardlands. Four more such owners appear after the enclosure: two were landowners on this scale for the first time (the Reverend John Watkin and Nicholas Heygate) and two had bought up more land in the interval (John Kilsby and John Walker). All paid all their tax. Watkin may have been a landlord paying his tenants' tax, but Kilsby, Heygate and Walker farmed for themselves before enclosure and may well have continued to do so on their larger holdings after it. Ward and Whitfield appeared on the returns for the first time after enclosure – the latter now owned nearly six hundred acres. Both could have been tax-paying landlords. A third possibility affecting Ward, Whitfield and Watkin is that they had not finally divided their new lands or finished their improvements. Until the site of their farms was fixed, landlords would pay the tax. The defective returns allow us to look at land*holding* in all its forms with some safety before enclosure but with increasing danger of mistaking landlords for owner-occupiers, and of losing tenants, after enclosure. *Ownership* can be studied both before and after enclosure using the list of owners (ZA 9053) for and against enclosure made *c.*1761 and the Award of 1765.

[46] A petition against enclosure presented to the Commons by landowners, 'and on behalf of the Poor Manufacturers of Broad Woollen Cloth', from Armley in Yorkshire in 1793 gave as a reason for opposing the enclosure of Armley Common the use of the Common for tenters and frames on which they stretched and dried their cloths, warps and wool after dying: *Jls House of Commons*, 26 Mar. 1793. West Haddon weavers may have used their common in the same way, and woolcombers may have taken fuel for their pots.

[47] Northants. RO, ZA 9053, Land Tax, West Haddon, 1759; Neeson, 'Common Right and Enclosure', p. 260, Table 5.3.

Table 7.2. *West Haddon: occupiers for and against enclosure*

Acreage	For	Against	Unknown (tenants)	Total
Under 10	3	16	8	27
10–17	1	2	7	10
18–45	6	5	0	11
46–60	1	0	2	3
61–90	0	0	9	9
91 and over	2	1	1	4
Totals	13	24	27	64

The tenants were solely that: they owned no land.

Source: Northants. RO, ZA 9053; Land Tax, West Haddon, 1759.

One in three owners let their land in West Haddon. As landlords they favoured the enclosure, regardless of how little land they owned and let: even four who owned less than a half yardland supported it. Most landlords opposed to enclosure owned relatively small amounts of land and said they were either too old or satisfied with things as they were; the landlord with least land argued that enclosure was wicked.[48]

If owner-occupiers generally opposed enclosure and landlords usually supported it what did tenants do? Table 7.2 groups all occupiers (owner-occupiers, owner-occupiers who also rented land, and tenants) according to their opinion of the enclosure and the size of the lands they worked. Figures are most complete for holdings of forty-five acres and less. Nearly half of these occupiers were against the enclosure. Only one in five supported it. But the opinion of the one in three who were mere tenants (owning no land of their own) is unknown. If they were divided on the issue in the same proportion as the other occupiers of forty-five acres and less, 70 per cent of them

---

[48] Northants. RO, ZA 9053, Land Tax, West Haddon, 1759. Opposed were William Moulton (18 acres), Richard Parnell (27 acres), Widow East (18 acres) and John Worcester (18 acres). The richest landlord opponent of enclosure was John Branston, who owned 63 acres which he sold before the Award was finished. He was old and blind and argued very convincingly that he was too tired to face the prospect of enclosure. The smallest landlord opponents of enclosure were Joseph James and James Green: James thought enclosure was wicked, Green thought he would not 'meddle' either way. Joseph James died before the Award was made.

would have opposed the enclosure and 30 per cent would have supported it.[49]

Those who owned no land at all may not have felt the same about enclosure as those who owned some land as well as renting more. But their dependence on common grazing would have been similar, and the fear of incurring extra costs was mutual. In particular small tenants probably feared rising rents. Tenants of larger estates may have been more ambivalent. But there is evidence that some of these opposed enclosure on the grounds that their rents would rise too. John Underwood, one of the leaders of the opposition in West Haddon, and sometime constable of the parish, opposed the change. He rented four yardlands (144 acres) 'at a low price' and owned only eighteen acres. Underwood said he would spend 'a Hundred Pounds of his own Money' to stop the enclosure.[50]

Landholding after enclosure

Supporters and opponents of enclosure were clearly differentiated in terms of landholding: most of those with more than forty-five acres supported enclosure, those with less opposed it. They also fared differently as enclosure went through. After enclosure the number of landowners in West Haddon fell by 18 per cent from fifty-seven in 1761 to forty-seven in 1765. The number of owners of below twenty-five acres fell furthest (28 per cent), despite compensation to cottage commoners. And all the loss of owners in this group occurred amongst those with less than ten acres, most of whom had resisted enclosure. At the other end of the scale the number of estates over a hundred acres grew from four (including one of 262 acres) to seven (including one of 600 acres).

Both before and after enclosure the structure of landownership was a pyramid with a wide base of owners of less than forty-five acres (usually less than a yardland). But after enclosure there were fewer very small owners and more very large: clearly polarization had intensified. A further change occurred in the estates of between fifty-one and a hundred acres where the number of owners fell from

---

[49]   The exact figures are 9.4 per cent of tenants in favour, and 21.6 per cent against. Of all occupiers the proportions pro and con are 30.4 per cent and 69.6 per cent respectively.

[50]   Northants. RO, ZA 9053. On open-field rent and the conflict of interest between landlords and tenants see Allen, 'Enclosure, Farming Methods, and the Growth of Productivity', pp. 22–3.

Table 7.3. *West Haddon: landowners before and after enclosure*

	to 25	26–50	Acreage 51–100	100–50	over 150
1761	36	9	8	3	1
1765	26	9	5	3	4

Source: Northants. RO, Awards Book B, 92; ZA 9053.

eight in 1761 to five in 1765, and again most of the fall occurred at the lower end of the range (Table 7.3). Now ownership lay more certainly in the hands of large owners than it had, and we may even see the beginnings of a squirearchy. Before enclosure the Lord of the Manor, Thomas Whitfield, owned 262 acres and the Great Tithe. After enclosure his heir, John Whitfield, owned six hundred acres (a quarter of the parish). Another six men with farms of between a hundred and two hundred acres formed a substantial owner-occupier or rentier group.

To achieve this the five years between the first gathering of support for the Act and the making of the Award had been years in which much land changed hands. Landlords in particular sold land, especially those opposed to enclosure. By the time the Award was drawn up most landlords (76 per cent) owned less land than they had, or none at all (62 per cent). Those who held on to their land tended to buy more in the interval, and they were also the richest landlords who had supported enclosure.[51]

Owner-occupiers also bought and sold land according to the size of their pre-enclosure holdings and their attitude to enclosure. The 40 per cent of them who no longer owned land in 1765 were overwhelmingly those opposed to enclosure in 1760. Another 40 per cent owned more land in 1765. Again, they had supported the enclosure and appear to have done so with an eye to expansion.[52]

How had cottage-commoners fared? Enclosure ensured their decline in two senses. First, by taking away common right it destroyed an economy based on the use of land that belonged to others. Second, it took land from those cottagers who were landowners. A

---

[51] Northants. RO, Awards Book B, 92, and ZA 9053; see also Neeson, 'Common Right and Enclosure', p. 268, Table 5.9.

[52] Northants. RO, Awards Book B, 92, and ZA 9053; see also Neeson, 'Common Right and Enclosure', p. 269, Table 5.10.

third of them – all quartern owners – lost everything. Of the remainder, two held roughly the same amount of land after enclosure as they had before (without rights and at some cost); two died; and three owned more land than they had before enclosure. None of those who petitioned for the enclosure lost land, all but two of those who petitioned against it either lost land or had to sell out altogether.[53]

Of the quartern owners only Jonathan Robins held on to his land and for it he was compensated with another nine acres and an acre or so in exchange for his cottage common. He was a weaver who before enclosure rented another fifteen acres and opposed enclosure on the grounds that the tithe compensation was too generous. After enclosure his holding carried no common grazing at all and cost him £9 or £10 before fencing. He no longer rented land in 1766, perhaps because he could not afford the new rents or perhaps because no landlord would rent to him. The other quartern owners may have sold out knowing that they could not afford this sort of transaction.

Just as some had sold out even before the Award was announced, others had bought land before receiving their allotments. Four of the cottage commoners had done this, ranging from Mary Burbidge who bought about two acres to John Walker who more than doubled his seventy-two acres. Again, as with owner-occupiers and landlords, the buyers already owned the largest of holdings or had received compensation in lieu of tithe.

To summarize: by 1765 half of the small owners of less than ten acres were gone and a third of the small owner-cottagers went with them. Owner-occupiers in general had opposed the enclosure, and many, regardless of size, sold out or cut down the number of acres they owned. Most landlords wanted the enclosure and many took the opportunity to sell their land, usually to other supporters. The landlords that held on to their land usually bought more, as did those owner-occupiers who had wanted the change. Both had gambled on enclosure and appear to have won.

Once the Act was law, then, its opponents took stock: they sold whatever they could not afford to enclose, or were not prepared to

---

[53] Two commoners died before the Award was made; they were Richard Hipwell and Benjamin Collis. Cottage commoners were not older than the other landholders: Northants. RO, Abstracts of Enclosure Awards by J. W. Anscomb, I, p. 32k; Awards Book B, 92; ZA 9053; and Neeson, 'Common Right and Enclosure', p. 364, Table 5.6.

mortgage or invest in. The enclosers bought this land, enlarged their holdings and expected to afford the costs of enclosure. Some of them sold too, but they did so voluntarily: they had, after all, welcomed the chance to enclose. The sales changed West Haddon's economy substantially. There were fewer small owners and fewer holdings of between fifty and a hundred acres, and there were more farms of over 125 acres: over half of the land was owned by seven men, one of whom owned a quarter of the parish. Enclosure in West Haddon frightened its opponents off the land. It made them sell even before it was complete.

BURTON LATIMER, NORTHAMPTONSHIRE, 1803–7

West Haddon was enclosed in the mid 1760s when the parliamentary enclosure movement began to take hold in Northamptonshire, just before the great peak of the 1770s. Burton Latimer underwent enclosure in 1803 in the second period of intense activity during the Napoleonic Wars. Lying above the Nene valley, between the river and the town of Kettering, the site of Burton Latimer was less exposed, its soil more fertile than that of West Haddon on the western scarp. The lower limestone of the northern half of the county was better drained than the lias clays and the soil was better adapted to mixed farming than West Haddon's, which was best suited to pasture. Burton Latimer's population was also slightly smaller at 669 in 1801, compared to 806. Each parish covered about 2,500 acres, of which nearly a quarter was a common or wold.[54]

Both villages depended on weaving to some extent, but by 1803 the industry had suffered a slow and final depression in Burton Latimer, and many of the weavers may well have been unemployed on the eve of the enclosure. Its proximity to Kettering prevented a retreat to a purely agricultural economy, the ultimate fate of West Haddon once the drove-route trade declined and weaving came to an end. Outwork in one form or another sustained the parish through the nineteenth century, as it did other Nene valley villages lying between Thrapston and Wellingborough. The woollen industry, based in Kettering, had prospered in the eighteenth century, partly because the town was closer to London than its East Anglian

[54] The total acreage was 2,690 in 1851, according to the census: *Parliamentary Papers* 1852–3, vol. 85; 2,583a 2r 28p was enclosed in 1803–4, according to the Award: Northants. RO, YZ 4594, Burton Latimer enclosure award.

and Yorkshire competitors at a time when transportation costs were high. It depended upon locally produced wool. Villagers turned out everlastings, moreens, tammies and calamancoes and sold them quite successfully until Yorkshire competition began to undercut them in the 1770s.[55] By the 1790s half of the five or six thousand people employed in Kettering, Rothwell and Desborough were out of work, and much the same must have been true of Burton Latimer. From the 1790s to the 1810s the whole area was depressed.[56]

If West Haddon was a village with the business of a small market town in 1764, Burton Latimer in 1803 was an agriculturally based parish, set in the suburbs of an economically depressed town, partially dependent on outwork from the town itself.

Opposition in Parliament

Joseph Harper of Chilvers Coton, Warwickshire, and his fellow enclosers at Burton Latimer first heard of the Petition against the enclosure Bill there in April 1803. Their Kettering solicitor, Thomas Marshall, had asked Sir William Dolben MP for support, but 'After looking over the printed Bill', Marshall wrote, Dolben still refused to sign 'and informed me he had received a Petition signed by several proprietors against the Bill and which on his return to Town he should certainly present.'[57] Dolben was Lord of the Manor of nearby Finedon; he owned no land in Burton Latimer but he was Patron of the Rectory there, and a trustee of Herbert's Charity. In March he had told another solicitor that he had been badly dealt with by the enclosers (who may have suspected he would be difficult to satisfy) because they had delayed showing him the Bill and had not informed him of their meetings.[58]

Dolben's subsequent appearance to present the case in the House of Commons was reported to Joseph Harper by his Warwick attorney, John Tomes. Harper was Lord of the Manor of Burton

[55] H. A. Randall, 'The Kettering Worsted Industry in the Eighteenth Century', *Northamptonshire Past and Present*, 4 (1971/2), pp. 352–3.

[56] The poor rate was 10s in the pound in 1806 and would go higher: Pitt, *General View ... Northampton*, pp. 240–3. Weaving returned to Burton Latimer in the 1810s in the form of silk manufacture. The census attributes to this an increase in population between 1811 and 1821 from 705 to 842: *Census* (1851), p. 45. Shoemaking also began late in this decade: Randall, 'Kettering Worsted Industry', p. 355.

[57] Northants. RO, ZA 891 in X3872, Accounts of Mr Marshall, n.d., April 1803.

[58] Northants. RO, ZA 892 in X3872, Accounts of Thomas Heydon, 16 Mar. 1803.

Latimer but lived fifty miles away in Chilvers Coton.[59] His Burton estate covered some 550 acres in 1803 and was mostly let to five tenants.[60] Tomes wrote to Harper that Dolben had made the mistake of keeping the committee sitting for far longer than was usual (all of two hours) during which he had proposed 'a vast number' of alterations to the Bill. He had not reckoned with a committee already well disposed to the enclosers, and each of his changes was rejected. Tomes described the support the Bill enjoyed: 'Mr. Dickins the Member for Northamptonshire was Chairman and friendly – my friends Mr. Mills, Mr. Farquhar, and Mr. Dugdale and a Mr. Hobhouse (an acquaintance of Mr. Mills) attended and took the active part for us.'[61]

The amendments Dolben proposed ('extremely absurd indeed', said Tomes) had been discussed by the sponsors of the Bill with Dickins, the friendly chairman of the committee, long before they reached the committee itself. There were three: that 'each pro-pr[ietor] shall plant a 40th part of his Allotm[ent] with Timber'; that the charity lands should be fenced free of charge; and that the *right* of the poor to the eight-hundred-acre wold should be given greater acknowledgement in the Bill, and compensation in the Award.[62] Tomes' (and presumably Dickins') arguments against these were that the first was 'injurious to the proprietors' because no *law* required anyone to plant woods on newly enclosed land. The second amendment – free fencing of the charity lands – was unjust because not all Trustees of charity land in Burton Latimer had asked for such a consideration, and because all were empowered to raise loans on their lands for fencing by the General Enclosure Act. Dolben's third amendment, that better compensation be given the poor for their rights on the wold, was dismissed out of hand by Tomes and the chairman of the committee; Tomes said simply that '*Mr. Dickins* thinks it cannot be put better than it is.'[63]

Sir William Dolben's objections to the Burton Latimer Bill were

[59] Harper's succession to the manor was disputed by the Duke and Duchess of Buccleuch and Mr William King of Colchester; the dispute was prevented from hindering the progress of the Bill by those interested entering all their competing claims in the opening sentences of the Bill itself: Northants. RO, ZA 886, Burton Latimer enclosure Bill.

[60] Northants. RO, Land Tax, Burton Latimer, 1803.

[61] Northants. RO, H(BL) 808, John Tomes to Joseph Harper, 18 May 1803.

[62] Northants. RO, H(BL) 804, 805, 'Reasons in Supporting Bill' and 'Reasons for Supporting Burton Inc. Bill'.

[63] *Ibid.*, my italics.

patriotic and humanitarian and close to contemporary opinion in favour of compensated enclosure.[64] For some time he had interested himself in forestry for naval purposes, and his wish to enforce by law the planting of woods in Burton Latimer was only one of a number of such attempts.[65] His defence of charity lands and commoners' rights was part of a more general reform interest (he was a steady supporter of Wilberforce in the slave trade debate), and a concern for equity in the rural community. Like many of those calling for compensated enclosure he was not an opponent of enclosure as such: his own manor of Finedon underwent enclosure two years after Burton, in 1805.[66] But in 1773 he and Sir Richard Sutton piloted through the Commons an Act 'for the better Cultivation, Improvement and Regulation of the Common Arable Fields, Wastes and Commons of Pasture, in this Kingdom'. It provided that a common-field parish's agriculture could be communally regulated by three-quarters in value and *number* of its occupiers, with careful consideration of the common rights of all inhabitants. This was a considerably more democratic proceeding than that for getting a private enclosure Act, in which, because land alone counted, a minority of owners could transform the agriculture of a majority of owners, occupiers and cottagers.[67]

As far as we know, commoners in the parish did not concern themselves with Dolben's schemes for timber. The other two issues were more important: the cost of fencing the many pieces of public land in the village – lands bequeathed to the poor for charity – and the loss of the wold.

There were thirteen pieces of publicly used land in Burton Latimer on the eve of the enclosure (Table 7.4), and the awarded allotments made for each of them would require fencing. With the exception of the wold, the land used by the pinder and the parish clerk as part of their wages and the Town Headlands, all were administered by

---

[64] See above Chapter 1, pp. 46–7.

[65] Dolben made a Commons speech in 1799 proposing that an order be made 'that when 50 acres and upwards should be allowed to be inclosed by Parliament a proportionable quantity of such land should be allotted for the growth of timber for the navy'. He was sorry to note that timber had not been planted on the lands 'inclosed of late years by the *authority of Parliament*', *Staffordshire Advertiser*, 5 Jan. 1799. The point of his speech was that Parliament made enclosure possible and in return it should command reciprocal aid – in this case timber for the navy.

[66] Slater, *English Peasantry*, p. 293.

[67] 13 Geo. III c.81; Sheila Lambert, *Bills and Acts: Legislative Procedure in Eighteenth-Century England* (Cambridge, 1971), pp. 142–3.

trustees. Despite Tomes' assertion that they did not oppose the enclosure it is certain that some of them did. Francis Robinson, a trustee for Scot's, Smith's and Bell Acres Charity lands, objected to the enclosure of the wold, although he was outnumbered by others whose opinion we do not know. Dolben himself was a trustee of the larger Herbert's Charity together with the Honourable Edward Bouverie, Sir Charles Cave, Rector of Finedon, the Earl Spencer and a Mr Gunning. All of them wanted the allotment granted in lieu of the charity's five yardlands to be fenced free of charge. They also wanted the enclosure charges waived. But they were not all adamant about it, unlike the commoners. Lord Spencer 'hoped the Propr[ietor]s at large meant to inclose this Estate free of Expence to the Charity tho[ugh]t it would be handsome in them but if they refused did not nor did he mean to say that he sh[oul]d conceive think it be a suff[icien]t gr[oun]d to oppose the Bill'. Bouverie was more determined, saying he expected the enclosure to be free of *any* expense, but at least to be free of the commissioners' fees and legal costs, and 'that if this was not agreed to shod most certainly oppose it on the grod of not having had sufft notice'. Gunning was more complacent: he *expected* free fencing but would not oppose the Bill and would even support it in committee. Sir Charles Cave as Rector of Finedon, one of Sir William Dolben's livings, made it clear he would act with his patron.[68] Two other trustees of Herbert's Charity seem to have signed the Bill without raising objections. But not all trustees of all boards were applied to, and for some it must have been difficult to get a majority to sign in favour. The trustees of Savage's Close numbered eleven, of whom eight opposed the enclosure by signing the petition against it. The commissioners made do with the agreement of only one and William Dickens signed for Savage's Close on 25 March 1803.[69] But Dickens was not entirely in their pockets and he soon wrote to Marshall to remind him of two other charities – Dryden's and Middleton's – and to ask if the proprietors would enclose the charity land without charge. And the enclosers knew that others might ask the same question. In April, as the Bill was going through Parliament, Heydon wrote to Marshall

---

Table 7.4. *Burton Latimer: publicly used land before and after
enclosure*

Name	Acres Before enclosure	In award
Wold	800	72.8
Herbert's Charity	100	71
Northampton Poor's Estate	100 (+2 closes)	37.8[†]
Burton Latimer		
Poor's Estate	40	40
Scot's Charity	30* (+2 closes)	0
Smith's Charity	10*	0
Bell Acres Charity	4	2.5
Savage's Close	5	0
Town Headlands	8*	0
Church Estate	10	10
Wellingborough School Land	10	9.3
Meeting House	15 (+2 acres in closes)	9
Pinner's Piece	2	0
Parish Clerk's land	1.3	0.5
Totals	1137.3 + 4 closes	252.9
Total award acreage		2,583a 2r 28p

* may have been consolidated into the Burton Latimer Poor's Estate (a common
practice at enclosure).
† assumes it formed part of William King's estate in 1808.
Source: Northants. RO, H(BL) 813, n.d. (eve of enclosure, compiled for Joseph
Harper); ZA 891 in X 3872, n.d. (mid enclosure, Surveyor's calculations); H(BL) 816,
'Burton Proprs', n.d. (eve of enclosure, compiled for Joseph Harper); YZ 4594,
Burton Latimer Enclosure Award, 1803; Book L, pp. 311–13, Enrolled Enclosure
Awards, Burton Latimer, 1804. All calculations at the rate of twenty acres to the
yardland (ZA 891 in X 3872). The fate of Dryden's and Middleton's charities is
unknown.

asking, 'Do you hear of any point being made for the Northampton
Charity being inclosed at the public Expence?'[70] If he had, it made
no difference: Dolben's amendment exempting the Charity lands of
all costs was dismissed, with the result that half of the various
boards of trustees sold land to cover the expense of enclosure.[71]

[70] Northants. RO, ZA 891 in X3892, 25 Feb. 1803; ZA 892 in X3872, 8 Mar. 1803;
and Heydon to Marshall 24 Apr. 1803.
[71] The trustees of Herbert's Charity sold land to Joseph Harper, Thomas Coleman,
William Miller, Rev. William Hanbury, and the trustees of Burton Latimer Poor's
Estate. The total amount sold before the Award was 20a 2r 3p or 20 per cent of the

Some, including the trustees of the Northampton Poor's Estate, seem to have sold everything. In the end charity land and common waste shrank from over eleven hundred acres in January 1803 to about two hundred and fifty in March. The trustees were divided, complacent, and no more than occasional advocates. Their demands on behalf of the poor went no further than free fencing for the allotments. Unlike them, commoners against the enclosure trusted the process not at all. Enclosure would 'take away from the poor a Wold or Common of nearly 800 acres which provides them with fuel and sustenance for their Cattle and for which there is no probability that an adequate compensation will be made to them'.[72]

And they had quite other demands. They asked that the Bill should not become law at all unless the wold was left open. It was an important common resource, in part because right to it was attached not to land but to residence in the parish. Thomas Daniels had lived in Burton most of his life and had 'stocked the Wolds with one, 2 or 3 Cowes as he thought proper without any Interuption as did every House Dweller who co[ul]d get a cow'. Every year after harvest landless and land-poor commoners could buy additional field pasture. Henry Eady, an owner-occupier who opposed enclosure, had lived sixty of his eighty years in the parish and told the Commissioners that 'every House Dweller' who kept a cow could pay 4s for this common or could have it free if he owned a cottage. Thomas Daniels told them the same, saying he had paid '4s formerly and lately 2s per head to the Fieldsman for going into the fields after harvest'.[73] Inhabitant-commoners who owned or rented little or no land were variously called house dwellers, poor inhabitants, pot-wobblers and paupers.[74] At the very least they could common a cow

estate. The Burton Latimer Poor's Estate land was reduced by some 6a 3r 39p; Bell Acres, the Church Estate, and the Meeting House land were all partly sold for enclosure costs: Northants. RO, YZ 4594; Burton Latimer enclosure Award, 1803, Book L, pp. 311–13; Enrolled Enclosure Awards, Burton Latimer, 1804.

72 Northants. RO, H(BL) 806, 'Petition against the Inclosure of Burton Latimer, 1803'; *Jls House of Commons*, 25 Apr. 1803, pp. 350–1.

73 Northants. RO, ZA 891 in X3872, especially claims of Francis and John Robinson, and Joseph Wood, trustees of the Meeting House. John Harper bought the right to common a cow and five sheep for a season from Thomas Daniels in 1773 for 10s – this was part of Daniel's cottage common right. H(BL) 649, Account Book, 1774–90.

74 Northants. RO, ZA 892 in X3872, Thomas Heydon to Thomas Marshall, Esq., solicitor, Kettering, 26 April 1803; Heydon called them pot-wobblers (householders and tenants of houses). H(BL) 808, John Tomes to Joseph Harper, Esq.,

on the wold free, and for a few shillings they could feed it on the corn stubble. Even the impropriator of the tithe recognized the right when he supported the claim made by the churchwardens and overseers for the 'right of Common for Cows and cutting of Furz for fuel on the Wold' on behalf of the 'poor Inhabitants' of the parish.[75] And the Reverend Sir Charles Cave, as Rector of Finedon, claimed the right to common without stint upon the Wold, calling it a 'garden right'.[76]

Cottagers, unlike house-dwellers, had right attached to their cottages – usually for a horse and ten sheep as well as a cow. They used the wold like house dwellers but put their animals into the harvested fields without paying a fee.[77] By 1803 most of the cottages in Burton Latimer were owned by landlords and absentee land-owners; only four were occupied by their owners.[78] Three of the cottage owners signed the petition against the enclosure, and some of the trustees of Herbert's Charity and of the Meeting House, who also held cottages, made objection to the nature of the Bill. But the enclosers had no fear of opposition from the cottage owners in general. They knew that other commoners and cottage-*tenants* were the principal source of opposition. And they relied on the Reverend Hanbury (who owned three cottages) to bring his influence to bear on the other owners to ignore the claims of their tenants.[79]

Despite the appearance of Dolben to oppose the Bill, and the

Chilvers Coton, 17 May 1803; Tomes called the petitioners against enclosure 'all the Paupers in the parish and a few freeholders'.
[75] Northants. RO, ZA 891 in X3872, Claims made at enclosure, 1803.
[76] Northants. RO, ZA 891 in X3872, 29 July 1803; Cave's patron was Sir William Dolben.
[77] Northants. RO, ZA 891 in X3872; Joseph Harper, Francis Robinson, Robert Capps and others made this claim for cottage common rights.
[78] Northants. RO, H(BL) 812, 813, 816, Lists of proprietors of land in Burton Latimer drawn up for Joseph Harper, Esq.; ZA 891 in X3872, Claims made at the enclosure, 1803. The claims are substantiated in Harper's lists. The occupying owners were Robert Capps, Joseph Sudborough, Francis Robinson, and Samuel Wright. Three owners were clerics – Rev. William Hanbury (3 cottages), Rev. Samuel Barwick (2) and Rev. Shaw King (1). Four others lived outside the parish – Thomas Partridge and Joseph Robinson (Wellingborough, 2 and 1), Mrs Eleanor Benford (Kettering, 1), and Joseph Harper (Chilvers Coton, 1). The trustees of Herbert's Charity, the Meeting House and Bell Acres each held one. Capps, Sudborough and Robinson opposed the Bill.
[79] Northants. RO, ZA 891 in X3872, 24 March 1803; ZA 892 in X3872, Heydon to Marshall, n.d., before 26 Apr. 1803; H(BL) 813, 'Burton Statmt of Property'. Hanbury claimed only 3 cottages but was listed by Harper's agents as being the owner of 5; see also H(BL) 812, 'Burton Inclosure – State of Property – Proprs – Old Inclosures – Open Field Lands – For-Vs. Neuter'.

petition itself with its seventy-eight signatures representing almost half the parish, the Bill became law, the Award was drawn up in 1803 and enrolled in the following year.[80]

The petitioners against enclosure

Who were the commoners against the Bill? Two-thirds of them appear not to have owned, rented, or let any land at all. It is this group which received least consideration at the time, and about which least is known now. Twenty-three can be traced and partially identified through Militia Lists for 1777, 1781, and the year of the enclosure, 1803.[81] Of these, four were tradesmen or artisans (a blacksmith, mason, carpenter and cordwainer), and five were weavers who may have been outworkers. Another four were described as servants (probably agricultural), six were labourers and one was a shepherd.[82] The remaining three were described simply as 'housekeeper' – that is, a householder who, in Burton Latimer, had grazing and fuel rights on the wold.[83] Unfortunately, the occupations of the younger landless petitioners (thirty men under the age of thirty-nine) are unknown; their families may have been those most harmed by the extinction of common right.[84] So the largest

---

[80] If each of the seventy-eight petitioners was a householder with a family size of about 4.3, the total number of persons they represented would have been 334 in a population of 669: *Census* (1801), p. 247. The Award was enrolled in September 1804: Northants. RO, Book L, Enrolled Enclosure Awards, Burton Latimer.

[81] Northants. RO, Militia Lists, Huxloe Hundred, Burton Latimer, 1777, 1781. Army of Reserve, Kettering Division, Burton Latimer, List of Men and Occupations, 1803, X281/3. A shortcoming is the quarter-century lag between the Militia Lists and the petition of 1803. See next note.

[82] Militia and Reserve Lists cited above; Northants. RO, Land Tax, Burton Latimer, 1803, H(BL) 13, 'Statement of property' (probably 1803). On the 1777 list appear Richard Croxen, Samuel Fox, John Burnaby, William Nutt, Thos. Bellamy (farmer; 1781 labourer), John Daniels (labourer; also 1781 servant), Charles Hodson (servant; also 1781 labourer), Jos. Miller (also 1781), Samuel Smith (also 1781), John Timpson (also 1781), Fraser Toulton (also 1781). On the 1781 list only appear John Ball, David Chamber, William Croxen, James Dickenson, Edey Langley, Thomas Shipley, John Styles, Thomas Vorley. Four men are listed as housekeepers on the 1803 list: James Mee, Wm Mitchell, Joseph Payne, and William Butlin. The last was also a shepherd: H(BL) 656, 'Account Book 1790–1800'. Occupations differ on two lists only for Bellamy, Daniels, Hodson, and only in Bellamy's case is the change significant.

[83] The *Oxford English Dictionary* cites H. Martineau, *Brooke Farm*, II (1833), p. 21, 'A piece of land will be given to every house-keeper in return for his right of common.'

[84] Huxloe Hundred Militia Lists end in 1781. The overall age distribution of identifiable landless petitioners (all men) was thirty-four between the ages of 18

group of petitioners against the Act were landless commoners, some of whom can be identified in the Militia Lists as artisans, weavers, servants and labourers. The remaining third of the petitioners (twenty-five) owned or rented some land. We know the occupations of nineteen. Six were artisans or tradesmen (a carpenter, a butcher, a miller, a victualler, two wheelwrights), one was a weaver, five were farmers; and there was one shepherd, a 'proprietor and occupier', a labourer, a lodger, a housekeeper and two servants. Two thirds of these men owned land, and all of them worked it. To the enclosers they were described as just a few freeholders, and classed with the 'Paupers' who also opposed the enclosure. Joseph Harper left half of them off his list of proprietors.[85]

The petitioners against the enclosure appear to have been farmers, tradesmen and artisans who held land, and weavers, servants and labourers who apparently did not. The opponents of the enclosure appear not to have worked only in agriculture. Agricultural and non-agricultural occupations were about equally represented among both the landed and landless. It is possible, however, that some (perhaps many) of the fifty-three petitioners who do not appear on the Land Tax return actually owned or rented land before the enclosure. Poor owners and tenants of land worth less than 20s a year in rent were legally exempt payment of the Land Tax.[86] If rents were low, plots of up to two acres may have been held without taxation. Tenants of such holdings will never be traced, and some of the 'landless' petitioners against the enclosure of Burton Latimer may be among them. Nor can we identify the owners of such plots from the Award because many would have sold out before it was made, such as Nathaniel Daniels, once a weaver, an owner of half a rood of old-enclosed land, who did not pay tax on his land and sold

and 45 and another nineteen between 40 and 71 years of age. A man whose name appeared only in 1777 and not in 1781 must have been in his mid sixties by 1803, for he would have been over 45 (upper age for the militia) in 1781. Those appearing on the 1781 list (between 18 and 45 years at the time) would be aged from 40 to 65 or so in 1803. Men found on the list of the Army of Reserve would have been between 18 and 45 in 1803. However, they were probably no older than 39 because they escaped the 1781 Militia List. For the Army of Reserve see Sir John Fortescue, *The Army and the County Lieutenancies* (1908), ch. 1.

85 Northants. RO, H(BL) 812, 'Burton Inclosure – State of Property. Proprs – Old Inclosures – Open Field Lands – for Vs. Neuter'.
86 38 Geo. III c.5; and see below, Appendix A, pp. 340–1.

Table 7.5. *Burton Latimer: owner-occupiers in 1803: size of holdings before enclosure, and resistance*

	to 5	5–10	10–25	25–50	50–100	Unknown	Total
			Acreage				
Owner-occupiers	7	6	3	2	1	3	22
Opponents	5	4	1	1	1	1	13
Supporters	0	2	1	0	0	2	5

Source: Northants. RO, Land Tax, Burton Latimer, 1803; H(BL) 806; H(BL) 812: this source incorrectly identified several petitioners as supporters of the enclosure; this may be true of its labelling of three more owners as supporters – Thomas Hughes, Henry Robinson jr and John Hughes.

it in 1803 before the Award was complete.[87] There may have been others who sold out to settle their tithe payment, or to avoid the cost of fencing and draining, or because the land was useless without commons, or for any number of reasons.[88]

Several owners of old enclosures, closes of no more than a rood or two, also suffered from the loss of the wold because, like cottage commoners and house dwellers, they used its unstinted acres for rough pasture. Five men owned no more than these closes in 1803 and two of them signed the petition against the enclosure. In any parish like Burton Latimer where common was open to the inhabitants, owners of old enclosures were badly affected by its loss at enclosure.[89]

The commissioners compensated the house-dwellers and cottage commoners for their eight-hundred acres of wold with about seventy-three acres situated in the same place. The area was less than a tenth of the wold and the quality of the land was unimproved. Whatever rents it brought in were to be applied to the relief of the poor at the discretion of the rector and the churchwardens. House-dwellers and cottage commoners had accurately predicted that no adequate compensation would be made to them. Nor had they been heard: the Commons' *Journal* failed to record their opposition; it

[87] Northants. RO, Land Tax, 1803; H(BL) 813, 'Statement of Property'; unfortunately this source is incomplete. Militia List, 1777, Burton Latimer.
[88] See above, pp. 205–7.
[89] Northants. RO, H(BL) 813, 'Burton State of Property', n.d. [1803]. George Braybrooke owned 3r; Thomas Vorley, 2r; John Neal, ½r; Nathaniel Daniels, ½r; and Benjamin Ireland, 1r. Thomas Vorley and Nathaniel Daniels signed the Petition: H(BL) 806, 'Petition against the Inclosure of Burton Latimer, 1803'.

Table 7.6. *Burton Latimer: changes in owner-occupiers' holdings after enclosure, 1803–8*

Acreage	Opponents of enclosure					Other owner-occupiers				
	(Total no.)	Gone	Less	Same	More	(Total no.)	Gone	Less	Same	More
to 10	10	5	3	1	1	5†	2	1		2
11–25	0					1†		1		
26–50	1				1	1		1		
51–100	1				1	0				
Unknown	1*					2#				

† includes one owner-occupier who rented additional land.
* part owned and part rented 140 acres in 1803; owned 51 acres in 1808.
# tax paid by the rector and Lord of the Manor is not specified in the 1803 return.

Source: Northants. RO, Land Tax, Burton Latimer, 1803, 1808; H(BL) 806.

listed only the total sum of land owned by opponents of the Bill, not the opposition of those whose only property was common right. This was a perfectly proper legal proceeding, but a misleading one. It meant that the opposition of fifty-seven commoners, who were at most the smallest of smallholders, and of eight tenants who owned no land worthy of taxation went unnoticed in Parliament.[90] Parliament's deaf ear may have made counter-petitions the least useful of all means of resisting enclosure.[91]

Opposition and landholding change at enclosure

Two-thirds or more of all the owner-occupiers in Burton Latimer and one third of the tenants signed the petition against enclosure.[92] Most of the former owned less than twenty-five acres, and many held less than ten[93] (Table 7.5). Five years later a third (seven out of twenty-two) of the owner-occupiers no longer owned or rented land. Another six owned less than they had in 1803, the year of the

[90] *Jls House of Commons*, 16 May 1803.   [91] See below, Chapter 9, p. 272.
[92] Of the owner-occupiers thirteen of the eighteen whose opinion was recorded signed the counter-petition, five were identified as supporters of the Bill by Joseph Harper's agents.
[93] Of the five who supported the Bill, two were principally landlords (Harper who was Lord of the Manor, and the Rector); a third (Henry Robinson, jr) was principally one of Harper's tenants and rented more land than he owned.

Table 7.7. *Burton Latimer: changes in tenants' holdings after enclosure, 1803–8*

Acreage	Opponents					Other tenants				
	(Total no.)	Gone	Less	Same	More	(Total no.)	Gone	Less	Same	More
to 50	7	2	4		1	7	5	2		
51–100	0					3	2	1		
100 plus	1				1	3		1		2
Unknown	0					3[†]				

[†] amounts of land not listed individually in 1803 (all tenants of Joseph Harper).

Source: Northants. RO, Land Tax, Burton Latimer, 1803, 1808; H(BL) 806, 'Petition against the Inclosure of Burton Latimer, 1803'.

Award. Fewer than half (nine out of twenty-two) of the owner-occupiers had held on to their lands or improved them (Table 7.6). Owner-occupancy and tenancy were virtually separate states in Burton Latimer on the eve of enclosure. Only four of the twenty-two owner-occupiers rented additional land from other landowners.[94] Five of the twenty-four tenants owned land too, but these owned lands were far smaller than their rented lands, too small to justify calling them owner-occupiers.[95] Eight of them signed the Petition against the enclosure in 1803. Most worked less – usually much less – than fifty acres of land; one (Thomas Burnaby) was the principal tenant of the glebe land. But opponents were the very small tenants on the whole: none of the three tenants of middling-size farms (fifty

[94] Northants. RO, Land Tax, Burton Latimer, 1803. They were Mrs Wood; Henry Robinson, jr; and George and John Robinson, who rented their land from other Robinsons and who all opposed the enclosure: H(BL) 806, 'Petition against the Inclosure of Burton Latimer, 1803'.
[95] Five of the twenty-four tenants owned very small plots of land in 1803 for which they received allotments at the making of the Award. None of these properties were taxed before enclosure, although all but one were taxed in 1808 – the exception was a holding of 6a 1r 2p belonging to William Miller, jr, which may have been sold soon after enclosure: Northants. RO, YZ 4594, Burton Latimer Inclosure Award, 1803. They were William Miller, jr (6a 1r 2p); William Miller, sr (1 acre) – the former bought from Kettering Charity, the latter from Kettering Rectory; Robert Capps (2a 1r 27p); Samuel Wright (2a 2r 27p); and Thomas Eady (3a 2r 2p). All of them (with the exception of William Miller, jr) were listed by Harper's agent as owning small plots before the enclosure: H(BL) 813, n.d., probably 1803.

to a hundred acres) signed the petition against the enclosure.[96] By 1808 – five years after the Award – almost half the small tenants no longer rented land; a third rented smaller estates than in 1803; only four rented more land than before, and all of them were tenants of the larger estates (Table 7.7).

To summarize: most of the owner-occupiers and many of the smaller tenants had petitioned against enclosure at Burton Latimer. Five years later, a third of the owner-occupiers and a half of the tenants no longer worked taxable land. Others worked less than before. In all, two-thirds of each group had either lost their land altogether or rented and owned less than they had on the eve of enclosure. Only the more substantial owner-occupiers and the tenants of larger estates had improved their acreage – and they tended to be the supporters of the enclosure.

Despite differences of agricultural and industrial region and enclosure period, landed, land-poor and landless commoners in Burton Latimer and West Haddon shared the same dependence on common right and the same loss of both rights and land at enclosure. Though neither was a fen or forest village, villages, that is, with extensive common waste, in both places commoning had not disappeared, and in Burton Latimer *inhabitants'* rights to common of pasture still flourished. In both villages enclosure met resistance. In West Haddon, small freeholders, tenants, trading and artisan-commoners organized both a parliamentary and an illegal opposition to enclosure. In Burton Latimer, owner-occupiers, artisans, virtually landless labourers and the poor drew up a local petition and found a defender in a paternalistic critic of enclosure. Despite this, in both places everyone lost the use of a valued common waste, and in both landholding changed markedly. The smallest occupying commoners, those with up to forty acres of owned or rented land, lost all or a significant amount of their land. The following chapters discuss the wider boundaries of opposition to enclosure and changes in landholding at enclosure, and show that West Haddon and Burton Latimer commoners were not alone in their resistance, any more than they were in their loss of lands and common rights.

---

[96] Northants. RO, Land Tax, Burton Latimer, 1803; H(BL) 806; Neeson, 'Common Right and Enclosure', p. 290, Table 5.14.

8. *Decline and disappearance*

Allow me first to consider a little the case of the *Poor* under inclosures. They feel the evil, and complain; but complain in vain. The common people, indeed, frequently murmur without cause; they quote Scripture improperly. Yet, my Lord, *interdum vulgus rectum videt*: and Scripture may be aptly adduced against this unchristian practice. It is not *doing as we would be done unto:* it is not *loving our neighbour as ourselves*; but is *removing his landmark*, contrary to his inclination; and therefore *joining field to field by iniquity*. The history of Ahab and Naboth is not altogether inapplicable here. It does not appear from the sacred pages, that the wicked prince intended to rob his subject of his vineyard; but to make him, as he supposed, a proper recompence. Under an act of parliament, the poor man's land is frequently taken from him; and what is allotted to him is by no means a compensation for his loss.

> Anon., *Reflections on the Cruelty of Inclosing ... letter to the Bishop of Lincoln* (1796), pp. 6–7.

In an important article published in 1979, J. M. Martin described changes in landholding taking place at parliamentary enclosure in Warwickshire.[1] Like Michael Turner, who had made a similar discovery in Buckinghamshire,[2] Martin was struck by the 'turnover', or replacement through land sales, of one set of small

---

[1] J. M. Martin, 'The Small Landowner and Parliamentary Enclosure in Warwickshire', *Economic History Review* 32 (1979), pp. 328–43.

[2] Turner, 'Parliamentary Enclosure and Landownership Change in Buckinghamshire', pp. 565–81; see also J. R. Walton, 'The Residential Mobility of Farmers and its Relationship to the Parliamentary Enclosure Movement in Oxfordshire', in A. D. M. Phillips and B. J. Turton, eds., *Environment, Man and Economic Change: Essays Presented to S. H. Beaver* (1975), pp. 238–52.

landowners by another. However, unlike Turner, he also found that both the engrossing of estates and an absolute numerical decline of small owners followed enclosure, and child mortality rates rose too. This was evidence of a more serious and far-reaching change than 'turnover' alone suggested.

The group of owners most affected by engrossing were not occupiers, they were landlords, often absentees. In fact landlords comprised 61 per cent of all owners paying between 5s and £3 in Land Tax just before enclosure, and they declined in absolute numbers by 39 per cent in its aftermath.[3] In contrast, small occupiers hung on after enclosure: 'The actual cultivator', Martin wrote, 'whether owner-occupier or tenant-farmer, appeared as elsewhere to be little affected as a class'.[4]

In a subsequent essay on the role of enclosure as a catalyst in rural proletarianization in Warwickshire Martin turned his attention to occupiers.[5] He identified the characteristic small occupiers in the most populous open-field villages as men with multiple occupations, most often small trades- or craftsmen. He went on to argue that enclosure, by reducing their holdings, and by impoverishing most of their customers, pushed them into the ranks of the poorest tradesmen or turned them into labourers. But, again, he argued that enclosure destroyed the livelihoods of the small traders and craftsmen rather than the small landowners as a class, though who remained was unclear.[6]

Despite some unanswered questions, Martin's is the most imaginative and well-contextualized account we have of the effect of enclosure on landholding in the most densely populated parishes of a large Midland county. He goes beyond the earlier accounts of 'turnover' to explain how the lives of small occupiers actually changed as a result of enclosure. If the ultimate fate of the class is

---

[3] Martin, 'The Small Landowner', p. 335, Table 5.

[4] *Ibid.*, p. 343. This was a puzzling conclusion to a study showing a numerical decline in small owners of 28 per cent, another in small owner-occupiers of 14 per cent, and the contraction of their shared acreage (my calculations from figures in Table 5, p. 335). And having established the decline of small landlords Martin also overlooked its possible significance. The function of little landlords in open-field parishes, and the implications of their decline for small occupiers, remain obscure. We cannot assume that they were overwhelmingly outsiders or that they were small versions of large landlords.

[5] Martin, 'Village Traders and the Emergence of a Proletariat in South Warwickshire', pp. 179–88.

[6] *Ibid.*, p. 188.

left unclear, its experience of enclosure is more exactly described than before.

In this chapter, like Martin and Turner, I look at turnover in original landholders at enclosure in a Midland county; and, like Martin, I also look at engrossing and the decline of small occupiers. But, unlike either Martin or Turner, my concern is with the question of what happened to the eighteenth-century English peasantry as a class. I argue that high rates of turnover, a striking contraction in size of original holdings, and an absolute decline in the number of small owner-occupiers, landlords and tenants were common in Northamptonshire at enclosure, and rare in villages that remained open. From this I go on to suggest why the turnover of individual landholders at enclosure did not mean the substitution of one cohort of smallholders for another. I argue that the economies of each were necessarily, and radically, different. Where the peasant economy had survived in open-field villages until enclosure it had depended on a particular agricultural practice, a set of social relations, a right to use common lands and a body of commoners large enough to support it: after enclosure all of these were either changed or lost. I argue that in most of the villages studied here parliamentary enclosure destroyed the old peasant economy. It did this not only by more than decimating small occupiers and landlords and by reducing their total acreage, but also by more completely separating the agricultural practice of small and large farmers, by pushing the smaller occupiers into the market more thoroughly than before, and by expropriating landless commoners on whom much of the old economy had depended.[7] The Northamptonshire evidence does more than qualify the optimistic view that enclosure benefited small farmers: it directly contradicts it.

For this discussion 2,179 entries on forty-six Land Tax returns were edited to yield detailed evidence of the owned and rented land of 1,598 individuals. Three-quarters of them lived in seventeen parishes enclosed at different times between 1778 and 1814; one quarter came from six parishes remaining open throughout.[8] Open-

---

[7] For Leicestershire evidence pointing to the same conclusion see Hoskins, *Midland Peasant*, ch. 10.

[8] Land Tax records were examined for all fifty-four enclosures taking place between 1778 and 1802 but suitable returns were found for only fourteen of the enclosures. They related to fifteen parishes (two of the parishes were enclosed together). Returns that failed to distinguish between proprietor and occupier could not be used (even after 1780 status was not invariably recorded); nor could returns which

field parishes were chosen for comparison rather than old-enclosed or recently enclosed parishes because they provide the best contrast in that, while newly enclosing parishes were undergoing whatever transformation an enclosure wrought, open-field ones were not.

All twenty-three parishes were in Northamptonshire, a Midland county remarkable for its large numbers of parliamentary enclosures, in W. E. Tate's words, '*the* county of parliamentary enclosure'.[9] Fully half of the county's 630,000 acres were enclosed in this manner in the eighteenth century alone.[10] At the height of the movement, in the 1770s, sixty Acts were passed, enclosing one fifth of all the parishes in the county and affecting considerably more than one fifth of the population.[11] In broad terms, the movement spread from the south west in the 1750s (by-passing the southern forests), through the scarp along the western side of the county, and into the central parishes between Northampton and Kettering in the sixties and seventies, reaching the Nene valley, Rockingham Forest and the fens in the 1790s and 1800s.

Parishes studied were located in areas undergoing enclosure between 1780 and 1815. It is one of the limitations of using the Land Tax as a source for a study such as this that (with a few exceptions such as Rushden and Bugbrooke, below) suitable returns exist only after 1780. Before 1780 the Land Tax collectors were required to list only the taxpayer, not to identify proprietors and occupiers. Of course much parliamentary enclosure took place before 1780, some with the intention of turning arable land to pasture, or to extend convertible husbandry, and with the potential to produce

grouped together several tenants as occupiers of the land of a landlord who paid all their tax in one lump sum; and nor could listings of tenants as 'John Smith and Others' or those which did not break down the individual holdings of landlords who let their lands to the same large tenant. In addition, two fenland parishes whose enclosure took place between 1809 and 1814 were examined. Missing from the study is an examination of scarpland parishes enclosed in the 1760s and a representative of Rockingham Forest or Salcey enclosures, although two Whittlewood Forest parishes are included. For a discussion of the significance of the omission of the pre-1780 enclosures see pp. 224–5 below. Throughout, the term 'open' is used to describe parishes not yet enclosed by Act.

[9] Tate, 'Enclosure Movements in Northamptonshire', p. 30.
[10] Turner notes that, when non-agricultural land is subtracted, as much as 70 per cent of Northamptonshire, Oxfordshire and Cambridgeshire was enclosed by Act: *English Parliamentary Enclosure*, p. 34.
[11] Open villages tended to be more densely populated than enclosed. In 1720, 87 per cent of the population lived in the 66 per cent of the county's parishes that were open: calculation from population estimates in Bridges, *History and Antiquities of Northamptonshire*.

unemployment and engrossment, two frequently lamented results of enclosure in the Midlands.[12] But because Land Tax returns are insufficiently detailed until 1780, it is not possible to measure land-holding change in terms of either the histories of individual land-holders or of numbers of landholders before and after an enclosure until then.[13] As a result *all* Land Tax based studies of the relation-ship between parliamentary enclosure and the decline of the peasantry, including this one, are, in effect, studies of that relation-ship only after 1780. A measure of the significance of this is that by 1780 most of the open-field arable Midlands and much of Lin-colnshire and up into the East Riding of Yorkshire were already enclosed.[14] Northamptonshire enclosures taking place before the late 1770s and early 1780s are missing from this study then, and in particular the enclosures of parishes on the western scarp.[15] Apart from these, all other major geographical regions are represented. The six open parishes chosen for the purpose of comparing changes in landholding in open and enclosing parishes lay in the same geographical regions as their enclosing counterparts and were exam-ined in the same years.

Two returns, one at the beginning and one at the end of a ten-year *method* period, were compared for each parish. In the enclosing parishes enclosure took place in the middle of the ten-year period. Ten years is an interval long enough to show most of enclosure's effects on landholding. If small owners sold some or all of their lands before the Awards burdened them with high costs this would be shown in the comparison of pre- and post-enclosure returns. Similarly, if particular tenancies were terminated, this would appear. And any enlarging of estates could be compared to the growth of estates in still-open parishes. Ten years is also short enough to let us assume that where an enclosure was made it was responsible for whatever changes took place that did not also happen in open parishes.

---

[12] Conversion to pasture and unemployment were common complaints in protests against enclosure: see below, pp. 252–3 and p. 285.

[13] Denis Mills and Richard Grover have used very early Land Tax returns to compare numbers of taxpayers they deduce to be owners, with owners identified as such in post-1780 returns; neither discusses the effect on ownership of parlia-mentary enclosure: Michael E. Turner and Dennis Mills, eds., *Land and Property: The English Land Tax, 1692–1832* (Gloucester, 1986).

[14] Turner, *English Parliamentary Enclosure*, pp. 72–6.

[15] The effects of enclosure in West Haddon, a scarpland parish enclosed in 1765, are discussed below, Chapter 9; for the limits of its Land Tax returns see pp. 201–2.

Clearly some long-term effects of enclosure, and in particular the sale of foreclosed holdings after 1814, escape this survey.[16]

The study falls into three parts. First, the rate at which landowners in enclosing parishes left the land is established, and compared to the rates Turner measured for Buckinghamshire villages. To this degree the study is much like Turner's and can endorse his findings, although a control group of still-open villages is used rather than the recently enclosing and old-enclosed villages he chose. But, having done this, it is necessary to refine the evidence by giving separate consideration to those owner-occupiers, tenants and landlords who disappeared from the Land Tax returns. The advantages of this are that the abstract, catch-all category of landowner can be jettisoned and instead the sometimes different strategies of landlords and owner-occupiers can be discussed; and the experience of tenants who did not own land, or who owned only part of their holdings can also be examined. In the second part of the study, the fortunes of the survivors of enclosure, those landholders who did not sell up or leave at enclosure, are investigated, and, in particular, changes in the size of their holdings are noted. In the third part, I argue that it is possible, and necessary, to count bodies rather than simply identify faces. Accordingly, I compare the numbers of owner-occupiers, tenants and landlords before and after enclosure. In conclusion, I begin to discuss the implications of these changes in landholding for the survival or decline of the English peasant – a discussion continued in the chapters that follow.

I

If we look first at the disappearance of landowners from the returns it appears that half (49 per cent) of the original owners in enclosing parishes no longer held any kind of land for which they paid tax at the end of the ten-year period during which enclosure had taken place. In open parishes the proportion was 29 per cent. In fact, if we assume a constant rate of attrition (due to illness, death, and the transfer of land to family members not sharing the original owner's name) in both kinds of parish, then the difference in rates of

[16] On the connection between earlier enclosure and the acceleration of land sales after the peace brought down agricultural prices, see Hoskins, *Midland Peasant*, pp. 263–6.

Table 8.1. *Comparison of parish rates of landowner disappearance in Northamptonshire (1778–1814) and Buckinghamshire (1780–1832)**

Old-enclosed parishes, Bucks.	Recently enclosed, Bucks.	Currently enclosing, Bucks.	Currently enclosing, Northants.	Open parishes, Northants.
17.9%	20.4%	38.7%	42%	26%

Note: * Northants. RO Land Tax returns for the following parishes: Bugbrooke (1774, 1784), Rushden (1774, 1783), Wollaston (1783, 1793), Roade (1786, 1796), Wadenhoe (1788, 1798), Abthorpe (1790, 1800), Stanwick (1790, 1800), Raunds (1791, 1802), Whitfield (1791, 1801), Greens Norton (1794, 1804), Whittlebury (1794, 1803), Islip (1795, 1805), Newton Bromswold (1795, 1805), Chelveston (1796, 1806), Hannington, (1797, 1807), Hargrave (1797, 1807), Sutton Bassett (1797, 1807), Weston by Welland (1797, 1807), Eye (1804, 1813), Maxey (1803, 1814), Helpston (1804, 1813), Naseby (1806, 1814), and Lutton (1796, 1806). Buckinghamshire figures from Michael E. Turner, 'Parliamentary Enclosure and Land Ownership Change in Buckinghamshire', *Economic History Review*, 2nd series, 28 (1975), pp. 567–8.

disappearance between open and enclosing parishes was even greater.

How does this compare to Turner's findings for Buckinghamshire? If we translate the Northamptonshire figures from mean individual to mean parish rates in order to produce comparable statistics,[17] the Northamptonshire mean parish rate of change was 42 per cent in enclosing parishes, compared to 38.7 per cent in Buckinghamshire; and 26 per cent in open parishes, compared to 17.9 per cent and 20.4 per cent respectively in old- and recently enclosed Buckinghamshire parishes. Table 8.1 shows that the Northamptonshire findings support those from Buckinghamshire, in fact they show that slightly more owners left the land at enclosure in Northamptonshire than in Buckinghamshire.

The rate at which owners gave up their lands varied with the size

[17] Turner calculated the percentage of owners who disappeared from the returns *in each parish* and then averaged all the results within categories (enclosing, recently enclosed, old-enclosed). In this way he measured the rate of disappearance in an average, but non-existent, parish, for each category. I have preferred to count all the owners in *all* the enclosing (or open) parishes who no longer held land at the end of the ten-year period, and to express that number as a percentage of the total number of landowners who held land at the beginning. In this way the experience of the majority of owners in enclosing and open parishes may be compared. The histories of individual parishes are not ignored, however: see pp. 231–4, 241–3.

Table 8.2. *Disappearance from the Land Tax returns of owners over a ten-year period, by size of owned land, 1774–1814*

	0–5 acres		5–25		25–50		50–100		Over 100		Totals	
	%	(no.)	%	(no.)	%	(no.)	%	(no.)	%	(no.)	%	(no.)
Enclosing parishes	62	(74)	55	(119)	51	(39)	44	(27)	28	(32)	49	$\left\{ \frac{291}{594} \right\}$
Open parishes	40	(20)	27	(10)	29	(5)	15	(4)	28	(11)	29	$\left\{ \frac{50}{172} \right\}$

of their holdings.[18] Owners of less than one hundred acres left the land in larger numbers than owners of more land, who seem to have sold up no faster than usual. It seems that substantial owners in enclosing parishes could hold on to their lands during an enclosure (which they themselves must have supported) as well as they could at any other time. Table 8.2 sets this out in detail.

Among landlords the pattern is repeated: half of the landlords in enclosing parishes sold all their lands after enclosure but only one

[18] In order to calculate the size of holdings from tax returns a sum of tax equivalent to an acre of land (an acreage equivalent) was calculated for each parish in each of the two tax years. Allowance was made for tax paid on tithe, office and dwellings. Enclosure Awards were used to cross-check the size of holdings and the sum of tax paid on them. For a detailed discussion of the problems of using the Land Tax, and the methods adopted here, see Appendices A and B, pp. 331–43. See pp. 245–7 below for a discussion of acreage equivalents, the taxation of small owners and the taxation of tithe. In the last year, D. E. Ginter's criticism of Yorkshire Land Tax returns has appeared (in his *A Measure of Wealth: The English Land Tax in Historical Analysis*, Kingston and Montreal, 1992). This is not the place to respond at length, but something may be said in brief. First, the recent work of a number of historians has confirmed the value of the source when used within the generally agreed boundaries respected here, notably Turner and Mills, eds., *Land and Property*. Second, in the present study the returns have been compared where possible to enclosure papers and Awards which provide an independent index of the size and status of landholdings and landholders. Third, the micro-studies of enclosing West Haddon and Burton Latimer described above in Chapter 7 *confirm* the trends in turnover of landholders, diminution in survivors' holdings (within size categories large enough to compensate for error), and absolute decline in numbers of landholders, seen in the larger study of twenty-three parishes presented here. Finally, the returns disclose significant differences in the experience of enclosing and still-open villages, differences one would not expect to find were the returns utterly unreliable guides to landholding – and differences corroborated in Martin's work on Warwickshire and Turner's on Buckinghamshire: see Martin, 'The Small Landowner and Parliamentary Enclosure in Warwickshire', and Turner, 'Parliamentary Enclosure and Landownership Change in Buckinghamshire'. In short: the Land Tax is a useful and usable source for studying these Midland parishes at enclosure.

Table 8.3. *Disappearance from the Land Tax returns of landlords over a ten-year period, by size of owned land, 1774–1814*

	0–5 acres		5–25		25–50		50–100		Over 100		Totals	
	%	(no.)	%	(no.)	%	(no.)	%	(no.)	%	(no.)	%	(no.)
Enclosing parishes	64	(28)	61	(72)	57	(33)	50	(18)	26	(17)	52	$\left\{\frac{168}{323}\right\}$
Open parishes	46	(13)	37	(7)	31	(4)	14	(2)	35	(9)	35	$\left\{\frac{35}{100}\right\}$

third did so in open parishes (Table 8.3). Like small owners, small landlords in enclosing parishes sold up more often than men with more land. And again, rates of disappearance merged in open and enclosing parishes in the largest holdings: substantial landlords promoted enclosure and most continued to hold land.

Landlords and landowners were often the same men. (For this reason their disappearance from the returns at the same times and in similar proportions is not surprising.) A better distinction is that between landlords and owner-occupiers. But owner-occupiers sometimes rented land to supplement their own holdings: in the open and enclosing parishes studied here approximately one third of owner-occupiers were also tenants.[19] The ubiquity of such owner-occupier/tenants led Professor Mingay to conclude that 'apparent shifts in the arbitrary categories of small owners, based only on the acreages of owned land as deduced from land tax assessments, may not be all that meaningful'.[20] In order to overcome this problem the rates of disappearance of both owner-occupiers who rented and those who did not have been studied together. The results are summarized in Table 8.4.

Owner-occupiers and owner-occupier/tenants in enclosing parishes gave up their holdings twice as often as those in open parishes. They were more likely to do so than landlords or owners *per se*: for every two landlords selling up in open parishes three did so in enclosing, whereas for every two owner-occupiers selling up in open parishes four did so in enclosing. Even occupiers of more than one hundred acres sold their lands more frequently in enclosing than

[19] The figures were 88 out of 266 in enclosing parishes (33 per cent) and 17 out of 56 in open parishes (30 per cent).
[20] G. E. Mingay, 'The Land Tax Assessments and the Small Landowner', *Economic History Review*, 2nd series, 17 (1964), p. 388.

Table 8.4. *Disappearance from the Land Tax returns of owner-occupiers and owner-occupier tenants over a ten-year period, by size of holding, 1774–1814*

	0–5 acres		5–25		25–50		50–100		Over 100		Totals	
	%	(no.)	%	(no.)	%	(no.)	%	(no.)	%	(no.)	%	(no.)
Enclosing parishes	61	(46)	48	(47)	29	(6)	36	(9)	29	(14)	46	{ 122 / 266 }
Open parishes	32	(7)	18	(3)	0	(0)	40	(2)	11	(1)	23	{ 13 / 56 }

open villages. But the occupiers most likely to leave were those with holdings of between five and twenty-five acres.

The Land Tax evidence shows that all kinds of occupying owners were more likely to sell up at enclosure than their counterparts in still-open villages. If we go on to compare the disappearance rates of owner-occupiers who rented additional land with those who did not, a further distinction may be drawn. Owner-occupiers who did not rent land were more mobile at enclosure than those who did: after enclosure half of them no longer owned any land compared to a little more than one third of owner-occupiers who were tenants as well.[21] The variation between the two may be explained in terms of size. On the whole those who did not rent land were owners of smaller landholdings than those who did: three-quarters of owner-occupiers owned and worked less than twenty-five acres compared to less than a quarter of the owner-occupiers who were also tenants.[22] As we have seen in the case of owners and landlords, movement out of the Land Tax returns after enclosure was most common amongst those with least land.

Tenants – distinguished here from other occupiers because they rented all their land and owned none – disappeared from the returns as fast as owners, landlords and both kinds of owner-occupies: half of them had gone before the ten years were up. But this surface similarity hides their habitual mobility, something brought out when the mobility of tenants in open parishes is compared. Even in

[21] Of the 179 original owner-occupiers, 90 (50 per cent) no longer appeared on the returns after enclosure; of the 87 owner-occupier/tenants, 33 (38 per cent) no longer appeared.

[22] The figures were 20 (23 per cent) of the 87 owner-occupier/tenants; 137 (77 per cent) of the 179 owner-occupiers.

Table 8.5. *Disappearance from the Land Tax returns of tenants over a ten-year period, by size of holding, 1774–1814*

	0–5 acres % (no.)	5–25 % (no.)	25–50 % (no.)	50–100 % (no.)	Over 100 % (no.)	Totals % (no.)
Enclosing parishes	74 (50)	47 (31)	50 (9)	44 (12)	27 (16)	50 $\left\{\dfrac{118}{236}\right\}$
Open parishes	50 (25)	38 (10)	10 (1)	64 (9)	14 (4)	38 $\left\{\dfrac{49}{129}\right\}$

open villages 38 per cent of tenants left their holdings, compared to the 50 per cent in enclosing villages (Table 8.5). Enclosure accelerated their customary mobility, it did not create it. Again, acceleration was most marked among small tenants of twenty-five to fifty acres; but substantial tenants with more than one hundred acres moved out as frequently as equivalent owner-occupiers and owner-occupier tenants. The creation of new consolidated farms at enclosure seems to have required new tenants too.

The Land Tax returns for Northamptonshire show that almost twice as many landholders of all kinds no longer held land in enclosing parishes, after enclosure, as in neighbouring open parishes. They also show that small landholders – and small owner-occupiers in particular – left the land more frequently than large. Equally significantly, the Land Tax returns show that, compared to open-field villagers, the kind of landholder most likely to leave the land at enclosure was not the small landlord or small tenant, who, it might be argued, were men most likely to leave easily if only because they did not work the land themselves or because they were accustomed to moving or selling. On the contrary, the landholder most likely to leave was the one hitherto most bound to the soil, and most reluctant to move – the small owner-occupier.

Although the general contrast of experience between open and enclosing parishes is valuable, some of the distinctions within each group are lost in drawing a conclusion based on an average of the changes within each of them. Some enclosing parishes saw more change than others. Rushden (enclosed in 1778), Bugbrooke (1779) and Wollaston (1788), the first of the survey parishes to be enclosed, each saw the disappearance of 60 to 70 per cent of their landholders in the 1770s and 1780s. In Wollaston almost all of the owner-

occupiers, landlords and tenants of less than twenty-five acres (90 of
a total of 108), disappeared from the post-enclosure tax return. In
nearby Rushden, from 60 to 70 per cent of every group, regardless
of size, left the land. Both parishes were in the Nene valley, lying on
land easily converted to pasture. Bugbrooke, lying to the south west
on land suited to crops but also well-adapted to pasture, shared this
higher rate of disappearance.[23] Eight of the nine tenants of under
fifty acres no longer held any kind of land after enclosure, although
more substantial tenants and owner-occupier/tenants survived the
enclosure in greater numbers.

The rate of disappearance seems to have slowed down after the
outbreak of war in 1792, if we can generalize from the evidence of
pre-war returns from only three parishes and war-time returns from
fourteen. The pre-war disappearance rate of 67 per cent for all
landholders fell to 41 per cent in parishes enclosed during the war.
In open parishes it fell from 40 per cent to 25 per cent.[24] Generally,
the decline in the size of surviving original landholders' lands – a
consequence of enclosure discussed at length below – also varied
with the time at which parishes were enclosed.[25] Half of the
surviving landholders in parishes enclosed before the war lost more
than 20 per cent of their land at enclosure. In comparison only 29
per cent of survivors in the war-time enclosures lost this much
land.[26]

Lowest rates of disappearance occurred in Weston by Welland
(enclosed in 1802 with Sutton Bassett) and Chelveston (enclosed in
1801). In both parishes the consolidation of land in the long run-up
to enclosure had created a majority of large and stable tenants. Only
one of the fourteen tenants in Chelveston no longer held land after
enclosure; and all but one of the five owner-occupiers and owner-

[23] Whellan, *Directory*, describes Bugbrooke as having 'a considerable portion ... in
pasture'.
[24] These rates are based on a comparison of the numbers of individual landholders in
the pre-war and war-time enclosing parishes. There were 285 landholders in
parishes enclosed before the war, 190 of whom no longer held land after enclosure;
in parishes enclosed during the war there were 545 landholders, 221 of whom no
longer held land after enclosure. In the open parishes for which pre-war returns
were examined there were 151 landholders, 60 of whom sold up; in those for which
war-time returns were examined there were 135, 34 of whom sold up.
[25] See below, section II.
[26] H. G. Hunt noted a similar trend in Leicestershire parishes: see Hunt, 'Landownership and Enclosure 1750–1830', *Economic History Review*, 2nd series, 11
(1958–9), pp. 503–4.

occupier/tenants in the parish also held on to their lands. In Weston all the owner-occupiers and owner-occupier/tenants survived the enclosure, although small and middling tenants fared less well.

But the war explains only part of this contrast. Not all enclosures taking place in war-time were as relatively benign as the aggregate figures suggest. Larger parishes with many small holders, like Raunds, may have seen almost as much of an exodus from Land Tax records as large parishes undergoing enclosure before the war. More than half Raunds' landholders disappeared from the returns after the enclosure. It appears, then, that at least two factors influenced the rate of disappearance: the timing of the enclosure and the number of small landholders at risk.

Like parishes of consolidated ownership enclosed during the war the forest villages of Whitfield, Greens Norton and Whittlebury also underwent smaller changes. Greens Norton shows the most stability in the event of enclosure of all three; only ten of its forty-six landholders disappeared from the returns.[27] In Whitfield, in Whittlewood, more properly a forest village than Greens Norton, there were no owner-occupiers of less than one hundred acres before enclosure. Small tenants of fifteen to twenty-five acres held on to their lands, as did their equally small landlords. Whittlebury's experience was something of a contrast: most owner-occupiers sold their lands, and most tenants of less than one hundred acres gave up their tenancies; but the smallest landlords did not take the opportunity to sell their lands; instead they held on to them during the enclosure and beyond. Some of the relative stability of these Whittlewood forest parishes may be due to the post-enclosure availability of forest commons. Some of Whitfield's common lands were left open; and access to commons in the Forest remained into

---

[27] V. M. Lavrovsky in 'Tithe Commutation as a Factor in the Gradual Decrease of Landownership by the English Peasantry', *Economic History Review* 1st series, 4 (1932–4), remarked on the 'numerous and rather powerful peasantry' of the parish; twenty-three proprietors (five of them called yeomen) owned 589 acres after compensation for tithe. Neeson, 'Common Right and Enclosure', pp. 62–6 presents evidence of the habit of resistance to authority of some Greens Norton woodstealers and parish officers in these years. Ian Gentles, 'The Purchasers of Northamptonshire Crown Lands', *Midland History*, 3 (1976), pp. 208, 210, describes the sale by Samuel Chidley, the Leveller, of Crown land to the 'tenants, local yeomen and minor gentry' in 1653, and their purchase of more Crown land from military purchasers; the local buyers kept the land after the Restoration, although they reverted to their former status.

the 1850s.[28] Some of the old agriculture could continue with the customary support of such pasture improved by the consolidation of strips brought about by enclosure. Indeed, the survival into the nineteenth century of enclosed villages with access to commons like this helps explain the relatively late incidence of peasant economies in areas like the Weald.[29]

To summarize: land sales accelerated in enclosing parishes, and many landholders either sold all their lands or gave up whatever land they rented; but enclosure led to such large-scale change in some rather than all of the enclosing parishes. Wherever there was a large body of smallholders, and of small owner-occupiers in particular, the prospect of enclosure encouraged the sale of whole estates. This was the experience of most enclosing parishes in this study: in eleven of the seventeen parishes a new landholding generation appeared after enclosure. In contrast, parishes in which consolidation had preceded enclosure (there were three in the survey) underwent relatively little change. One exception to this rule was the effect of enclosure on forest parishes, where smallholders held on to their lands either in whole or in part. In these parishes the survival of forest pasture, and relatively modest tithe compensation, enabled occupiers to pursue customary agriculture to a greater extent than anywhere else. Where common right remained, the old common-right economy could carry on and even flourish. In Northamptonshire such parishes were few.

II

Half of the landholders who paid tax on their land at the beginning of the ten-year period during which an enclosure was made did not

[28] Northants. RO, Whitfield Enclosure Award, 1797, Award Cupboard; J. W. Anscomb, 'Abstract of Enclosure Awards', II, p. 137, 'Whitfield'. Whittlebury lost seventy acres of forest commons at enclosure, but that forest land lying within the forest's ring mound, and in the parish, was left open: see PRO, CRES 2/1037, Whittlebury Inclosure Act Draft Report [by John Fordyce, Surveyor General] on the Memorial of John Malsbury Kirby, Gent., praying that his consent may be given to the said Bill, 5 April 1797. It is my impression that commons were more frequently left open in pre-parliamentary enclosures in Northamptonshire than they were later on, an impression confirmed by J. W. Anscomb (personal correspondence).

[29] See M. Reed, 'The Peasantry of Nineteenth-Century England: A Neglected Class?', *History Workshop Journal*, Issue 18 (Autumn, 1984), pp. 53–73, for an account of Wealden peasant economies dependent on commons and barter. Also see Bourne, *Change in the Village*, chs. 8, 9, for an account of the economic collapse of just such a Sussex peasant economy on the enclosure of its common;

sell their lands or leave the land for any other reason. They appeared at the end of the period still paying the Land Tax. But these 'survivors' may have owned or let smaller or larger holdings than they had before enclosure. Initially, decline in the size of holdings would be due to the loss of land in compensation to the tithe-owner for commutation of tithe, and an assessment of the changing size of holdings must take this into account. In a study of nineteen enclosure Awards, V. M. Lavrovsky found that the average rate of compensation to tithe-owners was 20.9 per cent of the general area of the allotments made, or 16.9 per cent of the area mentioned in the Awards (an area that presumably included old enclosures, commons and woods).[30] In twelve of fifteen enclosing parishes studied here the proportion of the total parish acreage awarded in compensation for tithe varied from as little as 11 per cent in Wollaston to as much as 26 per cent in Rushden, but on average the proportion was 17 per cent.[31] In order to account for the decline of holdings, apart from the customary loss to the tithe-owner, when change in size was measured it was defined as a loss only if it exceeded 20 per cent: that is, only if a landholder lost somewhat more than the land he exchanged with the tithe-owner for freedom from tithe.

The returns show that landholders who still owned or rented land at the end of the ten-year period in enclosing parishes often sold some of their land, or rented smaller holdings. One third of these 'survivors' (almost three times as many as those in open parishes) had given up more than 20 per cent of their land. Table 8.6 shows change in the size of holdings of all kinds of landholder in both kinds of parish.

Total numbers of surviving landholders may be disaggregated in

similarly J. H. Kent, *Remarks on the Injuriousness of the Consolidation of Small Farms and the Benefit of Small Occupations and Allotments* (Bury, 1844), quoted in D. J. V. Jones, *Crime, Protest, Community and Police in Nineteenth-Century Britain* (1982), p. 38.

[30] Lavrovsky, 'Tithe Commutation as a Factor', p. 283.

[31] The figures were Rushden (26 per cent); Bugbrooke (13 per cent); Wollaston (11 per cent); Wadenhoe (14 per cent); Whitfield (corn rent, no land given in compensation); Whittlebury (6 per cent and an annual corn rent); Raunds (17 per cent); Greens Norton (11 per cent); Islip (15 per cent); Newton Bromswold (20 per cent); Chelveston (16 per cent); Hargrave (21 per cent); Hannington (14 per cent); Weston by Welland (17 per cent); Sutton Bassett (22 per cent). Figures for Maxey and Helpston were unknown; those of Whittlebury and Whitfield were excluded from the calculation of the average loss of land because the former's was only one part of the tithe settlement (a corn rent completed the exchange), and the latter's was wholly corn rent, with no land settlement.

Table 8.6. *Change in survivors' lands: all landholders, 1774–1814**

	Over 20% loss		Stable or up to 20% loss		Gain		Total
	%	(no.)	%	(no.)	%	(no.)	(no.)
Enclosing parishes	34	(129)	37	(138)	29	(109)	(376)
Open parishes	12	(24)	69	(134)	18	(35)	(193)

Note: * All parishes except Whitfield and Whittlebury.

order to consider the histories of owners, owner-occupiers, landlords and tenants separately.

Relative decline, growth and stability in *owners'* lands in open and enclosing parishes were much like those landholders in general, with one exception. Owners in open parishes were remarkably stable compared to landholders in aggregate. But, for every surviving owner in an open parish who sold more than 20 per cent of his land, four or five did so in enclosing parishes (see Table 8.7). In other words, at enclosure, owners, generally the most stable of landholders, became as likely to lose land as anyone else.

Owners of least land – less than fifty acres – did not lose land on a greater scale than those who owned more than one hundred acres, though they did lose more than middling-sized owners. Between one quarter and one third of all size groups each suffered serious losses (Table 8.8). The fact that small owners' holdings shrank no more than their much larger neighbours' may be explained by the disproportionate amount of selling up of total holdings already noted among small owners.[32] Those who had remained on the land had to be sure of their ability to finance the change. Land would be sold for the best price before allotments were made final because the greatest possible number of buyers would be interested then. Once lands were apportioned, the number of men interested in buying a small plot of land would shrink to those with land lying next to it, and perhaps one or two others. Consequently, the decision to stay had to be taken very seriously indeed; and, once made, it may have made more sense to smaller owners to keep as large a holding as possible (at the cost of mortgaging it) than to sell enough to remain solvent.

Landlords' holdings showed losses and gains of the same order as owners'; and, as a group, larger landlords with more than one

[32] See pp. 227–8 above.

Table 8.7. *Change in survivors' lands: landowners, 1774–1814**

	Over 20% loss		Stable or up to 20% loss		Gain		Total
	%	(no.)	%	(no.)	%	(no.)	(no.)
Enclosing parishes	33	(89)	38	(102)	29	(76)	267
Open parishes	7	(7)	74	(80)	19	(21)	108

Note: * All parishes except Whitfield and Whittlebury.

Table 8.8. *Change in size of survivors' lands: landowners, 1774–1814, by size of owned land**

	0–50 acres				50–100 acres				Over 100 acres			
	% D	% S	% G	(no.)	% D	% S	% G	(no.)	% D	% S	% G	(no.)
Enclosing parishes	34	38	28	(218)	24	47	29	(17)	34	34	31	(32)
Open parishes	7	75	18	(73)	6	72	22	(18)	6	76	18	(17)

Note: * 'D' signifies a drop in acreage of more than 20 per cent; 'S' signifies a drop of less than 20 per cent, or no change; 'G' signifies a gain in acreage. All parishes except Whitfield and Whittlebury.

hundred acres registered a growth of estates no more often than small. Of course the scale of engrossment by large landlords is hidden from view in these tables, which take no account of the *degree* to which lands grew in size: they establish only the fact of growth. Tables 8.9 and 8.10 show the changes taking place in surviving landlords' holdings.

Owner-occupiers'[33] lands changed at much the same rate (Tables

[33] Owner-occupiers before enclosure may have become landlords or tenants after enclosure. Thus, measuring their post-enclosure land must account for any land they let or rented then. For this reason the later holdings of surviving owner-occupiers and owner-occupier/tenants included the land they let and rented as well as whatever land of their own they occupied. The unit studied here is the total holding of owner-occupiers and owner-occupier/tenants before and after enclosure. Unfortunately, the changing proportions of owned, rented and let land are not measured: thus an owner-occupier might become an owner-occupier/tenant after enclosure, perhaps selling some of his land too; or an owner-occupier/tenant may have rented more of his total holding after enclosure than before. Shifts in the proportions of owned and rented or let land are hidden in these figures, then, but a greater change is not obscured: very few owner-occupiers and owner-occupier/tenants gave up all their land in the ten-year period to become solely tenants of land: only ten such became tenants in all twenty-two parishes. Nor were they

238   *Commoners*

Table 8.9. *Change in survivors' lands: landlords, 1774–1814*

	Over 20% loss		Stable or up to 20% loss		Gain		Total
	%	(no.)	%	(no.)	%	(no.)	(no.)
Enclosing parishes	35	(46)	43	(57)	23	(30)	(133)
Open parishes	8	(5)	74	(49)	18	(12)	(66)

Note: * All parishes except Whitfield and Whittlebury

Table 8.10. *Change in size of survivors' lands: landlords, 1774–1814, by size of owned land**

	0–50 acres				50–100 acres				Over 100 acres			
	D	S	G		D	S	G		D	S	G	
	%	%	%	(no.)	%	%	%	(no.)	%	%	%	(no.)
Enclosing parishes	29	50	21	(78)	33	40	27	(15)	45	30	25	(40)
Open parishes	5	78	16	(37)	8	83	9	(12)	12	59	29	(17)

Note: * All parishes except Whitfield and Whittlebury

Table 8.11. *Change in survivors' lands: owner-occupiers and owner-occupier/tenants, 1774–1814**

	Over 20% loss		Stable		Gain		Total
	%	(no.)	%	(no.)	%	(no.)	(no.)
Enclosing parishes	41	(56)	28	(38)	31	(43)	(137)
Open parishes	20	(9)	48	(21)	32	(14)	(44)

Note: * All parishes except Whitfield and Whittlebury

Table 8.12. *Change in size of survivors' lands: owner-occupiers and owner-occupier/tenants, 1774–1814, by holdings**

	0–50 acres				50–100acres				Over 100acres			
	D	S	G		D	S	G		D	S	G	
	%	%	%	(no.)	%	%	%	(no.)	%	%	%	(no.)
Enclosing parishes	37	30	33	(91)	47	13	40	(15)	48	36	16	(31)
Open parishes	16	53	31	(32)	0	33	66	(3)	50	37	13	(8)

Note: * All parishes except Whitfield and Whittlebury

8.11 and 8.12): 41 per cent of the survivors lost more than 20 per cent of their holdings; almost one third (31 per cent) bought or were awarded more than their former acreage; the remainder lost up to 20 per cent of their holdings. In contrast, only half as many owner-occupiers in open parishes who still held land at the end of the ten-year period lost more than 20 per cent of their holdings. Owner-occupiers of fifty to one hundred acres lost land more often than in open villages: almost half of them lost more than 20 per cent of their lands. Proportionately fewer owner-occupiers in this group than in the sub-fifty acre group sold *all* their land at enclosure;[34] it seems likely that a greater proportion of those who remained would have needed to sell some of their land to finance the enclosure of their property.[35] But the experience of owner-occupiers in enclosing villages diverges most from that of other landholders in the holdings of over one hundred acres: owner-occupiers of lands larger than one hundred acres in enclosing parishes showed the same degree of decline, stability and growth of estates as those in open parishes. In other words, surviving large owner-occupiers weathered enclosure comfortably, they were no more mobile than their counterparts in open parishes, and enclosure suited them well.

Tenants show the most stability of all kinds of surviving landholder, only 25 per cent suffered a substantial cut in the size of their holdings. This is none the less a notable change if the fortunes of tenants in open parishes are compared. Only 11 per cent of these lost so much land (see Table 8.13). Tenants of less than fifty acres before enclosure lost land in the same proportions as those with holdings of between fifty and one hundred acres (about 30 per cent of each group) but larger tenants were more stable: only 21 per cent of them lost a significant amount of land. But more middle and large tenants worked larger holdings after enclosure than did tenants of less than fifty acres (see Table 8.14). For tenants, as for owner-occupiers, the larger the pre-enclosure holding, the larger and more assured the post-enclosure settlement.

We can summarize the findings on disappearance of landholders and decline of survivors' holdings as follows. First: half of all

concentrated in one or two parishes; only Rushden had more than one such owner-occupier; it had two.
34 See Table 8.4 above.
35 But perhaps most remarkable is how few owner-occupiers of this middling size lived in *any* village in the survey, open or enclosing, and see pp. 250–1 below.

Table 8.13. *Change in survivors' lands: tenants, 1774–1814**

	Over 20% loss		Stable		Over 20% Gain		Totals	
	%	(no.)	%	(no.)	%	(no.)	%	(no.)
Enclosing parishes	25	(30)	41	(40)	34	(33)	100	(103)
Open parishes	11	(9)	78	(64)	11	(9)	100	(82)

Note: * All parishes except Whitfield and Whittlebury

landholders sold all their lands in enclosing parishes during the enclosure period, compared to only one quarter of those in open parishes. Occupiers sold as frequently as owners who let their lands; and tenants left the land at the same rate. The smaller the holding, the more likely was the sale of land: accordingly, parishes with a large population of smallholders underwent more of a change than those with a high degree of consolidation of land before enclosure. One exception to this rule seems to have occurred in forest parishes, where smallholders stayed on the land in greater numbers than elsewhere, perhaps encouraged by continued enjoyment of common right.

Second: surviving landholders sold some of their land too, and tenants worked smaller holdings. One third of the remaining original landholders lost a significantly larger amount of their lands than would have gone to the tithe-owner for tithe compensation. In contrast only one eighth of open parish landholders lost land on this scale. With the exception of small tenants' lands, estates of less than one hundred acres shrank at roughly the same rate as those above. But owner-occupiers of more than one hundred acres sold land no

Table 8.14. *Change in size of survivors' lands: tenants, 1774–1814, by holdings**

	0–50 acres				50–100 acres				Over 100 acres			
	D	S	G		D	S	G		D	S	G	
	%	%	%	(no.)	%	%	%	(no.)	%	%	%	(no.)
Enclosing parishes	28	43	30	(47)	31	31	38	(13)	21	42	37	(38)
Open parishes	8	81	11	(53)	40	40	20	(5)	13	79	8	(24)

Note: * All parishes except Whitfield and Whittlebury

more frequently in enclosing than in open parishes, whereas smaller owner-occupiers sold up much more often than their counterparts in open villages. A somewhat higher frequency of partial land sales in the middle range of holdings (fifty to one hundred acres) may indicate an attempt to continue on the part of peasant farmers that would succeed during the war at least. Fewer land sales of this size amongst smaller landholders (under fifty acres) may have reflected the sale of whole estates among members of this group during the enclosure period: those who remained on the land had more certain means of survival. It is important to note here that this discussion of change in the size of holdings takes no account of the *exact* proportion of land sold, it deals only with changes greater or less than 20 per cent. It is possible, even likely, that the smaller holdings contracted further than did the larger, and that large holdings grew more than the smaller.

Third: average rates of change are most useful for the purpose of comparing two groups of parishes – in this case, open and enclosing parishes over ten-year periods. Within each group the Land Tax reveals different rates of change, and sometimes these have more to do with the particular parish than enclosure *per se* – or the lack of it (see Tables 8.15 and 8.16). The returns show that enclosure led to the thorough-going sale of land in most enclosing villages, but not in all.[36] And they also show that original pre-enclosure holdings were not broken up for partial sale on the same scale in every parish. The major determinants of variations in landholding change at enclosure again appear to be the degree to which land had been consolidated and smallholders diminished before enclosure, and the survival of usable adjacent commons after. To this extent the Northamptonshire evidence confirms J. M. Martin's view that enclosure 'meant quite different things in different localities and in

[36] See pp. 231–3 above. They also show different rates of change in open parishes. Relatively high rates of disappearance from the returns (though not of diminution of holdings) occurred in Abthorpe and Stanwick, for example. They were produced by the departure of all sizes of landholders, particularly of middling and large landholders. This is a reversal of the pattern of disappearance in enclosing parishes, where the smallest landholders, and a disproportionate number of owner-occupiers, left. J. R. Walton also found periodically high turnover rates amongst occupiers in old-enclosed Oxfordshire villages. His data was not disaggregated according to size of holding so comparison with these open villages is not possible: see Walton, 'The Residential Mobility of Farmers'.

Table 8.15. *Disappearance of landholders and decline in size of holdings over a ten-year period in seventeen enclosing parishes, 1774–1814*

Parish	Total landholders on pre-enclosure Land Tax return	Disappearance of Landholders		Decline of holdings		Total original landholders disappeared and holding diminished lands	
		no.	%	no.	%	no.	%
Rushden	(1774)	101	68	67	18	18	86	85
Bugbrooke	(1774)	66	39	59	13	20	52	79
Wollaston	(1783)	118	83	70	17	14	100	85
Wadenhoe	(1788)	8	4	50	0	0	4	50
Whitfield	(1791)	22	6	27	(8)*	36	14	63
Raunds	(1791)	143	79	55	27	19	106	74
Whittlebury	(1793)	41	13	32	(4)*	10	17	41
Greens Norton	(1794)	46	10	22	4	9	14	30
Islip	(1795)	35	10	29	17	49	27	77
Newton Bromswold	(1795)	12	4	33	7	58	11	92
Chelveston	(1796)	27	6	22	7	26	13	48
Hargrave	(1797)	27	16	59	3	11	19	70
Hannington	(1797)	19	10	53	3	16	13	68
Sutton Bassett	(1797)	14	4	29	2	14	6	43
Weston by Welland	(1797)	26	8	35	4	15	12	46
Maxey	(1803)	53	20	38	2	4	24	42
Helpston	(1804)	68	30	44	5	7	35	51
Totals (no.) Individual rates %	(826)	(410)	50	(141)	17	(553)	67

Note: Table includes all landholders. 'Decline' describes a fall in the size of original landholders' holdings of more than 20 per cent. Mean parish rate of decline was 19 per cent; mean parish rate of disappearance or decline in holding size of all original landholders was 61 per cent of the original landholding population; mean parish rate of disappearance of all landholders was 42 per cent.

* Not in survey of decline.

different periods'.[37] However, neither a sensitivity to nor an analysis of these distinctions should lose sight of the equally important observation that at any time, and in any place in the study, where smallholders owned or rented land in large numbers their experience at enclosure was the same. Thus, with the possible exception of

[37] Martin, 'The Parliamentary Enclosure Movement and Rural Society in Warwickshire', p. 39.

Table 8.16. *Disappearance of landholders and decline in size of holdings over a ten-year period in six open parishes, 1786–1814*

Parish	Total landholders on first Land Tax return		Disappearance of land-holders		Decline of holdings		Total original handholders disappeared and holding diminished lands	
			no.	%	no.	%	no.	%
Roade	(1786)	43	11	26	3	7	14	33
Stanwick	(1790)	46	20	43	5	11	25	54
Abthorpe	(1790)	62	29	47	7	11	36	58
Lutton	(1796)	21	5	24	1	5	6	29
Eye	(1804)	81	25	31	7	9	32	40
Naseby	(1806)	33	4	12	1	3	5	15
Totals (no.)								
Individual rates %		(286)	(94)	33	(24)	8	(118)	41

Note: 'Decline' describes a fall in the size of original landholders' holdings of more than 20 per cent. Mean parish rates and mean individual rates were the same in all cases.

parishes where part of the old common-right economy survived, many smallholders sold all their land at enclosure and most sold some of it. Although there was no common parish experience, there was a common smallholder experience.[38]

Contemporaries of the enclosure movement, and historians ever since, have argued about whether enclosure caused the disappearance of the English peasantry. 'Turnover' studies like this one address a different question: they consider the effect of enclosure on the individual landholders of currently enclosing parishes. Through them it becomes apparent that enclosure dealt small peasants a double blow, for not only did they lose common right, they lost land too. No argument about the rise and fall of classes can do justice to this effect of enclosure. Whether the English peasantry disappeared or not, the effect of enclosure on the last generation of open-field peasants was profound.

But coupled with a change of agricultural practice, a loss of

---

[38] For the same finding see the similar experience of two contrasting Midland parishes enclosed in different periods described in Chapter 7.

markets, and a decline in the number of small peasants, this dislocation may also indicate the end of the peasantry itself. It is to this question that we turn now.

III

Counting numbers of owners or owner-occupiers by size of holding has been the preferred method of revisionist agrarian historians when they have come to measure the decline of the English peasantry. It is a method which addresses the older Marxist argument that enclosure – both pre-parliamentary and parliamentary – expropriated small landholders as a class and brought about their transformation into a rural (and thence an urban) proletariat. Historians who have doubted the connection between enclosure and peasant decline have been most moved to count numbers. In doing so they have concentrated on *parliamentary* enclosure alone, and of that they have looked principally at those enclosures taking place after 1780. For example, in a famous article published in 1927, Professor Davies concluded (after an exhaustive count of owner-occupiers in several thousand villages) that the *greatest* decline of small owners preceded parliamentary enclosure and that, far from causing that decline, enclosure 'safeguarded the interests of those owning land'. In a smaller study, and in a lower key, Professor Chambers also exonerated parliamentary enclosure from the charge of causing the decline of the peasantry.[39] Despite serious criticisms of their use of the Land Tax returns,[40] and despite their concentration on parliamentary enclosure, and that in its later stages alone, their conclusions have been endorsed by later enclosure historians.[41]

The assumption has been made, then, that had numbers of landowners fallen after enclosure then enclosure would have been responsible for a serious diminution in property holding, and prob-

[39] E. Davies, 'The Small Landowner, 1780–1832, in the Light of the Land Tax Assessments', *Economic History Review*, 1st series, 1 (1927); J. D. Chambers, 'Enclosure and the Small Landowner', *Economic History Review* 1st series, 10 (1940).

[40] Mingay, 'The Land Tax Assessments'.

[41] For example, Mingay, while criticizing Davies' methodology, nevertheless endorsed both Davies' and Chambers' conclusions that 'small owners prospered between about 1780 and 1815, and were by no means washed away by the high tide of parliamentary enclosure': *ibid.*, p. 381.

ably for an increase in the rural labour supply. But, the reasoning continued, numbers did *not* fall, so enclosure was blameless. Indeed, numbers appeared to *rise* on enclosure. Both Davies and Chambers remarked on this augmentation of the small peasantry, and, more than anything, it served to prove the point that enclosure was benign. But the argument is built on weak foundations. First, it is clear from Northamptonshire, Warwickshire and Buckinghamshire evidence that the last generation of open-field landholders was profoundly affected by parliamentary enclosure, and I shall return to this later. Second, Davies' and Chambers' evidence was severely flawed: we know now that both misused the Land Tax. Most seriously, they assumed that the same rate of tax per acre was paid in all parishes.[42] But they also saw no difficulty in counting numbers of very small taxpayers. Both assumptions were wrong.

If we look at tax rates first, it seems clear that different parishes paid tax at different rates per acre: £1 paid to the tax collector in one Northamptonshire village represented a twelve-acre holding, in another it represented one almost three times as large.[43] The solution to this problem is to calculate individual parish tax rates per acre (acreage equivalents), and this has been done here.[44] When enclosure involved tithe commutation (as it often did) it is sometimes necessary to go one step further and calculate two acreage equivalents. This is because the tax formerly paid on tithe had now to be raised from land alone, with the result that tax rates often rose

[42] Mingay, 'Land Tax Assessments', pp. 384–7.
[43] The Northamptonshire examples come from Greens Norton and Whittlebury, parishes lying within a few miles of each other.
[44] Mingay, 'Land Tax Assessments', pp. 384–7, doubts that a uniform acreage equivalent can be assumed even within a parish, arguing that land was differentially and arbitrarily taxed *within* parishes. However, cross-checking against enclosure Awards shows that informed calculations from Land Tax returns may be made; on this and related points see J. M. Martin, 'Landownership and the Land Tax Returns', *Agricultural History Review*, 14 (1966); Richard Grover, 'Procedures for Exploiting the Land Tax', paper presented to the Conference on Land Tax, London, 1981: Open University and Portsmouth Polytechnic, and below, Appendix A, pp. 337–9.
Decline in overall numbers of landowners etc., and the disappearance from the returns of individuals, are unaffected by the acreage equivalent problem, except where the size of holdings is measured. Even where this occurs the range within each acreage category (five to twenty-five acres, for example) is large enough to cope with the inevitable variety of land quality and land size. Errors of omission and inclusion at the margins of size categories should remain constant between open and enclosing villages.

on tithe commutation.[45] When Davies and Chambers failed to calculate individual parish acreage equivalents they made nonsense of their numbers of owners categorized by size of holdings.

But they also counted sum totals of owners, regardless of size, incorrectly. They did so because they assumed that every landowner paid tax. Professor Mingay began chipping away at this assumption in 1964 when he showed that the 1797 Land Tax Act exempted poor owners of land worth less than 20s a year.[46] In fact, although Mingay did not know it, the provision for poor owners was not new in 1797 but applied throughout the eighteenth century and originated in the first Land Tax Act.[47] Poor owners of land worth less than 20s a year had *never* paid the tax and we shall never be able to count them using the Land Tax as our source.[48] That being so, can we assume that the number of small taxpayers who did *not* qualify for an exemption was constant, all else being equal? The answer appears to be no. First, as Chambers observed, enclosure *created* a number of new small owners who had previously owned untaxed common rights but had exchanged these for small plots of land. Second, the rise in tax rates caused by tithe commutation would also have brought previously exempt small landowners on to the tax

[45] See below Appendix B, Table B.1. Tax rates rose by as little as 9 per cent or as much as 63 per cent; the median was 17 per cent. See also, Hunt, 'Landownership and Enclosure', p. 498.

[46] Mingay, 'Land Tax Assessments', p. 383.

[47] The provision made in 4 William and Mary c.1, section XL, and repeated in all subsequent Acts was that 'noe poore Person shall be charged with or lyable to the Pound Rate imposed by this Act whose Lands, Tenements or Hereditaments are not of the yearly value of Twenty shillings in the whole': *Statues of the Realm* vol. VI (1685–94), p. 366. W. R. Ward misread this section and set the exemption level in the first, and all subsequent, Land Tax Acts at £20: Ward, *English Land Tax* p. 7. Richard Burn's *Justice of the Peace and Parish Officer* consistently notes the 20s exemption in all eighteen editions, 1755–97. The assumption that taxation began at 20s was made by the author of *The Case of the Salt-Duty and Land Tax Offered to the Consideration of Every Freeholder* [1732], p. 9.

[48] Berks. RO D/EHy E9/2, 'Bucklebury Inclosure. A Statement of Property . . .'. See also Ashby, *Changing English Village*, p. 219: 'In 1807, the 1,539 acres of the parish were divided into nineteen holdings beside some very small ones which did not pay land tax'; and Northants. RO, Land Tax, Burton Latimer, 1803, 1808, and H(BL) 813: Robert Capps and Samuel Wright both appear to pay tax on their land allotted in lieu of common right in 1808, but both owned land earlier on which they were not taxed: Capps owned three acres of 'oddlands' and a two-rood close, Wright owned two acres of 'oddlands' and a three-rood close. Eight small owners receiving allotments on the enclosure of Whittlebury were neither taxed before or after the award was made: Northants. RO Whittlebury Enclosure Award, CP 43/373 [1800], Land Tax, 1794, 1797, 1807.

Table 8.17. *Change in numbers of owners over a ten-year period, by size of owned land*

	5–25		25–50		Acreage 50–100		100–150		150+	
	F	L	F	L	F	L	F	L	F	L
Enclosing parishes	244	206	77	67	54	56	33	30	48	58
Open parishes	32	37	10	13	15	10	6	12	13	13

Note: F signifies first Land Tax return, L signifies last; in enclosing parishes enclosure occurred between the two dates.

returns at enclosure. Both groups would swell the ranks of the smallest taxpayers and in so doing would suggest, wrongly, that enclosure caused peasant ownership to grow. Because numbers of small landowners shift in response to these factors (their right to exemption, the compensation of common rights, the rise in tax rates after commutation) they are not included in the calculations that follow.[49] However, although we cannot count their numbers it seems unlikely that the very smallest landowners would have fared much better than those with a little more land, if anything they may have fared worse, something that should be borne in mind in the discussion that follows.

Having refined our use of the source to this degree, what can it tell us about numerical decline? Put briefly: in the enclosing villages studied here the number of landowners *fell* after enclosure by 9 per cent (from 456 owners to 417) and in open parishes numbers *rose* by 13 per cent (from 76 to 85). As Table 8.17 shows, the decline in enclosing villages was concentrated among owners of less than fifty acres: the smallest category of owners (five to twenty-five acres) shrank by 16 per cent; the next largest (twenty-five to fifty) by 13 per cent. In open villages the reverse was true: the smallest category

[49] This also has the advantage of screening out tax paid on dwellings without land, another problem of dealing with the Land Tax. Owners etc. of less than five acres are included in the discussion of land sales made by individuals (above, sections I and II). This is because, in the first part of the study, names not numbers are compared; and because, in the case of the names of small owners, they are (if anything) *more* likely to remain on the returns than they are to disappear at enclosure, given the inflation of tax rates, unless enclosure caused them to sell their lands. Numbers of small taxpayers owning land worth less than 20s and becoming legally exempt (on grounds of poverty) from tax in these years for reasons other than enclosure are likely to be constant in open and enclosing parishes.

Table 8.18. *Change in numbers of owner-occupiers and owner-occupier/tenants, by owner-occupied land only (no rented or let land*)*

	Acreage							
	5–25		25–50		50–100		Over 100	
	F	L	F	L	F	L	F	L
Enclosing parishes	133	105	26	29	19	20	31	27
Open parishes	19	27	2	6	7	6	5	4

Note: * If rented land is included, no significant change in numbers occurs.

grew by 16 per cent and the next largest by 30 per cent. Growth in the enclosing villages was confined to the very large landowners: those with a minimum of 150 acres grew from 48 to 58 (21 per cent). Half of the enclosing parishes gained at least one new large landowner.[50]

Amongst occupiers, those who owned land were more affected by enclosure than those who only rented. Total numbers of owner-occupiers (and owner-occupiers who also rented land) fell from 209 to 181, or by 13 per cent. Again, as Table 8.18 shows, decline was most marked in the smallest size category: the five to twenty-five acre group shrank in size by 21 per cent (28 individuals). In open parishes this group still flourished, its membership grew from 19 to 27, an increase of 42 per cent. Amongst *tenants* in enclosing villages there was an overall decline of 8 per cent. Once again this was concentrated among those renting from five to twenty-five acres: this group shrank by 14 per cent. But not all sizes of tenants were diminished by enclosure: tenants with large holdings of 150 acres and up were more numerous after enclosure. Eight enclosing parishes absorbed thirteen new large tenants.[51]

Not all parishes saw the same degree of decline in the five to twenty-five acre group. Of the seventeen enclosing parishes studied, numbers in this group of owner-occupiers fell in a majority (ten parishes); in three they were unchanged; and in four they grew very slightly. The most populous communities of small occupiers saw

[50] Hannington, Islip, Greens Norton and Whitfield each had one; Bugbrooke and Newton Bromswold each had two; Raunds and Rushden had three each.
[51] They are Hannington, Helpston, Chelveston, Newton Bromswold and Whittlebury, each of which had one new tenant; Rushden and Bugbrooke, each of which had two; and Raunds which had four.

most decline. In Rushden, Bugbrooke and Wollaston, for example, the five to twenty-five acre group shrank by 69 per cent, 38 per cent, and 40 per cent respectively. The only exception to this rule was Raunds, a parish with many small occupiers, much like nearby Rushden and Wollaston, and one where turnover of landholders and diminution of landholdings was common at enclosure. In Raunds the numbers of small occupiers in the five to twenty-five acre group actually grew from 32 to 37 (16 per cent). Perhaps the potential effect of enclosure here was unrealized because of its timing. Unlike Wollaston, Bugbrooke and Rushden, Raunds was enclosed in 1797, during the war, when the economic security of small farmers and artisans (and those who were both) was strengthened by the twin effects of high agricultural prices and a growing demand for army boots.[52] This may have created a market for smallholdings. Vigorous opposition to the enclosure may have brought some concessions too: Raunds petty landowners petitioned against the enclosure in the House of Commons and, when the Act was passed anyway, they tore down the enclosure fences and burnt them.[53] Rushden, Wollaston and Bugbrooke had the misfortune to be enclosed a decade earlier.[54]

Taken together, the detailed evidence of numerical change allows us to make three general observations. First, it is clear that there was some numerical decline in landownership and occupancy directly after an enclosure. Second, it is equally clear that this decline was concentrated amongst the small landowning and occupying peasantry, those with between five and twenty-five acres. Aggregate numbers of landowners show an overall decline of 9 per cent but the size of the most numerous class – the small owner-occupiers – fell further and fell fast. It fell by 21 per cent on average and it did so in a space of ten years or less. The change is most apparent when neighbouring still-open villages are compared. They saw no overall decline in numbers, and, emphatically, no decline in the small peasantry; rather the reverse. Finally, there is evidence of a trend to larger farms and more large landowners in the enclosing parishes. Eleven of the seventeen villages had gained either a new large

[52] Hatley and Rajczonek, *Shoemakers in Northamptonshire 1762–1911* p. 4.
[53] See below, p. 278.
[54] For local apprehension about the enclosure of Wollaston see Chapter 9, p. 291; in 1785 Arthur Young remarked on the 'depopulation' of farmers following the enclosures of Harford (1778) and Branton (1779–80) in nearby Huntingdonshire: *Annals of Agriculture*, VI (1785), pp. 452–506.

landlord or another substantial tenant. The trend was most marked in the villages that also saw most decline in numbers of small owners: Rushden had three new large landlords and two more large tenants. Again, the pattern was peculiar to enclosing rather than to open parishes.

Neither Davies nor Chambers uncovered a decline in numbers of small owner-occupiers; instead they recorded their growth, and this point alone carried much of the weight of the optimistic argument. However, Chambers was careful to add a disclaimer, later ignored. He argued that it would be wrong to conclude from the Lincolnshire evidence that 'enclosure was in *every case* followed by an increase of small owners. Local conditions varied widely, and the precise incidence of enclosure varied with them.'[55] He noted particularly that only two of the seven Derbyshire villages he studied saw a substantial increase in the number of owners. He also noted that some of the increase in numbers of owners in some villages would be due to their exchange of common right for small plots of land at enclosure.[56] But he remained convinced that no *decline* amongst small owners had been found. If, according to both Chambers and Davies, there had been a decline in any section of the landed community at enclosure it was not in the numbers of small owner-occupiers but in the ranks of middling landholders, those with from twenty to one hundred acres. This is a significant finding in itself, but not much was made of it in the popularization of the pro-enclosure argument that followed. Interestingly, in Northamptonshire this yeomanry and tenantry was already, on the eve of enclosure, only a pale shadow of its former self: it comprised only 21 per cent of all occupiers over five acres in contrast to the 64 per cent of occupiers who held less than twenty-five acres and more than five. In Northamptonshire this *small* peasantry was the most numerous landholding class and the one most seriously affected by enclosure.

Chambers' impression, gained from his foray into Derbyshire that this group may not have multiplied in every parish seems to have hardened into certainty by the time he and Mingay wrote about it in *The Agricultural Revolution, 1750–1880*. In discussing there J. M. Martin's work on high enclosure costs in Warwickshire, they wrote that it was

[55] J. D. Chambers, 'Enclosure and the Small Landowner in Lindsey', *The Lincolnshire Historian*, 1 (1947), p. 126.
[56] *Ibid.*, p. 123.

only the really small owners, *with holdings too small to be described as farms*, who were likely to have found the expenses too great for it to be worth keeping their land: they depended on some supplementary or alternative occupation in any case, and they may well have found the occasion of the enclosure a good time to sell. Many of these, it must be remembered, were absentee owners who had let out their land, and not occupiers. Indeed, some of the sales of absentee owners must have consolidated the holdings of small farmers and strengthened their position.[57]

We have seen that this description does not fit the experience of small Northamptonshire owners, whether landlords or occupiers. They were not overwhelmingly absentee owners, and they rarely enlarged the size of their holdings at enclosure. What *does* fit is the owner-occupiers' dependence on income from supplementary sources. Many were artisans or tradesmen as well as occupiers of land.[58] But this is the very fact that Chambers and Mingay produce in order to deny these landholders the status of small farmer and to preserve their own view of enclosure as generally advantageous to *real* small farmers, those with thirty or forty acres or more. It is a peculiar view of landholding that judges irrelevant the experience of the largest class of landholders in eighteenth-century England. It is also a curiously anachronistic one that ignores the integration of manufacture, trade and land so characteristic of early modern villages. But it must be said that the optimistic view of enclosure, expressed most powerfully by Chambers and Mingay, is built on precisely these foundations.

IV

We leave this forest of rates of disappearance from the returns, degrees of diminution of survivors' holdings, and numerical decline with two observations. First, that the last generation of open-field

[57] Chambers and Mingay, *Agricultural Revolution*, pp. 88–9 (my italics).
[58] For example, owner-occupiers of holdings smaller than twenty-five acres in Rushden, who gave up their land at enclosure, included two shoemakers, and two carpenters; almost half of the woolcombers and weavers in Kilsby held land or cottages with common right at enclosure; a weaver, a tailor, a carpenter, a 'dealer', two labourers and two wheelwrights all sold up at Wollaston after enclosure: Northants. RO, Land Tax: Rushden, 1774; Kilsby, 1772, 1775; Wollaston, 1783, 1793; Militia Lists: Kilsby and Rushden, 1771, 1774; Wollaston, 1774, 1777. In general, shoemakers and artisans in the wool trades were often occupiers of land in Northamptonshire at enclosure.

peasants was more than decimated at enclosure: two-thirds of them lost all or more than 20 per cent of their land within five years of an enclosure Act. Only one third of open-field villagers shared this experience. And the disparity between the two is greater if the constant proportion of sales due to death etc. is accounted for. The second observation is that enclosure accelerated the differentiation of the peasantry in the most populous landowning villages. After enclosure there were fewer small owner-occupiers and tenants, and more large tenants and landlords. The effect of the second wave of parliamentary enclosure on landholding structure was to change the names of most farmers and to reduce their numbers. Had the war not brought short-term prosperity, the effects of enclosure upon the populous villages of smallholders would have been even more dramatic. As yet the Land Tax returns have not been examined for the earlier period when cereal prices were not the cushion for small farmers that they later became, and when conversion to pasture or convertible husbandry was more common, but in Northampton-shire the evidence suggests that the first wave of parliamentary enclosure may have caused more disruption than the second. In both periods enclosure was far from benign in its effects and at all times, from the earliest period to the latest, was viewed by small owner-occupiers and tenants with apprehension.

Is this evidence of a crisis in the history of the small peasantry or only evidence of a period of adjustment? Until the survey of land-holding undertaken here is extended beyond 1814 we cannot know if the diminution in numbers of occupiers was permanent, although the post-war history of small farmers suggests that it was. But, putting the post-war depression aside, there are a number of good reasons to suspect that peasant farming declined. In many Midland villages in both enclosure periods the conversion of arable open fields to pasture was common.[59] For small farmers this was a serious

---

[59] Returns sent to the enclosure commissioners noting changes in the acreage of wheat following enclosures made between 1760 and 1800 discuss 93 of the 120 Northamptonshire parishes enclosed in this period. The figures show a fall in wheat acreage from 19,922 acres to 14,135 acres (29 per cent). Given the more thorough coverage of later enclosures, and the temporary rise in arable pro-duction due to high war-time prices, this is probably a serious underestimate of the acreage lost to temporary and permanent pasture or fodder crops. Rutland and Buckinghamshire lost more wheat acreage, 56 per cent and 33 per cent respectively; Warwickshire lost 25 per cent; Young, *General Report on Inclosures*, Appendix XI, 'The Culture of Wheat'. See also Turner, *English Parliamentary*

challenge not easily met. The vicar of Twywell, a Northamptonshire parish enclosed in 1780, made the point in 1801: 'Less corn is grown since the inclosure', he wrote. 'Small farms are abolished and poor rates much increased, much of the land being laid down in grass not properly, or not fitted for it'.[60] Dorothy George, no pessimist in these matters, quotes a Northamptonshire petition sent to the House of Commons in 1774: 'These farmers', it ran, 'know nothing of the grazing business, and they have not money to buy in a sufficient stock of cattle, much less to pay for an enclosure'.[61] Small owner-occupiers were under-capitalized at the best of times. Equally, they were short of pasture once common right was removed. And, as the petition makes clear, enclosure was expensive: even the cost of the Act and Award and the fencing of their allotments would be enough to push small farmers into early sales of all or part of their lands, or would burden them with debt for the foreseeable future.[62] Every rule has exceptions and those small occupiers of land near enough to towns to repay the cost of market gardening or poultry farming and dairying probably fared better; and the evidence of some forest villagers suggests that, where access to commons still remained after enclosure, small occupiers did not suffer as badly.[63] But these villages were vastly outnumbered by others where no common land survived enclosure, or that lay too far from sizeable towns, or on clays suited to pasture. For the last generation of open-field peasants the evidence of crisis, disappearance and diminution is clear.

But what of the smallholders who replaced those who left? We know there were fewer of them but were they not, in effect, much

Enclosure, p. 76; and for a contemporary account [Stephen Addington], *Inquiry into the Reasons for and against Enclosing Open Fields* (1772).

60 Communication from Twywell, Northamptonshire, to the Board of Agriculture, in 'The 1801 Crop Returns for England', ed. M. E. Turner, p. 364 (manuscript on deposit at the Institute of Historical Research, University of London, and at the Public Record Office).

61 Dorothy George, *England in Transition* (1965), p. 86.

62 J. M. Martin, 'The Cost of Parliamentary Enclosure in Warwickshire', *University of Birmingham Historical Journal*, 9 (1964); M. E. Turner, 'The Cost of Parliamentary Enclosure in Buckinghamshire', *Agricultural History Review* 21 (1973).

63 Of course, tenants of land near towns also paid much higher rent when that land was enclosed: newly enclosed common-field land near Kettering was let at £2 to £3 15s per acre, double its former level; and, at £8 per acre, garden ground near Northampton was costlier than the best meadows; Pitt, *General View ... Northampton*, pp. 37–9, 63. The need that would-be market gardeners had for capital is plain.

like their predecessors – another peasantry? Let us look again at those who left. It seems clear enough that those who sold up were first of all those owner-occupiers who could not afford enclosure; they were also the older landholders and the smaller landlords.[64] They were also tenants who were unwilling to pay higher rents either because they could find cheaper open-field land elsewhere (although this was shrinking too) or because they were unable to farm their smallholdings sufficiently profitably. In other words there may well have been a shake-out of the least productive occupiers and tenants. This throws some light on their replacements, the new generation, for, by extension, we can assume that these new owner-occupiers and landlords had access to enough capital to pay for enclosure; and we can guess that the new tenants were confident of their ability to manage a higher rent despite the loss of pasture rights and the shrinkage of their holdings.

But, by the same token, these newcomers – and those surviving from before enclosure – were also more dependent on their ability to turn a sufficient profit to repay their mortgages, to justify their investment of capital, to pay their higher rents and to stock their farms, and pay a disproportionately higher poor rate.[65] They were more firmly tied into the market than their predecessors: in Teodor Shanin's terms, their economies were less family-farm, more business.[66] This is a point worth emphasizing. A lack of capital led

[64] See above, Chapter 7, pp. 198–9 for the opposition to enclosure of older land-owners.

[65] Parishes with large numbers of smallholders paid a considerably higher rate for poor relief than those with few because settlement regulations enabled large landowners to avoid relieving unemployed, sick and aged labourers: see Anthony Brundage, *The Making of the New Poor Law 1832–1839* (1978), p. 3. George R. Boyer in 'The Old Poor Law and the Agricultural Labor Market in Southern England', *Journal of Economic History*, 46 (1986), p. 133, makes the same observation: large farmers 'used their power to pass some of their labor costs on to non-labor hiring rate payers'. It is likely that the consolidation of land at enclosure and the polarization of landholding that accompanied it further strengthened large farmers and landowners.

[66] Teodor Shanin, ed., *Peasants and Peasant Societies* (1971: 1979), pp. 14–16, and 'The Peasantry as a Political Factor', *ibid.*, pp. 241, 248–9. Central to the peasant family-farm, according to Shanin, is its independence of the need to maximize profit *at all costs*. Family welfare can, and must, be considered even if the consequence is economically unjustifiable. In contrast the business-like character-istic of non-peasant farming is its ability and need to make profits, and so shed labour and other costly liabilities at will. Without entering the debate on the proper definition of peasantry here (see below Chapter 10), it seems to me that the family-farm/business contrast has some value in the context of the transition from open-field to enclosed agriculture. On the significance of capital for the survival of

to borrowing, but loans required regular repayment in cash, and cash was forthcoming only if a farmer had enough land to produce a marketable surplus and a profit. In this way enclosure pushed small occupiers into the market more irresistibly than before. A viable holding could support a mortgage, but, as we have seen, the farms of the smaller survivors of enclosure shrank in size by at least a fifth, often much more. And on the smaller holdings the advantages of enclosure could not compensate for reduced acreage and the loss of common right. Small farmers, unlike large, had benefited from common pasture and the fallow; by their very nature they had no need to save labour, and they relied on low rents: enclosure was of dubious value.

There was another equally serious consequence of enclosure for post-enclosure occupiers that had less to do with debt and the market than it had to do with common-field agricultural practice and the social relations built around it. Small occupiers lost not only land at enclosure, they lost communal agriculture based on common of pasture, and they lost the hope of acquiring more land at low rent too. After enclosure common pasture was lost, and the agricultural practice of large and small farmers became at once more differentiated, more specialized, and more private. Shared use-rights and the collective regulation of agriculture were replaced by increasingly separate agricultures, which weakened the old custom of mutual aid between landholders. And at the other end of the village community the bonds of reciprocity between small occupiers and landless users of common right were similarly damaged. Here the mechanism was the loss of common right coupled with the loss of social mobility represented by the new high rents. Landless commoners could no longer feed pigs, geese and poultry on commons, lanes and roadsides; they could no longer gather fuel; in the fens they lost their fishing and fowling; in forest villages they could no longer hire a common right for their cattle, unless commons remained open. Nor did the landless former commoners have much hope any more of moving into the lesser landed classes because rents had risen, and because the likelihood of small pieces of land becoming available for rent diminished sharply with the substitution of self-contained farms for scattered open-field

small owner-occupiers see Hoskins, *Midland Peasant*, p. 264; on the effect of total integration into a money economy see Bourne, *Change in the Village*, ch. 9.

strips.[67] As a result it is possible that small occupiers were increasingly isolated on both sides: they no longer shared much of an economic identity with larger farmers, and too few small landless peasants were left with whom to usefully exchange labour, goods, special skills and strategies, or news of prices and markets. This is a large argument properly dealt with only at length. It is introduced here to indicate how complete a transformation took place at enclosure, to suggest that those who remained on the land after enclosure, and those who were newly arrived, lived in a new world, sharing a new economic function and a reduced social role. This is something that change in numbers and acreage alone cannot show.

Nor is it something that the existence of smallholders or traders in enclosed villages in the nineteenth century can dispute. I hope the argument here makes it clear that the scope for mutual aid, and the numbers of people able to practice it, diminished at enclosure in the eighteenth and nineteenth centuries along with the shared routines of common-field agriculture and the number of small occupiers. The *transformation* of social relations that followed the enclosure of villages where commoners had flourished is described in an anonymous letter sent 'To the Gentlemen of Ashill, Norfolk' in 1816, a year of reckoning for many small farmers. Ashill had been enclosed earlier in 1785 but the full brunt of enclosure was felt only gradually, perhaps because the war protected the smallest occupiers for a while – as it did in Raunds. By 1816, however, land in Ashill was consolidated into a few hands. Thanks to the low wages paid by the farmers, poor rates were high and small occupiers had to pay them though they hired no labour themselves. Even common grazing on the roads was brutally denied. And the farmers who could have helped their poorer neighbours felt no need, instead they jeered them at town meetings. But where meetings failed, an anonymous threatening letter might succeed: 'This is to inform you', it ran,

> that you have by this time brought us under the heaviest burden and into the hardest Yoke we ever knowed; it is too hard for us to bear ... You do as you like, you rob the poor of their Commons right, plough the grass up that God send to grow, that a poor man may feed a Cow, Pig, Horse, nor Ass; lay muck and stones in the road to prevent the grass growing. If a poor man is out of work and wants a day or two's work you will give him 6d. per week, and

---

[67] Orwin and Orwin, *Open Fields*, p. 172; for the levelling effect of scattered strips see Harriet Rosenberg, *A Negotiated World* (Toronto, 1988), p. 164.

then a little man that does not employ a labourer at all, must help
pay for your work doing, which will bring him chargeable to the
parish. There is 5 or 6 of you have gotten all the whole of the land
in this parish in your own hands and you would wish to be rich
and starve all the other part of the poor of the parish. If any poor
man wanted anything, then you will call a Town meeting about it,
to hear which could contrive to hiss him the most ...

Gentlemen, these few lines are to inform you that God
Almighty have brought our blood to a proper circulation, that
have been in a very bad state a long time, and now without
alteration of the foresaid, we mean to circulate your blood with
the leave of God.[68]

I shall return to consider the sense of betrayal felt in enclosed
villages.[69] At Ashill it indicated the breaking of a connection
between farmers and commoners. This, and the economic hardship
faced by landless and land-poor commoners when the commons
disappeared, suggests the reduced scope of mutual aid between the
petty-landed and everyone else. It does not, of course, necessarily
imply any loss of sympathy between smallholders, traders and
labourers, but it does imply an inability to substantially support one
another's economies.[70]

The first generation of post-enclosure smallholders were fewer in
number but probably more confident, and necessarily more individualistic, than their predecessors. Both characteristics were more
often attributed to larger farmers by the cartoonists and poets of the
time, and it is clear that both confidence and individualism were
moods matched among small farmers by great vulnerability should
prices fall, as they did in 1814. This vulnerability was itself as much a
product of enclosure as the disappearance of former landholders
from the Land Tax returns, the diminution of survivors' lands and
the decline in numbers of small owner-occupiers. Enclosure reduced
the size of holdings, extinguished common pasture and collective

68 PRO, HO 42.150, Anonymous letter, 'To the Gentlemen of Ashill, Norfolk',
enclosed in Rev. Edwards to Sidmouth. On the part played by the common in
preserving a peasant village see above Chapter 6.
69 See Chapter 10, pp. 326–8.
70 Compare Reed, 'Peasantry of Nineteenth-Century England' and 'Class and Conflict in Rural England: Some Reflections on a Debate', in M. Reed and R. Wells,
eds., *Class, Conflict and Protest in the English Countryside, 1700–1880* (1990). I am
not saying here that peasants disappeared from *all* of England; I am saying that
the parliamentary enclosure of common fields and common waste in the Midlands
caused peasant disappearance in villages with dispersed landholding.

agriculture, reduced the scope of mutual aid, and demanded an investment of capital, and often a change of techniques, least viable or profitable on smallholdings. Smallholders could best survive if they adopted their own specialized agricultures, or if their lands were solely adjuncts to trade. In either case they were implicated in an economy far removed from that of farmer-weavers and commoner-shoemakers in open-field villages. A few acres were less often the insurance kept by an artisan's family to get it through periods of high prices when corn could not be bought. They were less frequently eyed as a means to future independence by farm servants saving their wages. And it is in this sense that parliamentary enclosure caused the disappearance of the English peasantry.

9. *Resisting enclosure*

To the Right Honourable Lord Sonds –
The Humble Petition of the Major Part of the ffarmers
ffreeholders and Cottagers of the parish of Wilbarston in
the County of Northampton –
Sheweth
That your Petitioners having been informed some of the proprietors of Lands in the parish of Wilbarston, are about to
petition to Parliament for an Act to Inclose the said Parish, the
doing of which, Your petitioners apprehend, and believe, will
be very hurtful, if not ruin some of them, by reason of the
expence which will attend the same, and more particularly,
such who have but small quantities of Land in the sd parish,
which said small quantities, in the present situation, find Bread
Corn for their severall families. That the said parish, is now,
very much oppressed with poor, And as your Petitioners
believe, will be at a much greater yearly charge for the same, if
the sd parish should be inclosed, as the poor have now a
priviledge to Cut Bushes and gather Clots upon a very large
peice of Ground calld the Cow pasture, which priviledge will be
taken away and the parish obligd to provide for the poor
otherwise –
Your Petitioners therefore Humbly pray – that your Lordship
will be pleased to oppose and put a stop to a Bill for inclosing
the sd parish of Wilbarston.
And Your petitioners shall ever pray &c –
[signed Benjamin Humfrey and twenty-three others].[1]

---

[1] Northants. RO, Rockingham Castle MSS, B.7.55, n.d. [1798]

8. Extraordinary Expenses occasioned by the resistance
of the Mob against the Commissioners and Surveyor
on staking out the plain – including the expences of
two troops of Yeomanry Cavalry.   £105 5s 8d[2]

Not since the Hammonds wrote *The Village Labourer* have commoners seemed to act in their own defence at enclosure. Yet when
the Hammonds came to sum up the evidence of resistance they
found it relatively sparse. They attributed this to the realism of
enclosure's victims who, they said, knew only too well that legal
opposition was expensive and often quite futile. Given that Parliament turned a deaf ear to legal protest, opponents were left with
illegal protest, 'which made no impression at all upon Parliament,
and which the forces of law and order could, if necessary, be
summoned to quell'.[3] The result was that opponents began opposition only where it stood some chance of success, that is, said the
Hammonds, in relatively rare circumstances. The view did not go
long unchallenged for, writing a year later, Edwin Gonner came to a
radically different conclusion. Lack of resistance to enclosure, he
wrote, was the 'greatest testimony' to the advantage of enclosure
itself.[4] In other words, enclosure met little resistance because it
deserved little.

Since then historians have shown more agreement on the slight-
ness of opposition than on almost any other aspect of enclosure.
Optimistic historians, following Gonner and A. H. Johnson, have
considered opposition the product of unusual, exceptional situ-
ations because, they argue, enclosure itself was fair and generally
advantageous.[5] For this reason resistance occurred only in exceptional circumstances: where unusually large commons were lost, or

---

[2] Northants. RO, The Account of Robert Edmonds, Robert Weston, and Thomas
Eagle, Gentlemen Commissioners …, n.d., c.1799; Northants. RO, Wilbarston
Parish Chest, photostat no. 743.

[3] Hammond and Hammond, *Village Labourer*, pp. 39, 44–8, 73–4.

[4] Gonner, *Common Land and Inclosure*, p. 83.

[5] See Johnson, *Disappearance of the Small Landowner*, p. 147; Gonner, *Common
Land and Inclosure*, pp. 82–3, 94–5; Davies, 'Small Landowner, 1780–1832',
pp. 111–13; W. E. Tate, 'Opposition to Parliamentary Enclosure in Eighteenth-
Century England', *Agricultural History Review*, 19 (1945), pp. 137, 141–2; Chambers and Mingay, *Agricultural Revolution*, pp. 88–9; G. E. Mingay, *Enclosure and
the Small Farmer in the Age of the Industrial Revolution* (1968), pp. 23–5. E. J. Hobsbawm, 'The British Standard of Living, 1790–1850', in his *Labouring Men* (New
York, 1967), pp. 75–6, uses the terms 'pessimist' and 'optimist' to distinguish the
'classical (Ricardo-Marx-Toynbee-Hammond) view' of the standard of living
under early industrialism from the 'modern (Clapton-Ashton-Hayek) view'.

where small absentee owners let their lands, or where large pasture owners profited from local shortages of grazing, or where enclosure was forced through without due process.[6] More pessimistic historians, while agreeing that opposition was small, have looked for explanations of why what they see as a seriously impoverishing change should have provoked so little reaction.[7] On the whole they have concluded that enclosure's victims were too weak, too fearful, and too unfamiliar with parliamentary procedure to defend themselves. In Mantoux's opinion, 'Those who had most to complain of dared scarcely lift their voices. If they ventured to put forth a claim or send a petition to Parliament, the only probable result for them was money spent fruitlessly'. If they refused to sign a Bill they robbed their opposition of any effect by saying they would not oppose it further, 'an attitude showing that the villager, as the phrase goes, "knew his betters"'.[8] W. G. Hoskins agreed: 'How could they make a case, these humble village farmers who had, most of them, been no further than Leicester on market-days?'[9] And E. P. Thompson:

> Men in the social and cultural station [of small owners and cottage commoners] ... could only in the most exceptional circumstances – and with the advice of some men of education and substance – have had recourse to the costly and procrastinating procedures of an alien culture and an alien power. The fatalism of the cottager in the face of this ever-present power, and the uneven, piecemeal incidence of enclosure (when the enclosure of neighbouring villages might be separated by the passage of

6 Max Beloff, *Public Order and Popular Disturbances, 1660–1714* (Oxford, 1938), p. 76–80; Chambers and Mingay, *Agricultural Revolution*, p. 91; John Stevenson, *Popular Disturbances in England, 1700–1870* (1979), p. 43. Stevenson concludes that disturbances were few, but he argues in large part from what seems to be a misreading of Slater, *English Peasantry*, p. 112, where Slater wrote that disturbance was unlikely unless enclosure led to the loss of arable land to pasture and the loss of wastes. Stevenson assumes that Slater thought this did not happen. That Slater thought it did occur may be seen on pp. 106–7, where he writes of enclosure leading to conversion to pasture and depopulation in the eighteenth century in an arc of counties from Lincolnshire through Northamptonshire, Leicestershire and Warwickshire to Buckinghamshire and Oxfordshire. He argued that only in the nineteenth century did enclosure not lead to depopulation (p. 93).
7 Slater, *English Peasantry*, pp. 104–12, is an implicit exception to this rule.
8 Paul Mantoux, *The Industrial Revolution in the Eighteenth Century* (2nd edn, 1961), p. 174.
9 Hoskins, *Midland Peasant*, p. 249. See also Christopher Hill, *Reformation to Industrial Revolution* (1969), p. 270.

several decades), go some way towards explaining the seeming passivity of the victims.

Thompson alone went on to say that perhaps not enough work had been done at the local level to prove this passivity.[10]

This chapter follows Thompson's suggestion. It uses evidence from one densely enclosed Midland county – Northamptonshire – to look at resistance to enclosure at the local level. It agrees with the Hammonds that small owner-occupiers and tenants, cottagers and landless commoners were shrewd realists when enclosure came in sight: their opposition was less a product of unusual circumstances – the old optimist argument – than of their own assessment of their own strength. But it also argues that commoners were more active in their own defence than historians – including the Hammonds – have allowed. In more places in Midland England in the second half of the eighteenth century than either the pessimists or the optimists might suppose, commoners thought themselves strong enough to disrupt and delay enclosure.

I

Between 1750 and 1815 two-thirds of Northamptonshire's agricultural land was turned from open fields and commons to enclosed farmland.[11] Opposing this was a matter of time and opportunity, and of patience and staying power. It began long before a petition for a Bill was taken to the House of Commons and lasted long after Bills became Acts. The unfolding village history of argument and obstruction that this longevity represents is as instructive as the parliamentary record of petitions against enclosure and refusals to sign Bills, and the incidence of riots in enclosing villages – the kinds of opposition historians have looked at most closely. If we neglect it we get a truncated view of protest, and we lose the history of wars of attrition waged skilfully over a decade or longer. Some villages shared a tradition of enclosure protest, a tradition that looked back

[10] Thompson, *Making of the English Working Class*, pp. 240–1. Thompson's assumption of the passivity of enclosure victims is cited by Wells as evidence of the presence of a vast, depressed rural proletariat in eighteenth-century England able to engage in only covert social protest and conscious of no notion of a 'golden age': R. A. E. Wells, 'The Development of the English Rural Proletariat and Social Protest, 1700–1850', *Journal of Peasant Studies*, 7 (1979), pp. 120, 115, 134.

[11] Tate, 'Inclosure Movements in Northamptonshire', p. 30; Turner, *English Parliamentary Enclosure*, p. 34.

to earlier resistance to enclosure, one that owed much to the habits of communal agriculture, and one lost to view when the focus of the historian is on parliamentary procedure or riot alone.

But the unfolding village history of protest also suggests that parliamentary petitions and riots were the least effective, and probably least common, means of opposing enclosure. Their ineffectiveness (and the decision of commoners not to use them) is significant in itself.

For a year or two before plans progressed as far as a Bill, would-be enclosers weighed local support and opposition. At this stage, before spending too much time and money on the scheme, they were most inclined to alter or drop their proposals if they met serious resistance.[12] For this reason early local opposition may have been the most effective and most vocal of all. It is also the hardest to find, never more so than when at its most successful it thwarted a Bill altogether. It ranged from refusing consent and petitioning enclosers and sympathetic gentry to spreading false rumours and trying to frighten enclosure away with threats of parliamentary contest or attacks on property.

Stubborn non-compliance, foot-dragging and mischief were common. The early history of Wellingborough's enclosure is unusually well recorded because its surveyor, Thomas Cowper, kept a diary which has survived. According to this, when he surveyed Wellingborough fields prior to their enclosure in 1764 he found that no matter how conscientiously he worked he met hostility at every step. Dissentient landowners refused to sign the enclosure bills he brought them, and casually took their time to tell him so; tenants repeatedly neglected to mark out their lands for his survey. Even – or perhaps particularly – his customary drinking places gave him little pleasure, being noisy with 'warm Discourse' too often for comfort. He wrote to his daughter that he longed to be in the New World, surveying what must surely be less conflict-ridden land.[13]

Three years before the enclosure of Long Buckby someone sent the Reverend George Freeman, the largest landowner and tithe-owner, an anonymous threatening poem. A week or so later someone pulled down several of his fir and fruit trees, an oak and two

---

12 Turner, 'Cost of Parliamentary Enclosure in Buckinghamshire', p. 36, makes the same observation.
13 Northants. RO, X678, 26 Nov. 1763; Wake file, 'Wellingborough Letters and Other Papers, 1738–1817', Thomas Cowper to his daughter Mary, 21 Oct. 1760.

summerhouses. The poem warned Freeman and other enclosers not
to go out at night:

> dick hannal georg freeman Jack Coleman
> tom Eyare tom Robarsun and flyer
> wa valey nun of them a straw
> neither for them nor their *law*
> for as much muer mischief thel have dun
> which makes us laf now at the fun
> So take care who comes out at night
> for you have dun an on just part
> and *we will destroy what ear we can*
> *for we duent fear parson nor is man*
> nor dick hannol nor tos Eyare nor
> Jak Coman nor parson Freeman by God
> for we will do you all the mischief that we can
> So dam the parson and is puer man
> for his gun we do not fear sins no Shot
> he dare put there and *nun will elp him then*
> but Young Merill and weldu for him.[14]

Further south, in the village of Pattishall, opponents of enclosure
spread the rumour that the Bill was supported by neither a majority
of landowners in the parish nor even by the owners of most of the
land. They hoped to persuade the Duke of Grafton to renew his
opposition. The enclosers wrote quickly to the Duke to scotch the
rumour – perhaps with one of their own – saying, 'such report has
been as we have the greatest reasons to believe as artfully & indus-
triously propagated and Proclaimed by Persons who have no Property in the fields for the gratification of Neither the best of Passions
or Purposes'.[15] Letters flew back and forth. The enclosure of
Ravensthorpe in 1795 provoked one to the elderly father of an
encloser. It purported to come from a friend. It broke the 'news' that
the old man's son was dangerously ill 'of a Feavour in the Brain'.
This is a diagnosis one might suspect to have sprung from the
common belief or hope that enclosers met early deaths; or perhaps it

[14] *Northampton Mercury*, 17, 24 May, 13 Sept., 27 Dec. 1762; a sign of the longevity
of protest may be the destruction of yet another Freeman summerhouse, just built,
in July 1784, twenty-two years after the destruction of the first two: *Northampton
Mercury*, 5, 26 July 1784.

[15] Northants. RO, D8028, n.d., probably 1770; at least six years of discussion
preceded Pattishall's enclosure in 1771.

came from the more charitable observation that they were deranged. Whichever it was, it succeeded in worrying the enclosers, who complained that the letter 'much alarmd the old man & might have occasiond much more Anxiety & Trouble & Expence than it did'. Presumably, the old man might have changed his mind.[16] We may imagine the opinions of Ravensthorpe anti-enclosers to have resembled those of the West Haddon men and women, whose opinions were described in an earlier chapter.[17] Most of them said they would not benefit from the enclosure; some said they were too old. Others said bluntly that enclosure was unjust: Joseph James 'cant answer it to his conscience'; David Cox thought it 'would not answer but would tend to ruin ye nation'; it was a 'very wicked thing', a 'bad thing'. These butchers, innkeepers, cottagers and farmer-artisans owned no more than thirty-six acres each – though a few rented more – and most owned much less. They stood to lose some of their land, all their field-pasture rights and an eight-hundred-acre common which provided fuel as well as pasture. And they had to pay for the privilege. Before the commissioners had claimed their last expenses almost half of West Haddon's owner-occupiers had sold all their lands.[18]

Perhaps all this is no more than the 'passive grumbling' that John Stevenson, in his synopsis of enclosure disturbance, calls the most common kind of enclosure protest.[19] But it had a purpose that was far from passive. It allowed those opposed to an enclosure to find others of the same mind. Grumbling was the first stage of more effective opposition. In Wellingborough the 'warm Discourse' that greeted Thomas Cowper in the pub was followed by refusals to sign the enclosure Bill and the presentation of a counter-petition to the House of Commons. The petitioners ('several Freeholders, Copyholders, Owners and Occupiers of Lands and Houses ... in behalf of

---

16 Northants. RO, D2778, 12 June 1795. For the belief that enclosers could not prosper, see Cowper, *Essay Proving that Inclosing of Commons and Common Field Land is Contrary to the Interests of the Nation*, pp. 19–20; Scrutton, *Commons and Common Fields*, pp. 84, 131–3. Enclosers took care to repudiate the power of the curse in Anon., *The True Interest of the Landowners of Great Britain*, pp. 24, 27; and [Joseph Lee], *A Vindication of a Regulated Inclosure* (1656). On cursing enclosers and the reasons for cursing and its power see Keith Thomas, *Religion and the Decline of Magic* (1971), pp. 603, 608–10.

17 See above, Chapter 7, pp. 198–201.

18 Northants. RO, ZA 9053, n.d., probably 1760–2, and see above, Chapter 7, pp. 204–7.

19 Stevenson, *Popular Disturbances in England*, p. 42.

themselves and many poor Inhabitants') complained that they would lose their 'small but comfortable Subsistence' because they could neither do without their common rights nor afford to pay for an enclosure. When this failed, the newly completed plan of the fields and all the field books allotting the lands were stolen from the enclosure commissioner's house and another attempt was made to steal the quality or land-valuation books from the surveyor's house and so bring the enclosure to a standstill. A local poet captured the patience of enclosure's opponents:

> When grumbling *Dudgeon* seem'd to sleep,
> Which late play'd wanton at Bo-peep;
> When Jars, and Knotty Points were ended,
> And patient *Flamen's Panes* were mended
> When *Pro* and *Con* did well nigh cease,
> 'Sway'd by the Olive-Wand of Peace;
> When drooping *Ceres* was half slain,
> And *Grass* might grow instead of *Grain*;
> When *honest* labour was struck mute,
> And *Av'rice* gain'd the high Dispute;
> When Act of Parliament was o'er
> (As wise as hundreds made before)
> When Fr–m–n had the Field survey'd,
> And Numbers of Wise-Acres made;
> When Town was lulled in sweet Composure,
> And dream'd of Nothing – but In-c—re; –
> Forthwith fly VULCAN steps, and blows the Fire,
> In which – *Plan, Patience, Hope, and all expire.*[20]

All this cost the enclosers increased parliamentary fees and a year's improvement of the fields as well as the cost of making more maps and allotments.[21] In much the same way we have seen local grumbling in West Haddon translated into a parliamentary counter-petition which led to the withdrawal of the first enclosure Bill.[22] When the Bill finally became law at the third attempt, its opponents advertised a football match in the *Northampton Mercury*, to which

[20] *Northampton Mercury*, 10 Mar. 1766; Freeman was William Freeman the surveyor, Northants. RO, J. W. Anscomb's 'Abstracts of Enclosure Awards', I, p. 36; the poem hints at an earlier riot – when patient Flamen's panes were broken.
[21] *Jls House of Commons*, 26 Feb., 1 Mar. 1765; Northants. RO, Wake file, 'Wellingborough Letters and Other Papers, 1738–1817', 16 Feb. 1766.
[22] See above, Chapter 7, p. 190.

they invited 'Gentlemen Gamesters and Well-Wishers to the Cause now in Hand' – the cause, that is, of opposition to the enclosure – and, in the two-day riot that followed, the well-wishers gathered and burnt the posts and rails lying in the fields awaiting erection and did other serious damage.[23] This grumbling could serve a symbolic or demonstrative purpose too: after 'passively' advertising their disquiet at plans for the enclosure of Flore in 1777 and threatening a parliamentary counter-petition, commoners drove the message home by breaking down the squire's hall gates.[24]

Grumbling was also put down on paper and sent to enclosing landowners in the form of a local counter-petition. Commoners declared their opposition quite plainly, and signed their names to it – in one instance ninety-two people put their names to a petition from three parishes. The Duke of Buccleuch heard such a grumble in 1792 as his agent planned the enclosure of Geddington Chase in Rockingham Forest. Eighteen 'small Proprietors of Land and Cottages' from Brigstock – most of them artisans and tradesmen – explained at length that his plans would cost them time, trouble and money as well as drive the poor rate up in the winter and raise the overall level of unemployment. Unemployment was a consequence of the inevitable change in land use brought to forest parishes by enclosure. The extinction of common right deprived arable farmers of the large wood pastures on which they depended. In Rockingham they would have to convert their land to pasture. This had happened in Benefield already. Everyone knew that the consequence of conversion was the loss of as many as two-thirds of agricultural labouring jobs; 'We see whole Lordships', they wrote, 'managed by a Shepherd or two and their Dogs'. The labouring poor would suffer first, and those who presently contributed to their survival in winter would soon have to pay for their upkeep year in and year out.[25] Two years later they were still grumbling. In their second petition the Brigstock commoners were joined by more men from Stanion and

---

[23] *Jls House of Commons*, 18 Dec. 1760; *Northampton Mercury*, 29 July, 5 Aug. 1765; J. W. Anscomb, 'An Eighteenth-Century Inclosure and Football Play at West Haddon', *Northamptonshire Past and Present*, 4:3 (1968–9), pp. 175–8; for a longer discussion of events in West Haddon see Chapter 7.

[24] *Northampton Mercury*, 28 July, 13, 20 Oct. 1777.

[25] According to Pitt, *General View … of Northampton*, p. 253, the number of labourers needed on pastoral land was one-third of that needed on arable. For an account of unemployment following the clearing of forest see Linnell, *Old Oak*, p. 8.

Geddington, who were also under threat of losing their commons in Geddington Chase. This time they moved from a loyal, if strained, deference to something more like defiance and threatened to take their case to Parliament. They questioned Buccleuch's priorities directly:

> We are convinced that the Benefit, if any, arising from the inclosure, will not be reciprocal, but entirely in your Grace's Favour; and considering the Amplitude of Your Possessions it cannot be an Object worthy of Your Grace's Notice to endeavour to encrease Your Grace's income at the expence of so many necessitated Persons.

His Grace received more letters at 48 Albermarle Street, Piccadilly, putting the case of the commoners of Geddington Chase, and his petitioners advertised their intention of pursuing the matter in Parliament in the *Northampton Mercury*.[26]

A little later, in 1798, Lord Sondes received a similar petition against the planned enclosure of Wilbarston: 'The Major Part of the ffarmers, ffreeholders and Cottagers', explained that his plans would cost them their self-sufficiency in corn at times of dearth like the present, and cause the poor rate to rise too.[27] All but three of the twenty-four petitioners owned or rented less than five acres each, or nothing at all, and only one could be called a full-time farmer; a couple were victuallers, four were artisans and three had been farm servants a few years earlier.[28] Sondes ignored their petition, the enclosure went ahead, and in the summer of 1799, a few days before Lammas, three hundred commoners held up the fencing of the common until two troops of yeomanry cavalry were brought in from Loughborough.[29] Another petition came from Staverton, which in

---

[26] Northants. RO, Montagu (Boughton), X350, Box 10, no. 26, Petitions, 30 Nov. 1792, July 1794; James Walker and Thomas Vicars to the Duke of Buccleuch, 19 July 1794. In 1636 Rockingham commoners at Hougham and Deene had denounced Thomas, Lord Brudenell, to the Commissioners for Depopulation, for devouring 'the people with a sheapheard and a dog' by enclosing land; he denied the charge but the commissioners fined him £1,000. See Finch, *Five Northamptonshire Families*, p. 162; *Northampton Mercury*, 21, 28 Sept., 5 Oct. 1793.
[27] Northants. RO, Rockingham Castle MSS, B.7.55, photostat no. 752.
[28] Northants. RO, Land Tax Records, 1798–9, 1803; Wilbarston Civil Parish Records, i, 'Wilbarston Inclosure Rate ...'; photostat no. 743, 'Sums Paid to the Commissioners for the Inclosure by the Proprietors'; Militia List, 1781, Wilbarston – half of the petitioners could not be identified from the list.
[29] *Annual Register*, 'Chronicle', 25 July 1799; Northants. RO, Wilbarston Parish Chest, photostat no. 743, 'The Account of Robert Edmonds ... Gentleman

contrast to the trades and forest commons of Wilbarston, Brigstock, Stanion and Geddington was a more purely agricultural and fielden parish at the south-western end of the county. The parliamentary record describes the opponents here as owners of only 5 per cent of the land, who made no appearance before the Commons' committee to oppose the enclosure Bill. But the survival of this locally presented petition demonstrates both the incompleteness of this kind of 'official' evidence and the wider consequences of enclosure here: 'If these farms should be inclosed', it ran, 'it would be impossible for the small farmers to live on their produce and about sixty families of poor day labourers would for the most part have to be relieved by the Parish'.[30]

Why did opponents petition local landowners and how successful were they? After all, their interests and their experiences were very different. The Brigstock petitioners to the Duke of Buccleuch had observed of him that, 'in that exalted Situation' it had pleased God to put him, 'It is impossible Your Grace should know the extreme Distress many of the Poor with large Families are driven to'.[31] None the less they petitioned him because his family had defended common rights on other occasions. They had once shared the same interest and they might count on him again. Commoners opposed to the enclosure of Benefield in Rockingham Forest in 1710 made the point in a letter to the Duke of Montagu when they reminded him of an earlier attempt at enclosure:

> to which both yrs and our poor family were very great enemies, above an hundred and sixty years agoe, yrs by staving it off by ye prudent, but chargeable methods of Law, ours by heading ye Gentry that level'd their trenches when they attempted illegal enclosures.[32]

Commissioner', n.d., c.1799: the services of two troops of yeomanry cavalry cost the enclosers £105 5s 8d.

[30] *Reasons Humbly Offered against the Bill for Inclosing and Dividing the Common Fields within the Parish and Manor of Stareton, otherwise Staverton, in the County of Northampton*, 1 page, folio, no imprint [18th century]. Offered for sale by Francis Edwards Ltd, *Catalogue 966*, History of Economics, Commerce and Trade up to 1800, Item 102. Staverton was enclosed in 1774.

[31] Northants. RO, Montagu (Boughton), X350, Box 10, no. 26, James Walker and Thomas Vicars to the Duke of Buccleuch, 19 July 1794.

[32] Northants. RO, Montagu (Boughton), Box W28, Barton to Montagu, Nov. 1710. See also Northants. RO, Gowran of Upper Ossory uncatalogued collection, Petition, 13 Apr. 1739, asking for promised aid in paying for a law suit between Brigstock and Great Weldon over commonable lands.

The hope was that the older alliance could be called on again. Commoners were negotiators – they had always been so. They resorted to negotiation when faced with what must have looked like the ultimate threat – the loss of the commons themselves. For this reason a petition to landowners such as Buccleuch and Sondes may have been a frequent resort in the middle of the eighteenth century when parliamentary enclosures began.

As prices rose and the rural worsted manufacture declined it is possible that some gentry who were not themselves bent on enclosing lent a sympathetic ear – the sort of men who found the arguments of pamphleteer defenders of commons persuasive. We have seen that in Burton Latimer a local petition signed by seventy-eight commoners was turned into a parliamentary petition and presented by a sympathetic local gentleman – Sir William Dolben.[33] In other places similar responses may explain dissents to Bills made by local gentry whose material interest in an enclosure was small and who may have viewed a more dependent poor with some alarm.[34]

Grumbling, in the form of rumours, local petitions, newspaper advertisements, letters and the like, was more significant in its function of organizing opinion and expressing opposition than has been acknowledged. Through grumbling, opponents came to decide to refuse to sign Bills and to threaten parliamentary counter-petitions, and through grumbling they strengthened each other's resolution. Furthermore, local opposition like this may have been more successful than the alternative, which was to take opposition to Parliament.

Bringing counter-petitions to the Commons and refusing consent to the Bill at the report stage were the means that, in the somewhat sardonic words of the Brigstock commoners, 'the wisdom of the Legislature' had provided for contesting enclosure; they were the only legal means of defeating an enclosure Bill once it reached Parliament. In Northamptonshire, landowners and cottagers

[33] Chapter 7, 208–9.
[34] See, for example, Nether Heyford, Stowe and Bugbrooke (1750), Ledgers Ashby (1764), Braunston (1774–5), Kilsby (1777), Welton (1754), Guilsborough, Nortoft and Coton (1764), Wappenham (1760), Blakesley (1760), Hannington (1802) and Burton Latimer (1803); most of these were upland parishes where enclosure often led to reduced agricultural employment and where wastes were most common. Opposition to the enclosure of Atherstone, Warwickshire, a parish with a comparable agriculture, found the support of 'several neighbouring gentlemen and farmers' who were 'likely to be impair'd in Value by this Inclosure': Warwicks. RO, HR 35/25, Opinion of W. Murray, 19 Jan. 1738/9.

refused their consent in two-thirds of all successful enclosure Bills. Furthermore, in half of these cases those refusing to sign owned between 10 and 30 per cent of the land to be enclosed.[35] Because only land and cottages were measured, not numbers of owners and cottagers, it is impossible to identify these opponents from this source alone, but it should be remembered that even the smallest proportions of land could hide a majority of a village's proprietors. For example, in Wigston Magna, W. G. Hoskins found that opponents of enclosure owned only 16 per cent of the land but were an overwhelming majority of the landowners.[36]

Counter-petitions were less common than refusals: opponents of enclosure sent them from only 11 per cent of parishes in Northamptonshire between 1750 and 1815.[37] Twelve were sent by small owners and cottagers or acknowledged their support; half of these were presented during the wars as enclosers took advantage of high prices and enclosed what were perhaps the most recalcitrant villages.[38] A counter-petition from the smaller commoners and land-

---

[35] W. E. Tate found that half of Nottinghamshire's enclosure Bills were not unanimously supported by owners who were 'very rarely reported as having anything approaching 20 per cent of the property in the parish in their possession': '*Commons' Journals* as Sources of Information', pp. 87–8. In Northamptonshire, proportions of land owned by those against enclosure were much higher: one in six Bills was opposed by owners of 18 to 28 per cent of the land, one in three by owners of more than 10 per cent. Because waste land was included in the total acreage noted in the Journal of the House of Commons, these proportions underestimate the amount of land owned by opponents of enclosures since wastes were considered the property of the Lord of the Manor, who was usually in favour of enclosure. Proportions given here are based on an examination of all Northamptonshire enclosures taking place between 1750 and 1815. See also Neeson, 'Common Right and Enclosure', pp. 323–33.

[36] Sixty men and women owned this 16 per cent: Hoskins, *Midland Peasant*, pp. 247–9.

[37] Nine counter-petitions were sent from Nottinghamshire (7 per cent of Acts 1743–1845); W. E. Tate, 'Parliamentary Counter-Petitions during the Enclosures of the Eighteenth and Nineteenth Centuries', *English Historical Review* 59 (1944), pp. 398–9; eighteen were sent from Northamptonshire between 1750 and 1815 (11 per cent of Acts); Buckinghamshire counter-petitions were about as common as Northamptonshire ones: Turner, 'Some Social and Economic Considerations', p. 186.

[38] See also Turner, *English Parliamentary Enclosure*, pp. 169–70, where he suggests that in Buckinghamshire parishes there were more small owners in later-enclosed parishes. Northamptonshire counter-petitions came from Welton (1754), Sulgrave (1760), West Haddon (1761, 1764), Ashby St Ledgers (1764), Wellingborough (1765), Braunston (1777), Kilsby (1777), Great Addington (1781), Raunds (1797), Sutton Bassett and Weston by Welland (1802), Burton Latimer (1803), Rothersthorpe (1806, 1808, 1809) and Cottingham and Middleton (1815).

owners of Raunds in 1797 described how their common rights on waste and common fields got them through the winter by enabling them to keep cows year round; they also raised young or lean stock to sell cheaply to local graziers. On enclosure they would lose not only their four hundred acres of common pasture but some of their arable land to pasture too. The owner-occupiers of Welton, who were also tenants, petitioned against their enclosure in 1754, foreseeing the end of cheap land and the rise of poor rates; the commoners of Burton Latimer asked that their eight-hundred-acre wold be left open to feed their cattle and provide them with fuel in 1803; the small farmers of Sutton Bassett tried to stop the amalgamation of their lands with the neighbouring parish of Weston by Welland and the enclosure of the two together in 1802; and the Kilsby cottagers petitioned successfully for their own commissioner and an umpire to adjudicate between all the commissioners should they disagree.[39]

Parliamentary counter-petitions represent only a small part of the opposition to enclosure; they are useful as guides to what kinds of grievance were felt not measures of how much there was. They were few because, as pessimistic historians have argued, they were expensive and they needed a degree of familiarity with parliamentary procedures that most small commoners lacked. In 1845 opponents of the enclosure of Foulmere in Cambridgeshire raised £20 to pay a solicitor to take their case, but the difficulty of getting to London and the cost of appearing in the Commons were too much for them: 'we have injoyed Commons heretofore for many years Without eny molestation', they wrote, but 'The Distance From London to Foulmire is 42 miles.'[40] Petitions cost money and they cost time. But, above all else, they were *unsuccessful*, and this lack of success was a far greater discouragement to commoners than either cost or ignorance. Counter-petitions were presented to a Parliament of enclosers. Opponents needed no one to tell them this, but an avowedly reluctant supporter of Northampton's enclosure made the point anyway in a letter to the *Northampton Mercury* in 1777:

Both Houses of Parliament, Gentlemen, *it is well known*, give all

[39] *Jls House of Commons*, 30 June 1797; Hammond and Hammond, *Village Labourer*, p. 32; [Young], *General Report on Enclosures*, p. 245; *Jls House of Commons*, 22 Jan. 1754; Anon., *Case of the Petitioners against the Welton Common Bill*; *Jls House of Commons*, 29 Mar. 1802, 25 Apr. 1803, 9 Apr. 1777; Northants. RO, Anscomb, 'Abstracts of Enclosure Awards'.

[40] Cambs. RO, 292/029.

the Encouragement they can to Inclosures; and this, no Doubt, from a Conviction of their being of public Utility. Indeed, when we consider the great Number of Members of both Houses, who have had Occasion to apply to Parliament on the same Business for themselves, we cannot wonder at the almost constant Success these Applications meet with; for, at this Time, they are never unsuccessful ...[41]

Moreover, we know from other sources that numbers of enclosures had succeeded because Parliament waived its own rules or made them flexible in order to favour enclosers. It ignored the informal four-fifths rule, whereby land in support of a Bill should amount to four-fifths of the total to be enclosed, in fourteen Northamptonshire enclosures.[42] It allowed at least three Bills to proceed, despite contravening the 1774 standing order that Bills must be publicly displayed in the parish before going to Parliament.[43] And it gave the order 'That all who attend shall have Voices', which enabled interested MPs to vote when opposition was expected, on nine occasions.[44] Not every enclosure was so readily helped along, but, because quantities of land required to defeat a Bill were inexact, because standing orders were occasionally flexible, and because

[41] *Northampton Mercury*, 20 Jan. 1777 (my italics).
[42] Sulgrave (1760), Guilsborough, Nortoft and Coton (1764), West Haddon (1764), Wellingborough (1765), Earls Barton (1771), Braunston (1775), Halse Woodford (1758), Yelvertoft (1776), Kilsby (1777), Walgrave (1776), Denton (1770), Sutton Bassett and Weston by Welland (1802), Irthlingborough (1808) and Rothersthorpe (1809). On this point, see Hammond and Hammond, *Village Labourer*, pp. 43–4; Turner, 'Parliamentary Enclosure and Landownership Change in Buckinghamshire', p. 36, giving more evidence that the four-fifths rule of thumb was ignored; Lambert, *Bills and Acts*, p. 143, discussing the likely origin of the belief that there was a statutory minimum of consent. In at least two Northamptonshire enclosures (West Haddon and Sulgrave) enclosers calculated tithe as acres and added them to their own quantity of land to arrive at a respectable majority of land in favour of the Bills.
[43] The enclosures were of Evenley (1779), Whitfield (1796) and Wilbarston (1798). At the enclosure of Wilbarston, the House of Commons was informed that no notice of the intention to enclose the eight-hundred-acre common had been given in the Bill circulated for signature in the parish. The enclosers were allowed to go ahead with the enclosure none the less because the common belonged to Lord Sondes, who was in favour of the enclosure: *Jls House of Commons*, 14 Mar. 1798. As a result, no opposition was ever recorded in Parliament; of course it was opposed with a counter-petition to Sondes himself and a riot: see p. 259, above, and p. 278 below.
[44] The order was given at the passage of the following Acts: Upper and Lower Middleton Cheney (1769), Astrop (1772), Evenley (1779), Piddington and Hackleton (1782), Little Weldon (1792), Brigstock, Stanion and Geddington (1795), Raunds (1797), Sutton Bassett (1803) and Rothersthorpe (1809).

committees were easily packed, opponents of enclosure were encouraged to look for better means of resistance.[45]

But if Parliament's attitude to enclosure was so favourable and so well known, why did small owners *ever* threaten counter-petitions and occasionally even bring them? Perhaps the certainty of failure was never absolute, and some petitioners felt that in their case the Commons would be moved. It is possible that in the early years of parliamentary enclosure their chances were better than later on. Certainly Parliament was more divided on the issue than it would become, and conversion to pasture – the aim of many early Midland enclosures – had few friends. In the 1730s, as the very first Acts began, commoners at Atherstone in Warwickshire received the advice that their counter-petition might succeed because 'These Bills for Inclosing Commons have generally proceeded upon the Consent & Mutual agreement of *all* persons concerned', and the advice was good – enclosure took another generation. But in the 1760s their second attempt to thwart enclosure with a counter-petition failed.[46] After mid century, in the years of most enclosure, failure became the rule. In Northamptonshire, petitions delayed enclosure for anything from three to forty years, but overall only 3 per cent of all the county's enclosure Bills were successfully petitioned against. The odds against the success of a counter-petition brought by small owners alone, without other support, were ten to one; they were a little more favourable at three or four to one if small owners petitioned with more substantial interests, such as an aggrieved Lord of the Manor or tithe-owner.[47] It is possible that these odds were enough to make the threat of a counter-petition unwelcome to enclosers but not so good as to encourage opponents to send them in large numbers.

Petitions may have been one of the two major legal means of contesting enclosure provided by Parliament, but they were far too ineffective to be the major means of small owners and users of

[45] On the conflict of interest evident in the activity of Warwickshire MPs in support of enclosure Bills, see J. M. Martin, 'Members of Parliament and Enclosure: A Reconsideration', *Agricultural History Review*, 27 (1980).

[46] Warwicks. RO, HR 35/25, Opinion of W. Murray, 19 Jan. 1738/9 (my italics). Atherstone was finally enclosed in 1764.

[47] Five of the eighteen enclosure Bills opposed with counter-petitions were withdrawn: West Haddon (1761), Great Addington (1780), Hannington (1796), Southorpe (1800) and Rothersthorpe (1806). Three of the five were brought by an alliance of manorial lords and smaller owners; the participation of the former may have been the crucial determinant of success.

common lands. As a result they may represent (with refusals to sign
Bills) the last lawful stage of local opposition. Viewed in this light
they were useful negotiating weapons for use at home because
enclosers would prefer as smooth a passage as possible for their Bills
through the Commons.[48] Thus *threats* of counter-petitions, such as
those made in Flore and Brigstock, may have been more numerous
and may have enjoyed more success than counter-petitions themselves, and the same is true of locally expressed intentions of not
signing Bills.[49]

From this standpoint what we see in Parliament is only the
remnant of opposition mustered locally. It follows that the most
significant statistic of parliamentary opposition may be the 22 per
cent of Bills (1750–1815) withdrawn by their supporters before they
met any parliamentary opposition at all. If so many Bills reached
Parliament only to be dropped, there must have been quite some
argument going on at home.[50] Of course, not all withdrawn Bills
were thwarted by small landowners and landless commoners; larger
interests had their differences to settle too, but usually the key
signatures to a Bill (the tithe-owner and the largest landowners)
were gathered before approaching the Commons. The opposition
which led to the withdrawal of Bills may have been most commonly
brought by lesser interests: the enclosure of Northampton Fields in
1778, for example, was delayed for eight years by the opposition of
owners of less than one hundred acres each; two Bills were withdrawn before a third was successful. Corby enclosure was held up
for longer by commoners adept at foiling enclosers, and when the

[48] Not only did they risk losing a Bill, they incurred higher costs too: first, the fees for
private Bills rose with the number of interests involved in the enclosure (*Jls House
of Commons*, 11 Apr., 11 May 1775); second, all other costs rose too (surveying,
gathering support, parliamentary costs other than fees). On the last point, during
the 1770s when average legal costs were 15s per acre, the costs of enclosing
resisting parishes like Bugbrooke, Flore, Braunston and Northampton Fields
were almost twice as high: Northants. RO, Anscomb, 'Abstracts of Enclosure
Awards', II.
[49] *Northampton Mercury*, 13, 20 Oct. 1777, 21, 28 Sept., 5 Oct. 1793.
[50] In Nottinghamshire the proportion was also 22 per cent: Tate, 'Opposition to
Parliamentary Enclosure in Eighteenth-Century England', p. 138. Some Bills
would have been lost through lack of time; P. D. G. Thomas, *The House of
Commons in the Eighteenth Century* (1978), p. 61. But most would have reappeared
within the year. In Northamptonshire 16 per cent of all Bills were delayed for
longer than a year and 8 per cent were delayed from nine to fifty-seven years.
Almost half of all delayed enclosures needed more than two Bills before they were
successful. According to Lambert, *Bills and Acts*, p. 113, 14 per cent of enclosure
Bills failed between 1715 and 1774.

parish was finally enclosed in 1829 (after attempts as widely separated as 1766 and 1796) its forest commons were left open.[51]

More enclosures must have been discussed without agreement to bring in even one Bill. This impression is given substance when one looks – as Donald McCloskey and M. E. Turner have – for an economic rationale behind the timing of enclosure.[52] In Northamptonshire one is struck by the lateness of enclosures in particular areas. As many as a quarter of all parishes enclosed by Act were so enclosed long after the point at which enclosure would have been most profitable. For example, when large numbers of potentially pastoral parishes were enclosed in the 1750s, 1760s and 1770s, thirty parishes of exactly this description – prime for conversion to pasture or up-and-down husbandry – escaped enclosure. In some of these parishes there is evidence that unsuccessful attempts at enclosure had been made in the most profitable years: the mooted enclosures of Ringstead, Finedon and Aynho are three examples.[53] Here Bills, early surveys, or notices of enclosures posted on church doors had come to nothing. There is more evidence that when these out-of-step parishes were finally enclosed it was even then in the face of considerable opposition. Cottingham and Middleton were enclosed only after two counter-petitions and three Bills; Cold Higham's enclosure required two Bills and was delayed for six years; Croughton's needed six Bills and suffered an eight-year delay; Rothersthorpe's took four Bills over nine years, a counter-petition

[51] Northants. RO, Miscellaneous Quarter Sessions Records, Northampton Inclosure Papers, Accession 11969/14/91, 'Northampton Inclosure. A List of Property', and 'Bill on Northampton's Inclosure' (Aug. 1776–Feb. 1777); *Jls House of Commons*, 8 Feb. 1770, 3 Apr. 1778. Argument for and against enclosure filled the *Northampton Mercury* between December 1776 and February 1777. Two unsuccessful attempts to enclose Corby were made in 1766 and 1796; see *Jls House of Commons*, 25 Mar. 1766, 10 Feb. 1796. W. E. Tate makes a connection between the survival of large numbers of small proprietors and late enclosure in Cambridgeshire and Berkshire: see Tate, 'Cambridgeshire Field Systems with a Handlist of Cambridgeshire Enclosure Acts and Awards' reprinted from *The Cambridge Antiquarian Society Proceedings*, 40 (1939–42), p. 76, and 'Handlist of English Enclosure Acts and Awards relating to Lands in Berkshire', p. 73.

[52] McCloskey, 'Persistence of English Common Fields'; Turner, *English Parliamentary Enclosure*, ch. 5 and pp. 169, 173.

[53] Ringstead's forthcoming enclosure was announced in an advertisement published in 1782, but the parish remained open until 1829: *Northampton Mercury*, 18 Nov. 1782. Aynho's enclosure was discussed in 1766 without agreement, and enclosure did not go through until 1792: Northants. RO, Cartwright (Aynho) collection 3408. Thomas Cowper was busy surveying Finedon's fields in 1774, but no more was heard of enclosure until 1805: Northants. RO, X678.

was brought, the order that all should have voice was given, a clause setting a 40s minimum fine for fence-breaking was added and, throughout, owners of a fifth of the land refused support.[54] It seems likely that smaller owners were able to prevent earlier enclosure here just as P. A. J. Pettit thought they had done in Whittlewood Forest, as Turner suspected was the case in north Buckinghamshire parishes, and as Thirsk wrote of the Lincolnshire marshlands.[55]

Opposition seems to have been most often a local matter. Even where counter-petitions and refusals to sign Bills were brought to the Commons their purpose was less to impress Parliament than to impress enclosers with their opponents' determination. There is evidence that the threat did worry enclosers and cause them to abandon Bills. During the hearings on the Welton enclosure Bill the enclosers warned each other that their opponents were 'very suttle and vigilant' and they took pains to enlist stronger support: 'If you have any interest with Lord Hallifax', wrote one, 'now is the time to make use of it.'[56]

When, despite this opposition, Bills did become Acts, opposition remained local but became unlawful. Unlawful opposition either delayed and disrupted enclosure or it mitigated its terms and punished its supporters. Unfortunately surviving sources underestimate the amount of riot and covert malicious damage to fences, gates and walls. Assize records have been lost for the Midland Circuit, which included Northamptonshire, Leicestershire, Nottinghamshire and Warwickshire – some of the most densely enclosed Midland counties; moreover most fence-breaking and wood-stealing cases would have been heard summarily and left unrecorded; and, finally, newspapers reported riot only occasionally, and villages kept the identities of fence-breakers and rioters secret, making their detection difficult. It cannot be emphasized too strongly that the absence of records of illegal opposition makes any attempt to establish its dimensions impossible. It is entirely possible

[54] Cottingham and Middleton: *Jls House of Commons*, 1766, 1814, 1816; Cold Higham: *ibid.*, 1806, 1812; Croughton: *ibid.*, 1798, 1799, 1802, 1803, 1807 (April), 1807 (July); Rothersthorpe: *ibid.*, 1800, 1807, 1808, 1809.

[55] Pettit, *Royal Forests of Northamptonshire*, pp. 314–16; Turner, 'Some Social and Economic Considerations of Parliamentary Enclosure in Buckinghamshire', pp. 67, 172; Thirsk, *English Peasant Farming*, pp. 237, 292.

[56] Northants. RO, Wel. 26; fear of opposition to enclosure led Mordant to advise lords and stewards to keep the intention to enclose a secret (this was possible until a change in the Standing Orders for enclosure Bills in 1771) and buy up freehold land: Mordant, *Complete Steward*, pp. 170–1.

that both overt and covert resistance was never recorded and is forever lost to the historian of protest. It follows that we have to consider the evidence that remains as the rump of what may have been widespread activity.

The most persistent legal opposition was often followed by riot. After the defeat of their parliamentary counter-petition the West Haddon commoners, with help from nearby villages, had burned £1,500 worth of posts and rails; when the Wilbarston local counter-petition failed, three hundred men and women tried to prevent the fencing of the common; and when the Raunds parliamentary counter-petition was dismissed petitioners also became rioters: led by the village women and some shoemakers they pulled down fences, dismantled gates, lit huge bonfires and celebrated long into the night.[57] Rioters in Warkworth had less good fortune. Warkworth meadow was common to the inhabitants of three neighbouring villages, many of whom had refused to sign the enclosure Bill, knowing that no proper compensation would be made to them. When they made good their threat to march on the new fences they were met by a company of mounted gentlemen led by the local justice, who rode over them and 'broke their Disposition'. In a few minutes six men were taken. Four of the six were soon discharged for want of prosecution and three others who had threatened the riot earlier in the day were never arrested: the first concern of the proprietors was to prevent the bringing down of the fences, not to look for enemies. A month in gaol for some offenders and a gracious pardon for the others was thought sufficient punishment.[58]

Covert resistance was more difficult to thwart. In 1764, a year before the football match riot in West Haddon, the two principal landowners of neighbouring Guilsborough had suffered theft and arson even before their fences had gone up: Richard Clarke's brakes were burnt, and with them went the gate to his home close, some posts and their rails from his hayrick, and seventy perches of

---

[57] [Tyley], 'Inclosure of Open Fields', p. 5.

[58] *Jls House of Commons*, 2 Apr. 1764; *Northampton Mercury*, 16 Sept. 1765; PRO, War Office papers 4/7, p. 420–1; Northants. RO, Quarter Sessions Order Book, 8 Oct. 1765, p. 257, and Grand File, Michaelmas, 5 Geo. III, information of Thomas Taylor. On the effect of intercommoning on resistance to enclosure see John Walter, 'A Rising of the People? The Oxfordshire Rising of 1596', *Past and Present*, 107 (1985), p. 102; compare P. M. Jones, 'Parish, Seigneurie and the Community of Inhabitants in Southern Central France', *Past and Present*, 91 (1981), p. 87.

hedging from his fields. Ten days later justice John Bateman lost four gates and their locks.[59] In the following year, opponents of Hardingstone's enclosure began a systematic campaign of fence-breaking and tree-barking. They kept up their raids for years, destroying live hedges, throwing down posts and rails, digging up sand in the roads.[60] As the years went by angry men and women carried out more attacks: they felled young trees in a new plantation in Warmington's enclosed fields shortly after enclosure, provoking the advertisement of a reward large enough, at £20, to suggest the incident was one of many; they broke down the new fences of Duston four years after its enclosure; they sawed down most of the stiles and several gates on the footpath and horseway between Northampton and its neighbouring villages in 1786, a few years after the long-delayed enclosure of Northampton Fields.[61]

Other attacks on fences combined symbolic revenge after enclosure with immediate utility. Posts and rails were taken down and carried home to burn in the hearths of this fuel-scarce country. As a result it is hard to define where enclosure protest ends and the need for fuel begins. For example, when the men, women and children of Yardley Hastings, Denton and Grendon extended their wood-gathering rights in Yardley Chase to the fences of the newly enclosed fields and common of Denton in 1775, they cut and carried the wood home. They did so quite boldly, fearing no one, least of all the Earl of Northampton or the tenants he directed to stop them. But they had recently lost a seven-hundred-acre common rich in fuel and they had need of a new one. If they needed to justify their work they may have found justification enough in the loss of their common rights.[62] Hedge-breaking and wood-stealing were offences

[59] *Northampton Mercury*, 20, 27 Feb. 1764.
[60] *Ibid.*, 18 Feb. 1765, and esp. 25 May 1767, 27 Feb. 1775; Northants. RO, Quarter Sessions, Grand File, Easter, 14 Geo. III, 5 Apr. 1774; Grand File, Easter, 21 Geo. III, 28 Mar. 1781. Sand from commons was used for cleaning, building etc.; see above, Chapter 6, pp. 168, 173.
[61] *Northampton Mercury*, 22 Dec. 1777 (Warmington), 11 Dec. 1780 (Duston), 4 Mar. 1786 (Northampton); similar malicious damage to posts and rails, gates and mounts around the newly enclosed common was deplored and cautioned against frequently between 1785 and 1792; see, for example, *ibid.*, 26 Apr. 1785: 'Whereas, since the shutting up of the COMMON belonging to the Freemen ... several People have taken a Liberty to force a Way by Breaking down the Fences.'
[62] *Ibid.*, 27 Feb. 1775. At Butlers Marston, Warwickshire, payments for winter fuel made their appearance in the overseer's accounts within two years of the enclosure: Joan Lane, 'Administration of the Poor Law in Butlers Marston, Warwick-

with two motives in the enclosure period. A minute book (1819–34) belonging to the Walgrave Association for the Prosecution of Felons bears this out. The original had disappeared, but the Association's lawyer's descendant made this observation of its contents while it was in his hands:

> It appears from the minutes that persons were persecuted for pocket-picking, stealing horses, sheep or turnips, and for killing a number of sheep. The greater number of the proceedings were however taken against persons breaking or stealing hedge wood or throwing down a wall. Inasmuch as the greater part of the Inclosure Acts had then recently been passed, and the land inclosed, most of the offences were for hedge breaking – the feeling of the working men against the inclosures being very bitter.[63]

We come away from an investigation of unlawful resistance to enclosure with the feeling that enclosed fields and former commons were easy and long-term targets for enclosure's opponents. Enclosers' farms were plainly vulnerable despite the protection of seven-year transportation penalties for breaking their fences.[64] Who knows what kinds of understanding enclosers came to with former commoners during the long winter months or during harvest crises? The social separation of farmers and labourers so widely remarked upon after enclosure was accompanied by an intimacy in these questions that modified the power of one and the servility of the other. If landlords and farmers eventually won the battle for enclosure, rural artisans and agricultural labourers may have had some say in the terms of surrender.

But perhaps as significant as the (largely unknowable) dimensions of legal or illegal protest is the existence of *anger* in enclosed villages – the visceral hostility that the term 'grumbling' so effectively obscures. If we use the incidence of known protest as a measure of

shire, 1713–1822' (unpublished MA thesis, University of Wales, Cardiff, 1970), p. 19

[63] Northampton Public Library, no. 281, 'Walgrave Association for Apprehending etc. Thieves and Robbers. Notes made by Mr Markham'. Prosecuting Associations customarily included a cluster of parishes: eleven parishes within five miles of Walgrave were enclosed between 1800 and 1815: Orlingbury (1808), Hannington (1802), Burton Latimer (1803), Finedon (1805), Wilby (1801), Warkton (1807), Cranford (1805), Weekley and Geddington (1807), Kettering (1804) and Rothwell (1812).

[64] Under 9 Geo. III, c.29 (1769) anyone convicted of wilfully and maliciously damaging or destroying any enclosure fence was guilty of felony.

relations between farmers and labourers then we must also recognize the place of a sense of injustice and of conflicting interests – in the words of the last commentator, the 'very bitter' feeling of working men against enclosure. As an index of social relations this sort of hostility cannot be ignored, yet it is often neglected in a demand for the 'harder' evidence of riot or petition.[65] But, in terms of social antagonism, what is the difference between feeling and doing? What is the difference between the desperate *wish*, for example, of small farmers in Kilsby, Northamptonshire, to kill the butter dealer who cut their prices to the bone, and his murder?[66] Perhaps the difference is a matter of culture and risk: it was probably unusual in Kilsby to kill anyone, and it was certainly dangerous to do so. But it is important to note that the difference is not of degrees of injury and hatred: the butter dealer was just as much an enemy when he went unpunished. In fact he may have been hated *more* when he went unpunished because seeing him continue to go about his business must have stoked and preserved hostility. And the same would have been true of a hatred of enclosers and of the beneficiaries of enclosure.

II

From what kinds of village does protest survive? Riotous West Haddon, covertly resistant Guilsborough and Coton, counter-petitioning Welton, Braunston and Kilsby all lay in the worsted, stock, butter and crop region of the western uplands. Wellingborough, Northampton, Raunds and Burton Latimer were stock, crop, shoe and cloth towns and villages in the central Nene valley. Wilbarston, Brigstock, Geddington and Corby were all forest towns with forest trades, some cloth- and lace-making, and large forest commons. Resisting villages like these were often diffuse rather than consolidated in landownership; they were usually mixed agricultural and manufacturing rather than solely agricultural in economy; and

---

[65] R. A. E. Wells, 'Social Protest, Class, Conflict and Consciousness, in the English Countryside, 1700–1880', in M. Reed and R. A. E. Wells, eds., *Class, Conflict and Protest in the English Countryside, 1700–1880* (1990) p. 155.
[66] Northants. RO, R(K) 80, 26 Sept. 1796: 'Mr Watts has been about the place, bidding the farmers 10d per pound for their butter all the year round – and they talk of killing him'.

cf Richard in Whittlesford

many of them lost waste land and arable land to pasture after enclosure.[67]

It follows that the most active opponents of enclosure in Northamptonshire were the 'poor parishioners, both farmers, labourers and handicraftsmen' for whose future Thomas Cowper feared as he began to survey Wellingborough's fields.[68] They were the smaller farmers who occupied and owned or rented up to forty acres of common-field land and for whom enclosure represented high costs, raised rents, an individualistic agriculture, the loss of common pasture and a higher poor rate. Two-thirds of all the owner-occupiers living in West Haddon and Burton Latimer signed the petitions against enclosure sent to the Commons from their parishes in 1764 and 1803.[69] And, despite having no legal claim at enclosure, tenants or men who rented more land than they owned also resisted a change they predicted would raise their rents and deprive them of pasture. John Underwood of West Haddon, who owned eighteen acres and rented another 144, 'at a low price', said he would spend 'a hundred pounds of his own money' to stop the enclosure; and owner-tenants in Welton and Wellingborough sent counter-petitions to Parliament in the same spirit.[70]

The few remnants of the middling yeomanry who owned and

[67] Sources for the study of ownership and waste lands were originals and abstracts of enclosure awards made by J. W. Anscomb for the Northants. RO; Land Tax returns; [Young], *General Report on Enclosures*, supplemented with earlier and later enclosed wastes mentioned in enclosure awards and in Morton, *Natural History*. Landownership was considered consolidated when more than two-thirds of the open-field land belonged to a very small number of owners; it was considered diffuse when a third or more of the land belonged to owners of up to a hundred acres each. Enclosure was resisted in such places because, given the four-fifths or three-quarters rule of thumb, small owners of as much as a third of a parish stood some chance of persuading would-be enclosers to think again. Villages were considered agricultural when 60 per cent or more of their adult male populations were employed in agriculture; they were considered manufacturing and trades villages when less than 40 per cent were so employed; they were considered mixed agricultural and manufacturing when between 40 and 60 per cent of adult males were employed in agriculture: V. A. Hatley, ed., *Northamptonshire Militia Lists, 1777*, Publications of the Northamptonshire Record Society, 25 (1973) supplemented with other Militia Lists where the 1777 lists were incomplete or where enclosure occurred much later. See also Neeson, 'Common Right and Enclosure', pp. 375–88, and 'Opposition to Enclosure in Northamptonshire, c.1760–1800', p. 60 and map 16, p. 61.

[68] Northants. RO, X678, 26 Nov. 1763.

[69] See Chapter 7, pp. 187–220; and Neeson, 'Common Right and Enclosure', pp. 260, 288.

[70] Northants. RO, ZA 9053; *Jls House of Commons*, 22 Jan. 1754, 26 Feb. 1765.

occupied more than fifty acres were not often found in the ranks of enclosure's opponents, nor were landlords of more than fifteen or twenty acres. On the contrary, they hoped to profit from enclosure. In John Clare's opinion they were aspirant 'little tyrants', who dreamt of 'plunder in such rebel schemes' as enclosure and in dreaming forgot the welfare of their servants, labourers and poorer neighbours. In contrast, counter-petitioners were the small landed and land-poor commoners: 'the cottagers, the mechanic, and inferior shop-keepers', the small masters, innkeepers and butchers who used land in their trades; and they were the better-off of the artisans who combined a trade with stock-keeping or subsistence farming – almost half of the weavers and combers in Kilsby occupied land and cottages at enclosure.[71] It was the opinion of the Northamptonshire reporter to the Board of Agriculture that even as little as four acres of good land 'in the present defective common field system' would feed a family of four in the 1790s. Wilbarston counter-petitioners claimed that their 'small quantities' of land provided 'Bread Corn for their severall families' in years of dearth.[72] When they held land, such people were perhaps practitioners of the sort of farming that was 'soonest and most easily performed'.[73] Their land did not always support them entirely, but they were not divorced from the land: their few acres were not an eighteenth-century equivalent of cottage pig-keeping or modern vegetable allotments. Northamptonshire weavers, woolcombers and shoe-makers often had an important stake in land and common rights at enclosure, and said so. But land and rights were crucial supports of an economy dependent on more than land itself. In Northamptonshire the complementary resources were trades, manufactures and seasonal agricultural labour.

Entirely landless labouring families also opposed enclosure. As landless commoners they depended on commons in winter or at times of dearth and decline in trade. They gathered fuel, they gleaned

---

71 Anon., *Political Enquiry into the Consequences of Enclosing Waste Lands*, p. 43; Northants. RO, Land Tax, Kilsby 1772, 1775; Militia List, Kilsby, 1774.

72 Pitt, *General View ... Northampton*, p. 61; Northants. RO, Rockingham Castle MSS, B.7.55, photostat no. 752. And Hoskins, *Midland Peasant*, p. 245, writing of cottagers' and landed labourers' mixed economies, maintains that 'the early eighteenth-century inventories show that this satisfying economy ... was still profoundly characteristic of the open-field villages all over Leicestershire up to the very eve of enclosure'.

73 Samuel Bamford, *The Dialect of South Lancashire* (1850), p. 4, quoted in John Addy, *The Textile Revolution* (1976), doc. 14, p. 76.

after harvest, and their children went nutting and berrying, scared crows from the crops, watched the pigs at mast harvest, tended the sheep and gathered wool from the pastures. Where commons and custom allowed, even the landless put pigs, sheep or cows on to the common pastures. And, in many parts of the country, labouring families feared unemployment would follow enclosure if the clays were turned over to pasture. Commoners in the western uplands were particularly apprehensive and there is some evidence that unemployment did follow enclosure and conversion of arable to pasture there.[74]

Ultimately, appeals to landlords and yeomen to alter or drop their enclosure plans were of no use, and opponents turned instead to resident or neighbouring gentry who were not themselves materially interested in the enclosure, or they depended on their own resources. It seems logical to suppose that an economic independence of enclosing landowners helped those living in manufacturing villages or market towns to oppose enclosure independently. Here an economy of complementary employments freed commoners from complete dependence on landlords and farmers. It gave them versatility of resort in the face of economic hardship or social tyranny. It allowed some freedom of movement, including the power to resist enclosure itself. We have seen that eighteenth-century commentators remarked on this independence and either deplored or celebrated its loss at enclosure: the Shropshire reporter to the Board of Agriculture had observed in 1794 that 'The use of common land by labourers operates upon the mind as a sort of independence', but that after enclosure 'the labourers will work every day in the year, their children will be put out to labour early', and so there would follow that 'subordination of the lower ranks of society which in the present times is so much wanted'.[75] In Northamptonshire John Clare drew the same conclusion with regret:

74 For complaints from Staverton, Raunds, Brigstock, Stanion and Geddington, see pp. 269, 272, 267 and pp. 252–3 above. In Rothwell hundred numbers of labourers in parish Militia Lists fell by half after enclosure; see also Pitt, *General View ... Northampton*, pp. 248–9, for unemployment as a consequence of conversion to pasture; and J. Wedge, *General View of the Agriculture of the County of Warwick* (1794), pp. 21–2, for an account of conversion and unemployment at enclosure in neighbouring south and east Warwickshire driving 'the hardy yeomanry' into the manufacturing towns.
75 Bishton, *General View ... Shropshire*, quoted in Hammond and Hammond, *Village Labourer*, p. 31, and see above, Chapter 1, pp. 28–30; see also Thompson, *Making of the English Working Class*, pp. 242–3 (referring to small farmers and

> Inclosure came and trampled on the grave
> Of labours rights and left the poor a slave
> And memorys pride ere want to wealth did bow
> is both the shadow and the substance now ..[76]

But enclosure was not opposed everywhere. It may be misleading to generalize too far from the random survivals of enclosure protest, but it seems logical that the thinner evidence of resistance in more purely agricultural villages should reflect the truth of less opposition there. Enclosure was probably less disruptive in such places and probably harder to resist too. It was less disruptive because there were fewer wastes left to enclose by the eighteenth century, and because the conversion of arable land to pasture on these lands, lying between the uplands and the Nene valley, was less predictable.[77] It is also possible that land occupancy was more consolidated here, that there were fewer small commoners. These villages were significantly smaller than manufacturing villages, and the strict manorial control which could discourage worsted and shoemaking might have speeded up the disintegration of the co-operative or communal aspects of common-field agriculture.[78] Here substantial piecemeal enclosure of common-field land and the enclosure of uncultivated common may have begun early and proceeded quickly; and a contempt for petty rights may have hastened the wage dependence of agricultural labourers.

Moreover the social solidarities built in manufacturing villages

cottagers as well as labourers): 'To the argument of greed a new argument was added for general enclosure – that of social discipline.'

[76] John Clare, 'The Mores', *Selected Poems and Prose*, p. 170.

[77] At least 36 per cent of open field villages had wastes and commons of more than a hundred acres before enclosure; more would have had field pastures open to cottagers and even the smallest occupiers, but they were found twice as frequently in mixed agricultural and manufacturing/trades villages as in purely agricultural villages. According to [Young], Board of Agriculture *General Report on Enclosures*, parishes in Northamptonshire which lost a minimum of fifty acres to pasture were equally divided between the two economies (nineteen of each) but because there were more agricultural parishes (ratio to mixed non-agricultural parishes was three to two) conversion was more common in the latter. It should be noted that this source probably underestimates conversion in the pre-war enclosure period: see above, Chapter 8, p. 252n.

[78] The average size of the sixty-two mixed agricultural and manufacturing / trades villages in 1801 was 576 inhabitants (calculation excludes towns of 1,600 or more); that of the ninety-six agricultural ones was 354: *Census* (1801), pp. 244ff. Peterborough and the Northamptonshire fenland are not included in this part of the study because Militia Lists giving occupations there survive for 1762 only, whereas most fenland parishes were enclosed after 1800.

through trade associations, Friendly Societies, tramping fraternities, religious dissent, the organization of price setting at times of dearth and the shared regulation of common rights were all replaced in small agricultural villages by an economic dependence on enclosers themselves. Enclosers were more often than not employers and landlords as well.

Resistance here may have been less necessary, or more difficult, but when it occurred it did not take the form of 'covert' rearguard actions alone. Despite their relative scarcity, some very big commons were enclosed here and many small occupiers sold their lands after enclosure went through.[79] In anticipation of this, Staverton's small farmers drew up a local counter-petition, and Sulgrave, Sutton Bassett and Rothersthorpe farmers added their names to parliamentary counter-petitions. Many more refused to sign Bills and managed to delay enclosure. Later on, when covert post-enclosure attacks were made on fences, trees and walls in Duston, Staverton, Warmington and Newnham, the tactic may have been not so much proof of the disorganization and demoralization of these protesters as a reflection of their circumspection and a witness to their determination to punish enclosers.[80]

It is possible to tally the incidents described here, to count the numbers of local and parliamentary counter-petitions, the refusals to sign Bills, the Bills lost or delayed, the letters written to enclosers, the hostile fence-breaking before and after enclosure, the riots, the thefts of boundary marks and field books, the expressions of concern and apprehension found in diaries and poems, the malicious rumours, and the advertisements and letters sent to the *Northampton Mercury*. I have not done so because we cannot know the real dimensions of protest when it is as local as enclosure protest seems to have been: the Raunds riot is known only because a vicar from a

[79] For example, Ravensthorpe commoners lost 920 acres of waste at enclosure, Harpole commoners lost 930 acres, Astrop 800 acres, Warmington 762 acres: [Young], *General Report on Enclosures*; Northants. RO, Anscomb, 'Abstracts of Enclosure Awards'. In Rushden (1778) and Bugbrooke (1779) enclosures, 67 per cent and 59 per cent respectively of landowners sold their lands during the ten years of their enclosures; in Hargrave the proportion was 56 per cent, in Hannington 53 per cent (all these proportions refer to all landowners; proportions of small owners leaving the land were larger): see above, Chapter 8, Table 8.15, p. 242.

[80] Anon., *Reasons Humbly Offered against the Bill for Inclosing ... Stareton*; *Jls House of Commons*, 29 Mar. 1802, 9 Apr. 1806, 29 Mar. 1808, 28 Jan. 1760; *Northampton Mercury*, 11 Dec. 1780, 10 May 1784, 22 Dec. 1777, 5 Aug. 1765.

neighbouring parish wrote a poem about it many years after the event; much fence-breaking evidence turns up only because its victims advertised rewards in the vainest of hopes of attracting an informer; the Staverton counter-petition is known only because it was advertised for sale (and then sold without further trace) in an antiquarian bookseller's list in the 1970s; other counter-petitions survive only because their recipients were the largest of landowners with the largest of muniment rooms, who received enough petitions of all kinds to index them. In fact the only thing it is possible to count with any hope of accuracy is parliamentary activity (counter-petitions and refusals to sign Bills), which is no guide to protest at all. In all, 11 per cent of Bills were petitioned against and 66 per cent of Bills were refused approval by at least one owner; the number of enclosures meeting opposition probably fell somewhere between these two percentages.

But it is also possible (and more useful) to say that enclosure protest was not unusual, in the optimistic historians' sense. It was not typical only of 'special case' places, where very large wastes such as Otmoor in Oxfordshire were lost, or where gross abuses of procedure took place; nor did minority interests such as absentee landlords or large owners of pasture figure as opponents. The many towns and villages in Northamptonshire where we know enclosure was unpopular and resisted were not untypical of others enclosed throughout the lowland Midlands. After all, Northamptonshire itself – with Oxfordshire – was one of the two Midland counties most densely enclosed by Act of Parliament. The evidence of protest in this county seems to suggest that wherever large numbers of small occupiers, cottagers and tenants lived in Midland mixed-farming areas suited to conversion to pasture or convertible husbandry on enclosure, and dependent on field pastures and waste land, enclosure was probably unpopular and possibly resisted.[81]

So enclosure protest was not unusual or atypical, and optimists like Chambers, Tate and Mingay would not have thought it rare had they cast their nets wider. But they were concerned above all to test three pessimistic claims: first, that enclosure destroyed the peasantry as a class; second, that it created an industrial labour supply; and third, that members of Parliament and enclosure commissioners

[81] See Slater, *English Peasantry*, pp. 91–116, for a discussion of the possible extent of conversion and depopulation in the eighteenth century.

dismissed the lawful claims of small owners and cottagers.[82] As a result they did not consider that there might be other sources of hostility to enclosure. For example, they did not look at the sale of land and the turnover of tenancies after enclosure; they seriously underestimated the financial cost of the process; and they focussed primarily on the legal claims of landowners rather than on the equitable claims and accepted practices of the whole spectrum of commoners. All these areas are now under discussion in what may turn out to be a revision of the optimistic orthodoxy – so far as it applies to the Midlands at least. J. M. Martin and M. E. Turner, for example, have shown that enclosure in Warwickshire and Buckinghamshire was more expensive than Tate supposed and fell disproportionately heavily on smaller owners.[83] Turner has demonstrated that enclosure led to the rapid sale of land in Buckinghamshire, and we saw in the last chapter that this was also true of Northamptonshire, where small tenancies also changed hands with the same accelerated speed as rents rose.[84] Martin has found that in areas of Warwickshire prone to enclosure for conversion to pasture, enclosure led to twenty years of unemployment, higher infant mortality and emigration. K. D. M. Snell, in the broadest study to date of the standard of living of the rural poor in this period, has argued a strong connection between enclosure and the unemployment of women and the underemployment of men, and

[82] See especially Chambers, 'Enclosure and Labour Supply', in large part a rebuttal of Marx, Maurice Dobb, and Hermann Levy; Tate, 'Opposition to Parliamentary Enclosure', directed against the 'overdrawn' picture of enclosure opposition found in 'Some well-known and very scholarly books of the left'; Tate, 'Parliamentary Counter-Petitions during the Enclosures of the Eighteenth and Nineteenth Centuries'; W. E. Tate, 'The Cost of Parliamentary Enclosure in England (with Special Reference to the County of Oxford)', *Economic History Review*, 2nd series, 5 (1952–3); Chambers and Mingay, *Agricultural Revolution*, ch. 4. The optimists' revisions are now undergoing revision themselves, for example Chambers' work on labour supply is critically reassessed in N. F. R. Crafts, 'Enclosure and Labour Supply Revisited' *Explorations in Economic History*, 15 (1978); for an argument about enclosure and the end of peasantry see Chapter 10 below; and for an examination of the conflict of interest present in the actions of Warwickshire MPs at enclosure see Martin, 'Members of Parliament and Enclosure'.
[83] Martin, 'Cost of Parliamentary Enclosure in Warwickshire'; Turner, 'Cost of Parliamentary Enclosure in Buckinghamshire'.
[84] Turner, 'Parliamentary Enclosure and Landownership Change in Buckinghamshire', J. M. Neeson, 'Parliamentary Enclosure and the Disappearance of the English Peasantry, Revisited', in George Grantham and Carol S. Leonard, eds., *Agrarian Organization in the Century of Industrialization: Europe, Russia and North America*, Research in Economic History, Supplement 5, part A (1989), and Chapter 8 above.

he and Ann Kussmaul have associated enclosure with the decline of living-in – traditionally a route to landholding for the children of small farmers.[85] All these revisions of the optimists' view of enclosure suggest that it must have been widely unpopular.

Pessimists in the enclosure debate have never doubted enclosure's unpopularity, but they have doubted the ability of small owners, tenants and landless commoners to resist enclosure when faced with both the difficulty of taking opposition to Parliament and the fragmented incidence of enclosure itself. But we have seen that opponents could and did take petitions to Parliament and refused to sign Bills and that the futility of these protests when presented to a Parliament of enclosers may have deterred them far more than their difficulty or cost. Nor was the fragmented incidence of enclosure necessarily an insuperable obstacle. It was no deterrent to the opponents of enclosure in 1607 when they protested (in riots spreading through three Midland counties) at the effect of the repeal of the anti-enclosure statutes. J. E. Martin has told us that the most popular tactic of 1607 was a demonstrative assembly, explicitly directed at the King and his Parliament, during which the fences of recently enclosed, already depopulated villages were destroyed:

> The motivating force which unified the 'demonstrators' was their perception of the extent of enclosure requiring legal redress by the government. Hence they chose to destroy the enclosures in already depopulated parishes ... In rioting, the peasants felt, (as was thought in Kett's rebellion), that they were merely putting the King's law into execution.[86]

Little of this nature happened in the age of parliamentary enclosure. But it would have been remarkable if it had because, as far as small peasants were concerned, the crucial change in relations on the land between the early seventeenth and the mid eighteenth centuries was that the King's law had changed. Parliament increasingly supported the larger landowners; and, in particular, it was no longer hostile to

---

[85] J. M. Martin, 'Marriage and Economic Stress in the Felden of Warwickshire in the Eighteenth Century', *Population Studies*, 31 (1977); Martin, 'Warwickshire and the Parliamentary Enclosure Movement', pp. 147–9, 153–5, 205–6, 215–30; Snell, *Annals*, esp. chs. 2, 4; Kussmaul, *Servants in Husbandry*, esp. pp. 20–1, 171 for an account of the decline of living-in in Northamptonshire: servants in husbandry fell from a third of all farm workers in the 1770s to one fifteenth in 1851.

[86] John E. Martin, 'Peasant and Lord in the Development of Feudalism and the Transition to Capitalism in England' (unpublished Ph.D. thesis, University of Lancaster, 1979), p. 363.

enclosure. Instead, as the century went on, it became more than friendly, thereby ensuring that opposition to enclosure became a local affair between enclosers and their opponents.

III

Parliamentary enclosure marked a turning-point in the social history of many English villages. It struck at the roots of the economy of multiple occupations and it taught the small peasantry the new reality of class relations. John Clare's hatred of its symbol – the newly prosperous, socially aspirant former – is illustration of the growing separation of classes that enclosure embodied:

> That good old fame the farmers earnd of yore
> That made as equals not as slaves the poor
> That good old fame did in two sparks expire
> A shooting coxcomb and a hunting Squire
> And their old mansions that was dignified
> With things far better than the pomp of pride ...
> Where master son and serving man and clown
> Without distinction daily sat them down ...
> These have all vanished like a dream of good ...[87]

Perhaps this separation was a long time coming. But until enclosure it was masked by other relationships born of customary agricultural regulation and shared use-rights over land. The organization of work in the common-field system encouraged co-operation; and defence of common rights required the protection of lesser rights as well as greater. Enclosure tore away this mask not only to reveal more clearly than before the different interests of small, middling and large landowners but also to profit one at the expense of the other. It did so in a remarkably public way. In one ten-year period of village life, access to cheap land was at an end (rents commonly doubled or tripled at enclosure), lands were sold or mortgaged and wastes were fenced. The hostility to enclosure shown in Northamptonshire indicates that small owners knew how they lost their lands; that cottagers and landless commoners made no mistake about how they lost their winter fuel, the grazing for a cow and calf or a few sheep, the feed for pigs and geese. Enclosure had a terrible

---

[87] John Clare, 'The Parish: A Satire', in *Selected Poems of John Clare*, ed. Elaine Feinstein (London, 1968), p. 46.

but instructive visibility. It was seen in the societies and economies as well as in the landscapes of these Midland villages. Knowing this, David Hennell, a lace dealer living in Wollaston, Northamptonshire, wrote in his diary on the eve of Wollaston's enclosure: 'I lament that this field is now agoing to be enclosed. Some that have large quantities of land are set upon it, and pay no regard to the many little ones that may be injured, and I fear many ruined.'[88] The collective memory of the 'many little ones' informed all their social relations in the enclosed village in the years that followed.

There are two points. The first is that the deep hostility generated by enclosure was as corrosive of social relations as signing a petition or pulling down fences. The second is that counting signatures and riots is a wretchedly inadequate guide to the level of hatred in villages after enclosure. (It makes as much sense to measure the incidence of dearth by counting the number of food riots.) If protest is hard to quantify, a sense of injustice is harder. But it was surely more general and more long-lived than resistance. Resistance in the shape of petitions, riots and malicious damage required opportunity and a promise of satisfaction. As time went on both receded. Injustice is not always resisted; therefore to use resistance to measure it is absurd. Where would Norfolk incendiarism have been without the invention of the friction match?[89] But, with the match or without it, Norfolk labourers felt the same anger. In an effort to assert the consciousness of working men and women we have used the incidence of protest as a proxy to measure feeling. It can only underestimate it. Very often it required opportunity or the legitimizing blessing of authority – the moral economy shared with the gentry, the nationalism of the Irish rural arsonist.

Resistance is no guide to the extent of hostility to enclosure. The sense of loss, the sense of *robbery* could last forever as the bitter inheritance of the rural poor. For example, of all the verses of village poetry (and all the comment on enclosure) to survive into the twentieth century the rhyme about the common stolen from the goose must rank among the best known. It says nothing about riot but it says much about injustice:

[88] Amy Wichello, *Annals of Wollaston* (1930), p. 37.
[89] John Archer, *By a Flash and a Scare. Incendiarism, Animal Maiming, and Poaching in East Anglia 1815–1870* (Oxford, 1990), p. 73.

> The fault is great in man or woman
> Who steals a goose from off a common;
> But what can plead that man's excuse
> Who steals a common from a goose?[90]

Other counties have histories of resistance to parliamentary enclosure too, enough to lead a recent reviewer to conclude that 'peasant opposition has been badly underestimated'.[91] No doubt these histories of resistance vary, but it is unlikely that in any of them commoners found much protection in Parliament. It follows that in the eighteenth century resistance became local as a general rule.

When it did commoners had a tradition of negotiation over common right and of resistance to earlier enclosure to call upon.[92] In an earlier chapter we saw how Chippenham commoners reclaimed turbary in the 1830s, more than a generation after the parliamentary enclosure of the parish and the draining of some of the fen. They reopened the fen common, dug up soil, mowed grass, threatened the tenant, and when they were arrested they found counsel to act for them. But almost exactly two hundred years earlier other Chippenham commoners had resisted fen drainage in much the same way. They attacked the new works as they were put in, and when they were near completion some of them who were employed to deepen the river bed began 'flinging in the earth which they were paid to fling out'.[93] Common memory was long in English common-field villages – as it is in many peasant societies – and sharing or working common land strengthened it and made resisting enclosure easier.

[90] There are several versions, all questioning the justice of this kind of theft; this early nineteenth-century one is from *The Oxford University Press Dictionary of Quotations*, ed. B. Mitchell (2nd edn, Oxford, 1953; 1985), p. 10, citing *The Tickler Magazine*, 1 Feb. 1821.

[91] M. E. Turner, 'Benefits but at cost', in George Grantham and Carol S. Leonard, eds., *Agrarian Organization in the Century of Industrialization: Europe, Russia, and North America*, Research in Economic History, Supplement 5, Part A, (1989), p. 64. Discussions of resistance in counties other than Northamptonshire may be found in: Martin, 'Warwickshire and the Parliamentary Enclosure Movement'; Turner, 'Some Social and Economic Considerations of Parliamentary Enclosure in Buckinghamshire'; Martin, 'Members of Parliament and Enclosure', pp. 107–8; M. E. Turner, 'Economic Protest in a Rural Society: Opposition to Parliamentary Enclosure in Buckinghamshire', *Southern History*, 10 (1988).

[92] See above Chapter 3, pp. 100–1, 107–8, Chapter 5, pp. 153–6.

[93] Cambs. RO, R 55 7.117.16; and PRO, PC 2/40, f.239, cited in Keith J. Lindley, *Fenland Riots and the English Revolution* (1982), p. 41; and see above, pp. 75–7; for the effect of drainage on a commoning economy see Joan Thirsk, *English Peasant Farming*, pp. 118–19.

The 'argument' commoners shared when they organized common-field agriculture, and the alliances they made to protect customary rights, establish new usages, and to resist unregulated or parliamentary enclosure, have histories too. At parliamentary enclosure it is clear that commoners were divided. In Northamptonshire, occupiers of less than forty acres and landless commoners opposed enclosure, owners and tenants of more land than this supported it. Small commoners could no longer count on Lords of Manors, Impropriators of tithes and their vicars, or the middling and largest occupying commoners to protect common right. Such alliances had occurred in the past both in the daily regulation of agriculture and in disputes over trespass or intercommoning with neighbouring parishes, but at enclosure this common interest disappeared. The significance of that disappearance is the subject of the following chapter.

III

Conclusion

10. 'Making freeman of the slave'

Im swordy well a piece of land
Thats fell upon the town
Who worked me till I couldnt stand
& crush me now Im down

There was a time my bit of ground
Made freeman of the slave
The ass no pindard dare to pound
When I his supper gave

The gipseys camp was not affraid
I made his dwelling free
Till vile enclosure came & made
A parish slave of me

Alas dependance thou'rt a brute
Want only understands
His feelings wither branch & root
That falls in parish hands

From John Clare 'The Lament of Swordy Well', *c.*1822

Commoners were not labourers. Their defenders and critics agreed on this. Some laboured, some earned wages, but even they were independent of the wage. Their lands and common rights gave them a way of life quite unlike that of the agricultural labourers, outworkers or smallholders they might become at enclosure. Defining exactly what commoners were is difficult but it is important. They were peasants. I call them that reluctantly, but necessarily. The value of the name is that it emphasizes a continuity with the past, a continuity based on the occupancy of land and rights in the common-field system.

There are other words. As an alternative to peasant I could call commoners 'cottagers' as some contemporaries did. But in common-right terms 'cottager' has a very specific meaning; to use it here would be to exclude many commoners who were not cottagers.[1] Moreover, for all that Gregory King used it in 1688 to describe the very poor, cottager has a late eighteenth- and early nineteenth-century ring to it. It has an enclosure commissioner's stamp on it. Old Sally and her husband Dick in Flora Thompson's *Lark Rise* were cottagers. They were thrifty, and their dealings were often outside the cash nexus (they kept bees, brewed beer, had a large garden and a field), and they deplored farm labourers' big families. But they were remarkable because they were the only people behaving like this. They kept a cow, which gave them a tremendous advantage. But no one else did. They were cottagers because Sally's father was a commoner compensated at enclosure.[2] Sally's parents, not Sally and Dick, were commoners and peasants. 'Cottager' in the late eighteenth and nineteenth centuries carries an exclusivity and a privilege, and also an isolation, a minority status, that was less evident (though not absent) before enclosure. Worse, when both Thompson and Gregory King use it, it excludes any reference to common-field landholding or common right. It ignores all the reciprocity, the village dealing, the sense of self, the willingness to argue, the craft, the alliance with one lord against another, the collective celebration, collective memory and mutual aid properly associated with peasants, and with commoners.

In calling commoners peasants I am not saying that eighteenth-century England was feudal, that most agricultural production in unenclosed parishes was peasant. Clearly, it was not. I am aware also of the economic relations between commoners of the small peasant kind and their big tenant neighbours inside the village and in enclosed villages nearby. I am aware too of the important role of rural manufacturing in reinforcing and supporting or undercutting the power of this peasantry. Nor am I defining an ideal type when I call eighteenth-century commoners peasants. They were a very particular kind of English peasant, with a particular economy and culture. For that reason they are called commoners not peasants throughout this book. But they are the descendants of other English peasantries, not a rootless eighteenth-century phenomenon.

[1] See above, Chapter 2, pp. 61–4.
[2] Thompson, *Lark Rise to Candleford*, pp. 76–81.

It is necessary to make this point because orthodox enclosure history does not. It has turned the eighteenth century into a transit camp for peasant refugees from the seventeenth century. *Then* they were peasants, *now* they are cottagers waiting to disappear. In this chapter I want to argue that to deny the peasant nature of eighteenth-century commoners is to misunderstand what happened to them when the commons disappeared.

PEASANTS AND HISTORIANS

Defining a peasantry is difficult work. As a class it is rightly called awkward.[3] It lived too long, it changed too much in the process, its economic identity is unclear.[4] On the whole, historians avoid defining it at all. Most use the term to mean small landholders and leave it at that. The most common image is not of a class but of an individual, a small owner-occupier who looks remarkably like a modern small farmer.[5] He is self-sufficient and needs no other source of income. Should he rent land his tenure is secure, and his legal rights are growing. He has little to fear from parliamentary enclosure, but he *is* vulnerable to poor harvests, low prices and the sharpening appetite of the land market. In all, he is a very insular type, quite unlike his French counterpart, or his Irish. In general, we see not even as clear an image as this. Definitions are implied, not stated.

Given the difficulty of defining a peasantry, it may be wise, as Mick Reed has suggested, to begin by writing the histories of peasants instead.[6] And to define peasants themselves in broad terms. In the early modern period common-field peasants appear to have had at least three characteristics. First, they owned or occupied land and got their living from it. But the living they got did not enable them to accumulate much capital because their holdings were

---

[3] Teodor Shanin, *The Awkward Class: Political Sociology of Peasantry in a Developing Society: Russia 1910–25* (Oxford, 1972).

[4] Judith Ennew, Paul Hirst and Keith Tribe, '"Peasantry" as an Economic Category', *Journal of Peasant Studies*, 4 (1977).

[5] For example, Mingay writes about 'the peasantry proper, the small owner-occupiers': *Enclosure and the Small Farmer*, p. 9. Robert W. Malcolmson defines the lowest level of landed society to include only those with secure tenures living on a 'more or less self-sufficient farm', not cottagers or 'smallholders with one or two acres': Malcolmson, *Life and Labour in England, 1700–1780* (1981), p. 24. Scottish peasants have fared better: see Carter, *Farm Life in North-East Scotland*.

[6] Reed, 'The Peasantry of Nineteenth-Century England', pp. 70–1.

often very small, and rent, taxes and tithe creamed off any surplus.
And the degree of support they got from the land varied, not only
over the long term, from the sixteenth to the nineteenth century, but
also over the short term, through life-cycles, from decade to decade,
and from generation to generation. It follows that occupiers who
were also artisans, or who worked for a wage, and landless users of
common rights were peasants too.[7] Second, peasants worked the
land themselves, rarely employing anyone else for wages, though
probably depending on neighbours and friends at particular seasons
such as ploughing, lambing and harvest, and in widow- or widower-
hood and old age. And third, common-field peasants shared a
common culture. Their common rights supported customary
behaviour, joint agricultural practice, mutual aid, and, on occasion,
a sense of political solidarity.

It is also important to define what these peasants were not.
Always numerous, they were no longer a majority of the rural
population, although they had been once, and they still represented
the largest landholding group. Nor did they control either a majority of the land or of agricultural production. Consequently, neither
peasant production nor taxes were crucial to the state, and peasant
rents were only a part of the income on which landlords depended.[8]
In the eighteenth century English peasants were no longer revenue
and, in the Midlands at least, enclosure would ensure that they
never became scenery.[9]

Despite our reluctance to define them (or perhaps because of it), it
has become conventional wisdom that by the late seventeenth or

[7] Support for the idea that peasants might also labour is found in Shanin, *Peasants
and Peasant Societies*, pp. 14–16: in particular his comment that 'The definition of a
"general" type leads to a further delineation of *analytically marginal groups* which
share with the "hard core" of peasants most, but not all, of their characteristics. In
general, such differences can be presented on quantitative scales of more / less.
*Analytical marginality does not here in any sense imply numerical insignificance or
some particular lack of stability*' (my italics). His examples are agricultural labourers and rural artisans with land insufficient to provide complete subsistence. See
too J. Thirsk, 'Seventeenth-Century Agriculture and Social Change', in Thirsk ed.,
Land, Church and People. Essays Presented to Professor H. P. R. Finberg (Reading,
1970), p. 172. Even medieval peasants laboured: see R. H. Hilton, 'Lord and
Peasant in Staffordshire in the Middle Ages', *North Staffordshire Journal of Field
Studies*, 10 (1970), p. 7; in 1300 half-virgators (holders of twelve to fifteen acres of
land) in Kibworth Harcourt 'relied more or less heavily on supplementary earnings' to get money with which to pay rent: Cicely Howell, *Land, Family and
Inheritance in Transition* (Cambridge, 1983), pp. 167–8, 195.
[8] Cf. Hanawalt, *The Ties that Bound*, p. 5.
[9] Jeanette Winterson, *The Passion* (1987), p. 16.

early eighteenth century most English peasants had disappeared. I want to start by looking at this orthodoxy.

In *Captain Swing*, their study of agricultural labour and rural riot in 1830, Eric Hobsbawm and George Rudé open by saying that 'Agricultural England in the nineteenth century presented a unique and amazing spectacle to the enquiring foreigner: it had no peasants.'[10] The English peasantry had gone by 1750 at the latest, certainly 'before the start of the Industrial Revolution'. They make it clear that not only did the transition from feudalism to agrarian capitalism not take place in the eighteenth century, but not even so much as a transition from family subsistence cultivation to wage dependency took place then either.[11] Naturally, Ireland was an exception: peasants *did* survive in Ireland. They survived too in the 'thinly-populated' parts of Wales and Scotland, 'perhaps in parts of Northern England', and in 'local concentrations' elsewhere. But in most of England the rural proletariat was in place by 1750. Any peasants or smallholders hanging on later than this were, in Hobsbawm and Rudé's words, only 'unimportant minorities'.[12]

As evidence for this proposition they cite a rare convergence of opinion between most contemporary historians and Karl Marx.[13] And, indeed it is true that, while citing Marx, Hobsbawm and Rudé were at the same time expressing what had become, by the 1960s, the orthodox view of English landed society in the eighteenth century. The ultimate success of this orthodoxy was the work of J. D.

[10] Though Henry Meister in 1792 saw some: he noted the prevalence of commons and heaths, grass and sheep, and comfortable cottages in *Letters Written during a Residence in England* (1792), cited in R. Bayne-Powell, *Travellers in Eighteenth-Century England* (1951), p. 147. Also see Reed, 'A Neglected Class.''

[11] On an eighteenth-century transition see C. Searle, 'Custom, Class Conflict and Agrarian Capitalism: The Cumbrian Customary Economy in the Eighteenth Century', *Past and Present*, 110 (1986).

[12] Hobsbawm and Rudé, *Captain Swing*, pp. 23, 27, 21; see also E. J. Hobsbawm, *Industry and Empire* (1968), p. 78, for a similar thesis but a different terminal date: 'The fundamental structure of landownership and farming was already established by the mid-eighteenth century, and certainly by the early decades of the Industrial Revolution. England was a country of mainly large landlords, cultivated by tenant farmers working the land with hired labourers. This structure was still partly hidden by an undergrowth of economically marginal cottager-labourers, or other small independents and semi-independents, but this should not obscure the fundamental transformation which had already taken place. By 1790 ... a "peasantry" in the usual sense of the word no longer existed.'

[13] They note Marx's agreement that the landlord / tenant / labourer structure had been established before the start of the Industrial Revolution on p. 27; the reference is to Marx, *Werke*, XXIII, p. 750.

Chambers and G. E. Mingay, whose view of commons we have
encountered already. Although they identified the survival of large
numbers of *smallholders* into the mid nineteenth century, Chambers
and Mingay argued that the disappearance of the peasantry occurred before 1760. Thus early in the eighteenth century crippling
war-time taxation and low agricultural prices led to debt. Then
harvest failure, disease, and the competing attractions of trade and
industry accelerated decline. For some time small owners' land had
swelled the estates of the great landlords, but the trend became
marked in the first half of the century, and again in the depression
after the Napoleonic Wars. Mingay fixed the date more firmly in
*Enclosure and the Small Farmer in the Age of the Industrial Revo-
lution*: 'The major decline of small owners and of small farmers in
general must have occurred before 1760, probably between about
1660 and 1750.'[14]

Coupled with the older work of Johnson, Davies, Gonner and
Clapham, Chambers and Mingay, with the help of W. E. Tate,
managed finally to uproot the Hammond thesis that Parliamentary
enclosure starting in the second half of the eighteenth century was a
major cause of the disappearance of the English peasantry.[15]

The popularization of this view was so complete that ten years
after *The Agricultural Revolution*, in a discussion of rural social
protest from 1700 to 1850, Roger Wells could call it 'an elementary
fact in English agricultural history', that the 'vast bulk of the
inhabitants of the English countryside since the mid eighteenth
century were landless agricultural labourers and their families, who
have been described – with some economic justification – as "the
only real Marxian proletariat that England ever had".' This view
was shared by Corrigan and Sayer, sociologists otherwise aware of
the 'remarkable continuities' of English history in other respects. It
was the view too of Harold Perkin, who considered peasantry to be

---

[14] Chambers and Mingay, *Agricultural Revolution*, p. 19, 20; Mingay, *Enclosure and
the Small Farmer*, pp. 9, 31–2; the evidence cited came from Mingay's study of
estates in Nottinghamshire, Staffordshire, Bedfordshire and Sussex published in
'The Size of Farms in the Eighteenth Century', *Economic History Review*, 2nd
series, 14 (1961–2).

[15] Johnson, *Disappearance of the Small Landowner*; Gonner, *Common Land*;
Clapham, *Economic History of Modern Britain*, I; Tate, 'Opposition to Parlia-
mentary Enclosure'; 'Parliamentary Counter-Petitions'; Hammond and
Hammond, *Village Labourer*.

the antithesis of progress, and found none in Britain except on the 'Celtic fringe', where they lived 'still half-immersed in tribalism, dominated by near-feudal or alien landlords ... and almost without the varied, prosperous, energetic "middle ranks" which characterized Anglo-Saxon England'.[16] Even K. D. M. Snell, in a vindication of the Hammonds' interpretation of enclosure's 'social effects', remained unsure of the relationship between enclosure and peasant disappearance. His concern was with the 'cottager and other labouring classes'. Apart from a rejection of the Land Tax, which ignored the work of Turner and Martin, he did not talk about land at all.[17]

And, if historians of the eighteenth and nineteenth centuries have described them as centuries without peasants, historians of the seventeenth have assumed that the end of the English peasantry occurred then too. Robert Brenner argues his case for the determining power of class politics in effecting the different development of England and the rest of Europe partly from an assumption that the English peasantry not only lost political power in the sixteenth and seventeenth centuries but also ceased to exist.[18] In part this is due to the way agrarian history has been written as the history of individual villages. Thus in the last twenty years we have read that Terling, Chippenham, Orwell and Kibworth Harcourt all lost their peasants early. And we generalize their experience to the rest of England. But if we see only the early modernization of Kibworth we

16 Wells, 'The Development of the English Rural Proletariat and Social Protest', p. 115, quoting J. P. D. Dunbabin, *Rural Discontent in Nineteenth-Century Britain* (1974), p. 286. In their discussion of the slow progress of enclosure between the sixteenth and the nineteenth, even twentieth, centuries Philip Corrigan and Derek Sayer nevertheless found Wells' article 'very useful': see *The Great Arch: English State Formation as Cultural Revolution* (1985), p. 96, n. 9. Another example of the influence of this view is James Obelkevich, *Religion and Rural Society: South Lindsey 1825–1875* (1976), p. 25, which cites Hobsbawm and Rudé, *Captain Swing*, Chambers and Mingay, *Agricultural Revolution*, and John Saville, 'Primitive Accumulation and Early Industrialization in Britain', in R. Miliband and J. Saville, eds., *Socialist Register* (1979). Harold Perkin, *The Origins of Modern English Society, 1780–1880* (1969), pp. 91, 97: this repudiation of peasantry as an un-English phenomenon anticipates Alan MacFarlane's *The Origins of Modern English Individualism* (Oxford, 1978); on this see Philip Abrams, *Historical Sociology* (Shepton Mallet, 1982), pp. 322–5.
17 Snell, *Annals*, pp. 143–4.
18 Robert Brenner, 'Agrarian Class Structure and Economic Development in Pre-Industrial Europe', *Past and Present*, 70 (1976), pp. 63–4, 70.

forget the eighteenth-century 'peasant system' of Wigston Magna lying just six or seven miles away.[19]

If I overstate the case, if I ignore the work of Alan Everitt on farm labourers-with-land in the seventeenth century, and of Joan Thirsk on the Lincolnshire peasantry and E. P. Thompson on the history of the field labourers, it is because others have done so too.[20] The examples I have given (the most widely used textbook on the agricultural revolution, an influential study of rural social protest in the early nineteenth century, one of the most provocative recent historical debates, and the most detailed monographs of sixteenth and seventeenth-century lowland English villages) are themselves evidence that the work of Everitt, Thirsk, Hoskins and Thompson, in this respect, has been by-passed. In Hobsbawm and Rudé's terms, they have described the histories of unimportant minorities found only here and there in local concentrations.

And yet there are at least two reasons why we owe the question a little more of our attention. First, it is possible to show that a large landholding population *did* survive in much of eighteenth- and early nineteenth-century common-field England. Second, a majority of these landholders shared an economy grounded in communal land use until parliamentary enclosure. England may well have had an eighteenth-century peasantry after all.

PEASANTS AND LAND

More than thirty years ago, W. G. Hoskins showed that in Wigston Magna, Leicestershire, on the eve of enclosure in 1765, no less than half of the population occupied some land, and half the population owned it.[21] But Wigston Magna, though large and located in an area

---

[19] Keith Wrightson and David Levine, *Poverty and Piety in an English Village: Terling 1525–1700* (1979); Spufford, *Contrasting Communities*, esp. pp. 50, 118, 165–6; Howell, *Land, Family and Inheritance*, p. 69; see also A. C. Chibnall, *Sherington: Fields and Fiefs of a Buckinghamshire Village* (Cambridge, 1965); Hoskins, *Midland Peasant* (the term is his, p. 215). The records of early enclosed or engrossed villages may also survive more plentifully than those of villages of diffuse landholding, so encouraging their more thorough study.

[20] Everitt, 'Farm Labourers', pp. 396–465; Thirsk, *English Peasant Farming*, and 'Agriculture and Social Change in the Seventeenth Century', in Thirsk, ed., *Land, Church and People* (1970), pp. 172, 176–7; Thompson, *Making of the English Working Class*, ch. 7.

[21] Hoskins, *Midland Peasant*, pp. 217–18. Out of 200 families, 99 owned land; while the number of occupiers is unknown it was at least 99 when the smallest occupiers are included.

typical of much of the land lying along the borders of Leicestershire, Warwickshire and Northamptonshire, is only one village, and it was enclosed in 1765. It could be a local concentration, and one not surviving much after Hobsbawm and Rudé's mid century terminus. It seems important then to look at larger numbers of villages and to look at them later in the century.

Until Mingay's criticism of Johnson's use of Land Tax returns was published in the mid 1960s, this would have been a relatively simple thing to do using studies like Johnson's, Gray's on Oxfordshire, and Davies' national survey. But Mingay's discovery that different parishes had different tax rates, coupled with Chambers' observation that small owners appearing on Land Tax evidence after enclosure were untaxed cottagers and commoners before – and more recent criticism – makes using earlier work hazardous.[22] Since then landholding history has necessarily become parish rather than county based, leading to a fragmentation of information that makes generalization difficult. Accordingly, I look again at the enclosure records and Land Tax and census returns of twenty-three unenclosed parishes in Northamptonshire in the period 1778–1815 – the parishes examined in the study of landholding and enclosure described in Chapter 8.[23]

They suggest that a large proportion of the population held land in late eighteenth- and early nineteenth-century common-field Northamptonshire. In fact, proportions of occupiers and landlords ranged from a minimum of 22 per cent of the population of a parish to a maximum of 73 per cent. Expressed as a proportion of the total population of these villages in 1801, landholders were 53 per cent, or, as in Wigston Magna, roughly half of the population.[24] Largest proportions occurred in fenland parishes. But, if fen parishes are

22 Davies, 'The Small Landowner, 1780–1832'; Johnson, *Disappearance of the Small Landowner*; H. L. Gray, 'Yeoman Farming in Oxfordshire from the Sixteenth Century to the Nineteenth', *Quarterly Journal of Economics*, 24 (1910); Mingay, 'The Land Tax Assessments'; Chambers, 'Enclosure and the Small Landowner'; Chambers, 'Enclosure and the Small Landowner in Lindsey'; and see above, Chapter 8, pp. 245–6.

23 For a discussion of the basis of their selection see above Chapter 8, pp. 221–5; for a discussion of the use of the Land Tax in this chapter see above pp. 228n, 245–7, and below, Appendices A, B and C.

24 Total population of the twenty-three villages, using the 1801 census, was 9,087; divided by a (conservative) family-size factor of 4.3, this becomes 2,113. Total landholders on the Land Tax returns for the parishes was 1,112, or 53 per cent of the total population.

excluded, the proportion of landholders in all the other parishes falls no further than to 49 per cent, so proportions were high outside the fens too.[25] The numbers of landholders in Nene valley parishes, for example, often exceeded half.[26] The size of this landed population indicates how deeply landholding was still imbricated in the rural economy. If proportions like these were observed of shoe-makers or weavers instead of landholders we would consider the economy to be dominated by rural manufacturing.

The impression of a lasting connection between population and land strengthens when we consider *small* landholders separately. I shall define 'small' to be fifty acres or less, an amount large enough to include family farms providing subsistence, but not the farms of substantial owner-occupiers or large tenants.[27] It is also a category which includes the smallest occupiers and users of common right who were only partly supported by their holdings, and it would include some landed artisans and tradesmen too. Defined like this, small landholders were 35 per cent of the total population; small occupiers were 22 per cent. And these average figures underestimate the degree of sub-fifty-acre occupancy in a third of the villages in the study.[28]

There are obvious shortcomings in a calculation like this and these figures are offered as no more than very rough estimates. Quite apart from the deficiencies of the 1801 census, numbers of landhold-ers taken from the tax returns may be inflated by the inclusion of absentee landlords and non-resident occupiers. They are deflated by the omission of sub-tenants and some poor owners of less than three

[25] Total population in 1801, excluding the three fen parishes of Eye, Maxey and Helpston, was 7,972 or 1,854 families. Total landholding families were 909 or 49 per cent of the population.

[26] They were Wollaston (67 per cent), Hargrave (73 per cent), Stanwick (60 per cent), Lutton (58 per cent). Large proportions were also found in villages on the scarp (Kilsby, West Haddon, Yelvertoft – evidence from other sources); and in Abthorpe (69 per cent) and Roade (55 per cent) on the boundaries of Whittlewood and Salcey Forests. But not all forest parishes were populated by large numbers of landholders: Whitfield and Whittlebury, both in Whittlewood Forest, had below average numbers.

[27] See also Allen, 'The Growth of Labour Productivity in Early Modern English Agriculture', University of British Columbia, Department of Economics, Discussion Paper no. 86–40, pp. 5–6: Allen suggests that farms worked with largely family labour were no bigger than fifty to sixty acres.

[28] Total of sub-fifty-acre occupiers was 467 (22 per cent); total of sub-fifty-acre landlords was 282 (13 per cent). For the range from parish to parish see Appendix D.

acres or so.[29] And they are deflated again because the landholding figures of some parishes predate the census significantly: the chances are good that their populations had grown by 1801.[30]

Having said that, the Northamptonshire evidence still suggests that there was a substantial number of small owners and occupiers among the roughly 50 per cent of the population who held land in late eighteenth-century open-field villages. And evidence from nineteenth-century villages corroborates this. Mick Reed has gone so far as to argue that a substantial peasantry survived well into the second half of that century, and that, again, it was not one confined in the outer darkness of the 'Celtic fringe'. *Where* this peasantry survived, and what the strength of its relationship was to labouring families both need elaboration. Certainly it was smaller than its eighteenth-century counterpart. But it seems reasonable to assume that in areas of unenclosed waste, or in still-open common-field villages where land remained cheap and both landed and landless commoners were numerous, a peasant economy could continue. Bourne's Surrey heathland village survived as late as 1900.[31] And there are other reasons why a peasantry might survive into the nineteenth century: Ian Carter's work on Aberdeenshire describes a Scottish peasantry living into the 1870s in symbiosis with much larger tenants, who needed them in order to reclaim land.[32] None of these places was enclosed by Act of Parliament.

Although a substantial *number* of peasants lived in open-field England in the eighteenth and early nineteenth centuries, it should be made clear that they were not the occupiers of most of the land. The rural economy was not primarily a peasant one in 1750 for a number of reasons. First, the middling peasant occupiers of forty to eighty acres were relatively few. Second, the small peasantry that

---

[29] For the deficiencies of the Land Tax in omitting sub-letting and the poorest owners see above, Chapter 2, pp. 60–1, and below, Appendix A, pp. 340–1.

[30] The parishes were Rushden (1774), Bugbrooke (1774), Wollaston (1783), Roade (1786) and Wadenhoe (1788).

[31] M. Reed, 'Nineteenth-Century Rural England: A Case for "Peasant Studies"?', *Journal of Peasant Studies*, 14 (1986), and 'The Peasantry of Nineteenth-Century England'. For the use of common land by nineteenth-century labourers and small farmers see also Brian Short, '"The Art and Craft of Chicken Cramming": Poultry in the Weald of Sussex', *Agricultural History Review*, 30 (1982), p. 17. For unenclosed forest commons and their effect on landholding in neighbouring enclosed villages see Chapter 8, pp. 233–4; for the importance of landless and landed commoners for the working of mutual aid see Chapter 6, pp. 180–4, and Chapter 8 pp. 255–8. See too Bourne, *Change in the Village*.

[32] Carter, *Farm Life in North-East Scotland*, pp. 52–60.

remained, though numerous, did not control a majority of the land. Owner-occupiers and tenants of fifty acres or less usually held no more than perhaps a quarter or a third of all the land in open-field villages. For example, in Wigston a large majority of occupiers (of the order of 75 per cent) held less than fifty acres each, and most worked less than twelve. Together they held a little more than 20 per cent of the land in the parish. In Cumbria the proportion was about a third. In Oxfordshire Gray noted that one third of the county was in the hands of owner-occupiers of all sizes. Hunt calculated that in Leicestershire 32 per cent of the land in forty-four enclosures belonged to small owners.[33] But even these proportions are larger than the 10 to 20 per cent sometimes assumed to be general and proportions would rise if small tenants were included.[34] In fact proportions were not much smaller than in parts of France at the same time: Arthur Young estimated that one third of France lay in the hands of peasant proprietors in the 1780s.[35]

The evidence from these counties makes it clear that small occupiers did not hold most of the land, although they did hold more than we have supposed. In terms of productive power, in Northamptonshire, Oxfordshire and Leicestershire, most production came from farms of at least one hundred acres in the hands of tenants or freeholders. But it is equally clear that access to land was not restricted to these farmers. Instead, a substantial proportion of a village held land, fed itself to some degree, and supplied young stock to farmers and food to local markets.[36]

---

[33] Hoskins, *Midland Peasant*, p. 219: peasant farms of 100 acres or less comprised 30 per cent of the parish. Searle, 'Custom, Class Conflict and Agrarian Capitalism', p. 1; Hunt, 'Landownership and Enclosure', pp. 499–501.

[34] Citing F. M. L. Thompson's interpretation of Gregory King's figures of income from land, Mingay suggests that owner-occupiers received about one third of the income from land at the end of the seventeenth century. His own investigations suggest that 10 to 20 per cent of the cultivated acreage was in the hands of owner-occupiers at the end of the eighteenth century. A rough alignment of income and landownership suggests a fall in landownership or landed income to owner-occupiers of from 30 per cent in the 1680s to 20 per cent or even 10 per cent in the late eighteenth century. Northamptonshire evidence of owner-occupancy in the later eighteenth century suggests that owner-occupiers still held a third of the land or more on the eve of enclosure: Mingay, *Enclosure and the Small Farmer*, pp. 13–16.

[35] Arthur Young, *Travels During the Years 1787, 1788 and 1789; undertaken more particularly with a view of ascertaining the cultivation, wealth, resources, and national prosperity of the Kingdom of France* (2nd edn, 1794), I, p. 412.

[36] On the late survival of peasantry and its coexistence with capitalism in agriculture see the review essay by H. Newby, 'Rural Sociology and its Relevance to the

How would historians who describe a relatively peasantless eighteenth century view these commoners? They would argue that, although commoners were more numerous than they had thought, they were not peasants. Instead, they were one of two distinct groups: they were either smallholders, or they were labourers-with-land. In the case of smallholders, there is some disagreement about both their numbers and the nature of their economies.[37] The disagreement need not detain us here; what matters is that all agree that smallholders in no way represented a substantial proportion of a village population by the middle of the eighteenth century.

They would also agree that the second group, the labourers-with-land, were more numerous than smallholders. Nevertheless, in their case, *poverty* rules them out as contenders for peasant status. Holding less than a farm, and working for wages seemingly disqualify small landholders from peasant status in England (though not apparently in Ireland), despite the fact that peasants have often needed multiple sources of income, including wages, from whatever source.[38] Hobsbawm and Rudé describe a more abject poverty, an independence that was only precarious, and, again, survival on the meagre proceeds of labour and the right to keep sheep, pigs, a cow or some geese on the common waste. Enclosure, when it came, would administer the *coup de grace*: dissipating 'the haze which surrounded rural poverty' it would leave that poverty 'nakedly visible as propertyless labour'.[39]

But the evidence of petty landholding suggests a different view. A large number of families in common-field England lived, in part, off the income from working or letting very small amounts of land: at least a third of the population of the open-field Midlands did so. It seems unlikely that they were confined to this region alone. Within

Agricultural Economist: A Review', *Journal of Agricultural Economics*, 33 (1982), pp. 141–2.

[37] Chambers and Mingay, for example, have argued that although they had declined in the early eighteenth century and could no longer be called a peasantry they were still numerous and were real farmers, if small. Hobsbawm and Rudé, Harold Perkin and others have argued that there were relatively few of them, and that they were largely involved in trade, using land only as an adjunct to it. Hobsbawm and Rudé go on to say that these men did not think of themselves as farmers: Chambers and Mingay, *Agricultural Revolution*, pp. 88–9; Hobsbawm and Rudé, *Captain Swing*, p. 24; Perkin, *Origins of Modern English Society*, pp. 91, 97; Martin, 'Village Traders and the Emergence of a Proletariat in South Warwickshire'.

[38] Chambers and Mingay, *Agricultural Revolution*, p. 88.

[39] Hobsbawm and Rudé, *Captain Swing*, p. 35.

open-field England the same kinds of small peasant economies probably stippled the clays, the loams and the downs; and they characterized heathland, forest and fen more thoroughly. Outside the lowlands, the more plentiful common waste of highland England and Wales supported more again.

But the question for these historians is 'Were they poor?'. We must forget for the moment that peasants often *are* poor and instead assess the value of a couple of acres in the eighteenth century. (If we take as small an acreage as this we can assume that larger holdings were correspondingly more useful.)

First, a couple of acres would keep a cow, if the cow could be bought. A cow in the middle of the eighteenth century cost anything from 45s to £9, depending on quality, age and region.[40] The cost and risk could be reduced by sharing cows between households.[41] Calves cost much less, between £1 and £2 each, again depending on age. A calf bought by a farm servant or a labourer could be raised by a neighbour or a friend. Once grown, she could be fed on only an acre and a half of grassland, if her owner kept half a dozen ewes to help manure it.[42] With generous commons, in fenland for example, she could survive and give milk on even less. During the winter, hay and straw were expensive fodder, and a cow in calf needed as much as fifteen pounds a day, but cows were turned into the stubble and fallow fields, and they were fed on straw and chaff supplemented with fodder from commons in the shape of furze and browse wood, and all manner of woodland foliage. Rivers provided weed: one Hampshire parson wrote to the *Annals of Agriculture* in 1803, in praise of the weeds in his local river which fed many commoners' cows.[43] Villages near the coast used seaweed – a substance high in calcium and magnesium.[44] Robert Trow-Smith argues that the

[40] William Squire of Wigston, Leicestershire, left two cows on his death in 1678, each worth about 45s: Hoskins, *Midland Peasant*, p. 308. The cost of cows in the middle of the eighteenth century ranged from around £4 in Cheshire and Lancashire to £5 or £8 or more in Hertfordshire and Buckinghamshire: Broad, 'Cattle Plague', p. 109.

[41] The inventory of Edward Brown of Kilsby made in April 1769 included 'Part in a Cow' worth £3: Northants. RO, Rd(K) 10.

[42] Testimony to Henry Pilkington, Poor Law Assistant Commissioner, in 1832, cited in Hoskins, *Midland Peasant*, p. 270.

[43] The Rev. Willis of Sopley, Hants, 'On Cows for Cottagers', *Annals of Agriculture*, 40 (1803), pp. 555, 564–7.

[44] John Seymour, *The Smallholder* (1983), p. 63: 'We do buy fertiliser, but it is organic natural seaweed fertiliser which can be spread on the land to about five hundredweight to the acre, for pastures. The cows can eat it, so you can leave the

calving percentages on good medieval farms were 'extraordinarily high', suggesting that 'winter keep for the cow was in fact more adequate than many modern historians ... would have one believe'.[45] These medieval cows were fed in much the same way as eighteenth-century commoners' cows.

The value of the cow lay in her calves and in the milk she gave. In season, between spring and autumn in each year, she would give anything from under one to three gallons of milk a day. Owning more than one cow would bring winter milk too if one of them was set to calve after Christmas.[46] In the late eighteenth century Arthur Young put the value of three gallons a day at £5 a year.[47] In the hungry 1790s Nathaniel Kent put it higher at 3s 6d a week, or £9 2s a year, if the value of the calf was included.[48] A recent estimate of the average yield of poor cows before enclosure suggests an annual output of 330 gallons or 3 cwt of cheese. This is substantial, but even the most conservative estimate (and perhaps the most likely for a cottager's cow) of a gallon of milk a day in season would bring in the equivalent of half a labourer's annual wage. Milk was turned into butter too, and cheese, which was readily sold; the whey was drunk, or fed to pigs.[49] Finally, the price of the calf in the autumn would go some way to paying the rent and Land Tax.

But, if a cow was too expensive, if its cost could not be shared, or if it died and could not be replaced, a few acres easily supported sheep, which were cheaper to buy than cows, and produced wool,

cows in while you are spreading – unlike the chemical fertilisers where you have to take the cattle off. And if the cows lick at the seaweed they are getting the added calcium and magnesium which they need. The reports from other farmers, who have used it for long periods, are that they get no milk fever or magnesium deficiency; it is staggering.'

[45] Trow-Smith, *History of British Livestock Husbandry*, p. 117.
[46] B. A. Holderness, 'Prices, Productivity and Output', in Mingay, ed., *The Agrarian History of England and Wales*, VI (Cambridge, 1989), p. 162; Hartley, *Lost Country Life*, p. 102.
[47] Howell, *Land, Family and Inheritance in Transition*, pp. 165–6, cites G. Fussell, 'Four Centuries of Leicestershire Farming', *Transactions of the Leicestershire Archaeological Society*, 24 (1949), p. 164, quoting Arthur Young on Leicester longhorns fed on hay in winter, producing three gallons of milk a day, worth £5 a season. Inferior cows produced less milk, hence the estimate here of £2 and up. Howell also notes that in 1623 Gervase Markham reckoned on a gallon a day from Whitsun to Michaelmas (p. 165).
[48] Kent, 'The Great Advantage of a Cow to the Family of a Labouring Man', p. 22: 'setting the profit of the calf versus the loss sustained when the cow is dry'. He assumed a high rent of 30s per acre but still reckoned on a profit of 30 per cent.
[49] Holderness, 'Prices, Productivity and Output', pp. 162–3.

ewe's milk, lambs and meat. Ewes gave milk (one to three pints a day) from the end of lambing to some time in August; then milking ceased to give the ewes time to strengthen before they went to the ram in late autumn, and the onset of winter. Lambing began again after Christmas.[50] The small common-field breeds were hardy, and thought to eat less in proportion to their size than the larger breeds. They were said to bear extreme hunger with less of a reduction in flesh than the larger sort, and when turned on to poor land would fatten faster.[51]

Livestock may have been the easiest and most profitable way to use a very small acreage, but even strips amounting to as little as two or three acres were sown with barley, rye, oats, wheat, peas and beans, and, increasingly, with potatoes. Small commoners at Maulden in Bedfordshire grew all these and turnips or rape too. Those tithed in 1775 included one who grew two acres each of wheat, barley and beans; another who grew this and two acres of rye and two roods of potatoes. Others grew only an acre each of oats, rye and potatoes.[52] Petitioners against the enclosure of Wilbarston in Northamptonshire, a parish in wood pasture not arable, claimed that their few acres provided 'Bread corn for their severall families' in years of dearth.[53] Cicely Howell has calculated that, to feed itself, a family needed at least twelve acres in south east Leicestershire in the middle ages. Because corn yields doubled between the middle ages and 1800, as little as two or three acres would provide as much as a third or a half of a family's food, in the mid eighteenth century.[54] William Pitt, the Reporter to the Board of Agriculture for

[50] Howell, *Land, Family and Inheritance* (1983), p. 166; Hartley, *Lost Country Life*, p. 61.

[51] Mr Price of Appledore, Kent, in *Annals of Agriculture*, 31 (1798), p. 344; John Morton also noted the hardy small sheep of the Northamptonshire scarp, in *Natural History of Northamptonshire*, pp. 9–10; for an opposing view see Wedge, *General View ... Warwick*, pp. 34–6.

[52] Beds. RO, P31/3/7 (1775); on cereals, vegetables, flax and hemp in the mixed farming of small peasants in Staffordshire see Angus McInnes, 'The Village Community 1660–1760', *North Staffordshire Journal of Field Studies*, 22 (1983) pp. 52–3. Even a rood or two was useful: typically half of a labourer's allotment in Flora Thompson's enclosed Oxfordshire village was sown with wheat or barley: Thompson, *Lark Rise to Candleford*, p. 63.

[53] Northants. RO, Rockingham Castle MSS, B.7.55, photostat no. 752, and see above, Chapter 8, pp. 268–9.

[54] An anonymous correspondent to the *Annals of Agriculture* in 1799 argued that, when well dunged and fed with lucern and turnips, a two-acre plot in Hertfordshire had produced 124 bushels and half a peck of barley, 33 (1799), p. 302. For crop yields see Mark Overton, 'Estimating Crop Yields from Probate Inven-

Northamptonshire, agrees: four acres would feed a family in the 1790s. This was a substantial contribution to an economy in which the overwhelming expense was food. And, unlike enclosed small-holdings, strips of land in open fields suffered little diseconomy of scale because they could rely on external sources of common pasture to some degree.

This is only the beginnings of a description of the value of even very small acreages to the smallest peasants who also depended on wage work, those whose seeming poverty has deprived them of peasant status in the literature. The value of a couple of acres suggests that this poverty is only relative: it was far better to hold land, even land burdened with debt, than not. Moreover, English peasants, whether landholders or not, had common right too, which brings me to the second part of the argument.

PEASANTS AND COMMON RIGHT

At common law, common right was the right to share the produce of land, not the ownership of the soil, but the right to pasture over it (common of pasture), to cut peat or turf for fuel (common of turbary), and to collect firewood and repair wood (common of estovers).[55] We have seen that this definition ignores the complexity of local custom and usage. In reality, on the ground, the range of common produce was magnificently broad, the uses to which it was put were minutely varied, and the defence of local practice was determined and often successful.

The obvious example is the gleaning by women and children of corn and straw from wheat fields after harvest. In some places they gleaned peas and beans too. Gleaning was a common practice, universally regarded as a common right. Indefensible at common law after 1788, in most villages with some arable fields it survived and prospered none the less. Commentators reckoned that gleaned corn would provide enough flour for at least a couple of months' bread in the autumn, usually enough to last till Christmas. In Canterbury gleaning brought in a 'whole winter's corn'.[56] Long

tories: An Example from East Anglia, 1585–1735', *Journal of Economic History*, 39 (1979) p. 375; Howell, *Land, Family and Inheritance*, p. 152; Holderness, 'Prices, Productivity and Output', p. 138.

55 *Halsbury's Laws of England* (2nd edn, ed. Viscount Hailsham, 1932), IV, p. 531, s. 983.

56 Baker, *Folklore and Customs*, p. 162.

Buckby gleaners were said to store their gleaned corn up in the bedrooms when the space downstairs ran out.[57] At Atherstone in the 1760s gleaning was worth 15s, more than twice a woman's harvest wage.[58] F. M. Eden calculated that gleaners in Roade, Northamptonshire, gathered enough corn after harvest to make bread to last the rest of the year, worth about 6 per cent of the family's annual income.[59] The value of this was even greater in the 1790s, when flour for a family cost from 5s to 8s a week. Besides the corn, the straw could be burnt on cottage hearths, or used to fire bread ovens, to dry malt or to brew. If long, it was turned into thatch or thrown into stalls and yards to be mixed with dung and used for manure. Gleaning persisted longer than any other right or custom. In the 1870s in more than fifty Northamptonshire parishes the gleaning bell still rang out to open and close the fields.[60]

But uncultivated commons in forest, fen, heath and even on the smaller wastes of arable parishes, or in the common fields at particular times, are the best example of the variety of advantages, besides grazing, that were won from shared land use. We have seen that they offered not one but many harvests.[61]

Despite this abundance, the value of common right in the eighteenth century, like the existence of a small peasantry, is in doubt. We have seen that eighteenth-century critics thought it was worth less than regular employment in an enclosed village, though they also said that it was widespread and tenaciously defended. Chambers and Mingay agreed that common right had only limited value but argued that few people enjoyed it. Garrett Hardin theorized that the end of common right was due to its inevitable overuse, itself a result of sharing property in common. Hobsbawm and Rudé, and Chambers

[57] Anon., 'The Folklore of Long Buckby', *The Library List. Journal of the County Library*, 5:54 (January, 1939), Northampton Public Library, no. 49.
[58] Warwicks. RO, Compton Bracebridge, HR/35: women's wages were 25s.
[59] Eden, *State of the Poor*, II, p. 547.
[60] Anon., 'A Letter from a Vale Farmer to the Editors, on the Disadvantages of Plowing in Stubble', *Museum Rusticum et Commerciale*, 2:72 (1764), pp. 35–6; on peas and beans see Northants. RO, Fitz. Misc., vol. 746, p. 25, November 1722; FH 991, Great Weldon by-laws, 1728; Thomas North, *The Church Bells of Northamptonshire* (Leicester, 1878), *passim*. For the regulation of gleaning see Neeson, 'Common Right and Enclosure', pp. 72–5. For an explanation of the longevity of gleaning see Peter King, 'Gleaners, Farmers and the Failure of Legal Sanctions in England 1750–1850', *Past and Present*, 125 (1989); cf. Neeson, 'Common Right and Enclosure', pp. 405–8; in Lawshall, Suffolk, the practice may have been re-established by force: *London Evening Post*, 3–5 Sept. 1772.
[61] See above, Chapter 6.

(before Mingay), with their metaphors of hazes and squalid curtains, thought it was better than nothing, but not a lot better.[62] This interpretation is undergoing important and far-reaching revision. In *Whigs and Hunters*, E. P. Thompson began a re-evaluation of use-rights in royal forests, one continued by Charles Searle in looking at the customary economy of eighteenth-century Cumbria and Jane Humphries in considering the significance of commons to women and children.[63] The Midland opponents of enclosure whose resistance I described in the last chapter were moved as much by the need to preserve common right as by fear of losing land or paying high costs – rights we have seen them protect and regulate with some care in the century before enclosure. And defenders of commons (and even their critics) were aware of the income value as well as the social value of commons. I want to continue the argument here by looking once more at common of pasture, the right most supportive of small peasant economies, and to look at it again in the Midlands, an area more thickly populated than rural Cumbria and more agriculturally productive than the forests of Berkshire and Hampshire; in other words, an area closer to the heart of agrarian capitalism.

Can a cash value be put on access to common pastures in the eighteenth century? Some observers thought that it could. When Henry Homer, no defender of commons, assessed the retail value of commons in the late 1760s he put it at a quarter to a third of the rent.[64] Obviously value varied from place to place, and no average figure will do, but Homer did not exaggerate. Here are some estimates made in woodland, fen, marsh, hill and vale.[65] First, woodland: Mrs Barbara Welch, a tenant to the Duke of Montagu, estimated the value of her common right in his two-hundred-acre wood in 1716 at 'almost one third of the value of the estate'. In other words, in her opinion her lands were effectively one third larger than their actual acreage.[66] In the fenland, common right was, if any-

[62] See above, Introduction, p. 6; Chapter 1, pp. 16–17.

[63] Thompson, *Whigs and Hunters*; Searle, 'Custom, Class Conflict and Agrarian Capitalism'; Humphries, 'Enclosures, Common Rights, and Women'; Neeson, 'Common Right and Enclosure'.

[64] Homer, *Essay*, p. 76.

[65] For an overview of village by-laws and a discussion of common rights from Domesday to the seventeenth century in the east Midlands, see Thirsk, 'Field Systems of the East Midlands', pp. 232–80.

[66] Northants. RO, Boughton papers, W28; also B67 (Brooke of Great Oakley), notes on Robinson's case (n.d. probably 1790s): Ossory calculated the value of field

thing, more useful. Common pastures in fen villages were in themselves sufficient for raising a household cow or some sheep, and common-pasture rights belonged to resident householders without land as well as those with. Substantial husbandmen there might hold no land at all. The most conservative estimate of value – made by the Cambridgeshire reporter to the Board of Agriculture – put the right for a cow common in the fen at 30s to 40s a year. He thought this was derisory, but noted that commoners did not: 'a surveyor would be knocked on the head, that went with a view to enclosure'.[67] Marsh villagers had some of the same advantages, William Stout thought the value of marsh common for his family's sheep worth a quarter the value of the holding:

> My father then could have kept one hundred sheep all summer on that marsh; and about the seventh month yearly the high tides brought the sheep's dung and sea tangle to the side, which was gathered by the Inhabitants, evry house at the sand Knowing how far their liberties for gathring extended.[68]

Forest, fen and marsh commons such as these were often generous, but hill and vale parishes benefited from common right too. In Long Buckby on the Northamptonshire scarp the rent of meadow with common right was higher than that of meadow without.[69] Cottage commoners in the Warwickshire village of Atherstone refused compensation of 20s a year each for their commons in the common fields in 1738. They thought they were worth more than a cash payment could cover. They also enjoyed grazing rights over another eight hundred acres of uncultivated common waste. The value of this in the market was the equivalent, in cash terms, of 15 per cent of a labourer's annual income, perhaps more.[70] In practical terms its value was greater because it saved some of the rent of

pasture at 10s per acre, wood pasture at 2s per acre or 5s per head of cattle. Open-field rents were from 7s to 10s per acre at this time: Pitt, *General View ... Northampton*, p. 38.

[67] Spufford, *Contrasting Communities*, p. 165, on the ability to stock without having much land in the fen parish of Willingham, which remained a peasant village in the eighteenth century; Gooch, *General View ... Cambridge*, cited by Arthur Young in *Annals of Agriculture*, 43, pp. 92–3, discussing Cottenham.

[68] William Stout, *The Autobiography of William Stout of Lancaster, 1665–1752*, ed. J. D. Marshall (Manchester, 1967), p. 67.

[69] Northants. RO, SG 235, rental of the lands of Mrs Peyto.

[70] On Atherstone see Warwicks. RO, HR 35/25, and Thompson, *Customs in Common*, pp. 152–8; Malcolmson, *Life and Labour in England*, p. 37. I have assumed a generous working year of 250 days at an average 1s a day.

pasture land, which was as much as a third of the rent of an average holding. Finally, two examples taken from downland. On the Wiltshire downs Thomas Davis, reporter to the Board of Agriculture, noted in the early 1790s that the sheep and corn economy of small farmers was devastated when they lost their commons at enclosure because they could no longer keep enough sheep to manure their arable land. And at Bucklebury in the Berkshire downs in 1834 almost two hundred petitioners against enclosure argued that the value of their common was substantial, and gave as evidence the fact that 'renters of small pieces of land adjoining the Common' paid rents 50 per cent higher than tenants of farms in the parish because they had the right to common their stock.[71] The value of commons varied across this range of agricultures from a quarter to a half or more of the rental paid for the land.

If common of pasture was valuable in as wide a range of locations and agricultures as this then it becomes important to know who actually enjoyed it in the eighteenth century. Was the right to keep a cow rare? And were *cottagers* with common right few? These questions have been dealt with at length in Chapter 2, so I shall summarize the argument made there briefly. Common right was more widely enjoyed than historians have thought. In Northamptonshire, customary court by-laws, presentments and stinting agreements show that all occupiers of common-field land, and all or most householders in forest, fen, and some heathland parishes enjoyed the right to pasture cows or sheep in the eighteenth century. Pasture rights in open-field arable villages outside the forest and fen were restricted to those with land or cottage rights, but they may have been of little use without them. To pasture a cow here the poorest commoners often had to occupy land, as much as six to ten acres by the end of the century, or to occupy a cottage to which common right was attached. Occupiers with no more than an acre or two might make up any shortfall with a payment of about 6d an acre. Of course pasture rights for sheep required less land, only an acre per sheep, and sheep were also easy to place with a farmer, so even landless labourers could (and did) keep a few. Rights to pasture pigs and geese rarely related to land or cottage-holding: they existed where pasture and custom allowed.

71 T. Davis, *A General View of the Agriculture of Wiltshire* (1794), p. 80, quoted in Yelling, *Common Field and Enclosure*, p. 102; Berkshire RO, D/E Hy E9/1,

I have suggested that a quarter or more of the population of open-field villages in Northamptonshire were small occupiers in the late eighteenth century. It is likely, then, that all of these, even the smallest, were entitled to pasture rights to some degree. But counting numbers of *cottagers* who had access to commons by virtue of their occupancy of a common-right cottage is difficult. Whereas rights appendant to land were inseparable from it, those appurtenant to cottages could be bought and sold. So, although cottages with common rights were often a half or a third of a parish's housing stock, and were well provided with grazing rights, they were also vulnerable to tenementization, to engrossment, to the permanent removal of their rights through sale, and to the separation of the use of their rights from occupancy.

On the face of it there was plenty of scope here for the devaluation of cottage rights long before the late eighteenth century, and with it the dispossession of cottagers themselves. Yet, despite engrossment, these rights were not easily marketable. In several parishes manorial court orders explicitly forbade the separation of occupancy from use: whoever occupied a cottage was alone allowed to stock for the rights. In any case cottages let *with* rights were more valuable to their owners than cottages let *without* them. This is because they brought in higher rents and at the same time remained clearly eligible for compensation at enclosure. Only in royal forests, or on substantially consolidated estates, were these advantages outweighed by the value of ridding the forest of cottagers' cattle by buying up cottages. Finally, evidence of the separation of cottages from their rights is almost always coincident with enclosure, when, because common right was about to end, cottagers began to sell their rights to speculators. There is only a little evidence of earlier separation. Cottage commons were likely to remain intact then, though cottages were bought up by farmers and landlords, and they were often divided to create two or more dwellings sharing the original rights – thereby increasing the number of cottage commoners eligible for right.[72]

Common of pasture was more valuable than contemporary pro-enclosure opinion admitted, and more widely enjoyed than some

Bucklebury Petition, 1834: 47 were identified as freeholders, 124 as 'occupiers'.
[72] For a discussion of why common of pasture survived until enclosure see above, Chapter 3.

historians have thought. If it was not everywhere the patrimony of
the poorest, it was critically important to the economies of small
occupiers. Combined with rents lower than those in enclosed villages, and relatively easy access to land, it gave some independence
of prices and wages. Even for landless labouring families it held out
some hope for the future: 'an Inability to stock at present', wrote an
Atherstone opponent of enclosure, 'does not necessarily imply the
same for the future'. In fact, hoping for land was in the very nature
of commoners, as we shall see.[73]

PEASANTS AND PRACTICE

I said at the beginning of this chapter that there is an historical
orthodoxy that the English peasantry had disappeared by 1750 at
the latest. I went on to say that the survival of petty landholding and
common right into the first half of the nineteenth century might
show that this orthodoxy was wrong. Then I added that the survival
until enclosure of *common right* in particular was evidence of a
peculiarly peasant economy. I want to return to that point now,
looking first at common-field agriculture and village relations and
then at reactions to enclosure, again bringing together arguments
presented separately in earlier chapters.

Before enclosure, but not after it, Midland peasant agriculture
required co-operation and the protection of common interests.
Sharing common pasture and working plots scattered over the
length and breadth of a parish each called for collective regulation.
Every spring and autumn occupiers made by-laws to set aside
pasture, to throw fields open to commonable beasts, to impose
stints, to brand the herd and arrange its coming and going, to
provide bulls and impound sick animals, and to clear water-courses.
They set rotations (and departures from them), they punished trespass and overstocking. They elected officers to enforce the by-laws,
and employed pinders and haywards to summarily fine offenders or
to bring them to court.

And, although the jurors were almost certainly the most substantial commoners,[74] the interests of the smallest were usually

[73] Warwicks. RO, HR 35/14, 15.
[74] For a recent discussion of the Laxton jury see J. V. Beckett, 'The Disappearance
of the Cottager and the Squatter from the English Countryside', in B. A. Holderness and M. E. Turner, eds., *Land, Labour and Agriculture* (1991), p. 65.

considered: their grazing rights were relatively secure. Thus, when new stints reduced the levels of stocking, juries often aimed them at the larger herds, leaving the smallest occupiers' rights relatively untouched. Equally, they upheld the poorest commoners' rights to fuel or browse wood. Sometimes we can hear common need and the obligations of neighbours in the language of field orders. At Sowe in Warwickshire no man was to bring waggons, carts or any other implements on to any balk and 'Damnify his Nieghbour thereby'; there would be no riding along any balks except one's own, so that no man may 'do his Neighbour Damage'; no grass borders should be left in any of the fields to 'defraud the Common herd'.[75] And in every parish at least once a year commoners heard the words of the Bible make the same point. Rogation – after the Reformation the only procession left in the Anglican calendar – was a progress around the parish boundaries of minister and congregation to give thanks to God for the fruits of the earth and to proclaim 'Cursed is he that removeth his neighbours land-mark', to which all the people should say Amen.[76]

Common-field villages did not house serenely self-regulating democratic communities. Economic and political changes affected the behaviour of open-field farmers, divided their interests, and led them to act independently in all kinds of ways. In some parishes the workings of the land market, or the ability of landlords to consolidate holdings, reduced the number of small peasants to nothing long before enclosure. In others, large owners and substantial tenants may have been more eager than small commoners to innovate and to consolidate land. In still others they may have tried to overstock the commons. The point is that they did not deny common pasture to small occupiers and cottagers. Landlords did not annul leases and raise rents two or three times over in the space of a year; nor did they drive land sales up to record levels. It took a parliamentary enclosure to do all this. Before enclosure the larger owners could (and did) alter the terms of landholding relations in this or that respect, but they could not tear up the contract. This limit to agrarian capitalism favoured the small and middling occupiers most. They took from it

---

[75] Warwicks. RO, CR 556/299 (5).

[76] H. Crossman, *An Introduction to the Knowledge of the Christian Religion* (SPCK, new edn, n.d. [pre-1841]), pp. 64–5. The verse is Deuteronomy XXVII.17, King James' version; earlier the words were more specific: 'Curseth is he that translateth the bounds and doles of his neighbour.' On Rogation see Thomas, *Religion and the Decline of Magic*, pp. 71–5.

vitally important pasture, some risk sharing, a sense of common purpose with richer men – however tenuous – and a tradition of mutual aid. The *social* efficiency of this common-field collectivism is overlooked by historians who consider enclosure's efficiency in narrowly economic terms – measuring only what Keith Snell has called 'growthsmanship'.[77]

That commoners recognized their mutual dependence on this shared economy is evident in their reaction to enclosure. In the last chapter I argued that an alliance of small occupiers and landless commoners resisted parliamentary enclosure in Northamptonshire. They contested enclosure Bills with petitions, threats, foot-dragging, the theft of new landmarks, surveys and field books; with riotous assemblies to destroy gates, posts and rails; and with more covert thefts and arson. It is entirely possible that a similar search of estate correspondence, enclosure papers, newspapers and court records would turn up evidence of opposition in other Midland counties too.[78] Opposition was long-lived, successful in impeding and delaying enclosure Bills, and not confined to 'special case' places where common lands were unusually large.

I think we can recognize a peasant consciousness in collective action like this. But it is also evident in the forum commoners chose for their resistance. They rarely took their opposition to Parliament, and then only as a last resort. Resistance was intensely, and most successfully, a local matter. This was not due to any restricted peasant world view but rather because commoners saw Parliament itself as part of the problem. In the Midlands its value as a defender of their economy had waned ever since the late sixteenth century, when it allowed anti-enclosure statutes to lapse.[79] Peasants, more

[77] On the bonds forged by collective agriculture see Marc Bloch, *French Rural History* (1966), p. 180. Eric Wolf emphasizes the dependence of small and middling peasants on mutuality, and their consequent vulnerability: Eric Wolf, 'On Peasant Rebellions', *International Social Science Journal*, 21 (1969); for the loss of the poor's potato land in common fallows at enclosure see Young, *General View ... Oxfordshire*, p. 185. K. D. M. Snell, 'Agrarian Histories and our Rural Past', *Journal of Historical Geography*, 17 (1991), pp. 195–203.

[78] Cf. 'In order for enclosure to be undertaken at all, agreement had first to be reached among the owners of the majority of the community's land, and that left the people without property politically isolated': John Bohstedt, *Riots and Community Politics in England and Wales 1790–1810* (Cambridge, Mass., 1983), p. 197.

[79] On the evolution of parliamentary attitudes to enclosure see D. C. Coleman, *The Economy of England* (Oxford, 1977), pp. 175–8; on the failure of crown protection in the 1630s see Martin, *Feudalism to Capitalism*, pp. 144–50. Parliament rejected the last Bill to regulate enclosure in 1656: Coleman, *Economy of England*, p. 175.

than their pamphleteer defenders, knew they mattered very little to the state, and they shared this knowledge of their own insignificance. At enclosure they understood very well where Parliament stood. And enclosers underlined it: 'It wou'd be tedious to reckon up the inconveniencys of open Fields', they said to Atherstone commoners; 'it hath been long the avow'd sense of Parliament that they are the occasion of frequent Trespasses and disputes and a hindrance to Industry & Improvmts: of Land'.[80] Commoners were up against a Parliament of enclosers and they knew it.

Accordingly, they directed their opposition to the *local* enclosers and couched it in revealing terms. Notions of sufficiency and accusations of greed filled the language of enclosure's opponents. West Haddon peasants argued that their lands supported them well *enough*, that they needed no more; that enclosing itself was a wicked thing, unjust, it could not answer to conscience. It promoted private profit not public welfare. Brigstock commoners accused the Duke of Grafton of unseemly and unnecessary greed. They expected better of him. At Atherstone commoners claimed the purpose of the enclosure was 'to serve the Particular end of two or three Private Persons whereas Lands in Common duely consider'd are as they was first design'd a Benefit to the Publick without Exception'. They asked the Lord of the Manor to act in that spirit and so

> restore to the Town that peace and tranquillity which your attempt to the contrary has made such Melancholy breaches upon; the more opposite this is to your Interest the more Noble and Generous wou'd be the Sacrifice you make for so valuable a blessing and the higher wou'd it raise you in the esteem and good will of all wise and Vertuous Persons.[81]

Commoners continued a dialogue with enclosers that was older than the present crisis. They expected to be heard.

I have said that the expectation sprang in part from the negotiation and argument of daily routine in common-field agriculture –

[80] Warwicks. RO, H35/11, 'Answer to the Paper of Grievances', n.d., probably 1760s; *Northampton Mercury*, 20 Jan. 1777; Berks. RO, D/EHy08/1, 'The History of a Secret Committee' [n.d., *c*.1768].

[81] Warwicks. RO, HR 35/15, beginning, 'We have before us a Paper entitled the Inclosure Vindicated ... '; HR35/14, 'Some Observations upon a Paper entitled The Inclosure Explain'd and Vindicated'. See also Everitt, 'Farm Labourers', pp. 439–40, for examples of sixteenth-century gentry willing to go to law to defend their labourers' commons. John Tharp, responsible for the fen enclosure in Chippenham (see above pp. 76–7) had run his mill free of toll one day a week: Gooch, *General View ... Cambridge*, pp. 294–5.

the constant dealing of neighbours working the same land. But surely the expectation was shared by those who were not yet commoners too. Farm servants and day labourers who were children of commoners expected to become commoners themselves. Others who stood little chance of inheritance perhaps hoped to get land or rights through saving, skill or good luck. In the meantime they behaved as if this was likely: they lived in hope. George Cornewall Lewis noticed this living-in-hope when he described Irish labourers in the early nineteenth century as men who worked on the assumption that they would have land at some point: 'though they may not have a present, yet they have a future interest in the matter; though they may not be personally concerned, yet their kinsmen and friends and fellows are concerned'. Fewer English labourers could be as certain of land as the Irishmen Lewis described, but in common-field villages more looked forward to it than we have allowed.[82] Their 'future interest' made commons their business. It made an attack on common right more difficult: it had to withstand the resistance of commoners *and* those who would become commoners. Not only commoners spoke on common right's behalf: their children and neighbours did too.

This web of connection could have some eminent threads woven into it. In early seventeenth-century Orwell, Margaret Spufford noted that the prosperous and poor sides of families did not drift apart:

> There seems to have been a close family network, and a remarkably unexclusive amount of give-and-take between cousins, one group of whom were acquiring plate, books, university education, and ex-monastic lands, and the other group of which were continuing to live in Orwell on between fourteen and thirty-five acres apiece.[83]

Similarly, at Wigston on the eve of the eighteenth century gentry families were related to peasant farmers and even cottagers. Here is

---

82 George Cornewall Lewis, *Local Disturbances in Ireland* (1836), p. 188 – I am grateful to Dorothy Thompson for this reference; and see D. Walker, *General View of the Agriculture of the County of Hertford* (1795), pp. 52–3, describing a village in which very few cottagers could afford to buy a cow: 'if the cottager cannot purchase now he cherishes the hope that he may be able to purchase thereafter'; and Beckett, 'The Disappearance of the Cottager and Squatter', p. 66, for the conclusion that labourers in Laxton climbed the 'farming ladder' until the 1950s.

83 Spufford, *Contrasting Communities*, pp. 111, 299; Cressy, 'Kinship and Kin Interaction in Early Modern England', pp. 50, 68; Hoskins, *Midland Peasant*, pp. 199–200.

another reason why juries protected small commoners' rights, why they allowed the local poor to glean but not the certificate poor from outside, why the landless as well as the landed signed counter-petitions, why some gentlemen supported them too, and why labourers as well as landowners pulled down fences.

Kinship and sharing the same fields and commons in as intimate a way as common-field agriculture demanded probably discouraged overt displays of social difference too. Clothes, houses, language and leisure divide or unite people of different wealth and social standing. But when farmers dressed as plainly as husbandmen and put pewter on their tables not silver, when their wives and daughters worked with other women, and when they ate with their labourers and servants at the same table every day, and drank too, when contact was as regular and as personal as this perhaps a sense of obligation and connection was there also. Clare's poem 'The Parish' describes the polarization at enclosure of labourers and the landed; in particular he describes the decline of farmers like Ralph Wormstall, 'a very rich plain and superstitious man'. Clare remembered his thrift (he went to market himself, sold even the apples and pears from his orchard when he had a bumper crop, and after forty years still wore his wedding suit every Sunday) but he also remembered his meticulous observation of ceremony:

he was always punctual in having the old bowl of frumitory at sheepshearing ready in time for the shepherds suppers and never let the old year go out without warming the old can of ale for the ringers well peppered with ginger and he woud always have his Yule cake cut at Twelfth night for the Morris dancers to taste of with their beer let the old dame mutter as she might he always got the fattest goose for Christmass and a couple of the best ducks in the yard for lammass tide and he kept almost every Saint day in the almanack with an additional pitcher after dinner and another pipe at night with the Vicar which he called 'honoring the day'.[84]

Clare remembered him after enclosure when the customs he honoured survived in a changed social setting, and on a short lease, but the same celebrations (and more) occurred before enclosure in a village full of commoners. To Christmas, Twelfth Night and Lammas they added beating the bounds, feasts at the division of lot meadows, and the hundred smaller and more private occasions

<hr>

[84] John Clare, in *Selected Poems and Prose of John Clare*, p. 28.

when labour was shared and rewarded with food, drink and evenings spent together.[85] Village celebrations were acknowledgements that wages alone could not pay for labour. They brought together those with very little land or commons and those with the lion's share. They mediated an otherwise strictly economic relationship. They made it harder to dance with people on Saturday night and overstock their common pastures on Monday morning.[86] After enclosure the occasions for celebrations like these declined. It is not surprising that complaints of superciliousness among the farmers grow strongest at the end of the eighteenth century and in the first decades of the nineteenth. Doubtless they were the bitter fruits of dearth and the denial of moral economy, but they came too from the experience of parliamentary enclosure.[87]

By the middle of the eighteenth century any kinship between gentry, yeomen and commoners may have failed; in Northamptonshire in particular the absence of middling farmers of sixty to a hundred acres is striking.[88] But there is little reason to think that the kinship of peasants and labourers changed. Moreover, they still shared a history of collaboration with the very men who would decide to enclose the village, a history of past favours, common interests and daily routines. We have seen some of this earlier when commoners reminded gentry that they had stood together against common enemies, or reminded them of their obligations, for example Brigstock commoners' terse assertion that

antient rights given to the Poore for the generall good of a Towne

---

85 The division of Warkworth lot meadows was marked by a weekend-long feast: Thirsk, 'Field Systems of the East Midlands', p. 248, citing Bridges, *History and Antiquities*, I, p. 219; commoners from several parishes rioted against Warkworth's enclosure: see above Chapter 9, p. 278. On smaller celebrations marking the sharing of labour see Brody, *Inishkillane*, pp. 27, 134.

86 This is not to deny social hierarchy, rather to describe how its unequal power relations were managed in a society sharing commons; cf. Beckett, 'The Disappearance of the Cottager and the Squatter', p. 65. Celebration had other functions too, of course: see Malcolmson, *Popular Recreations in English Society*, pp. 83–4.

87 John Clare, 'The Parish: A Satire', in *Selected Poems* ed. J. W. and Anne Tibble (Everyman edn, 1965), pp. 140–67. For a defence of the historical specificity of both nineteenth-century ballads and pastoral poetry see Howkins and Dyck, '"The Time's Alteration": 'Popular Ballads, Rural Radicalism and William Cobbett', p. 22, and Barrell and Bull, *Penguin Book of English Pastoral Verse*, pp. 380–1; as an example of the decline of celebration see the prosecution of mop-and-pail day at Rushden in 1846 (*Northampton Mercury*, 23 May 1846), which provoked the complaint that 'We shan't be allowed to play at marbles next.'

88 See above, Chapter 8, pp. 250–1, 283–4.

ought to be safely preserved & keept to their owne proper use and uses but not to be perverted by the richer Sort of ye same to private Ends and Sinister Respects.[89]

But collaboration transcended mere emergencies, it was a way of life. Commoners collaborated with 'the richer Sort' not only for a particular, finite end – a piecemeal enclosure or the removal of the lord's flocks from the common, for example – but as a general insurance policy. They worked at building a connection, a mutuality that emphasized common interests. How they did it is no more than suggested here, but common-field agriculture, sharing common waste, living-in-hope of getting commons or land, kinship, ceremony and celebration were important parts of it, together with an assertive local consciousness, the provision of skilled and timely labour, and votes.[90] Even a lord's duty to keep a bull for the commoners' cows, or to contribute to the ale the jury drank after the court adjourned, was a point of contact that could be turned by commoners into a relationship of obligation.[91]

This explains why, as enclosures went through and protest letters and petitions were ignored, the tone of opposition changed. There was increasingly about it a sense of the violation of expected behaviour, an accusation that the customary rights and needs of commoners had once been acknowledged but were now denied. 'Where is *now*', ran a letter sent to the Marquis of Anglesey, 'the degree of virtue which can resist interest?'

... Should a poor man take one of Your sheep from the common, his life would be forfeited by law. But should You take the common from a hundred poor mens sheep, the law gives no redress. The poor man is liable to be hung for taking from You what would not supply You with a meal & You would do nothing illegal by depriving him of his subsistance; nor is Your family

---

[89] Northants. RO, Box X360.

[90] On voting behaviour and its reward in Whittlewood and Salcey forests, see Linnell, *Old Oak*, pp. 89–90.

[91] See above, Chapter 6, pp. 181–2. Ian Carter notes the same in Aberdeenshire: 'a systematic blurring of class lines was a central element of peasant defensive tactics, and hence an important element in the culture generated by that peasantry': *Farm Life in North-East Scotland*, p. 5. The relationship worked both ways of course, especially at enclosures: when, at the second attempt to enclose Atherstone in the 1760s the commoners asked Justice Littleton of Tamworth to intercede on their behalf, he wrote to the enclosers that he would put *their* side of the case to the commoners, though privately, for if he did so publicly he would lose the commoners' trust: Warwicks. RO, HR 35/19, 22.

supplied for a day by the subtraction which distresses his for life!
... Yet the causers of crimes are more guilty than the perpetrators.
What must be the inference of the poor? when they see those
who should be their patterns defy morality for gain, especially
when, if wealth could give contentment, they had enough wher-
with to be satisfied. And when the laws are not accessible to the
injured poor and Government gives them no redress?

But the Marquis was unmoved and from Uxbridge House he
announced the end of dialogue:

Excepting as to the mere fact of the Inclosure, the forming of
which no one has a right to contest, All your statements are
without foundation & as your language is studiously Offensive I
must decline any further communication with you.[92]

At Atherstone commoners asked:

What must we think of those who can Cloak themselves with
Indifference and Neutrality while an affair of such importance to
the said Town is depending what must we look upon those to be
who byass'd by some sinister and selfish ends and views will give
their vote for such an Inclosure?[93]

And at Ashill in Norfolk:

you have often times blinded us saying that the fault was all in the
Place-men of Parliament; but now you have opened our eyes, we
know they have a great power, but they have nothing to do with
the regulation of this parish.[94]

The call to remember the old peasant community went unheard.
John Clare's poetry is full of fury at the repudiation of customary
expectation, the denial of connection between the strong and the
weak: he called it 'the kindred bond'. His charge to the enclosers,
the 'petty tyrants', the 'spoilers', was that they were turning their
backs on the major part of the village. He wrote, 'Old customs usage
daily disappears'. Another poet agreed and took as his example the
end of celebration: 'Feast of the happy Village! where art thou?',
wrote Ebenezer Elliott,

---

92 Staffs. RO, D603/K/16/104, C. Landor to the Marquis of Anglesey, 26 Apr. 1824,
and 3 May 1824, Anglesey to the Rev. C. Landor.

93 Warwicks. RO, HR 35/14; see also *The Case of the Major Part of the Owners and
Proprietors of Lands in Sympson, in the County of Bucks.* [Goldsmith's Library,
GL 1770].

94 PRO, HO 42.150, Anonymous letter enclosed in Rev. Edwards to Sidmouth, 22
May 1816.

> Phsaw! thou wert vulgar – we are splendid now.
> Yet, poor man's pudding – rich with spicy crumbs,
> And tiers of currants, thick as both my thumbs, –
> Where art thou, festal pudding of our sires? –
> *Gone, to feed fat the heirs of thieves and liars.*

Much later, a peasant in another village put it this way:

> Do you know ... what the trees say when the axe comes into the
> forest? .... When the axe comes into the forest, the trees say:
> 'Look! The handle is one of us!'[95]

Perhaps peasant consciousness, lived daily in the routines and expectations of common-field agriculture and common right, was nowhere so well expressed as when peasant economy was in the process of being extinguished.

To conclude: we may have to call a substantial proportion of eighteenth-century English society peasants. This is not sentimental.[96] On the contrary, it defines a large part of rural England more accurately. It frees it from the marginal, minority status associated with terms like poor cottagers, or labourers-with-land, or smallholders. The first two are terms which define only the poorest parts of the peasantry, and ignore their connection to those with a bit more land, to whom they were related, with whom they shared common right and a common agriculture. It ignores the stages in a peasant's life, from farm servant or labourer to husbandman. It disregards the effect of relatively easy access to land on this kind of mobility. Unless we recognize the connections between small and very small landholders, the poorest commoners remain no more than a proto-proletariat, a stage in a process, only two-dimensional, and the larger commoners become 'smallholders', with all the sense of apartness and individualism so inappropriate to common-field villages.

Calling eighteenth-century common-field landholders and landless commoners peasants would also acknowledge that relatively easy access to land, common right, and common-field agriculture

---

[95] John Clare, 'Remembrances', *Selected Poems and Prose of John Clare*, p. 175; 'The Parish', *Selected Poems of John Clare* (1968), p. 70, line 845; Ebenezer Elliott, 'The Splendid Village', in Barrell and Bull, eds., *Penguin Book of English Pastoral Verse*, p. 421 (my italics); John Berger, 'Boris is Buying Horses', *Once in Europa* (1983), p. 69.

[96] Mingay, *Enclosure and the Small Farmer*, p. 10.

provided the determining framework of their social relations and their way of life. Land and common right came first. They were considered the most desirable, most satisfactory basis for a living. Agricultural labour or rural trade and manufacture enhanced or even enabled this economy to continue, but land itself came first. Long after enclosure had created compact farms, and renting more than an allotment had become almost impossible, labourers still felt a longing for land. Well into the second half of the nineteenth century, in E. P. Thompson's words, 'the ground-swell of rural grievance came back always to access to the *land*'.[97]

Finally, the survival of this peasantry until enclosure in many common-field villages also helps establish the social meaning of parliamentary enclosure in more dramatic terms than the orthodox version of a much earlier peasant disappearance allowed. Between 1750 and 1820, 20.9 per cent of England was enclosed by Act of Parliament, or some 6.8 million acres; as a proportion of agricultural land the area was much greater, perhaps 30 per cent of the total. Moreover, in the Midlands, enclosure affected the most densely populated rural areas.[98] It was no small event; it affected large numbers of men, women and children who lived and worked in what was still the largest sector of the economy – agriculture. Ann Kussmaul and Keith Snell have argued that enclosure seriously disrupted the employment patterns of farm servants, labourers and women.[99] Now it is clear that enclosure transformed the customary economies of occupiers and cottage-commoners as well. Moreover, enclosure was an institutional or political intervention. No other attack on common right succeeded as well as enclosure. No other means could be found to raise rents as far or as fast. Enclosure, sanctioned by law, propagandized by the Board of Agriculture, and

97 Thompson, *Making of the English Working Class*, p. 253, and a sense of time itself came out of the changes enclosure brought: 'Times used to be better before Bledlow was enclosed'; Chase, *The People's Farm*; Snell, *Annals*, p. 12, on letters from rural emigrants: 'After the family, almost every letter voiced another major concern – land.'

98 Turner, *English Parliamentary Enclosure*, p. 32. Hoskins suggests that perhaps half of the arable land in England in 1700 later came to be enclosed by Act: Hoskins, *The Making of the English Landscape*, p. 178. A more recent sample of 10 per cent of the enclosure Awards in England estimates a total of 7.25 million acres enclosed by Act. Of this, 61 per cent was common waste but in the Midlands roughly 75 per cent was common arable: John Chapman, 'The Extent and Nature of Parliamentary Enclosure', *Agricultural History Review*, 35 (1987), pp. 28–30.

99 Kussmaul, *Servants in Husbandry*, pp. 15, 120–1; Snell, *Annals*, ch. 4.

profited in by Members of Parliament, was the final blow to peasants in common-field England. The result was a memory of expropriation that informed, legitimized, and sharpened the class politics of nineteenth-century villages.

Appendix A. *Using the Land Tax*

Two major problems make the use of Land Tax returns for the study of landholding difficult. First, the need to find an accurate acreage equivalent – a sum of tax representing acres – which can be used for all the land in a parish. Second, the need to be certain that all, or nearly all, landholders were taxed, allowing the influx (or exit) of particular groups of landholders to be identified and measured.

ACREAGE EQUIVALENTS

A sum of tax paid per acre, or acreage equivalent (AE), is calculated by dividing the total parish tax sum by the number of acres of taxable land in the parish. But the accuracy of the result depends on a satisfactory answer to four questions. First, whether the tax on tithes was included in the pre-commutation returns. Second, whether common land or waste was taxed before and after its enclosure. Third, whether differing values of land in a parish led to different tax assessments and thus to different rates of tax per acre. Fourth, whether the inclusion of unidentified houses and buildings (with their lands) on the returns, and their misidentification as land, undermines the study of changes in smallholdings.

Taxation of tithes

The evidence of Northamptonshire Land Tax returns shows that before enclosure the value of the tithes was taxed, and that after enclosure wherever the tithe was commuted for land it was taxed also. In the returns of the parishes of Raunds, Eye and Abthorpe, the exact sum paid for tithe before enclosure is listed, and distinguished from the other taxes paid by the tithe-owner. Expressed as a percentage of the total parish tax the tithe was 14.5 per cent in Raunds, 10 per cent in Abthorpe and 2 per cent in Eye.[1] Elsewhere, in five parishes where the tithe-owner paid tax on glebe land and tithe together (but paid tax on no other land), the acreage equivalent (AE), and the proportion of this tax paid on tithe alone, may be calculated using the evidence of the total parish tax, and the tithe-owner's tax in the returns, the evidence of the size of the glebe land in the enclosure Award, and the evidence of the total parish acreage in either the Award or the 1851 *Census* (whichever more accurately represents the size of the parish). Thus –

$$\text{Since} \quad AE = \frac{\text{glebe tax}}{\text{glebe acreage}} \tag{1}$$

$$\text{and} \quad AE = \frac{\text{total tax} - \text{tithe tax}}{\text{total acreage}} \tag{2}$$

$$\text{and glebe tax} = AE \times \text{glebe acreage} \tag{3}$$

$$\text{and tithe tax} = \text{tithe-owner's tax} - \text{glebe tax} \tag{4}$$

Substituting in (2) above,

$$AE = \frac{\dfrac{\text{total tax}}{\text{total acreage}} - \dfrac{\text{tithe owner's tax}}{\text{total acreage}}}{1 - \dfrac{\text{glebe acreage}}{\text{total acreage}}} \tag{5}$$

Using the acreage equivalent calculated in formula (5) above, tithe tax as a percentage of total tax may be calculated:

$$AE \times \text{total acreage} = \text{tax on land} \tag{6}$$

$$\text{total tax} - \text{tax on land} = \text{tithe tax} \tag{7}$$

$$\text{tithe tax as \% of total tax} = \frac{\text{tithe tax}}{\text{total tax}} \times 100 \tag{8}$$

In this way the tax paid on tithe before commutation may be calculated for the following parishes: Newton Bromswold (28 per cent), Rushden (20 per cent), Wadenhoe (12 per cent), Greens Norton (7 per cent), and Hannington (18 per cent). Thus the exact sum paid for tithe was known for each of eight parishes in the survey of twenty-two.

---

[1] The low percentage in Eye may indicate that only the tax paid on small tithes was identified, instead of the tax paid on both small and great tithes.

The returns of the other fourteen parishes[2] listed tithe, glebe, and other land belonging to the tithe-owner, in one sum making separation of the tax paid on tithe alone impossible.

This problem is one not usually dealt with by those using the Land Tax as a source. J. M. Martin alone offers the opinion that 'Enclosure would ... leave [the relationship between the tax assessment] and the acreage unchanged (except insofar as it was *slightly* affected by the intake of common or exclusion of land granted in lieu of tithe.)'[3] Northamptonshire returns, however, taxed the tithe before commutation in the pre-enclosure returns. And they also taxed the land given to the tithe-owner in lieu of tithe after enclosure. Thus the relationship between the return and the acreage is affected by the transformation of tax on tithe into tax on land. (Of course, neither the total acreage in the returns, or the global sum of tax paid, changed.) Leaving the tithe tax in the pre-commutation returns, and so calculating acreage equivalents which include a sum of tax paid on money not land *underestimates* the size of holdings before commutation (and enclosure) by a proportion equal to the proportion that the tithe tax is of the total parish tax. The evidence of the eight parishes in which the size of the tithe tax is known suggests that this underestimate would vary from 2 per cent of a man's holdings to 28 per cent. A mean of all eight parishes would produce an underestimate of 14 per cent per holding.[4] Thus a pre-commutation holding of 5 acres would appear from the uncorrected Land Tax to be one of 4.3 acres. The size of the error grows with the size of the holding: for instance, a 50-acre holding, when diminished by the 14 per cent of the tithe, would appear to be only 43 acres; 100 acres would become 86 acres.

2 For the purpose of the survey, Weston by Welland and Sutton Basset, enclosed together in 1802, were computed separately but their results were consolidated because their landholders often held land in both parishes.

3 Martin, 'Landownership and the Land Tax Returns,' p. 99, my italics.

4 The exact figure is 13.9 per cent. The median is 13.25 per cent. The tithe tax of Wollaston was discovered too late for inclusion in the calculation of this mean and median of tithe tax as a proportion of total parish tax. As a proportion the tithe tax in Wollaston was 8 per cent. Similarly, Islip's tithe was accurately calculated, by glebe formula at 18 per cent, too late for inclusion here. If both Wollaston's and Islip's percentages had been included the mean would have changed from 13.9 per cent to 13.75 per cent and the median would have remained unchanged at 13.25 per cent. In view of the advanced stage of the work at that point, and the closeness of the new mean and median to the former figures, Wollaston's and Islip's tithe figures were left out of the calculation of the mean.

If the error is allowed to remain in pre-commutation calculations it produces another distortion when pre- and post-commutation acreages are compared.[5] When a comparison of one man's holdings of 100 acres before and after commutation is made it appears that he has paid tax on a holding of 86 acres before commutation, but that after it he pays tax on a larger holding of roughly 100 acres. Thus he would seem to have gained land in the process of enclosure and commutation.

Even if the amount of land 'lost' before commutation (because tithe was included in the calculation of the acreage equivalent) was equal (at 14 per cent) to the amount each owner gave to the tithe-owner on commutation, the fall shown in the uncorrected records would underestimate the real change. For instance, the 100-acre holding would actually have fallen to 86 acres, but, because it would have appeared to be an 86-acre holding to begin with, no change would be revealed. More likely, the value of land given in exchange for tithe was *higher* than the original tithe. If such a landowner gave 20 per cent of his land, the apparent change would be from an 86-acre holding to an 80-acre one, instead of from a 100-acre holding to an 80-acre one – again, the drop is grossly underestimated by the uncorrected returns.[6]

The effect of leaving the tax on tithe in Land Tax returns before commutation and enclosure is to minimize the change in the size of farms after enclosure, and (if little was lost in compensation to the tithe-owner) even to show an increase in the size of holdings. Even when the probable loss of land given in lieu of tithe is calculated at 15 per cent the effect of leaving the earlier records uncorrected is to underestimate the real fall in size of farms.

For this reason in each of the fourteen parishes for which the size of tax paid on tithe was not available a deduction of 14 per cent of

[5] Post-commutation acreage equivalents are accurate simply because in most returns the tithe tax has been replaced with tax paid on *land* awarded in lieu of tithe.

[6] At the other end of the ownership scale, an owner of 10 acres would appear to own only 8.6 acres before enclosure and commutation, falling to 8 acres after. But the real drop would have been from 10 acres before to 8 acres after. At this end of the scale the importance of the error lies more in the way the figures are interpreted than the actual size of loss. A 10-acre owner would be thought to have undergone *little change* in size of holding (probably none at all when considerations of tithe compensation are included), whereas, in fact, he *lost* land.

the total parish tax (the mean figure where the tithe was known) has been made from the tithe-owner's tax. An acreage equivalent based on the reduced parish tax was then made. The inaccuracy resulting from the use of one proportion (14 per cent) for all parishes is less serious than that of leaving pre-commutation returns uncorrected. Similarly, in open parishes used for comparative purposes, tithe tax has been deducted where possible both before and after enclosure.[7]

If the 14 per cent estimate is too great in a minority of parishes it will exaggerate the size of holdings before commutation and enclosure, but probably by no more than about 7 per cent or so because at least 7 per cent of parish tax would have been paid on tithe. In this case a 100-acre holding would rise to one of 107 acres, or a 10-acre holding to 10.7 acres. But these overestimates are small in comparison to the possible underestimate of 14 per cent in the pre-enclosure size of holdings, and the resultant minimization of change, if tithe were not accounted for. If anything, an overestimate produced by allowing too much for tithe tax would exaggerate the shrinkage of estates a little. Thus a holding of 100 acres would appear to be one of 107 acres, which on enclosure might fall to 80 acres, if compensation to the tithe-owner took 20 per cent of the holding. Instead of dropping by the true percentage of 20 per cent the holding would then seem to drop by 25 per cent. Such an exaggeration is smaller than the underestimation which results from leaving tithe tax in the pre-commutation returns. Moreover the results of changes in the size of an individual's holding in the eight parishes where the *exact* tithe tax is known may be used to check exaggeration in the parishes where the tithe tax has been estimated.

A deduction for tithe tax of 14 per cent might also underestimate the proportion of tithe tax in some parishes – in four parishes where the exact tithe tax is known it was more than 14 per cent.

But in either case the alternative of not deducting tithe tax would underestimate the size of holdings before commutation and enclosure in *all* parishes; and it would underestimate the degree of change

---

[7] See Appendix B. In two open parishes (Roade and Lutton) the tithe had to be left in the return, but the effect of this is constant because no commutation took place. Of the enclosing parishes: Whitfield and Whittlebury continued to pay a corn rent which was taxed, tithe tax was not subtracted either before or after enclosure; tithe was also left in the pre-enclosure returns of Helpston and Maxey.

in the size of holdings over the ten-year period. It would produce a stable pattern of landholding despite all the other evidence of a reduction in the size of holdings due to land sales for payment of compensation to the impropriator, the cost of securing the Act, paying for the Award and building fences.

Taxation on uncultivated common

Doubts that the common was taxed before and after enclosure arise on two counts. First, the land was in need of serious investment if it was to become more than rough pasture. Any tax put upon it might seem a deterrent to improvement, or a penalty upon it. According to David Grigg, the fact that the global assessments were never increased was due to a desire *not* to penalize improvers.[8] Second, as land it was not owned or rented in the way that cultivated land was owned and rented. If anyone paid the tax it would have been the Lord of the Manor. But if the tax was assessed locally by the assessors on the basis of the then current rental of the land how could they assess the value of, for example, the eight hundred acres of heath, common, wasteground, and two rye hills in West Haddon? Unless a nominal sum was based on some other way of assessing the value of such land, it seems likely that it was not taxed before enclosure.

But what of *after* the enclosure, when the land was fenced and potentially marketable? Martin, in discussing the likelihood of general reassessment of taxes after enclosure, suggests that 'small differences [in taxation] can be accounted for by the addition of common or subtraction of land in lieu of tithe'.[9] But in North-amptonshire, the returns themselves do not mention the inclusion of waste land after enclosure. Nor is there any evidence of the kind of thoroughgoing reassessment this would have required. If common land was not included before enclosure, it seems safe to guess that it was not included after. Comparison of awarded acreages and the

---

[8] D. B. Grigg, 'A Source on Landownership: The Land Tax Returns', *Amateur Historian*, 6 (1964), p. 154. Also Pitt *General View ... Northampton*, pp. 150–1. Pitt thought that Whittlewood Forest should be sold in one hundred 500-acre sections, reimbursing landowners and freeholders for their common rights and arranging the Land Tax so as to *encourage* cultivation and penalize the leaving of the land in its natural state or leaving it as pasture for longer than seven years.

[9] Martin, 'Landownership and the Land Tax Returns', p. 98, n. 2.

amount of tax a manorial lord paid in the same year is a useful check.[10]

Changing rental values

When land was first assessed for taxation the rental values on which the assessment was based would have varied with the type of land and the kind of tenure. For this reason Grigg has stressed the need to look at places with 'a fairly uniform rent per acre within the parish'.[11] In all parishes, anywhere, closes and good meadow would have been worth more than common-field land. But, beyond that, in Northamptonshire there were few parishes with greater contrasts of land types within them. Even the forest assarts of the royal forest parishes were well cultivated by the eighteenth century.[12]

Furthermore, there was no recognition of the change in the rental value of land after the first assessments of the 1690s, despite the fact that recently enclosed or newly drained land would have risen in value. Thus enclosure did not change the basis on which the tax was assessed, and this makes comparison of pre- and post-enclosure returns possible.

Nevertheless, some differences of tax rates per acre may have existed within a Northamptonshire parish. Good closes and rich meadow may have been assessed at a higher value than tilled land. And a uniform *parish* acreage equivalent would smooth out those distinctions by assuming that the same tax per acre was paid for good land as for poor. But perhaps this problem is not as great as it appears. Rent may well reflect value. If so, although the calculations of relative acreage would be wrong, the conclusions drawn of relative value would be accurate. Thus a man paying more per acre for five acres of meadow than another paying tax for five of arable

---

10 When this is not a satisfactory check it is possible to estimate two acreage equivalents and compare the structure of landholding each produces. For example, in West Haddon an acreage equivalent after enclosure which assumed that no common was newly included came to 1s 5d per acre; an acreage equivalent that included the common as taxed land came to 1s 2d per acre. Holdings estimated at 10 acres using the former acreage equivalent rose to 12 acres using the latter. In this survey greatest attention is given to holders of less than 100 acres, thus this size of difference is unimportant. At its widest, the gap between the two acreage equivalents puts a 103-acre estate (no common included in acreage equivalent) at 120 acres (when common was included).

11 D. B. Grigg, 'The Land Tax Returns', *Agricultural History Review*, 11 (1963).

12 Pettit, *Royal Forests of Northamptonshire*, p. 3.

would (using a uniform parish acreage equivalent) appear to own seven acres of land instead of five. In fact his five of meadow would have been worth seven of ordinary land; so the comparison of values is accurate. Of course, land improved after the assessments of the 1690s would not have been reassessed so the problem remains of differences in value between land undergoing little improvement and other land undergoing much. Again, during the enclosure period, the comparison of Land Tax returns with the enclosure Award serves as a means of avoiding gross exaggeration of individual holdings.

The same kind of comparison of two sources makes it possible to estimate the margin of difference in tax rates per acre paid by large and small landowners. Mingay has shown that in one Nottinghamshire parish the landlord, who owned much of the parish, paid a lower rate of tax than the smallest landowners. From this he has argued that the structure of landownership cannot be deduced from Land Tax returns.[13] Responding to Mingay, Martin has found that the margin of error in a study of Warwickshire landowning is small, although it increased with the smaller the amount of land owned. The maximum error he found was 33 per cent: one Cubbington man owned 21 acres but an estimate based on his tax put it at 28.[14] A similar check made for the Northamptonshire parish of Burton Latimer shows the same degree of error (Table A.1). The degree of error in estimating the acreage grows rapidly when the smaller holdings are considered. In Burton Latimer, Henry Eady owned 5.3 acres in 1803 but an estimation based on the Land Tax return gives him a holding of 8 acres – a margin of error of 56 per cent. Other holdings of a similar size showed the same degree of exaggeration.

The exaggeration is greatest at the sub-20-acre level, but it need not prevent use of the Land Tax returns to investigate the changes in these holdings. First, the exaggeration is not enormous: a 5-acre holding appears to be 7 or 8 acres. Second, it is constant over time, which enables comparison of a man's pre-enclosure holding with his post-enclosure one. Third, although the acreage is wrongly inflated it may reflect the *value* of the land to its owner – home closes, meadow land, paddocks adjoining inns, etc., were all worth more than the equivalent acreage of tilled lands, probably as much as the inflated acreage produced by the use of a uniform parish acreage

[13] Mingay, 'Land Tax Assessments and the Small Landowner', pp. 381–3.
[14] Martin, 'Landownership and the Land Tax Returns', p. 102.

Table A.1. *Acreages owned compared to acreages estimated from Land Tax returns*

Name	Acres owned	Acres estimated from Land Tax	% Error
J. Harper	591.25	576	2.6
Rev. Hanbury	156	147.3	5.7
J. Sudborough	86	85.5	0.5
Buccleuch & Cave	64.5	58.25	9.6
Rev. Knight	48	37.5	21.3

Source: Northants. RO, Land Tax, Burton Latimer, 1803; ZA 891 in X3872, List of allotments, 1803.

equivalent. Fourth, the size categories used in comparing numbers of landholders before and after enclosure are large enough (the smallest includes those with as little as 5 and as much as 25 acres) to make even substantial variations in taxation insignificant. Finally, it is still possible to record the disappearance of landholders from the returns (on sale of land or death) over the enclosure period, or at any other time.

Tax on houses and buildings

Although originally assessed on office, 'the yearly value of houses, land quarries, mines, iron and salt works, profits from land' and personal property, the Land Tax became a tax on land almost immediately.[15] As such it was very unpopular. Walpole tried to lower the rate to a minimum 1s in the pound in 1733, declaring 'No man contributes the least share to the tax but he that is possessed of a landed estate.' The difficulty of continually assessing any goods and property other than land played a large part in changing the original balance of the tax from personal property to office and land alone.[16] Despite this, writing of the Kentish parish of Ripple in 1816, H. G. Hunt supposed that 'The assessments of four shillings

---

[15] Stephen Dowell, *History of Taxation and Taxes in England*, 4 vols. (1884, 3rd edn, 1965), II, p. 47.

[16] *Ibid.*, p. 98; Davies, 'The Small Landowner in the Light of the Land Tax Assessments', p. 88: 'with the exception of easily detected taxes on office it had become a pure Land Tax'.

and under were most likely for buildings and adjacent land.'[17] In Northamptonshire some houses were taxed and identified as such in the returns, and so pose no problem. Others may have been taxed without identification. But substantial houses were more likely to be taxed than the homes of the poor. As such they had closes, plots of old inclosure, rights over common land, and perhaps a couple of acres as well. Thus they were not only residential, nor would they disappear at enclosure and so exaggerate the decline of small landholders.[18]

ESCAPING THE TAX

Exemptions

Every Land Tax Act exempted the poor smallholders of land who paid less than 20s in rent for it every year. M. K. Ashby, writing of Bledington in 1807, says that the parish's 1,539 acres were divided into nineteen holdings, 'beside some very small ones which did not pay land-tax'. Similarly, in Bucklebury, Berkshire, where enclosure was resisted in 1834 by petition, there were 'sundry small proprietors not assessed to the Land Tax'.[19] Such men were often the owners of small old-enclosed bits of land laying near their cottages. For example, there were five men (possibly more) in Burton Latimer in 1803 who each owned between a half rood and three roods of old enclosures and who paid no Land Tax.[20] Owners of very small old enclosure were to be found in most parishes.

We do not know how rigorously the law was enforced.[21] If

---

[17] H. G. Hunt, 'Land Tax Assessments', *English Historical Review*, Short Guides to Records, no. 16, p. 284.

[18] Nevertheless, some sub-five-acre tax equivalents are excluded from the study: see p. 247.

[19] Ashby, *Changing English Village*, p. 219. Berks. RO, D/Elly E9/2, 'Bucklebury Inclosure, A Statement of the Property of Persons claiming Rights over the Land to be enclosed and of the proportions which the Consents Dissents and Neuters bear to each other'. Owners of 4a 1r 9p opposed the Bill, owners of 0a 2r 17p supported it, and owners of 3a 2r 4p were neutral.

[20] They were George Braybrooke (3 roods). Thomas Vorley (2r), John Nearl (½r), Nathaniel Daniel (½r), and Benjamin Ireland (1r). Northants. RO, H(BL) 813, 'Burton State of Property'; Land Tax, 1803. This list was drawn up for Joseph Harper, Lord of the Manor, and may not have been exhaustive.

[21] Turner suggests that the law was not observed, or even uniformly enforced, in every Buckinghamshire parish: 'Parliamentary Enclosure and Land Ownership Change in Buckinghamshire', p. 570, n. 3, although he may have made this judgement in the erroneous belief that the 1798 Land Tax Act was the first to carry the exemption clause (see Chapter 2, p. 246).

enforced, it applied to open-field holdings of less than three acres.[22] Owners of closes were probably still eligible for tax because their land was worth more per acre, although some who owned less than an acre may also have been excused payment. Such owners were to be found in most parishes. Their experience at enclosure depended on whether old enclosures were reallotted with the common-field land. But they did use large unstinted commons (eight hundred acres of wold in Burton Latimer for example) and suffered from its loss on enclosure.

These non-tax-paying smallholders must join those commoners who enjoyed commons without entitlement of right as they too slip through the most commonly used surviving records. And their loss is a reminder that our knowledge of the shape of petty landholding is incomplete if the Land Tax is our only source. The implication for the survey made in Chapter 8 is that the names of small landholders are incomplete, and their numbers, before and after enclosure, are underestimates. But it is unlikely that there were *more* exempt after enclosure than before: enclosure was a devastating blow to the small taxed landholders; why would it not be equally or more devastating to the smallest?

Compensation to landless cottagers at enclosure

Some cottagers who could prove their right of common were compensated with small plots of land at enclosure and so are to be found on the Land Tax returns after the making of the enclosure Award.[23] Because they were not taxed before enclosure their sudden appearance after it leads to an artificial increase in the number of landowners after enclosure. They may be identified by comparing the enclosure Award with the Land Tax returns. In Northamptonshire their numbers were small.[24]

[22] James Donaldson put the average open-field rent at 8s an acre in the early 1790s, William Pitt put it higher in 1806 at between 10s and 15s, depending on the location and quality of the land; Donaldson, *General View ... Northampton*, Appendix, p. 4; Pitt, *General View ... Northampton*, pp. 38–9.

[23] See Mingay, 'Land Tax Assessments', p. 383; Martin, 'Landownership and the Land Tax Returns', p. 97; and Grigg, 'Land Tax Returns', p. 83.

[24] A search of awards for twenty enclosures (1778–1807) produced only thirty-seven landless commoners who were compensated with land (six of whom *may* have held land in addition); nine of them shared 7a 0r 38p together: Northants. RO, Book G, 65, Wootton Award; Book F, 238, Rushden Award; Book F, 336, Isham Award; D 1085 (ML 679), Badby Award; Book G, 548, Bugbrooke Award; Award Cupboard, Grendon Award; Book I, 1, Wollaston Award; Book I, 347, Polebrooke Award; Book K, 109, Wadenhoe Award; Flat folder, Whitfield Award; Book K, 215, Bozeat Award; M 36, Whittlebury Award; Award Cupboard, Weston by Welland and Sutton Bassett Award; Book K, 251, Islip Award; Book K, 327, Newton Bromswold Award; Book K, 370, Raunds Award; Book K, 297, Hannington Award; Book L, 163, Hargrave Award; Award Cupboard, Greens Norton Award; X3475, Chelveston cum Caldecott Award.

Appendix B. *Acreage equivalents*

Table B.1. *Acreage equivalents of enclosing parishes before and after enclosure*[25]

Parish	Total parish acreage A (Award) C (1851 Census)	Total parish Land Tax (minus tax on houses etc.) (£)	Tax on tithes (£)	Acreage Equivalents pre-Enclosure (£)	Equivalents post-Enclosure (£)
Rushden	3,425 (A)	172.06 (1774) 225.28 (1783)	33.68 none	0.0404	0.0658
Bugbrooke	2,420 (C)	153.67 (1774) 204.90 (1784)	21.25 none	0.055	0.085
Wollaston	3,640 (C)	275.94	24.67	0.069	0.083
Wadenhoe	1,170 (C)	88.60	10.56	0.0667	0.0757
Whitfield	1,210 (C)	30.75	not subtracted	0.0254	0.0254
Whittlebury	2,870 (C)	88.51	not subtracted	0.0308	0.0308
Raunds	4,700 (A)	302.86	44.0	0.0551	0.0644
Greens Norton	1,895 (1851 Acreage, minus 595 acres waste)	168.18	11.97	0.0824	0.0902
Islip	1,370	83.16	15.06	0.0497	0.0683
Newton Bromswold	841 (A)	49.53	14.18	0.042	0.0589
Chelveston	1,730 (C)	87.82	13.85	0.0427	0.0572
Hargrave	1,210 (A)	79.00	11.06	0.0561	0.0653
Hannington	1,270 (C)	84.35	15.18	0.0544	0.0664
Weston by Welland	959 (A)	70.95	9.93	0.064	0.074
Sutton Bassett	711 (A)	46.80	6.55	0.056	0.065
Maxey	2,280 (C)	167.04	not subtracted	0.0732	0.0732
Helpston	1,860 (C)	91.79	not subtracted	0.0495	0.0495

[25] See Bibliography: 'Sources for the landholding survey', and Appendix A.

Table B.2. *Acreage equivalents of open parishes*[26]

Parish	Total parish acreage (A) Award (C) Census	Total parish Land Tax (minus tax on houses etc.) (£)	Tax on tithes (£)	Acreage equivalents (£)
Roade	1,570 (A)	70.80	constant left in	0.045
Naseby	3,255 (A)	88.87	unknown but subtracted with tax of J. Maddock	0.0273
Eye	2,670 (C)	252.05	6.00	0.0922
Abthorpe	1,919 (C)	87.15	7.77	0.0414
Stanwick	1,830 (C)	140.00	25.63	0.0625
Lutton	1,509 (C)	80.60	constant left in	0.0534

[26] *Ibid.*

Appendix C. *Correcting and editing the Land Tax*

CORRECTING

Slight changes of name between tax years (William Brown and William Browne), and miscodings (Wm. Allen, and William Allen) were corrected when the individual involved was clearly the same person.

EDITING INDIVIDUAL NAMES

Many landholders disappeared from the returns over the ten-year period because they had died, or had given their land to sons or other relatives in old age. Their land was not sold, it was inherited. Thus the returns were edited in order to assess the disappearance of owners who had *sold* their land more accurately. Inheritance was assumed if:

a) a former landowner no longer appeared in the later return

and b) a person with the same family name appeared on the later return;

and c) the newcomer owned at least one parcel of land which was taxed at the same sum as the former owner, and a total holding which was very nearly the same.

Similarly, the incumbents who changed from the earlier return to the late, who owned the same amount of land, and paid the same tax, were treated as one man. Publicly held lands (charity land, towns lands etc.) were counted as the same from one return to the next, and compared. Editing of this kind is obviously a source of error, but one that remains constant between open and enclosing parishes, thus conclusions as to relative change remain reasonably accurate.[27]

---

[27] Turner edited his returns in a similar fashion: 'where it can be established that a son or widow inherited the land it is counted as uninterrupted ownership'; church land and land belonging to university, school and charity estates were treated in the same way. In Turner's opinion this is a source of error 'but minimal as a percentage of the total change': 'Parliamentary Enclosure and Land Ownership Change in Buckinghamshire', p. 567.

Appendix D. *Landholding estimates*

Table D.1. *Landholding and parish populations*

Parish	All Occupiers as % of parish population, 1801	Occupiers of up to 50 acres as % of parish population, 1801	All Landholders as % of parish population, 1801
Hannington	18	15	48
Wollaston*	39	33	67
Maxey	45	33	73
Helpston	60	50	94
Rushden*	35	24	54
Chelveston	31	16	44
Islip	28	20	35
Greens Norton	22	14	32.5
Whitfield	30	16	46
Wadenhoe	18	2	22
Hargrave	38	19	73
Whittlebury	13	6	24
Raunds	39	28	52
Sutton Bassett	32	14	41
Weston by Welland	23	11	49
Newton Bromswold	30	17	52
Bugbrooke*	26	16	45
Stanwick	39	27	60
Eye	49	39	70
Lutton	33	14	58
Naseby	26	13	26.8
Abthorpe	38	32	69
Roade	25	14	55

* *c.*20 or more years between Land Tax assessment and *Census*
Source: Northants. RO, Land Tax returns and enclosure Awards (for parish acreage equivalents see Appendix B); 1801 *Census*; and see above pp. 305–7 for commentary.

Bibliography

SOURCES FOR THE LANDHOLDING SURVEY: LAND
TAX RETURNS AND ENCLOSURE AWARDS IN THE
NORTHAMPTONSHIRE RECORD OFFICE

Enclosing parishes

	(Date of encl. Act)	Returns	Awards
Rushden	(1778)	1774, 1783	Book F, 335, 1779
Bugbrooke	(1779)	1774, 1784	Book G, 548, 1781
Wollaston	(1788)	1783, 1793	Book I, 74, 1789
Wadenhoe	(1793)	1788, 1798	Book K, 109, 1793
Whitfield	(1796)	1791, 1801	Award Cupboard, 1797
Whittlebury	(1797)	1793, 1804	CP 43/373 (M36), 1800
Raunds	(1797)	1791, 1802	Book K, 370, 1800
Greens Norton and Duncott	(1799)	1794, 1804	Award Cupboard, 1807
Islip	(1800)	1795, 1805	Book K, 251, 1801
Newton Bromswold	(1800)	1795, 1805	Book K, 327, 1800
Chelveston cum Caldecott	(1801)	1796, 1806	X3475, 1801
Hargrave	(1802)	1797, 1807	Book L, 197, 1804
Hannington	(1802)	1797, 1807	Book, K, 297, 1802
Weston by Welland and Sutton Bassett	(1802)	1797, 1807	Award Cupboard, 1804
Maxey with Deepingate, Northborough, Glinton with Peakirk, Etton and	(1809)	1803, 1814	
Helpston		1804, 1813	

Open parishes	*(Date of encl. Act)*	*Returns*	*Awards*
Roade	(1816)	1786, 1796	J. W. Anscomb, 'Abstracts from Enclosure Awards', 3 vols., typescript, located in Northants. RO, p. 183
Naseby	(1820)	1806, 1814	Anscomb, p. 188
Eye	(1820)	1804, 1813	
Abthorpe	(1823)	1790, 1800	Anscomb, p. 190
Stanwick	(1834)	1790, 1800	Anscomb, p. 198
Lutton	(1864–7)	1796, 1806	

PARLIAMENTARY PAPERS AND GOVERNMENT PUBLICATIONS

Abstract of Answers and Returns, pursuant to an Act [41 Geo III] ... for taking an account of the population of Great Britain, Parliamentary Papers, 1801–2, VI, pp. 244 ff.

Board of Agriculture, *The General Report on Enclosures Drawn up by the Order of the Board of Agriculture* [ed. Arthur Young], 1808

Census of 1851 ... Population Tables. Part I ... Vol. I Report ..., Parliamentary Papers, 1852–3, LV, pp. 38 ff.

House of Commons, *Journals*, 1727–1815

House of Commons Sessional Papers of the Eighteenth Century, ed. Sheila Lambert (Wilmington, 1975)

House of Lords, *Journals*, 1760–1815

Land Utilization Survey of Britain, *Land Classification* (map; 1944)

Parliamentary Register, 1781

Report from HM Commissioners for Inquiring into the State of the Poor Laws in England and Wales, Parliamentary Papers, 1834, Answers to Rural Questions, XXX [Northamptonshire evidence abstracted, Northants. RO, YZ 6325/1–4]

Report of the Select Committee on Waste Lands [ed. Sir John Sinclair] (1795)

Royal Commission on Common Land, 1955–8, *Report* (Command 462)

Select Committee on Commons' Inclosure, Parliamentary Papers, 1844, V (583), pp. 1–99

OTHER PRINTED PRIMARY SOURCES

Place of publication is London unless otherwise stated.

[Addington, Stephen], *Inquiry into the Advantages and Disadvantages Resulting from Bills of Enclosure* (1780)
   Inquiry into the Reasons for and against Enclosing Open Fields (1772)
Andrews, C. Bruyn, ed., *The Torrington Diaries. A Selection from the Tours of the Hon. John Byng (later Fifth Viscount Torrington) between the years 1781 and 1794* (1954)
Andrews, Thomas, *An Enquiry into the Encrease and Miseries of the Poor of England; Which are shewn to be, I, Taxes . . . II, Luxury . . . III, Absence of Great Men from their Counties . . . IV, Inclosures of Commons* (1738)
Annals of Agriculture and Other Useful Arts, 1–46 (1784–1815)
Anon., *The Advantages and Disadvantages of Inclosing Waste Lands and Open Fields. Impartially Stated and Considered. By a Country Gentleman* (1772)
Anon., *Agricultural History, Gazetteer and Directory of the County of Huntingdon* (1854)
Anon., *The Case of the Major Part of the Owners and Proprietors of Lands in . . . Sympson, in the County of Bucks, who have petitioned the Honourable House of Commons to be heard against a Bill there depending . . . and answer to the case . . .* (1771) [Goldsmith's Library, GL 1770]
Anon., *The Case of the Petitioners against the Welton Common Bill*, n.d. (*c.* 1754) (Northampton Public Library)
Anon., *The Case of the Salt-Duty and Land Tax Offered to the Consideration of Every Freeholder* [1732]
Anon., *Cursory Remarks on Inclosures, Shewing the Pernicious and Destructive Consequences of Inclosing Common Fields &c. By a Country Farmer* (1786)
Anon., *An Enquiry into the Advantages and Disadvantages Resulting from Bills of Inclosure in which Objections are Stated and Remedies Proposed: the whole is humbly recommended to the attentive consideration of the legislature, before any more Bills (for that purpose) be enacted into laws* (1780)
Anon., *An Enquiry into the Reasons for and against Inclosing the Open Fields Humbly Submitted to All who Have Property in them, and Especially the Members of the British Legislature* (Coventry, 1767)
[Anon.], *Inquiry into the Advantages and Disadvantages Resulting from Bills of Enclosure* (1780)
Anon., *The Law of Commons and Commoners* (2nd edn, 1720)
Anon., 'A Letter from a Vale Farmer to the Editors, on the Disadvantages of Plowing in Stubble', *Museum Rusticum et Commerciale*, 2:72 (1764), pp. 35–6
Anon., 'A Letter to the Editors, on the Uses of Furze or Goss as Food for Cattle', *Museum Rusticum et Commerciale*, 2:39 (1764), pp. 118–19
Anon., *Observations on a Pamphlet entitled An Enquiry into the Advantages and Disadvantages Resulting from Bills of Inclosure to which Are Added*

Outlines of a Proposed Act of Parliament for a General Inclosure of Commons or Waste Lands (Shrewsbury, 1781)

Anon., *A Political Enquiry into the Consequences of Enclosing Waste Lands, and the Causes of the Present High Price of Butchers Meat. Being the Sentiments of a Society of Farmers in —shire* (1785)

Anon., *Reasons Humbly Offered against the Bill for Inclosing and Dividing the Common Fields within the Parish and Manor of Stareton, otherwise Staverton, in the County of Northampton*, 1 page, folio, no imprint [eighteenth century]. Offered for Sale by Francis Edwards Ltd, *Catalogue 966*, Item 102 (not traced)

Anon., *Reflections on the Cruelty of Inclosing Common-Field Lands, Particularly as it Affects the Church and Poor; in a letter to the Lord Bishop of Lincoln by a clergyman of that diocese* ... (1796)

Anon., *The True Interest of the Land Owners of Great Britain or the Husbandmen's Essay* ... [n.d., early eighteenth century]

[Arbuthnot, John], *An Inquiry into the Connection between the Present Price of Provisions and the Size of Farms ... by a farmer* (1773)

Baird, T., *General View of the Agriculture of the County of Middlesex* (1793)

Bamford, Samuel, *The Dialect of South Lancashire* (1850)

Batchelor, Thomas, *General View of the Agriculture of the County of Bedford* (1813)

Bewick, Thomas, *A Memoir*, ed. Iain Bain (1862; 1975 edn)

Billingsley, J., *General View of the Agriculture of the County of Somerset* (1797)

Bishton, J., *General View of the Agriculture of Shropshire* (1794)

Blackstone, William, *Commentaries on the Laws of England* (12th edn, 1794)

[Blane, Gilbert Dr], *Inquiry into the Causes and Remedies of the Late and Present Scarcity and High Price of Provisions in a Letter to the Right Honourable Earl Spencer, KG, First Lord of the Admiralty* (1800)

Bridges, John, *History and Antiquities of Northamptonshire*, ed. P. Whalley (Oxford, 1791)

Burn, Richard, *The Justice of the Peace and Parish Officer* (14th edn, 1780)

Byng, John (5th Viscount Torrington), *The Torrington Diaries*, ed. C. Bruyn Andrews (1954)

Clare, John, *John Clare*, ed. Eric Robinson and David Powell (Oxford, 1984)

   Selected Poems, ed. J. W. and Anne Tibble, Everyman edition (1965)

   Selected Poems of John Clare, ed. Elaine Feinstein (1968)

   Selected Poems and Prose of John Clare, ed. Eric Robinson and Geoffrey Summerfield (1967)

Clark, John, *General View of the Agriculture of the County of Hereford with Observations on the Means of its Improvement* (1794)

   The Nature and Value of Leasehold Property (1808)

Cobbold, T. S., *Entozoa* (1864)

Cowper, John, *An Essay Proving that Inclosing of Commons and Common Field Land is Contrary to the Interests of the Nation* (1732)

Crabbe, George, *George Crabbe: Tales, 1812 and Other Selected Poems*, ed. Howard Mills (Cambridge, 1967)

Crossman, H., *An Introduction to the Knowledge of the Christian Religion* (SPCK, new edn, n.d. [pre-1841])

Davies, David, *The Case of the Labourers in Husbandry Stated and Considered* (1795)

Davis, T. (senior), *A General View of the Agriculture of Wiltshire* (1794)

de Monchy, Salomon, *Remarks upon the Mortality among the Horned Cattle* (Rotterdam, 1769, trans. London, 1770)

Defoe, Daniel, *A Tour through the Whole Island of Great Britain* (1724–6; 1962 edn)

Donaldson, James, *General View of the Agriculture of the County of Northampton, with Observations on the Means of its Improvement . . . to which is added, an appendix containing a comparison between the English and Scotch systems of husbandry as practised in the counties of Northampton and Perth* (Edinburgh, 1794)

A General View of the County of Northampton (1795)

Eaton, Daniel, *The Letters of Daniel Eaton to the Third Earl of Cardigan 1725–32*, ed. Joan Wake and D. C. Webster, Publications of the Northamptonshire Record Society, XXIV (Kettering, 1971)

Eden, F. M., *The State of the Poor, and History of the Labouring Classes in England* (1797)

[Ellman], 'On Folding Sheep: Extract of a Letter from Mr Ellman to Sir John Sinclair', *Annals of Agriculture and Other Useful Arts*, 38 (1801)

Foot, Peter, *General View of the Agriculture of the County of Middlesex* (1794)

Gooch, W., *General View of the Agriculture of the County of Cambridge* (1811)

[Goode, Thomas, Rector of Weldon], *A Letter to the Commoners in Rockingham Forest, by a Commoner* [Stamford, 1744]

Hampton, Christopher, ed., *A Radical Reader: The Struggle for Change in England 1381–1914* (1984)

Harrison, Edward, 'An Inquiry into the Nature of the Soil, and the Circumstances which Induce and Prevent the Rot', *Annals of Agriculture and Other Useful Arts*, 40 (1803), pp. 19–30

Hatley, V. A., ed., *Northamptonshire Militia Lists, 1777*, Publications of the Northamptonshire Record Society, 25 (1973)

Hilman, Daniel, *Tusser Redivivus* (1710)

Historical Manuscripts Commission, *Dartmouth III* (Ser. 20, 15th Report, 1896)

Homer, Henry, *An Essay on the Nature and Method of Ascertaining the Specifick Shares of Proprietors, upon the Inclosure of Common Fields. With observations upon the inconveniencies of open fields, and upon the objections to their inclosure particularly as far as they relate to the publick and the poor* (1766; 2nd edn, Oxford, n.d.)

Howlett, John, *Dispersion of the Gloomy Apprehensions, of Late Repeatedly Suggested, from the Decline of our Corn Trade, and Conclusions of a Directly Opposite Tendency Established upon Well-Authenticated Facts: to which are added, Observations upon the First Report from the Committee on Waste-Lands, &c.* (1797)

Enclosure and Population (1973, ed. and introduction by A. H. John)
Enclosures a Cause of Improved Agriculture (1787)
An Enquiry into the Influence which Enclosures Have Had upon the Population of this Kingdom (1781)
An Essay on the Population of Ireland (Dublin, 1786)
An Examination of Dr Price's Essay on the Population of England and Wales (Maidstone, 1781)
The Insufficiency of the Causes to which the Increase of our Poor, and of the Poor's Rates Have Been Commonly Ascribed; the True One Stated ... (1788)
Hoyle, Henry, 'Advantage of Inclosures', *Annals of Agriculture and Other Useful Arts*, 32 (1799), pp. 530–9
James, W., and Malcolm, J., *General View of the Agriculture of Buckinghamshire* (1794)
Jefferies, Richard, *The Gamekeeper at Home* (1878; 1948)
Kalm, Pehr, *Kalm's Account of his Visit to England on his Way to America in 1748*, trans. Joseph Lucas (1892)
Kent, J. H., *Remarks on the Injuriousness of the Consolidation of Small Farms and the Benefit of Small Occupations and Allotments* (Bury, 1844)
Kent, Nathaniel, *The Great Advantage of a Cow to the Family of a Labouring Man* (broadsheet), and also in *Annals of Agriculture and Other Useful Arts*, 31 (1798), pp. 21–6
Hints to Gentlemen of Landed Property (2nd edn, 1776)
Kett, Henry, *An Essay on Wastes in General, and on Mosswold in Particular* (Norwich, 1792)
Laurence, Edward, *The Duty of a Steward to his Lord ... Methods Likely to Improve their Estates* (1727; 2nd edn, 1731)
The Duty and Office of a Land Steward (3rd edn, Dublin, 1731)
The Complete Steward (1761)
Laurence, John, *A New System of Agriculture and Gardening* (1726)
Lawrence, John, *The Modern Land Steward* (1801)
Lawson, G., 'Hints Favourable to the Poor', *Annals of Agriculture and Other Useful Arts*, 40 (1803)
[Lee, Joseph], *A Vindication of a Regulated Inclosure. Wherein is Plainly Proved, that Inclosure of Commons ... are Both Lawful and Laudable* (1656)
Lewis, George Cornewall, *Local Disturbances in Ireland* (1836)
Malthus, Thomas, *An Essay on the Principle of Population, as it Affects the Future Improvement of Society* (1798), and *An Essay on the Principle of Population, or, A View of its Past and Present Effects on Human Happiness* (1803), both repr. in Gertrude Himmelfarb, ed., *On Population. Thomas Robert Malthus* (1960)
Manwood, John, *A Treatise of the Lawes of the Forest ...* (1615)
Marshall, William, *Draught of a General Act, for the Appropriation of Parochial Wastes* (1801)
On the Landed Property of England, an Elementary and Practical Treatise, Containing the Purchase, the Improvement, and the Management of Landed Estates (1804)

Rural Economy of Gloucestershire (1789; 2nd edn, 1796)

Rural Oeconomy of the Midland Counties, including the Management of Livestock, in Leicestershire and its Environs, together with Minutes on Agriculture and Planting in the District of the Midland Station (2nd edn, 1796)

Marsters, Thomas, jr, *A View of Agricultural Oppressions: and of their Effects upon Society* (2nd edn, 1798)

Martineau, Harriet, *Brooke Farm*, II (1833)

Mavor, W., *General View of the Agriculture of Berkshire* (1813)

Meister, Henry, *Letters Written during a Residence in England* (1792)

Middleton, J., *General View of the Agriculture of the County of Middlesex* (1807)

Monk, John, *General View of the Agriculture of the County of Leicester* (1794)

Mordaunt, John, *The Complete Steward* (1761)

Morton, John, *The Natural History of Northamptonshire* (1712)

Norden, John, *Speculi Britanniae pars Altera; or a Delineation of Northamptonshire; being a brief historicall and choriographicall description of that county ... by the travayle of J. Norden, in the year 1610* (1720)

Nourse, Timothy, *Campania Foelix, or a Discourse of the Benefits and Improvements of Husbandry* (1700; 2nd edn, 1706)

Paul, George Onesiphorus, *Observations on the General Enclosure Bill* (1796)

Pennington, W., *Reflections on the Various Advantages Resulting from the Draining, Inclosing and Allotting of Large Commons and Common Fields* (1769)

Phillips, J., *A General History of Inland Navigation* (5th edn, 1805; repr. New York, 1970)

Pitt, William, *General View of the Agriculture of the County of Leicester* (1809)

General View of the Agriculture of the County of Northampton (1809)

General View of the Agriculture of the County of Stafford (1796)

Topographical History of Staffordshire (Newcastle-under-Lyme, 1817)

Plot, R., *The Natural History of Oxfordshire. Being an Essay towards a Natural History of England* (Oxford, 1677)

Power, E., and R. H. Tawney, *Tudor Economic Documents, I, Agriculture and Industry* (1924; new edn, 1951)

Pratt, Samuel Jackson, 'Cottage-Pictures' [1801] in *Sympathy and Other Poems Including Landscapes in Verse, Cottage-Pictures, Revised, Corrected, and Enlarged* (1807)

Price, Richard, *Essay on the Population of England from the Revolution to the Present Time* (1780)

Observations on Reversionary Payments (2nd edn, 1771; 6th edn, 1805)

Richmond, Duke of, 'On the Use of Furze, by His Grace the Duke of Richmond', *Annals of Agriculture and Other Useful Arts*, 41 (1804), pp. 193–6

Rudge, Thomas, *General View of the Agriculture of the County of Gloucester* (1807)

Sinclair, Sir John, *An Address to the Members of the Board of Agriculture, on the Cultivation and Improvement of the Waste Lands of this Kingdom* (1795)

The Code of Agriculture (5th edn, 1832)

'Observations on the Means of Enabling a Cottager to Keep a Cow, by the Produce of a Small Portion of Arable Land', in *Communications to the Board of Agriculture*, IV, no. 18 (1805), pp. 358–67

Smith, Adam, *An Inquiry into the Nature and Causes of the Wealth of Nations* (1776; New York, 1937 edn)

Stone, Thomas, *Suggestions for Rendering the Inclosure of Common Fields and Waste Lands a Source of Population and Riches* (1787)

Stout, William, *The Autobiography of William Stout of Lancaster, 1665–1752*, ed. J. D. Marshall (Manchester, 1967)

Stow, John, *The Annales, or Generall Chronicle of England, Begun first by Maister John Stow, and after him continued . . . unto the ende of the present yeere 1614, by E. Howes* (1615)

Tusser, Thomas, *Five Hundred Points of Good Husbandry* (1573; 1580; repr. Oxford, 1984, with an introduction by Geoffrey Grigson)

[Tyley, the Rev. James], 'Inclosure of Open Fields, in Northamptonshire, translation by Miss Dorothy Halton, of a Latin Poem by the Rev. James Tyley, Rector of Great Addington, 1799–1830', ed. Joan Wake, *The Reminder*, 3: 94 (Feb. 1928), pp. 5–6 (copy in Northamptonshire Record Society, Miscellaneous Pamphlets)

Vancouver, Charles, *General View of the Agriculture of the County of Cambridge* (1794)

General View of the Agriculture of Hampshire (1813)

Wake, Joan, and D. C. Webster, see Daniel Eaton

Walker, D., *General View of the Agriculture of the County of Hertford* (1795)

Wedderburn, Alexander [later Lord Loughborough], *Essay upon the Question What Proportion of the Produce of Arable Land Ought to Be Paid as Rent to the Landlord* (Edinburgh, 1776)

Wedge, J., *General View of the Agriculture of the County of Warwick* (1794)

Whellan, William, *History, Gazetteer, and Directory of Northamptonshire* (1849)

White, Gilbert, *The Essential Gilbert White of Selborne*, ed. H. J. Massingham (Boston, 1985)

Gilbert White's Journals, ed. Walter Johnson (Cambridge, Mass., 1970)

The Natural History of Selborne (1788–9; 1977)

Williams, J., *The Historical and Topographical View . . . of Leominster* (Leominster, 1808)

Willis, James, 'On Cows for Cottagers', *Annals of Agriculture and Other Useful Arts*, 40 (1803), pp. 554–67

Woodhouse, A. S. P., ed., *Puritanism and Liberty. Being the Army Debates (1647–9) from the Clarke Manuscripts with Supplementary Documents* (1938)

Young, Arthur, *The Autobiography of Arthur Young*, ed. M. Betham Edwards (1898; repr. New York, 1967)

'Dairy Farms', *Annals of Agriculture . . .* , 5 (1786), pp. 222–4

General View of the Agriculture of Oxfordshire (1813)
General View of the Agriculture of Lincolnshire (1813)
'An Inquiry into the Propriety of Applying Wastes to the Better Mainte-
nance and Support of the Poor: with Instances of the Great Effects
which have Attended their Acquisition of Property in Keeping them
from the Parish even in the Present Scarcity', *Annals of Agriculture and
Other Useful Arts*, 36 (1801), pp. 497–547
'Introduction', *Annals of Agriculture and Other Useful Arts*, 1 (1784)
'Minutes Concerning Parliamentary Inclosures in the County of Cam-
bridge', *Annals of Agriculture and Other useful Arts*, 42 (1804),
pp. 471–502
'Mischiefs of Commons', *Annals of Agriculture and Other Useful Arts*, 8
(1787), pp. [437–9] misprinted 347–9
'On the Application of the Principles of Population, to the Question of
Assigning Land to Cottages', *Annals of Agriculture and Other Useful
Arts*, 41 (1804), pp. 208–31
*Travels During the Years 1787, 1788 and 1789; undertaken more par-
ticularly with a view of ascertaining the cultivation, wealth, resources,
and national prosperity of the Kingdom of France* (2nd edn, 1794)
[Young, Arthur], Board of Agriculture, *General Report on Enclosures.
Drawn up by Order of the Board of Agriculture* (1808)
[Young, A.], 'Waste Lands' [a digest of the Reports to the Board of
Agriculture], *Annals of Agriculture and Other Useful Arts*, 33 (1799)

SECONDARY SOURCES

Abrams, P., *Historical Sociology* (Shepton Mallet, 1982)
Addy, John, *The Textile Revolution* (1976)
Albion, R. G., *Forests and Sea Power* (1926)
Alexander, George Glover, 'The Manorial System and Copyhold Tenure',
Publications of the Thoresby Society, 33, *Miscellanea* (Leeds, 1935),
pp. 283–305
Allen, G. C. K., *Law in the Making* (Oxford, 7th edn, 1964)
Allen, R. C., *Enclosure and the Yeoman* (Oxford, 1992)
'Enclosure, Capitalist Agriculture, and the Growth in Corn Yields in
Early Modern England', University of British Columbia, Department
of Economics, Discussion Paper no. 86-39 (1986)
'Enclosure, Farming Methods, and the Growth of Productivity in the
South Midlands', University of British Columbia, Department of
Economics, Discussion Paper no. 86-44 (1986)
'The Growth of Labour Productivity in Early Modern English Agri-
culture', University of British Columbia, Department of Economics,
Discussion Paper no. 86-40 (1986)
'Inferring Yields from Probate Inventories', *Journal of Economic History*,
48 (1988), pp. 117–25
Allen, R. C., and C. O'Grada, 'On the Road Again with Arthur Young',
Journal of Economic History, 48 (1988), pp. 93–116

Allison, K. J., 'The Sheep-Corn Husbandry of Norfolk in the Sixteenth and Seventeenth Centuries', *Agricultural History Review*, 5 (1957), pp. 12–30.

Allison, K. J., M. W. Beresford and J. G. Hurst, *The Deserted Villages of Northamptonshire*, Leicester University Department of English Local History, Occasional Paper no. 18 (Leicester University Press, 1966)

Anon., 'The Folklore of Long Buckby', *The Library List. Journal of the County Library*, 5:54 (January, 1939), Northampton Public Library, no. 49

Anon., 'Gleaning', *Scottish Law Times*, 1 (1893–4), p. 655–6

Anon., *List of Inclosure Awards and Enrolments of Awards now in the Office of the Clerk of the Peace of the County of Northampton* (Northampton, 1904)

Andrews, William, ed., *Bygone Northamptonshire* (1891)

Anscomb, J. W., 'An Eighteenth-Century Inclosure and Football Play at West Haddon', *Northamptonshire Past and Present*, 4:3 (1968–9), pp. 175–8

Appleby, Joyce Oldham, *Economic Thought and Ideology in Seventeenth-Century England* (1978)

Archer, John, *By a Flash and a Scare: Incendiarism, Animal Maiming, and Poaching in East Anglia 1815–1870* (Oxford, 1990)

Arlaachi, Pino, *Mafia, Peasants and Great Estates: Society in Traditional Calabria* (Cambridge, 1983)

Ashby, M. K., *The Changing English Village: A History of Bledington, Gloucestershire, in its Setting 1066–1914* (Kineton, 1974)

Joseph Ashby of Tysoe, 1859–1919: A Study of English Village Life (Cambridge, 1961; 1974)

Ashton, T. S., *An Economic History of England: The Eighteenth Century* (1955; 1969)

Ault, W. O., *Open-Field Farming in Medieval England: A Study of Village By-Laws* (1972)

'Open-Field Husbandry and the Village Community: A Study of Agrarian By-Laws in Medieval England', *Transactions of the American Philosophical Society*, new series, 55, part 7 (1965)

Baker, A. R. H., and R. A. Butlin, eds., *Studies of Field Systems in the British Isles* (Cambridge, 1973)

Baker, Margaret, *Folklore and Customs of Rural England* (1974)

Bales, Robert, 'Attitudes towards Drinking in the Irish Culture', in D. Pitmann and C. R. Snyder, eds., *Society, Culture and Drinking Patterns* (1962), pp. 157–87

Ballard, A., 'The Management of Open Fields', *Report*, Oxfordshire Archaeological Society (1913), pp. 131–44

Barrell, John, *The Dark Side of the Landscape* (1980)

The Idea of Landscape and the Sense of Place 1730–1840: An Approach to the Poetry of John Clare (Cambridge, 1972)

Barrell, John, and John Bull, eds., *The Penguin Book of English Pastoral Verse* (1982)

Bayne-Powell, R., *Travellers in Eighteenth-Century England* (1951)

Beckett, J. V., *The Aristocracy in England* (Oxford, 1986)
'The Decline of the Small Landowner in Eighteenth and Nineteenth-Century England: Some Regional Considerations', *Agricultural History Review*, 30 (1982), pp. 97–111
'The Disappearance of the Cottager and the Squatter from the English Countryside: The Hammonds Revisited', in B. A. Holderness and M. E. Turner, eds., *Land, Labour and Agriculture: Essays Presented to Gordon Mingay* (1991), p. 49–67
A History of Laxton: England's Last Open-Field Village (Oxford, 1989)
'Regional Variation and the Agricultural Depression, 1730–50', *Agricultural History Review*, 35 (1982), pp. 35–51
Beckwith, Ian, 'The Re-modelling of a Common-Field System', *Agricultural History Review*, 15 (1967), p. 109–12
Beecham, H. A., 'A Review of Balks as Strip Boundaries in the Open Fields', *Agricultural History Review*, 4 (1956), pp. 22–44
Bell, Vicars, *To Meet Mr Ellis: Little Gaddesdon in the Eighteenth Century* (n.d. [1955])
Beloff, Max, *Public Order and Popular Disturbances, 1660–1714* (Oxford, 1938)
Berger, John, *Once in Europa* (1983)
Bloch, M., *French Rural History* (1966)
Bohstedt, John, *Riots and Community Politics in England and Wales 1790–1810* (Cambridge, Mass., 1983)
Bonser, K. J., *The Drovers* (1970)
Bourne, George, *Change in the Village* (1912; 1966 edn)
Bowden, P. J., 'Agricultural Prices, Wages, Farm Profits and Rents', in J. Thirsk, ed., *Agrarian History of England and Wales*, V, part II (Cambridge, 1985), pp. 1–118
Boyer, George R., 'The Old Poor Law and the Agricultural Labor Market in Southern England', *Journal of Economic History*, 46 (1986), pp. 113–35
Brenner, Robert, 'Agrarian Class Structure and Economic Development in Pre-Industrial Europe', *Past and Present*, 70 (1976), pp. 30–75
Broad, John, 'Cattle Plague in Eighteenth-Century England', *Agricultural History Review*, 31 (1983), pp. 104–15
'The Verneys as Enclosing Landlords', in John Chartres and David Hey, eds., *English Rural Society: Essays in Honour of Joan Thirsk* (Cambridge, 1990), pp. 27–54
Brody, Hugh, *Inishkillane: Change and Decline in the West of Ireland* (1973)
Brundage, Anthony, *The Making of the New Poor Law 1832–1839* (1978)
Bushaway, R. W. *By Rite: Custom, Ceremony and Community in England 1700–1880* (1982)
'"Grovely, Grovely and All Grovely". Custom, Crime and Conflict in the English Woodland', *History Today*, 31 (1981) pp. 37–43
Campbell, B. M. S., 'The Regional Uniqueness of English Field Systems? Some Evidence from East Norfolk', *Agricultural History Review*, 29 (1987), pp. 16–28

Campbell, John, Lord, *Lives of the Lord Chancellors and Keepers of the Great Seal of England, from the Earliest Times till the Reign of King George IV* (5th edn, 1868)

Campbell, R. H., and A. S. Skinner, *Adam Smith* (1982)

Carter, Ian, *Farm Life in Northeast Scotland 1840–1914: The Poor Man's Country* (Edinburgh, 1979)

Chalkin, C. W., *Seventeenth-Century Kent* (1965)

Chambers, J. D., 'Enclosure and Labour Supply in the Industrial Revolution', *Economic History Review*, 2nd series, 5 (1953), pp. 319–43, and in *Agriculture and Economic Growth in England 1650–1815*, ed., E. L. Jones (1967), pp. 94–127

'Enclosure and the Small Landowner', *Economic History Review*, 1st series, 10 (1940), pp. 118–27

'Enclosure and the Small Landowner in Lindsey', *The Lincolnshire Historian*, 1 (1947), pp. 15–20

Nottinghamshire in the Eighteenth Century. A Study of Life and Labour under the Squirearchy (1932; repr. 1966)

Chambers, J. D., and G. E. Mingay, *The Agricultural Revolution, 1750–1880* (1966)

Chapman, John, 'The Extent and Nature of Parliamentary Enclosure', *Agricultural History Review*, 35 (1987), pp. 25–35

Charlesworth, Andrew, ed., *An Atlas of Rural Protest in Britain 1548–1900* (1983)

Chase, Malcolm, *The People's Farm: English Radical Agrarianism 1775–1840* (Oxford, 1988)

'Thomas Spence: The Trumpet of Jubilee', *Past and Present*, 76 (1977), pp. 75–98

Chatwin, Bruce, *The Songlines* (1987)

Chibnall, A. C., *Beyond Sherington* (1979)

Sherington: Fields and Fiefs of a Buckinghamshire Village (Cambridge, 1965)

Clapham, J. H., *An Economic History of Modern Britain: The Early Railway Age 1820–1850* (Cambridge, 1926; 2nd edn, 1930, repr. 1950)

Clark, Gregory, 'Productivity Growth without Technical Change in European Agriculture before 1850', *Journal of Economic History*, 47 (1987), pp. 419–32

Coleman, D. C., *The Economy of England* (Oxford, 1977)

Collins, Kins, 'Marx on the English Agricultural Revolution: Theory and Evidence', *History and Theory*, 6:3 (1967), pp. 351–81

Collis, John Stewart, *The Worm Forgives the Plough* (1973)

Cone, C. B., *The English Jacobins: Reformers in Late Eighteenth-Century England* (1968)

Cooke, James Herbert, 'Timber-Stealing Riots in Whittlebury and Salcey Forests, in 1727–8', *Northamptonshire Notes and Queries*, 1 (1886), pp. 123–7

Corrigan, Philip, and Derek Sayer, *The Great Arch: English State Formation as Cultural Revolution* (1985)

Cox, J. C., *The Royal Forests of England* (1905)

Crafts, N. F. R., 'Enclosure and Labour Supply Revisited', *Explorations in Economic History*, 15 (1978), pp. 172–83

'Income Elasticities of Demand and the Release of Labour by Agriculture during the British Industrial Revolution', *Journal of European Economic History*, 9 (1980), pp. 153–68

Cressy, David, 'Kinship and Kin Interaction in Early Modern England', *Past and Present*, 113 (1986), pp. 38–69

Croot, Patricia, and David Parker, 'Agrarian Class Structure and Economic Development', *Past and Present* 78 (1978), pp. 37–47

Cross, A. L., *Eighteenth-Century Documents Relating to the Royal Forests, the Sheriffs and Smuggling (selected from the Shelburn MSS in the William L. Clements Library)*, University of Michigan Publications, History and Political Science, XVII (New York, 1928)

Darby, H. C., *The Draining of the Fens* (1940)

Davidson, Caroline, *A Woman's Work is Never Done: A History of Housework in the British Isles 1650–1950* (1982)

Davies, E., 'The Small Landowner, 1780–1832, in the Light of the Land Tax Assessments', *Economic History Review*, 1st series, 1 (1927), pp. 87–113

Deane, Phillis, and W. A. Cole, *British Economic Growth 1688–1959* (2nd edn, 1967)

Dickinson, H. T., *Liberty and Property: Political Ideology in Eighteenth-Century Britain* (1977)

Ditchfield, Peter H., *Country Folk: A Pleasant Company* (1974)

Dobson, M. J., 'When Malaria was an English Disease', *The Geographical Magazine*, 54 (1982), pp. 94–9

Dowell, Stephen, *History of Taxation and Taxes in England*, 4 vols. (1884; 3rd edn, 1965), II

Dunbabin, J. P. D., *Rural Discontent in Nineteenth-Century Britain* (1974)

Dyer, Christopher, *Standards of Living in the Middle Ages* (Cambridge, 1989)

Ehrman, John, *The Younger Pitt: The Years of Acclaim* (1969)

Ennew, Judith, Paul Hirst, and Keith Tribe, '"Peasantry" as an Economic Category', *Journal of Peasant Studies*, 4 (1977), pp. 295–322

Ernle, R. E. Prothero, Lord, *English Farming Past and Present* (1948; 6th edn, 1961)

'Obstacles to Progress', in *Agriculture and Economic Growth in England 1650–1815*, ed., E. L. Jones (1967), pp. 49–65; originally published as chapter 3 of *The Land and its People* (1925)

Everitt, Alan, 'Farm Labourers', in Joan Thirsk, ed., *The Agrarian History of England and Wales*, IV (1967), pp. 396–466

Finch, M. E., *The Wealth of Five Northamptonshire Families 1540–1640*, Publications of the Northamptonshire Record Society, 19 (Oxford, 1956)

Fortescue, Sir John, *The Army and the County Lieutenancies* (1908)

Fussell, G., 'Four Centuries of Leicestershire Farming', *Transactions of the Leicestershire Archaeological Society*, 24 (1949), pp. 154–76

Gay, E. F., 'The Midland Revolt of 1607', *Transactions of the Royal Historical Society*, new series, 18 (1904), pp. 195–244

Gentles, Ian, 'The Purchasers of Northamptonshire Crown Lands', *Midland History*, 3 (1976), pp. 206–31

George, Dorothy, *England in Transition* (1965)

Gilbey, Sir Walter, Bt, and E. D. Cumming, *George Morland his Life and Works* (1907)

Ginter, D. E., *A Measure of Wealth: The English Land Tax in Historical Analysis* (Kingston and Montreal, 1992)

'Measuring the Decline of the Small Landowner', in B. A. Holderness and Michael Turner, eds., *Land, Labour and Agriculture. Essays Presented to Gordon Mingay* (1991), pp. 361–83

Glass, D. V., 'King's Population Estimates of England and Wales, 1695', *Population Studies*, 3 (1950), pp. 338–74

Godber, Joyce, *History of Bedfordshire, 1066–1888* (Luton, 1969)

Goddard, N., 'Agricultural Literature and Societies', in G. Mingay, ed., *Agrarian History of England and Wales 1750–1850*, VI (Cambridge, 1989), pp. 361–83

Gonner, E. C. K., *Common Land and Inclosure* (1912; 2nd edn, with introduction by G. E. Mingay, 1966)

Gray, H. L., *English Field Systems*, Harvard Historical Studies, XXII (1915)

English Open Fields (1955)

'Yeoman Farming in Oxfordshire from the Sixteenth Century to the Nineteenth', *Quarterly Journal of Economics*, 24 (1910), pp. 293–326

Grieve, M., *A Modern Herbal* (1931; 1982)

Grigg, D. B., *The Agricultural Revolution in South Lincolnshire* (Cambridge, 1966)

'The Land Tax Returns', *Agricultural History Review*, 11 (1963), pp. 82–94

'A Source on Landownership: The Land Tax Returns', *Amateur Historian*, 6 (1964), pp. 152–6

Grover, Richard, 'Procedures for Exploiting the Land Tax', paper presented to the Conference on Land Tax, London, 1981: Open University and Portsmouth Polytechnic

Habakkuk, H. J., 'English Landownership, 1680–1740', *Economic History Review*, 1st series, 10 (1940), pp. 2–17

Haldane, A. R. B., *The Drove Roads of Scotland* (Newton Abbot, 1973)

Halevy, E., *England in 1815* (2nd edn, 1949)

Hallam, H. E., 'The Fen Bylaws of Spalding and Pinchbeck', *Lincolnshire Architectural and Archaeological Society*, 10 (1963), pp. 40–56

Halpin, Brendan, *Patterns of Animal Disease* (1975)

Halsbury's Laws of England Being a Complete Statement of the Whole Law of England (2nd edn, ed. Viscount Hailsham, 1932)

Hammond, J. L., and Barbara Hammond, *The Village Labourer* (1911; repr. 1966)

Hanawalt, Barbara, *The Ties that Bound: Peasant Families in Medieval England* (Oxford, 1986)

Hardin, Garrett, 'The Tragedy of the Commons', *Science*, 162 (1968), pp. 1243–8

Harman, H., *Buckinghamshire Dialect* (1929; repr. 1971)

Hartley, Dorothy, *Food in England* (1954)

Lost Country Life (New York, 1979 edn)

Made in England (1939; 1987)

Water in England (1964)

Hasbach, Wilhelm, *A History of the English Agricultural Labourer* (1908; 1966)

Hatley, V. A., and Joseph Rajczonek, *Shoemakers in Northamptonshire, 1762–1911: A Statistical Survey*, Northampton Historical Series, no. 6 (Northampton, 1971)

Havinden, M. A., 'Agricultural Progress in Open-field Oxfordshire', *Agricultural History Review*, 9 (1961), pp. 73–83; reprinted in E. L. Jones, ed., *Agriculture and Economic Growth in England 1650–1815* (1967), pp. 66–79

Hay, D., 'Poaching and the Game Laws on Cannock Chase', in D. Hay, P. Linebaugh, E. P. Thompson, eds., *Albion's Fatal Tree: Crime and Society in Eighteenth-Century England* (1975), pp. 189–254

Crown Side Cases in the Court of King's Bench, (Staffs. Record Society (forthcoming)

Hay, Douglas, and Francis Snyder, eds., *Policing and Prosecution in Britain, 1750–1850* (Oxford, 1989)

Hill, Christopher, *Reformation to Industrial Revolution* (1969)

Society and Puritanism in Pre-Revolutionary England (1964; 1966 edn)

Hilton, H., 'Lord and Peasant in Staffordshire in the Middle Ages', *North Staffordshire Journal of Field Studies*, 10 (1970), pp. 1–20

Hobsbawm, E. J., *Industry and Empire* (1968)

Labouring Men (New York, 1967)

Hobsbawm, E. J. and George Rudé, *Captain Swing* (1969)

Holderness, B. A., 'Prices, Productivity and Output', in G. Mingay, ed., *The Agrarian History of England and Wales*, VI (Cambridge, 1989), pp. 84–189

Holderness, B. A., and Michael Turner, eds., *Land, Labour and Agriculture. Essays Presented to Gordon Mingay* (1991)

Hont, Istvan, and Michael Ignatieff, eds., *Wealth and Virtue: The Shaping of Political Economy in the Scottish Enlightenment* (Cambridge, 1985)

Horn, Pamela, 'An Eighteenth-Century Land Agent: The Career of Nathaniel Kent (1737–1810)', *Agricultural History Review*, 30 (1982), pp. 1–16

Hoskins, W. G., 'The Leicestershire Farmer in the Seventeenth Century', *Agricultural History*, 25 (1951), pp. 9–20; reprinted in Hoskins, *Provincial England* (1963), pp. 149–69

'The Leicestershire Farmer in the Sixteenth Century', *Transactions* of the Leicestershire Archaeological Society, 22 (1941–5), pp. 33–94

The Making of the English Landscape (1955; 1970)

The Midland Peasant: The Economic and Social History of a Leicestershire Village (1957; 1965)

Howell, Cicely, *Land, Family and Inheritance in Transition: Kibworth Harcourt 1280–1700* (Cambridge, 1983)

Howkins, Alun, and Ian C. Dyck, '"The Time's Alteration"': Popular Ballads, Rural Radicalism and William Cobbett', *History Workshop Journal*, issue 23 (1987), pp. 20–38

Hudson, W. H., *The Illustrated Shepherd's Life* (1910; 1987)

Humphries, Jane, 'Enclosures, Common Rights, and Women: The Proletarianization of Families in the Late Eighteenth and Early Nineteenth Centuries', *Journal of Economic History*, 1 (1990), pp. 17–42

Hunt, H. G., 'Land Tax Assessments', *English Historical Review*, Short Guides to Records, no. 16, pp. 283–86

'Landownership and Enclosure 1750–1830', *Economic History Review*, 2nd series, 11 (1958–9), pp. 497–505

Hyslop, N. St. G., 'Observations on Pathogenic Organisms in the Airborne State', *Tropical Animal Health and Production*, 4:1 (1972), pp. 28–41

John, A. H., ed., *Enclosure and Population* (1973)

Johnson, A. H., *The Disappearance of the Small Landowner* (1909; new edn, with an introduction by Joan Thirsk, 1963)

Jones, D. J. V., *Crime, Protest, Community and Police in Nineteenth-Century Britain* (1982)

Jones, E. L., *Agriculture and the Industrial Revolution* (Oxford, 1975)

Jones, E. L., ed., *Agriculture and Economic Growth in England 1650–1815* (1967)

Jones, P. M., 'Parish, Seigneurie and the Community of Inhabitants in Southern Central France', *Past and Present*, 91 (1981), pp. 74–108

Kerridge, Eric, *The Agricultural Revolution* (1967)

The Farmers of Old England (1973)

King, Peter, 'Gleaners, Farmers and the Failure of Legal Sanctions in England 1750–1850', *Past and Present*, 125 (1989), pp. 116–50

'The Origins of the Gleaning Judgement of 1788: A Case Study of Legal Change, Customary Right and Social Conflict in Late Eighteenth-Century England', *Law and History Review*, 10 (1992)

Kussmaul, Ann S., *A General View of the Rural Economy of England, 1538–1840* (Cambridge, 1990)

Servants in Husbandry in Early Modern England (Cambridge, 1981)

Lambert, Sheila, *Bills and Acts: Legislative Procedure in Eighteenth-Century England* (Cambridge, 1971)

Lane, Carolina, 'The Development of Pastures and Meadows during the Sixteenth Century', *Agricultural History Review*, 28 (1980), pp. 18–30

Lavrovsky, V. M., 'Parliamentary Enclosures in the County of Suffolk (1797–1814)', *Economic History Review*, 1st series, 7 (1936–7), pp. 186–208

'Tithe Commutation as a Factor in the Gradual Decrease of Landownership by the English Peasantry', *Economic History Review*, 1st series, 4 (1932–4), pp. 273–89

Lennard, Reginald, *Rural Northamptonshire under the Commonwealth: A Study Based Principally upon the Parliamentary Surveys of the Royal Estates* (Oxford, 1916; repr. New York, 1974)

Leonard, E. M., 'The Inclosure of Common Fields in the Seventeenth

Century', *Transactions of the Royal Historical Society*, new series, 19 (1905), pp. 101–42

Lindley, Keith J., *Fenland Riots and the English Revolution* (1982)

Linnell, John Edward, *Old Oak: The Story of a Forest Village* (1932)

Mabey, Richard, *Food for Free* (1972)
  Gilbert White: A Biography of the Author of The Natural History of Selborne (1986; 1987)
  Plants with a Purpose: A Guide to the Everyday Uses of Wild Plants (1977)

McCay, Bonnie M., and James M. Acheson, eds., *The Question of the Commons: The Culture and Ecology of Communal Resources* (Tucson, Ariz., 1987)

McCloskey, Donald N., 'The Persistence of English Common Fields', in W. N. Parker and E. L. Jones, eds., *European Peasants and their Markets* (Princeton, 1975), pp. 73–119

Macfarlane, Alan, *The Origins of English Individualism* (Oxford, 1978)

McInnes, Angus, 'The Village Community 1660–1760', *North Staffordshire Journal of Field Studies*, 22 (1983)

Malcolmson, Robert W., *Life and Labour in England, 1700–1780* (1981)
  Popular Recreations in English Society 1700–1850 (Cambridge, 1973)

Mantoux, Paul, *The Industrial Revolution in the Eighteenth Century* (2nd edn, 1961)

Markham, C. A., ed., *Acts of Parliament Relating to Northamptonshire* (reprinted from *Northamptonshire Past and Present*, n.s., I–IV, 1905–20

Martin, John E., 'Enclosure and the Inquisitions of 1607: An Examination of Kerridge's Article "The Returns of the Inquisitions of Depopulation"', *Agricultural History Review*, 30 (1982), pp. 41–8
  Feudalism to Capitalism. Peasant and Landlord in English Agrarian Development (1983, 1986)

Martin, J. M., 'The Cost of Parliamentary Enclosure in Warwickshire', *University of Birmingham Historical Journal*, 9 (1964), pp. 144–62; reprinted in E. L. Jones, ed., *Agriculture and Economic Growth in England, 1650–1815*, (1967), pp. 128–51
  'Landownership and the Land Tax Returns', *Agricultural History Review*, 14 (1966), pp. 96–103
  'Marriage and Economic Stress in the Felden of Warwickshire in the Eighteenth Century', *Population Studies*, 31 (1977)
  'Members of Parliament and Enclosure: A Reconsideration', *Agricultural History Review*, 27 (1980), pp. 101–9
  'The Parliamentary Enclosure Movement and Rural Society in Warwickshire', *Agricultural History Review*, 15 (1967), pp. 19–39
  'The Small Landowner and Parliamentary Enclosure in Warwickshire', *Economic History Review*, 32 (1979), pp. 328–43
  'Village Traders and the Emergence of a Proletariat in South Warwickshire, 1750–1851', *Agricultural History Review*, 32 (1984), pp. 179–88

Martin, R. A., 'Kettering Inclosure 1804–5', *Northamptonshire Past and Present*, 5 (1977), pp. 413–26

Marx, Karl, *Capital* (Everyman, 2 vols., 1962)

Miller, W. C., and G. P. West, *Black's Veterinary Dictionary* (10th edn, 1972)

Mingay, G. E., 'The Agricultural Depression, 1730–50', *Agricultural History Review*, 8 (1956), pp. 323–8

'The East Midlands', in *Agrarian History*, ed. Joan Thirsk, V, part I, (Cambridge, 1984), pp. 89–128

Enclosure and the Small Farmer in the Age of the Industrial Revolution (1968)

English Landed Society in the Eighteenth Century (1963)

'The Land Tax Assessments and the Small Landholder'. *Economic History Review*, 2nd series, 17 (1964), pp. 381–8

'The Size of Farms in the Eighteenth Century', *Economic History Review*, 2nd series, 14 (1961–2), pp. 468–88

Mingay, G. E., ed., *The Agrarian History of England and Wales*, VI (Cambridge, 1989)

Arthur Young and his Times (1975)

The Unquiet Countryside (1989)

Moir, Esther, *Local Government in Gloucestershire 1775–1800: A Study of the Justices of the Peace*, Publications of the Bristol and Gloucestershire Archaeological Society, VIII (1969)

Moreau, R. E., *The Departed Village: Berwick Salome at the Turn of the Century* (1968)

Morgan, David, 'The Place of Harvesters in Nineteenth-Century Village Life', in Raphael Samuel, ed., *Village Life and Labour* (1975), pp. 27–72

Neeson, J. M., 'The Opponents of Enclosure in Eighteenth-Century Northamptonshire', *Past and Present*, 105 (1984), pp. 114–39

'Opposition to Enclosure in Northamptonshire *c*. 1760–1800', in Andrew Charlesworth, ed., *An Atlas of Rural Protest in Britain, 1548–1900* (1983)

'Parliamentary Enclosure and the Disappearance of the English Peasantry, Revisited', in George Grantham and Carol S. Leonard, eds., *Agrarian Organization in the Century of Industrialization: Europe, Russia, and North America*, Research in Economic History, Supplement 5, Part A (1989), pp. 89–120

Newby, H., 'Rural Sociology and its Relevance to the Agricultural Economist: A Review', *Journal of Agricultural Economics*, 33 (1982), pp. 125–65

Nicholls, H. G., *The Forest of Dean* (1866, new edn with an introduction by Cyril Hart, 1966)

North, Thomas, *The Church Bells of Northamptonshire* (Leicester, 1878)

Obelkevich, James, *Religion and Rural Society: South Lindsey 1825–1875* (1976)

Orwin, C. S. and C. S., *The Open Fields* (Oxford, 1938; 3rd edn, 1967)

Overton, Mark, 'Agricultural Revolution? Development of the Agrarian Economy in Early Modern England', in A. R. H. Baker and D. J. Gregory, eds., *Explorations in Historical Geography*, (Cambridge, 1984), pp. 124–32

'The Diffusion of Agricultural Innovations in Early Modern England: Turnips and Clover in Norfolk and Suffolk, 1580–1740', *Transactions of the Institute of British Geographers*, new series, 10 (1985), pp. 205–21

'Estimating Crop Yields from Probate Inventories: An Example from East Anglia, 1585–1735', *Journal of Economic History*, 39 (1979), pp. 363–78

The Oxford University Press Dictionary of Quotations, ed. B. Mitchell (2nd edn, Oxford, 1953; 1985)

Page, J. T., 'West Haddon', *Northampton Herald*, 11 January 1907

Palliser, David, *The Staffordshire Landscape* (1976)

Parry, E., 'Helmdon Stone', *Northamptonshire Past and Present*, 7 (1986–7), pp. 269–70

Partridge, Eric, *A Dictionary of Historical Slang*, abridged by J. Simpson (1972)

Payne, E. O., 'Property in Land in South Bedfordshire, 1750–1832', *Publications of the Bedfordshire Historical Record Society*, 23 (1941) (whole volume)

Peacock, A. J., *Bread or Blood* (1965)

Pearson, M. K., *Chipping Norton in Bygone Days* (Chipping Norton, 1909)

Perkin, Harold, *The Origins of Modern English Society, 1780–1880* (1969)

Pettit, P. A. J., *The Royal Forests of Northamptonshire: A Study in their Economy 1558–1714*, Publications of the Northamptonshire Record Society, XXIII (1968)

Philpot, Gordon, 'Enclosure and Population Growth in Eighteenth-Century England', *Explorations in Economic History*, 12 (1975), pp. 29–46

'Parliamentary Enclosure and Population Change in England, 1750–1830: Reply' [to M. E. Turner], *Explorations in Economic History*, 13: 4 (1976), pp. 46–71

Pine, Richard, *Brian Friel and Ireland's Drama* (1990)

Polanyi, Karl, 'Our Obsolete Market Mentality', *Commentary*, 3 (1947), pp. 109–17

Pollock, Griselda, *Millet* (1977)

Postgate, M. R., 'The Field Systems of East Anglia', in A. R. H. Baker and R. A. Butlin, eds., *Studies of Field Systems in the British Isles* (Cambridge, 1973), pp. 281–324

Potter, Dennis, *The Changing Forest* (1962)

Potter, T. R., *The History and Antiquities of Charnwood Forest* (1842)

Poynter, J. R., *Society and Pauperism: English Ideas on Poor Relief, 1795–1834* (1969)

Raban, Jonathan, *Coasting* (1986)

Ramsey, Peter, *Tudor Economic Problems* (1963)

Randall, Adrian, *Before the Luddites. Custom, Community and Machinery in the English Woollen Industry, 1776–1809* (Cambridge, 1991)

Randall, H. A., 'The Kettering Worsted Industry in the Eighteenth-Century', *Northamptonshire Past and Present*, 4 (1971–2), pp. 349–56

Reaney, Bernard, *The Class Struggle in Nineteenth-Century Oxfordshire:*

The Social and Communal Background to the Otmoor Disturbances of 1830 to 1835, History Workshop Pamphlet No. 3 (Oxford, 1970)

Reed, M., 'Class and Conflict in Rural England: Some Reflections on a Debate', in M. Reed and R. Wells, eds., *Class, Conflict and Protest in the English Countryside, 1700–1880* (1990), pp. 1–28

'Nineteenth-Century Rural England: A Case for "Peasant Studies"?', *Journal of Peasant Studies*, 14 (1986), pp. 78–99

'The Peasantry of Nineteenth-Century England: A Neglected Class?', *History Workshop Journal*, Issue 18 (Autumn, 1984), pp. 53–76

Richardson, Rosamond, *Hedgerow Cookery* (1980)

Richardson, T. L., 'Agricultural Labourers' Wages and the Cost of Living in Essex: A Contribution to the Standard of Living Debate', in B. A. Holderness and Michael Turner, eds., *Land, Labour and Agriculture 1700–1920. Essays Presented to Gordon Mingay* (1991), pp. 69–89

Rosenberg, Harriet, *A Negotiated World* (Toronto, 1988)

Rosensweig, Roy, *Eight Hours for What we Will. Workers and Leisure in an Industrial City 1870–1920* (Cambridge and New York, 1983)

Russell, Rex C., *The Logic of Open Field Systems: Fifteen Maps of Groups of Common Fields on the Eve of Enclosure* (Standing Conference for Local History, 1974)

Rymer, L., 'The History and Ethnobotany of Bracken', *Botanical Journal of the Linnaeus Society*, 73 (1976), pp. 151–76

Sabean, David, *Power in the Blood: Popular Culture and Village Discourse in Early Modern Germany* (Cambridge, 1984)

Sahlins, Marshall, *Stone Age Economics* (Chicago, 1972; London, 1974)

Salaman, R. N., *The History and Social Influence of the Potato* (1949)

Saville, John, 'Primitive Accumulation and Early Industrialization in Britain', in R. Miliband and J. Saville, eds., *Socialist Register* (1979), pp. 247–71.

Scrutton, Thomas Edward, *Commons and Common Fields; or the History and Policy of the Laws Relating to Commons and Enclosures in England* (1887; repr. New York, 1970)

Searle, Charles, E., 'Custom, Class Conflict and Agrarian Capitalism: The Cumbrian Customary Economy in the Eighteenth Century', *Past and Present*, 110 (1986), pp. 106–33

Seymour, John, *The Smallholder* (1983)

Shanin, Teodor, *The Awkward Class: Political Sociology of Peasantry in a Developing Society: Russia 1910–25* (1972)

Shanin, Teodor, ed., *Peasants and Peasant Societies* (1971; 1979)

Shaw-Lefevre, G., *English Commons and Forest* (1874)

Short, Brian, '"The Art and Craft of Chicken Cramming": Poultry in the Weald of Sussex, 1850–1980', *Agricultural History Review*, 30 (1982), pp. 17–30

Simpson, Alan, 'The East Anglian Fold Course: Some Queries', *Agricultural History Review*, 6 (1958), pp. 87–96

Slater, Gilbert, *The English Peasantry and the Enclosure of Common Fields* (1907; repr. New York, 1968)

Smollett, Tobias, *Humphry Clinker* (1771; Harmondsworth, 1967)

Snell, K. D. M., 'Agrarian Histories and our Rural Past', *Journal of Historical Geography*, 17 (1991), pp. 195–203

Annals of the Labouring Poor: Social Change and Agrarian England 1660–1900 (Cambridge, 1985)

Spufford, Margaret, *A Cambridgeshire Community: Chippenham from Settlement to Enclosure*, University of Leicester, Department of English Local History, Occasional Paper no. 20 (Leicester, 1965)

Contrasting Communities: English Villagers in the Sixteenth and Seventeenth Centuries (Cambridge, 1974)

Stamm, G. W., *Veterinary Guide for Farmers*, ed. R. C. Klussendorf (New York, 1975 edn)

Stamp, L. D., and W. G. Hoskins, *The Common Lands of England and Wales* (1963)

Steiner, George, *After Babel* (Oxford, 1975)

Stevenson, John, *Popular Disturbances in England, 1700–1870* (1979)

Sturge Gretton, Mary, *Three Centuries in North Oxfordshire* (Oxford, 1902)

Tate, W. E., 'Cambridgeshire Field Systems with a Handlist of Cambridgeshire Enclosure Acts and Awards', *The Cambridge Antiquarian Society Proceedings*, 40 (1939–42), pp. 56–88

'The *Commons' Journals* as Sources of Information Concerning the Eighteenth-Century Enclosure Movement', *Economic Journal*, 54 (1944), pp. 75–95

'The Cost of Parliamentary Enclosure in England (with Special Reference to the County of Oxford)', *Economic History Review*, 2nd series, 5 (1952–3), pp. 258–65

A Domesday of Enclosure Acts and Awards, ed. Michael Turner (Reading, 1978)

'Handlist of English Enclosure Acts and Awards Relating to Lands in Berkshire', *Berkshire Archaeological Journal*, 47 (1943), pp. 57–90

'Inclosure Movements in Northamptonshire', *Northamptonshire Past and Present*, 1 (1949), pp. 19–33

'Land Enclosures in Nottinghamshire, 1748–1868', *Thoroton Society Record Series*, 5 (1935)

'Opposition to Parliamentary Enclosure in Eighteenth-Century England', *Agricultural History Review*, 19 (1945), pp. 137–42

'Parliamentary Counter-Petitions during the Enclosures of the Eighteenth and Nineteenth Centuries', *English Historical Review*, 59 (1944), pp. 393–403

Tawney, R. H., *The Agrarian Problem in the Sixteenth Century* (1912; repr. 1967)

Thirsk, Joan, 'Agrarian History', *Victoria County History, Leicestershire*, II (1954), pp. 199–264

'Agriculture and Social Change in the Seventeenth Century', in Thirsk, ed., *Land, Church and People: Essays Presented to Professor H. P. R. Finberg* (Reading, 1970), pp. 148–77

'The Common Fields', *Past and Present*, 29 (1964), pp. 3–25

English Peasant Farming: The Agrarian History of Lincolnshire from Tudor to Recent Times (1957)

'Field Systems of the East Midlands', in A. R. H. Baker and R. A. Butlin, eds., *Studies of Field Systems in the British Isles* (Cambridge, 1973), pp. 232–80

Tudor Enclosures (Historical Association, 1958; repr. 1967; new edn, 1989)

Thirsk, Joan, ed., *The Agrarian History of England and Wales*, IV, *1500–1640* (Cambridge, 1967); V, Parts I and II (Cambridge, 1984, 1985)

Land, Church and People. Essays presented to Professor H. P. R. Finberg (Reading, 1970)

Thomas, Keith, *Religion and the Decline of Magic* (1971)

Thomas, P. D. G., *The House of Commons in the Eighteenth Century* (1978)

Thompson, E. P., 'The Crime of Anonymity', in D. Hay, P. Linebaugh and E. P. Thompson, eds., *Albion's Fatal Tree: Crime and Society in Eighteenth-Century England* (1975), pp. 255–344

Customs in Common (1991)

The Making of the English Working Class (1963)

'The Moral Economy of the English Crowd in the Eighteenth Century', *Past and Present*, 50 (1971), pp. 76–136

Whigs and Hunters: The Origin of the Black Act (1975)

Thompson, Flora, *Lark Rise to Candleford* (1939; 1973)

Thompson, F. M. L., *English Landed Society in the Nineteenth Century* (1963)

Trow-Smith, Robert, *A History of British Livestock Husbandry 1700–1900* (1959)

A History of British Livestock Husbandry to 1700 (1957)

Turner, Michael E., 'Benefits but at Cost', in George Grantham and Carol S. Leonard, eds., *Agrarian Organization in the Century of Industrialization: Europe, Russia, and North America*, Research in Economic History, Supplement 5, Part A (1989), pp. 49–68

'The Cost of Parliamentary Enclosure in Buckinghamshire', *Agricultural History Review*, 21 (1973)

'Economic Protest in a Rural Society: Opposition to Parliamentary Enclosure in Buckinghamshire', *Southern History*, 10 (1988), pp. 94–128

English Parliamentary Enclosure. Its Historical Geography and Economic History (Folkestone and Hamden, 1980)

'Parliamentary Enclosure and Land Ownership Change in Buckinghamshire', *Economic History Review*, 2nd series, 28 (1975), pp. 565–81

'Parliamentary Enclosure and Population Change in England, 1750–1830', *Explorations in Economic History*, 13:4 (1976), pp. 463–8

Turner, Michael E., and Dennis Mills, eds., *Land and Property: The English Land Tax, 1692–1832* (Gloucester, 1986)

Underdown, David, *Revel, Riot and Rebellion. Popular Culture in England 1603–1660* (1987)

Victoria County History, Northamptonshire, ed. W. Ryland, D. Adkins and R. M. Serjeantson, I, II, III (1902; repr. 1970)

Walter, John, 'A Rising of the People? The Oxfordshire Rising of 1596', *Past and Present*, 107 (1985), pp. 90–143

Walton, J. R., 'The Residential Mobility of Farmers and its Relationship to the Parliamentary Enclosure Movement in Oxfordshire', in A. D. M. Phillips and B. J. Turton, eds., *Environment, Man and Economic Change: Essays Presented to S. H. Beaver* (1975), pp. 238–52

Ward, W. R., *The English Land Tax in the Eighteenth Century* (Oxford, 1953)

Warriner, Doreen, *The Economics of Peasant Farming* (Oxford, 1939; 1964)

Watson, Stephen, *The Reign of George III 1760–1815* (Oxford, 1960)

Wearmouth, R. F., *Methodism and the Common People of the Eighteenth Century* (1945)

Webb, Nigel, *Heathlands* (1986)

Webb, S. and B., *English Local Government*, I, *The Parish and the County* (1906; repr. 1963)

Wells, R. A. E., 'The Development of the English Rural Proletariat and Social Protest, 1700–1850', *Journal of Peasant Studies*, 7 (1979), pp. 115–39

'Social Protest, Class, Conflict and Consciousness, in the English Countryside, 1700–1880', in M. Reed and R. A. E. Wells, eds., *Class, Conflict and Protest in the English Countryside, 1700–1880* (1990)

Wichello, Amy, *Annals of Wollaston* (1930)

Wigens, Anthony, *The Clandestine Farm* (1980)

Williams, Michael, 'The Enclosure and Reclamation of Waste Land in England and Wales in the Eighteenth and Nineteenth Centuries', *Transactions and Papers of the Institute of British Geographers*, 51 (1970), pp. 55–69

Winterson, Jeanette, *The Passion* (1987)

Wolf, Eric, 'On Peasant Rebellions', *International Social Science Journal*, 21 (1969), pp. 286–93

Wrightson, Keith, and David Levine, *The Making of an Industrial Society: Whickham 1560–1765* (1991)

Poverty and Piety in an English Village: Terling 1525–1700 (1979)

Wrigley, E. A., and R. S. Schofield, *The Population History of England 1541–1871: A Reconstruction* (Cambridge, 1981)

Yelling, J. A., *Common Fields and Enclosure in England, 1450–1850* (1977)

Unpublished theses

Havinden, M. A., 'The Rural Economy of Oxfordshire, 1580–1730', (B. Litt. thesis, University of Oxford, 1961)

Lane, Joan, 'Administration of the Poor Law in Butlers Marston, Warwickshire, 1713–1822' (MA thesis, University of Wales, Cardiff, 1970)

Martin, John E., 'Peasant and Lord in the Development of Feudalism and the Transition to Capitalism in England' (Ph.D. thesis, University of Lancaster, 1979)

Martin, J. M., 'Economic and Social Trends in the Rural West Midlands 1770–1825' (M.Com. thesis, University of Birmingham, 1960)

'Warwickshire and the Parliamentary Enclosure Movement' (Ph.D. thesis, University of Birmingham, 1965)

Neeson, J. M., 'Common Right and Enclosure in Eighteenth-Century Northamptonshire', (Ph.D. thesis, University of Warwick, 1978)

Searle, Charles E., ' "The Odd Corner of England": A Study of Rural Social Formation in Transition, Cumbria c. 1700–c. 1914' (Ph.D. thesis, University of Essex, 1983)

Turner, Michael E., 'Some Social and Economic Considerations of Parliamentary Enclosure in Buckinghamshire, 1738–1865' (Ph.D. thesis, University of Sheffield, 1973)

Index

Aberdeenshire, 13, 307, 326n
Abington Piggotts (Cambs.), 73, 77n
Abthorpe (N'hants.), 241n, 243, 306n, 331–2
access, 3, 5–6, 171–2, 194
Adston (N'hants.), 112n, 148n
agriculture: 7, 26, 157, 199, 226n; and industrialization, 12–14; labour market in, 13–14, 245; productivity of, 13, 27, 43, 113, 156–7; *and see* common agricultural regulation; common fields; common waste; smallholders.
Agriculture, Board of, 7, 8, 11, 31, 40, 46n, 48, 51, 52, 283, 284, 329; *and see* Reporters' names.
Ailesworth (N'hants.), 112n, 132, 146n
Aldwinckle (N'hants.), 62
Allen, Robert C., 12n, 157n, 306n
Althorp (N'hants.), 163, 188n
Ampthill (Beds.), 105
Andrews, Thomas, [viii], 19, 43, 45
animals, commoners': 11, 17, 23, 24, 39, 310–12; asses, 56; boars, 131–2; bulls, 127, 131–2, 326; cows, 17n, 20, 39, 124n, 132, 135, 149, 310–11; geese, 3, 35, 56, 67–8, 72n, 94, 115, 149, 171n, 173, 317; horses, 34, 124, 131n, 132, 138, 145, 146; pigs, 3, 39, 66–7, 70, 125, 135, 141, 171, 317; poultry, 39, 67–8, 70; rams, 131–2; ridgels, 131–2; sheep, 3, 37, 66, 69, 91, 94, 118–20, 123, 129, 132, 135, 139, 146, 168–9, 310, 311–12; turkeys, 68; young stock, 69–70, 72n, 94, 130–2, 173, 272; *and see* common of pasture: stinted
animals, diseases of: 16, 17, 118, 122–33, 137, 149n; bacillary hemoglobinuria, 128; blackleg, 128; bloat, 129;

brucellosis, 127–8; cattle plague (rinderpest), 123, 127n, 128, 129n, 130; foot and mouth, 128, 130; leptospirosis, 127, 128; pleuropneumonia, 130; redwater, 128; scrapie, 128; sheep rot, 123, 124, 129, 130
Annals of Agriculture, 25, 48, 49
Anscomb, J. W., 174n
Appleby, Joyce, 19n, 43n
Arbuthnot, John, 168
Arden, Forest of, 72
Armley Common (Yorks.), 202n
Ashby, M. K., 17n, 181, 246n, 340
Ashill (Norfolk), 256–7, 327
Ashton (N'hants.), 70, 91n, 119, 135, 137, 138, 140, 141, 145, 146
Astley (Warks.), 72, 135n
Atherstone (Warks.), 69n, 79, 85n, 125n, 135n, 165, 270n, 274, 314, 316, 322, 326n, 327
Audley End (Essex), 50n
Avon Valley, 106
Axholme, Isle of (Lincs.), 31n
Aynho (N'hants.), 106, 123, 276

Bacon, Francis, 18
Baird, Thomas, 36, 37, 40
Barford (Warks.), 75
Barford St Martin (Wilts.), 184
Barkham (Berks.), 165
Barrell, John, 10n, 31n, 325n
Barwick, Rev. Samuel, 214n
Bassingbourne (Cambs.), 74
Batchelor, Thomas, 37
Bateman, John, JP, 195, 196, 279
beating the bounds, 2, 320, 423
Beckett, J. V., 319n, 323n, 325n
Bedford, Duke of, 49

370

commoners (*cont.*)
military reserve, 13, 20–5; migrations
of, 23, 28–9; mischief of, 4, 35;
mutuality between, 2, 74, 90, 93–4, 99,
102, 104–8 *passim*, 147, 153–60 *passim*,
162n, 174–6, 180–4, 192, 197, 200, 233n,
255–8, 319–28, *and see* common
agricultural regulation: communal
levies; and non-local poor, 175, 176;
occupations of, 179, 189–90, 197, 201,
215, 222, 251, 265; pattern of survival,
72–80; poverty of, 6, 33n, 41, 42; and
parliamentary enclosure, 17, 18, 21, 23,
108, 221; and productivity, 35;
proletarianization predicted, 27–35, 45,
and Chapter 1 *passim*; as promotors of
tillage, 22; as a race, 34; as rustics, 52;
self-interest of, 144, 145; sentimentality
about, 10–11, 328; threats of larger,
Chapter 3 *passim*, 108–9, 155; thrift of,
25, 177, 178; ubiquity of, 9, 42, 55–7,
60–1, Chapters 2, 3 *passim*, 72–80,
108–9, 174–6, 188, 189; *and see* animals,
commoners'; commoners (names);
enclosure; engrossment; labourers,
agricultural; peasants; women
commoners (names): Ball, John, 215n;
Beale, Richard, 195, 196; Bellamy,
Thomas, 215n; Benford, Eleanor, 214n;
Boyes, Thomas, 201; Branston, John,
198, 199, 203n; Braunt, William, 195;
Brown, Edward, 310n; Bull, John,
325n; Burbridge, Mary, 206; Burnaby,
John, 215n; Butlin, Charles, 215n;
Butlin, William, 215n; Capps, Robert,
214n, 246n; Cave, Edward, 190n;
Chamber, David, 215n; Chamberlain,
George, 150; Chapman, Treshman, 140;
Clark, Edward, 195n; Clarke, John, 63;
Collis, Benjamin, 201, 206n; Cox,
David, 200, 265; Cox, Oliver, jr, 147,
150; Corby, Edward, 140; Crick,
Thomas, 14; Croxen, Richard, 215n;
Croxen, William, 215n; Currin,
Laurence, 198, 199; Daniels, John,
215n; Daniels, Nathaniel, 216; Daniels,
Thomas, 213; Dickenson, James, 215n;
Eady, Henry, 213, 338; Earle, Robert,
199, 200; East, Widow, 203n; Ekins,
Robert, 131n, 147, 150; Evans,
Thomas, 24n; Facer, Nehemiah, 189,
190n; Fisher, John, 194, 197; Ford,
Thomas, 200; Fox, Samuel, 215n;

Freeman, Rev. George, 263; Frisby,
John, 149, 150, 152; Furniss, Jonathan,
150; Green, James, 200, 203n; Harper,
John, 201n; Heydon, Thomas, 211;
Heygate, Nicholas, 202n; Hipwell,
John, 190n; Hipwell, Richard, 198,
206n; Hipwell, William, 190n; Hodson,
Charles, 215n; James, Joseph, 200,
203n, 265; Joans, John, 140; Kenny,
John, 198; Kilsby, John, 202n; King,
William, 209n; Langley, Edey, 215n;
Loale, Samuel, 195n; Lovelock, John,
153; Martin, Samuel, 176–7; Martin,
William, 190n; Mee, James, 215n;
Miller, Jos., 215n; Mitchell, William,
215n; Moulton, William, 201, 203n;
Murden, Matthew, 194; Newton,
Henry, 190n; Newton, John, 189, 190n;
Nutt, Robert, 83; Page, William (alias
Walton), 190n, 200; Parnell, Richard,
198, 203n; Partridge, Thomas, 214n;
Payne, Joseph, 215n; Reed, Grace, 184;
Richardson, William, 195n; Robins,
Benjamin, 200; Robins, Jonathan, 189,
190n, 206; Robins, Richard, 189;
Robinson, Francis, 211, 214n;
Robinson, Joseph, 214n; Shipley,
Thomas, 215n; Smith, Thomas, 198;
Squire, William, 310n; Stout, William,
316; Streets, Thomas, 83; Sudborough,
Joseph, 214n; Styles, John, 215n;
Tabernar, Ann, 200–1; Timpson, John,
215n; Toulton, Fraser, 215n; Towers,
Thomas, 198, 199; Tucker, Henry, 150;
Underwood, John, 200, 204; Vaux,
William, 190n; Vorley, Thomas, 215n;
Walker, John, 202n, 206; Ward, John,
195; Weekley, James, 150, 151; Welch,
Barbara, 315; West, John, 200; West,
William, 200; Wimpress, John, 84;
Wood, Joseph, 195n; Wood, Roger,
195n; Worcester, John, 200, 203n;
Wright, Samuel, 214n, 246n
Corby (N'hants.), 275–6, 281
Corrigan, Philip, 303, 304n
Corringham (Lincs.), 106
Corse Chase (Glos.), 37
Coton, *see* Guilsborough
Cottenham (Cambs.), 173n, 316n
Cottingham (N'hants.), 270n, 276
court, assizes, 147, 148n, 277
court, quarter sessions, 145, 147, 148,
150, 151

Grigg, David, 336, 337
Grover, Richard, 245n
Guilden Morden (Cambs.), 77
Guilsborough (N'hants.), 189, 196, 197,
  270n, 278, 281
Gunning, Mr, 211
Gunthorpe (N'hants.), 68

Hackelton (N'hants.), 174n, 273n
Hales, John, 18
Hall, John, 63
Hall v Harding, 88–9
Hallam, H. E., 170n
Hammond, B. and J. L., 6, 16, 17, 47, 55,
  191, 260, 262, 302, 303
Hampshire, 28, 33, 100, 162, 164, 315;
  downs, 173, 178, 181
Halifax, Lord, 277
Hanawalt, Barbara, 111n
Hanbury, Rev. William, 214
Hannington (N'hants.), 242, 270n, 274n,
  286n, 332
Hardin, Garrett, 6, 314
Hardingstone (N'hants.), 279
Harford (Hunts.), 249n
Hargrave (N'hants.), 112, 242, 286n
Harlestone (N'hants.), 164n
Harpole (N'hants.), 62, 69n
Harrold (Beds.), 100
Harston (Cambs.), 77, 84n
Hartley, Dorothy, 69n, 159, 167, 168–9
Hartwell (N'hants.), 70, 91n, 135, 138,
  141, 143, 145, 146
Haselbeach (N'hants.), 196
Havinden, Michael, 98, 113n, 121n
Hay, Douglas, 144n, 170n
Helmdon (N'hants.), 183
Helpston (N'hants.), 3, 5, 91n, 112n, 115,
  118, 121, 122, 132, 138, 141n, 142, 172,
  179, 242, 306n, 335n
Hemingford Abbots (Hunts.), 92, 107,
  123n
Hennell, David, 291
Herbert's Charity, 208
Herefordshire, 28, 33, 36
Hertfordshire, 310n, 312n
Hilman, Daniel, 19
Hilton, R. H., 300n
Hinxton (Cambs.), 68, 77–8
Hobhouse, Mr, MP, 209
Hobsbawm, E. J., 8, 260n, 301, 304–5, 314
Holcot (N'hants.), 62
Holland Fen (Cambs.), 72n

Homer, Henry, 153, 315
Hoskins, W. G., 223n, 226n, 261, 271,
  283n, 304, 310n, 329n
Hougham (N'hants.), 268n
Hounslow Heath (Mddx.), 31, 36, 37
Howell, Cicely, 300n, 311n, 312
Howkins, Alun, 325n
Howlett, Rev. John, 25–7, 28, 39, 43, 48,
  49–50
Hull (Yorks.), 130
Humphries, Jane, 177n, 315
Hunt, H. G., 232n, 308, 339–40
Huntingdonshire, 97n

improvement, improvers: 11, 31, 32, 40n,
  81; ideology of, 31n, 44–5, 50–1; *and
  see* enclosure: pamphleteers
Ireland, 192n, 301, 309, 323
Irthlingborough (N'hants.), 62, 273n
Isle of Wight, 31
Islip (N'hants.), 242, 333n
Isted, Mr, 211n
Ivinghoe (Bucks.), 170

James Deeping (N'hants.), 142, 150
Jefferies, Richard, 162
Johnson, A. H., 260, 305
juries, 2, 9, 111n, 122, 124, 126, 144, 319,
  324, 325; *and see* common agricultural
  regulation

Kalm, Pehr, 66, 69, 164, 167n, 168n, 171n
Kempston (Beds.), 107n
Kennet, river (Berks.), 159
Kent, 4
Kent, Nathaniel, 27, 39, 43, 47, 311
Kerridge, Eric, 33n, 103
Kettering (N'hants.), 73, 78, 174n, 176–7,
  194, 207, 208, 224, 253
Kibworth Beauchamp (Leics.), 196
Kibworth Harcourt (Leics.), 300n, 303
Kilsby (N'hants.), 62, 251n, 270n, 271n,
  272, 273n, 281, 283, 306, 310n
King, Gregory, 298, 308n
King, Rev. Shaw, 214n
King's Cliffe (N'hants.), 90n
Kirtling (Cambs.), 74, 92
Kussmaul, Ann, 289, 329

labourers, agricultural: 12, 14, 49, 301n,
  302, 323; allotments for, 45n; deference
  of, 37; diet after enclosure, 11; drinking
  after enclosure, 50; early marriage after

Meister, Henry, 301n
Middlesex, 4, 33, 37–8, 39
Middleton (N'hants.), 276
Middleton, J., 37
Midgham (Berks.), 160
Midland Revolt (1607), 58, 289
Midlands, 57, 94, 97n, 104, 106, 114n,
170n, 172–3, 187–3, 222, 225, 228n,
262, 277, 300, 309, 315, 329
Millbrook (Beds.), 48–9
Millet, J.-F., 10n
Mills, Dennis, 228n
Mills, Mr, MP, 209
Mingay, G. E., 56, 229, 244n, 245n, 246,
250, 251, 299n, 302, 314, 338
Mitcham (Surrey), 85n
Monchy, Saloman de, 127
Moore, Rev. John, 18, 43
Mordant, J., 277
More, Thomas, 18
Moreton Pinkney cum Membris
(N'hants.), Chapter 4 *passim*, 111–12,
123n, 131, 136, 139, 141, 143, 146, 148,
150, 175
Morland, George, 10, 12
Moron, John, 97, 312n
mouchers, 183–4

Naseby (N'hants.), 243
national interest, 7, 15, 20, 21, 25, 42–6,
51
Needwood Forest, 72, 166n, 167n
New Forest, 72
Newark (N'hants.), 114n
Newbury (Berks.), 160n
Newby, H., 308n
Newnham (N'hants.), 286
Newton Bromswold (N'hants.), 242, 332
Norden, John, 1, 19, 66–7
Norfolk, 45n, 291
North administration (1771–4), 26
North Crawley (Bucks.), 116
Northampton, 151, 189, 221n, 224, 253n,
275, 279, 281
Northampton, Earl of, 279
Northampton Mercury, 61, 191–2, 194,
195, 266, 268, 272
Northamptonshire: 13, 57–71 *passim*, 91,
139, 165, 191, 207, 223–7 *passim*, 234,
241n, 245, 250, 252, 262, 271, 273n,
275n, 277, 284, 287, 305, 337, 341;
common-field agriculture in, 58, 98,
111–12, 313; enclosure Acts in, 58–9,

188, 207; heath and fen, 57–71 *passim*,
84, 96–7, 160, 224, 305–6; hogs in,
66–7, 125; landholding structure, 60–1,
305–8; manors, 111–12; Nene valley,
57–71 *passim*, 84, 97, 112, Chapters 4, 5
passim, 207, 224, 232, 281, 285, 306;
opposition to enclosure in, Chapter 9
passim; population of, 58–9, 305; Royal
forests, 57–71 *passim*, 84, 97, 109, 161;
rural manufacture in, 13, 58, 189–90,
207–8, 249, 283, 284, 285; scarp, 188,
207; waste, 96–7, 172–3; woods, 163–4
Northborough (N'hants.), 112n
Northmore (Oxon.), 108n
Nottinghamshire, 271n, 275n, 276
Nourse, Timothy, 19, 20–1, 32

Oakley, Little (N'hants.), , 62
Obelkevich, James, 303n
O'Grada, Cormac, 157n
Old (N'hants.), 90n, 91, 123, 139–40
opponents of enclosure: 194, 195, 197,
198–9, 215–16, 269, 315, 321; cottagers,
213–14, 215–16, 217–18, 220, 265, 268;
defined, 259, 265, 268, 272, 282–4;
economies of, 281–4; gentry, 208–9,
214, 220, 270, 274n, 284, 322n, 325;
inhabitants, 213, 214, 215–16, 217–18,
220, 268; landlords, 203; neighbours,
191–2, 278; old, 198–9;
owner-occupiers, 202, 217, 218, 220,
231, 265, 268; poor, 259, 261, 283–4;
small owners, 271, 274, 276–7, 282–3;
tenants, 204, 219–20; *and see*
opposition to enclosure
opposition to enclosure: 5, 8, 10, 11, 52,
58, 65, 100n, 106, 107, 109, 164, 187,
Chapters 7, 9 *passim*; anonymous, 155,
263, 278–80; by Commons'
counter-petition, 190–1, 192, 202n,
208–20 *passim*, 253, 263, 266, 270–5,
286–7; destruction of posts, rails,
hedges, 191–5, 196–7; and football,
191, 194; illegal, 260; and landholding,
202–7; little, 260–2; local, 263–70,
274–80, 286–7, 321–2; longevity of,
262–3; and Parliament, 260, 273–4,
288–90; pattern of, 281–7; and private
Bills, 190–1, 275–7; and property
damage, 263–4, 266, 267; reasons for,
198–204, 209–10, 213–14, 259, 265, 267,
269–70, 283–4; recorded at engrossing
of Bills, 62n, 191, 217–18, 269; rewards

Selborne (Hants.), 176
Seymour, John, 310n
Shanin, Teodor, 254, 300n
Shelburne, Lord, 26n
Short, Brian, 307n
Shropshire, 284
Shutlanger (N'hants.), 59, 70, 84, 91n,
 112n, 113, 119, 121, 135, 136, 137
Silsworth (N'hants.), 188n
Silverstone (N'hants.), 113n
Sinclair, Sir John, 31, 47
Slater, Gilbert, 55
smallholders: 10, 18, 45n, 199, 204–5, 223,
 253–8, 301–2, 309, 328; post-enclosure
 agriculture of, 10, 18, 199, 223, 253–8,
 328
Smith, Adam, 26, 67
Snell, K. D. M., 17n, 288, 303, 321, 329
Snitterfield (Warks.), 106
Soham (Cambs.), 74
Somerset, 39
Somersham Heath (Hunts.), 73, 87n, 91n,
 92
Sonning (Berks.), 87
Sowe, Walsgrave on (Warks.), 69n, 73,
 320
Spalding (Lincs.), 170n, 173n
Speen (Berks.), 160
Spelsbury (Oxon.), 121n
Spence, Thomas, 24n
Spencean Philanthropists, 52
Spencer, Earl, 163–4, 211
Spufford, Margaret, 316n, 323
Staffordshire, 67, 165, 173n, 189, 300n,
 312n
Stanbridge (Beds.), 77, 99n
Stanford on Avon (N'hants.), 188n
Stanion (N'hants.), 62, 267, 269, 273n,
 284n
Stanwick (N'hants.), 241n, 243, 306n
statutes: 32 Hen. VIII, c.18 (horses),
 124n; 13 Geo. III c.81 (common fields
 and wastes), 210n; 38 Geo. III, c.65,
 (sheep), 125n; 4 William and Mary c.1
 (Land Tax), 246n; statute law, 124n,
 125
Staughton, Little (Beds.), 91
Staverton (N'hants.), 268–9, 284n, 286–7
Stevenson, John, 261n, 265
Stoke Bruerne (N'hants.), 59, 70, 84, 91n,
 113n, 114, 119, 120n, 121, 123n
Stone, Thomas, 27, 39
Stony Stratford (Bucks.), 107

Stour Valley, 106
Stretham (Cambs.), 77
Suffolk, 45n
Suffolk marsh, 36n
Sulby (N'hants.), 188n
Sulgrave (N'hants.), 286
Surrey, 307
Sussex, 234n
Sutton, Sir Richard, MP, 210
Sutton Bassett (N'hants.), 232, 242, 272,
 273n, 286, 333n
Sutton Coldfield (Warks.), 39, 73
Sydenham (Beds.), 100
Sywell (N'hants.), 164n

Tamworth (Staffs.), 326n
Tate, W. E., 191, 224, 271n, 288, 302
Teeton (N'hants.), 83
Temple Balsall (Warks.), 98n
Terling (Essex), 303
Thatcham (Berks.), 160
Thirsk, Joan, 111n, 277, 300n, 304, 315n
Thomas, Keith, 265n, 320n
Thompson, E. P., 17n, 31, 261–2, 284n,
 304, 315
Thompson, Flora, 298, 312n
Thompson, F. M. L., 308n
Thrapston (N'hants.), 207
Tilbrooke (Beds.), 91n
timber, 29, 160, 163, 164, 179
Titchmarsh (N'hants.), 62
Tomes, John, 208, 209
Torrington, Viscount, 47
Tottington (Norfolk), 88, 156
Towcester, 87n
Turner, M. E., 17n, 153n, 221, 223, 224n,
 226, 227, 228n, 273n, 276, 277, 288,
 303, 340n, 345n
Tusser, Thomas, 19, 81, 154, 156
Twywell (N'hants.), 253

Underdown, David, 194n

Vancouver, C., 28, 33, 36, 37, 51, 65, 162,
 164, 181

Wadenhoe (N'hants.), 242, 332
Wales, 301
Walgrave (N'hants.), 273n, 280
Walker, D., 323
Wallingford (Oxon.), 91n
Waltham Chase, 109
Walton (N'hants.), 68

Past and Present Publications

General Editor: PAUL SLACK. *Exeter College*, Oxford

Family and Inheritance: Rural Society in Western Europe 1200–1800, edited by Jack Goody, Joan Thirsk and E. P. Thompson*

French Society and the Revolution, edited by Douglas Johnson

Peasants, Knights and Heretics: Studies in Medieval English Social History, edited by R. H. Hilton*

Towns in Societies: Essays in Economic History and Historical Sociology, edited by Philip Abrams and A. E. Wrigley*

Desolation of a City: Coventry and the Urban Crisis of the Late Middle Ages, Charles Phythian-Adams

Puritanism and Theatre: Thomas Middleton and Opposition Drama under the Early Stuarts, Margot Heinemann*

Lords and Peasants in a Changing Society: The Estates of the Bishopric of Worcester 680–1540, Christopher Dyer

Life, Marriage and Death in a Medieval Parish: Economy, Society and Demography in Halesowen 1270–1400, Zvi Razi

Biology, Medicine and Society 1840–1940, edited by Charles Webster

The Invention of Tradition, edited by Eric Hobsbawm and Terence Ranger*

Industrialization before Industrialization: Rural Industry and the Genesis of Capitalism, Peter Kriedte, Hans Medick and Jürgen Schlumbohm*

The Republic in the Village: The People of the Var from the French Revolution to the Second Republic, Maurice Agulhon

Social Relations and Ideas: Essays in Honour of R. H. Hilton, edited by T. H. Aston, P. R. Coss, Christopher Dyer and Joan Thirsk

A Medieval Society: The West Midlands at the End of the Thirteenth Century, R. H. Hilton

Winstanley: 'The Law of Freedom' and Other Writings, edited by Christopher Hill

Crime in Seventeenth-Century England: A County Study, J. A. Sharpe†

The Crisis of Feudalism: Economy and Society in Eastern Normandy c. 1300–1500, Guy Bois†

The Development of the Family and Marriage in Europe, Jack Goody*

Disputes and Settlements: Law and Human Relations in the West, edited by John Bossy

Rebellion, Popular Protest and the Social Order in Early Modern England, edited by Paul Slack

Studies on Byzantine Literature of the Eleventh and Twelfth Centuries, Alexander

Kazhdan in collaboration with Simon Franklin†

The English Rising of 1381, edited by R. H. Hilton and T. H. Aston*

Praise and Paradox: Merchants and Craftsmen in Elizabethan Popular Literature, Laura Caroline Stevenson

The Bremner Debate: Agrarian Class Structure and Economic Development in Pre-Industrial Europe, edited by T. H. Aston and C. H. E. Philpin*

Eternal Victory: Triumphal Rulership in Late Antiquity, Byzantine, and the Early Medieval West, Michael McCormick†*

East-Central Europe in Transition: From the Fourteenth to the Seventeenth Century, edited by Antoni Maczak, Henryk Samsonowicz and Peter Burke†

Small Books and Pleasant Histories: Popular Fiction and its Readership in Seventeenth-Century England, Margaret Spufford*

Society, Politics and Culture: Studies in Early Modern England, Mervyn James*

Horses, Oxen and Technological Innovation: The Use of Draught Animals in English Farming 1066–1500, John Langdon

Nationalism and Popular Protest in Ireland, edited by C. H. E. Philpin

Rituals of Royalty: Power and Ceremonial in Traditional Societies, edited by David Cannadine and Simon Price*

The Margins of Society in Late Medieval Paris, Bronisław Geremek†

Landlords, Peasants and Politics in Medieval England, edited by T. H. Aston

Geography, Technology, and War: Studies in the Maritime History of the Mediterranean, 649–1571, John H. Pryor*

Church Courts, Sex and Marriage in England, 1570–1640, Martin Ingram*

Searches for an Imaginary Kingdom: The Legend of the Kingdom of Prester John, L. N. Gumilev

Crowds and History: Mass Phenomena in English Towns, 1780–1835, Mark Harrison

Concepts of Cleanliness: Changing Attitudes in France since the Middle Ages, Georges Vigarello†

The First Modern Society: Essays in English History in Honour of Lawrence Stone, edited by A. L. Beier, David Cannadine and James M. Rosenheim

The Europe of the Devout: The Catholic Reformation and the Formation of a New Society, Louis Chatellier†

English Rural Society, 1500–1800: Essays in Honour of Joan Thirsk, edited by John Chartres and David Hey

From Slavery to Feudalism in South-Western Europe, Pierre Bonnassie†

Lordship, Knighthood and Locality: A Study in English Society c.1180–c.1280, P. R. Coss

English and French Towns in Feudal Society: A Comparative Study, R. H. Hilton

An Island for Itself: Economic Development and Social Change in Late Medieval Sicily, Stephan R. Epstein

Epidemics and Ideas: Essays on the Historical Perception of Pestilence, edited by Terence Ranger and Paul Slack

Commoners: Common Right, Enclosure and Social Change in England, 1700–1820, J. M. Neeson

The Political Economy of Shopkeeping in Milan, 1886–1922, Jonathan Morris

* Published also as a paperback

† Co-published with the Maison des Sciences de L'Homme, Paris